Rose Georgina Kingsley

South by West

Or, winter in the Rocky Mountains and spring in Mexico

Rose Georgina Kingsley

South by West
Or, winter in the Rocky Mountains and spring in Mexico

ISBN/EAN: 9783337251925

Printed in Europe, USA, Canada, Australia, Japan

Cover: Foto ©Andreas Hilbeck / pixelio.de

More available books at **www.hansebooks.com**

MONUMENT PARK.—Page 89.

SOUTH BY WEST

OR

*WINTER IN THE ROCKY MOUNTAINS
AND SPRING IN MEXICO*

EDITED WITH A PREFACE
BY THE REV. CHARLES KINGSLEY, F.L.S., F.G.S.
CANON OF WESTMINSTER

With Illustrations

W. ISBISTER & CO.
6 LUDGATE HILL, LONDON
1874

PRINTED BY T. AND A. CONSTABLE, PRINTERS TO HER MAJESTY,
AT THE EDINBURGH UNIVERSITY PRESS.

To my Father and Mother

PREFACE.

This unassuming volume will, I trust, prove interesting to that fast-increasing class of readers who look eagerly for any fresh information about the New World. To some, I venture to believe, it may have a solid value, on account of the novel facts about Mexico and its capabilities which will be found in it. Such persons may find it worth while to peruse, likewise, a paper on Mexico in *Ocean Highways* for May 1873, by the " M." who is so often alluded to in this book. The time for developing the vast resources of that country is surely close at hand. It possesses every earthly gift, save—for the present at least—the power of using them. Alone of all the countries of the world, it can produce in abundance, in its Tierra Templada and its Tierra Caliente, the riches both of the Temperate and of the Tropic Zones. Its position, between the Atlantic and the Pacific, ought to make it, some day, one of the most important highways of the world; and when the city of Mexico is joined by a railroad to some port on the Pacific, as it is already joined —by honourable English enterprise—to Vera Cruz on the Atlantic, it ought to become the entrepôt of a vast traffic, not only between California and New York, but even—so some think—between China and Europe. Heaven grant that that and all wholesome developments may be effected from within, by the Mexicans themselves, under the guidance of some wise and virtuous President; and anarchy and brigandage be peacefully exterminated, by the extermination of their true causes—ignorance and want. If not, the work will have to be done—perhaps in rougher fashion, and perhaps sorely against their will—by the American people. However much the wisest of them may shrink from the thought of annexation, they are growing less and less inclined to tolerate, along the whole frontier of Texas and New Mexico, a state of society which is as injurious to the Mexicans themselves as to the American settlers, and which has, in the last few years, given a pretext for armed invasion and usurpation by the Ultramontane party in Europe. That experiment, it is true, is not likely soon to be repeated. But it will be the duty of the patriotic President of the United States to prevent even the chance of its repetition; and to carry out at all risks—as far as Mexico is concerned—the "Monroe doctrine." However, we must hope better things for that fair but hapless land. We must hope that her government will so conduct itself toward foreign statesmen as to re-enter honourably the comity of Nations; and toward foreign capitalists, so as to attract the wealth—American, Dutch, and English—which is ready to flow into and fertilize and pacify the whole country.

But there is another object, of even deeper interest, which I cannot but help hoping that this book may further: namely, that better understanding between American and British citizens, which is growing so fast just now.

Every one who knows anything of the Americans of the older States, knows also that they are a generous, affectionate, and high-minded people, who put a courteous and modest visitor under heavy obligations, not only for the bounty of their hospitality, but for the pleasure of their society. But too many, I fear, misled by the reports of cynics and bookmakers, are unaware that the same good qualities are to be found in the distant territories, in the very wilds of the Rocky Mountains themselves, as well as in the older East and South; and that the border-fringe of ruffianism—which must exist on the frontier of any vast country—which is no worse now in Texas or New Mexico than it was two centuries ago in many border districts of England, Scotland, and Ireland, rapidly retreats before that most potent of civilizers, the railroad, as it pours in, from the distant regions of the old States, a perpetual reinforcement of the good, to drive the bad further and further into yet more desolate wildernesses. Much which the authoress may have longed to say, she could not say, for fear of trenching upon private confidences: but she has said enough, I trust, in her sketch of the foundation and rapid growth of a colony in Colorado, at the foot of the very wildest part of the Rocky Mountains, to show that, even there, face to face with the most brutal Red Indian, not only hospitality and humanity, virtue and probity, but cultivation and refinement are to be found among men and women who are not ashamed to labour with their own hands, ennobled by the sense that they are doing a great work—replenishing the earth and subduing it. And even of those who may have less cultivation or refinement, I know that I can say this at least. As long as the man of the Far West is not ashamed of honest toil, and as long as his courtesy and chivalry toward women is as perfect as I am assured it is, so long he will find that every real English gentleman who visits him will recognise in him a gentleman likewise.

I am bound to add—in my pleasant capacity of editor to this book—that it owes nothing whatsoever to my pen, beyond the mere correction of the press, and the scientific names of a few animals and flowers. The whole of the physical facts—botanical, zoological, or geological—were observed or collected by the authoress herself.

CHARLES KINGSLEY.

CONTENTS.

CHAPTER I.

NEW YORK, NIAGARA, AND WEST POINT.

First land—Our pilot—New York harbour—The doctor—A puzzled official—The streets of New York—Central Park—Hellgate Ferry—Maples—Picture of Washington—Fast trotters—A drive in a buggy—Start for Niagara—The Kenisteo Valley—" Run over a keaow "—Portage—The train-boy—Niagara—English service—The rapids—A horrible story—Des Vaux College—The Whirlpool—Leave Niagara—The smoke of Chicago—A friend in need—West Point—The Gatling gun—A terrible little shot—Our first American service, ... 1

CHAPTER II.

FROM EAST TO WEST.

Down the Hudson—Trains in the streets—Parlour cars—Baltimore—An American country-house—The Convention of 1871—Start for the West—St. Louis—" Arctic Soda "—Mustang fever—Kansas city—The Plains—Prairie dogs—An old " rattler "—Buffalos—United States forts—A railroad feat—Denver and the Rocky Mountains—The pioneer narrow-gauge railroad—Pike's Peak, ... 24

CHAPTER III.

LIFE IN A NEW TOWN.

A series of surprises—The young town—Our shanty and its fittings—How we live—Glen Eyrie—Tea in a loft—Bird-cage making—

A "scare"—House-warming—The Soda Springs—A trapper—
Walk to Mount Washington—School—Move to our new quarters—Staging and stage-drivers, ... 47

CHAPTER IV.

LIFE IN A NEW TOWN—*continued.*

The weather—Washing and cooking—The penalties of a free country
—Visitors from Denver—A snowy pillow—The cold "snap"—
A presentiment—Sunshine again—The Falls of the Fountain—
Starting a reading-room—Colonist-catching—The Garden of the
Gods—Pete shows his wisdom, ... 65

CHAPTER V.

CAÑONS AND COLD.

My first Cañon—Wild beasts—Pleasant society—A spelling match—
Camp Creek Cañon—Exploring by moonlight—Mountain air—
Snow drifts—Triumph of the Narrow Gauge—The Fountain
ditch—A Westerner—Antelope-shooting—A grand view—A
change in our plans, ... 77

CHAPTER VI.

MONUMENT PARK.

Expedition to Monument Park—A cheap dinner—The monuments—
A rough road—School-keeping a failure—Locating the skating
pond—Snow-birds—A second Monument Park—The southern
mountains—"Over the Ratons," 87

CHAPTER VII.

CHRISTMAS AND NEW YEAR.

A Christmas treat—Stock-farmers' troubles—The western metropolis
—Parlour skates—The fall of the Ulsters—Sleighing—A warm
Christmas day—Christmas tree—God save the Queen—My first
Indian—A wind storm—New Year's Day—Our new hotel—
Ute Indians—A "surprise party"—Cow-catching a dangerous
amusement, ... 98

CHAPTER VIII.

MOUNTAIN EXPLORATIONS.

Bronco manners — Mountain appetites — The Rainbow Fall — A scramble — The new road — Trailing Arbutus — Glenwood Mills — Beavers — A cold bath — Arkansas hospitality — The Ute pass — A scare — A "washing bee" — Our first Episcopal service — The ditch full at last — Growth of the town — A ride over the mesa — An exploring expedition — The "Pike's Peak gold fever" — A "cold snap" — Our concert, ... 108

CHAPTER IX.

LAST DAYS IN COLORADO.

Valentine's Day — The "Iron Ute" — Move to Glen Eyrie — The Servant Question — Snow blockade on the Union Pacific — A perilous path — The land of surprises — Cheyenne cañon — A distant view — Prospecting on Pike's Peak — Colonists — The irate market-gardeners — Indians and their doings — Farewell to Colorado, ... 125

CHAPTER X.

COLORADO — ITS RESOURCES AND PROGRESS.

Surface features — Climate — Irrigation — Timber — The mining interest — Coal beds — Attractions to settlers — The snowy range — Population — Denver — The Denver and Rio Grande Railway — Colorado Springs: its foundation and growth — The Soda Springs — Pueblo — Cañon City — Difference between the Old and New Worlds, ... 137

CHAPTER XI.

THE PACIFIC RAILROAD.

Denver Pacific Railroad — A pigs' paradise — The highest railroad point in the world — Snowbucking — How to keep well — Sagebrush and sandstones — The Mormon Railroad — Great Salt Lake City — Angelic architects — Commerce and holiness — Shoshonee Indians — A lofty breakfast-room — Miners — Flowers — Poison-oak — California — The Pacific at last, ... 152

CHAPTER XII.

CALIFORNIA.

Californian oysters—The Seal Rocks—A Western play—Chinese opium-eaters and temple—An opera "buffa"—Earthquakes—Sacramento Bay—San Raphael—A council of war—Seal and salmon—Preparations for journey—Yo Semite photographs—The San José Valley—A Californian country-house—The successful millionnaire—Chinese servants—*Adios California*, . 166

CHAPTER XIII.

DOWN THE PACIFIC.

The "peaceful ocean"—A tumble—Sea-gull and Spanish lessons—An odious child—Orchilla—The new "Earthly Paradise"—A narrow escape—Sunday—An addition to our party—Gloomy forebodings, ... 178

CHAPTER XIV.

FROM THE COAST TO COLIMA.

The Puerto de Manzanillo—*Frijoles* and *tortillas*—Mexican meals—The exports of the port—Our start for the interior—The Laguna de Cuyutlan—The delights of a night journey—Guadalupe—Salt collecting—Don Ignacio Lagos—Lace and embroidery—Tropic woods—Rumours of the Revolution—Tecolapa—A rough road—The volcano of Colima—Colima—Feast-day sights—Martial music—Easter decorations—A *huerto*—The Alameda—Hacienda de San Cayetano—The eruption of February 26th—More news of the Revolutionists, . . 184

CHAPTER XV.

ROBBERS AND REVOLUTIONS.

Our start—An ill-broken team—La Quesaria—Chicken wine—Barrancas—San Marcos—Mule trains—An uncomfortable luncheon—The "*Pedrigal*"—A break-down—Zapotlan—A revolution—The baffled bridegroom—Rough lodgings—Pulque—Severo—An early breakfast—A "scare"—Onions—"*Los bonitos rifles*"—Pronunciados—Alkali flats—A dry lake—"A friend indeed"—Our escort—La Coronilla—Robber towns—Guadalajara at last, ... 206

CHAPTER XVI.

GUADALAJARA.

The Paseo—Barricades—The Belen Cemetery—Attractive baths—
A fortunate escape—The Cathedral—Confessionals—*El Hospicio*
—Señor Menesses—A clean kitchen—Embroidery—The *Cuau*—
A wonderful contralto—*Helados*—A wicked bull—Pottery—
The opera—The States Prison—An embarrassing present—
Mexican troops—How to make a *pronunciamiento*, . . 232

CHAPTER XVII.

UP THE VALLEY OF THE LERMA.

The Rio Grande de Santiago—Ocotlan—Ordering dinner—The robbers—La Barca—An escape—A luxurious bed—Dug-out canoes—Buena Vista—A dead robber—Wine-growing and pedrigal—" *Una Señorita tan grande*"—The faithless negro—Farms and farming—The Padre's "boys"—An indigestible meal—Hanging a robber—Irapuato—Molasses candy—Swape wells—Cereus and nopals—Salamanca—Singing birds—The churches of Celaya—Indian music—A story of the "*Plaqueros*"—Peru pepper—Jumping cactus—A pretty leap—Approach to Queretaro, ... 244

CHAPTER XVIII.

QUERETARO TO MEXICO.

A bet—The Hercules Factory—Cheap labour—Arrival of the engineers from Colorado—Las Campanas—Leave Queretaro—Spearing a dog—The Divide—San Juan del Rio—Thunderstorm—An unlucky choice of routes—Ill-requited kindness—Barred out—An Indian school—The valley of the Tula—The broken break—Gathering nopal leaves—The capital of the Toltecs—An early start—On Cortez's track—The valley of Mexico—The railroad track—Arrival in the city, . . 268

CHAPTER XIX.

LIFE IN MEXICO.

The Hotel Iturbide—Flowers—Tacubaya—The Paseo—Aztec calendar stone—The Inquisition—Cathedral of Mexico—A ride round the city—*Cinco de Mayo*—Chapultepec—The *Pronunciamiento* of October 1871—El Peñon del Agua Caliente—Executions by the Liberals—Breakfast at the San Cosme—Speeches—The Habanera—Mexican salutations, . . 285

CHAPTER XX.

LIFE IN MEXICO—*continued*.

Indios and their costumes—Street cries—Guadalupe—Arrival of the engineers—Trying a gun—An *agua cerro*—Drainage—The Academia—Aztec arts—The Palacio—A Mexican debate—Chills and fever—Gizzard tea—The Monte Pio—The tree of the *Noche Triste*—A narrow bridge—Departure of the engineering party—Feast of Corpus Christi—Tacubaya—The Museum—A "useful man"—The considerate *compadre*, . . . 309

CHAPTER XXI.

LIFE IN MEXICO—*continued*.

Visit to Guadalupe—Origin of the miraculous serape—The collegiate church—Votive offerings—Church of Tepayac—Sulphur spring—Letter from M.—Popotla and Tacuba—Molino del Rey—The battles of August and September 1847—An unfortunate hacendado—Last evening in Mexico, ... 336

CHAPTER XXII.

A RECONNAISSANCE IN THE SOUTHERN TIERRA CALIENTE.

Preparations—Breakfast at Santa Fé—The unreasonable commandante—Over the Sierra—"*Escolta*"—*Pueblos* of the Toluca valley—Tenancingo—My new guide—The *barrancas*—A bad ford—The old pack-horse takes a swim—A curious phenomenon—The cave of Cacahuamilpa—Bananas and sugar-cane—The Mexican Sindbad—An army of bats—Stoning iguanas—Hacienda of San Gabriel—Ixtapan de la Sal—"A bad place"—The romance of the skunk—Back to Mexico, . . 357

CHAPTER XXIII.

THE CITY OF MEXICO TO VERA CRUZ.

Teocallis of the Sun and Moon—Pulque—Puebla de los Angelos—Churches and relics—Sta. Florenzia—Muddy roads—The steel works of Amozoc—Cacti—A midnight start—The Peak of Orizaba—Down the *cumbres*—Orizaba—A wild team—The railroad again—Vera Cruz—The *Vomito* and the *Norte*—Gachupines and parrots—Farewell to Mexico, . . 382

CHAPTER XXIV.

MEXICO AND ITS RESOURCES, . 399

LIST OF ILLUSTRATIONS.

MONUMENT PARK,	*Frontispiece.*
HORSE-SHOE BEND, ALLEGHANY MOUNTAINS,	PAGE 29
DRUG AND BOOK STORE,	33
PRAIRIE RANCHE NEAR SALINA,	35
PRAIRIE DOGS,	37
STREET IN DENVER,	43
OUR SHANTY,	49
THE CAÑON IN GLEN EYRIE,	51
THE GATE OF THE GARDEN OF THE GODS.	74
CROSSING A TRESTLE BRIDGE,	75
MONUMENT CREEK,	88
THE MONUMENT ROCKS,	90
INDIANS,	105
PIKE'S PEAK,	114
THE ROCKS NEAR GREEN RIVER,	157
WOMAN MAKING TORTILLAS,	187
BELL TOWER AT COLIMA,	198
THE CATHEDRAL, GUADALAJARA,	235
THE CATHEDRAL, MEXICO,	282
THE PALACE OF CHAPULTEPEC,	296
THE TREE OF THE NOCHE TRISTE,	325

CHAPTER I.

NEW YORK, NIAGARA, AND WEST POINT.

First land—Our pilot—New York harbour—The doctor—A puzzled official—The streets of New York—Central Park—Hellgate Ferry—Maples—Picture of Washington—Fast trotters—A drive in a buggy—Start for Niagara—The Kenisteo Valley—" Run over a keaow"—Portage—The train-boy—Niagara—English service—The Rapids—A horrible story—Des Vaux College—The Whirlpool—Leave Niagara—The smoke of Chicago—A friend in need—West Point—The Gatling gun—A terrible little shot—Our first American service.

IN the autumn of 1871 the Episcopal Church Convention of the United States was held in Baltimore, and the Dean of Chester accepted the invitation of many Americans to attend as one of the representatives of the Church of England. He most kindly asked me to join him and his family in their journey to America. We left Liverpool on September 22d, and on Sunday morning, October 1st, after a prosperous voyage, we sighted the shores of the New World.

First appeared Far Island, and then Long Island, which gradually became more and more distinct, till we could see houses upon it. Land-birds came flying round the ship, a large one like an oriole settling on the mast; and a shoal of sharp-nosed dolphins played round us, leaping four or five feet out of the water.

The evening before, while we were at dinner, still 300 miles from New York, for the first time since leaving Queenstown the engines had slackened their ceaseless beat, and a general stampede for the deck ensued, to see our pilot come on board. The good-natured captain allowed M. and me to come up on the bridge; and there, half a mile ahead on the starboard bow, lay a pretty little schooner of fifteen or twenty tons, and on the port bow a tiny rowing-boat. We went slower and slower, till as the little boat slid alongside, looking as if she must be sucked under the huge ship, the engines stopped for just one minute. The great man, in purple kid gloves, a tall hat, and a pilot jacket, climbed up the side; a dozen hands were stretched out to help him over the bulwarks; and as his feet touched the deck, "Full speed ahead!" roared the captain, and away we went again.

About 1 P.M. on Sunday we passed Sandy Hook lighthouse, and found ourselves in the outer bay of New York. The sky was cloudless, the sun intensely hot, and the sea like glass. Away to the left beyond Sandy Hook rose the heights of New Jersey, lost in mist at the furthest point of a huge semicircle of many miles, joined to Staten Island by a bit of low swamp land, covered, I was told, with red cedars and cranberries, in which you may get good shooting and bad fever.

Staten Island was on our left bow, clustered with charming villas buried in trees down to the very water's edge, ending at the Narrows or entrance into the inner bay in an escarped hill, with Fort Tomkins above and Fort Wadsworth in the water. On our north, opposite Sandy Hook, lay Far Rockaway, Rockaway, and Coney Island, famed for clams, in front of Long Island, which ended on our right bow at the Narrows with two more forts bristling with 22-inch guns. The part of Long Island between the forts and Brooklyn is where Washington was defeated by the English after Saratoga, and forced to retire upon New York through a swamp where Brooklyn now stands, in which he lost a great number of his men.

Passing the Narrows about 1.30, we anchored inside New York harbour, and waited patiently for the Health officers and Custom-house authorities to come on board.

The scene was marvellously beautiful,—Brooklyn on the right; then beyond East River lay New York itself, the spire of Trinity Church rising far above all the other many spires and towers; then the mouth of the Hudson or North River, as it is called at New York, with Jersey City on its further side; and as a background the blue ridge of the Palisades, 300 feet high.

We were soon summoned below to the saloon to be inspected by the doctor; and, crowding in, sat positively suffocating for some time, no doctor appearing; till at last a voice at the door announced, "You have been inspected, and the doctor has passed you all," and out we trooped again. But how it was managed—whether the doctor marked us down as we went in, or took a telescopic view of us through the windows—no one ever found out.

Our good luck did not end here; for the Custom-house officers, being in an amiable frame of mind, decided to send us ashore with our baggage, about which matter there had been great doubts and many discussions. So the Company's tender, with its black funnel and white band ("The Parson's Tie," the sailors call it), came off; and by three we started across the bay for the Custom-house. We flew through the water in the strange low-decked little boat, with a platform between the paddles, and the "walking beam" working above the deck, as is the case in all the low-pressure engines, which are exclusively used for river boats. The ferry-boats we passed looked most grotesque to our eyes, white painted, with deck piled on deck, and surmounted by their walking beam and tall funnels. Arrived at last at the Custom-house, we found Dr. C. awaiting us on the gangway. After two large waggon-loads of mail-sacks had been cleared out, the luggage began to come on shore; and how anything got through safe I cannot imagine. Truck after truck was run to the edge, and the hapless boxes dashed down upon them with a crack that made one's bones ache in very sympathy. After all our things were collected, Dr. C. took one of the officials aside, and, in a confidential and impressive manner, said to him, "Now, look here, the Dean of C. has just come over from England; so I'm sure you will pass his things out as quick as possible." The poor man, who did not the least know what sort of a creature a Dean was, thought he must at least be some tremendous foreign potentate, and looked duly impressed. The consequence therefore was, that our boxes were hardly opened, but chalked and passed in no time; a great contradiction to the accounts we had been hearing of the severity and rudeness of the New York Custom-house. The building itself is a huge shed, 50 feet high and 200 yards long, and at the end was an iron grille, through which men were thrusting their hands with cards of hacks, and screaming to the new-comers to take them. We forced our way through the noisy crowd to the two carriages which were waiting for us, and drove off.

The streets near the river had a strangely foreign look, reminding me more of some West Indian town, with their green jalousies and shady side-walks, than of any English city. But when at last we got into Fifth Avenue we began to see the full magnificence of this splendid city. The houses are very lofty, built of a rich dark-brown sandstone, with a great deal of mica in it, which comes from Ohio; or of a yellowish white New Jersey stone; or of beautiful white marble, which, owing to the purity and clearness of the air, never seems to get dirty. Up the houses Wistaria grew with an almost tropical luxuriance, and Virginia creeper, just turning red, climbed right up to the roofs. Many houses had a tiny bit of garden, with brilliant green turf and bright flowers in front. On each side of the streets trees were planted, ailanthus, maple, sumach, catalpa, broad-leaved birch, and weeping willows, which last grow to a prodigious size.

Monday, 2d.—After breakfast, unpacking, and writing letters, we wandered out down Fifth Avenue a little way. We passed some eight churches, all of different denominations, including Episcopal, Presbyterian, Unitarian, Catholic, Universalist, and a magnificent Jewish Synagogue just opposite our host's house. It is built of red stone, relieved by the most delicate white stonework, giving it quite a Moorish look, and two cupolas on the street side tower high into the air. The Jewish population of New York is estimated at 60,000, and they seem very much respected.

We were greatly struck by the enormous wealth which all this quarter represents. The rents are perfectly fabulous. One of our friends told us that the whole yearly rent of a large house he lived in, in one of the flourishing New England cities, was less than the rates and taxes he pays yearly on his own house which he has built on Thirty-eighth Street.

In the afternoon we were taken a drive through Central Park. It is beautiful, and unlike anything one has ever seen before. Broken ground with large sheets of water blasted out of the grey rocks, which are covered with Virginia creeper, just turning red, and crawling all over the ground. The trees are well grouped: black walnut, now turning purple; maple, sumach, oaks, and birches. Beds of flowers are scattered here and there; the red salvia especially, in masses of blazing scarlet. On the right of the main road is the beginning of a Zoological Garden, with elands, buffalos, and deer, grazing peaceably close to the carriage-way, and children riding camels over the grass. The roads are perfect, made of pulverized stone rolled down with heavy two-horse rollers. The horses look so well fed and groomed, and the rollers and water-carts in the park are so neat, that they might belong to some gentleman's garden, with his carriage-horses harnessed to them.

October 4.—This afternoon we drove with Dr. H. through Central Park to the Hellgate Ferry, over East River, which

is an arm of the sea connecting the harbour with Long Island
Sound. The river, though navigable above and below, is so
blocked up at this point with masses of rock under water, as
to make the passage impossible for large ships. This is a
serious disadvantage to shipping, forcing the Atlantic ships
and steamers to come far out of their way round the outside
of Long Island, with the dangerous bar to cross before they
can reach the harbour; and the Government are now carrying
out a scheme for removing the obstacle to make a safe passage
for the largest steamers. Under the water large bodies of
men are working, blasting innumerable galleries through the
rock, and in a few years they hope the whole bed will be
cleared.

We crossed over to Astoria on Long Island in the ferry-
boat, which runs every half hour, Dr. H.'s two spirited horses
standing like rocks the whole way over; and on landing
drove up through the village of charming villas, buried in
trees and gardens. Turning to the left through an avenue of
high trees, we came down to the side of the East River again,
and drove some way along a road between the houses and
the water. The views across to the land were beautiful in
the extreme. It was a hazy, warm afternoon, and the trees
were just beginning to turn. Certainly no description or
even painting has ever given one an idea of what the autumn
tints are in reality. The maples were here and there perfectly
dazzling—pure clear amber below, then every shade through
orange till the tips of the branches and tops of the tree were
bright scarlet. It is the clearest colouring I ever saw : nothing
to remind one of death or decay; the live healthy tree
becomes transformed into a flame of fire. We paid several
visits. One dear old Dutch cottage, a perfect museum of
treasures of art, paintings and sculptures inside, had in its
garden a rock on which Washington had smoked many a
pipe, for he was quartered at the house during the War of
Independence. Another house near by, belonging to Mr. W.,

was just the ideal of the American country-house one reads of in books; large and roomy, with a broad raised wooden piazza without any balustrade, running all round it, upon which was scattered every variety of rocking chair. There we were shown a small portrait of Washington, painted while he was President. It was very beautiful: a noble steadfast face in profile, looking away into the future with deep-set earnest eyes—a man, indeed, to found a new nation. Mr. W.'s grandfather was one of those who signed the Declaration, and held a distinguished post in the first American government; and he bought the picture soon after Washington's death.

We turned homewards after this visit, meeting many of the city men driving from their work to their country-houses, in their delightful spider-wheeled waggons, with fast-trotting horses. When we were safe on the broad streets across the ferry, Dr. H. showed us how fast his horses could trot, and gave me the reins when they were trotting as fast as a good gallop. It was the most curious sensation, as the traces were quite slack, and the waggon, with four souls in it, was pulled by my hands. I held on for about five minutes, using the whole of my strength, and then had ignominiously to give up the reins, or I should have just dropped them.

Thursday, 5th.—Directly after breakfast I had a drive in a buggy with a thoroughbred trotter through Central Park, and across the Haarlem river, by a wooden bridge, to a lovely bit of wild country, past the High Bridge which brings the water of the Croton aqueduct into New York, through winding lanes, with pretty cottages here and there, festooned with vines, and gardens full of squashes and Indian corn. Here corn is always called "wheat," and maize is known as "corn" *par excellence*. I hardly know whether I most enjoyed the country or the mere fact of passing through the air, for as we came home "Kentucky" was made to show off his paces, and trotted at the rate of a mile in 2 minutes 50 seconds.

Friday, 6th.—After our few charming days in New York, during which we met with kindness and hospitality on all sides that we can never forget, we started for Niagara by the 5 P.M. train, on the Erie Railway. Crossing from New York to Jersey City in one of the huge river ferry-boats, we pushed our way to the train, through a crowd of the great unwashed, along the dirty, ill-lighted depot: but, once in the luxurious sleeping car all discomfort ceased. We had the compartment for four at the end of the car all to ourselves, with arm-chairs, sofa, footstools, and even our own washstand and looking-glass; with liberty to walk through the rest of the car, or the whole train, if we wished: though no one, save the conductor, could invade our little room.

The evening was dark and wet, so we saw nothing of the country, except where here and there the great bell on the engine began to toll, and the red light from the blazing furnace fire was reflected on the houses as we ran through the open streets of some town, with no protection for the passers-by save their own wits.

At Turner's, a station forty-eight miles from New York, we stopped a quarter of an hour for supper, and got an excellent one of tongue, coffee, and delicious bread, for 25 cents each; after which we turned in for the night, tempted by the snowy pillow-cases, clean sheets, and gay Californian blankets with which the car-porter had invitingly spread our berths. I should doubtless have slept the whole night through, had not the house-flies in New York bitten my face and hands till I was nearly wild; and had not showers of sand, not to say cinders, flown in my face through the ventilators: but these were only slight discomforts; and I woke at 5.30 quite refreshed, and very glad to wash hands and face with clean water and good soap, provided in the ladies' dressing-room outside our compartment.

As the day dawned we became gradually aware of the

wonderful beauty of the scenery through which we were passing. We had left the valley of the Chemung, and were running up the Kenisteo river. Wooded hills on each side, covered with forests of maple, birch, oak, hickory, tulip, chestnut, pine, hemlock, and willow—like our English black willow—by the water; the undergrowth composed chiefly of raspberry, sumach, cypress, asters, and golden rod. On either side of the river were fields of maize in shocks, with bright orange pumpkins lying between the rows; or open pastures, in which fine horses and cattle were feeding. The fields were divided by "worm" fences—known in Canada as Snake-fences—or by root-fences, made of the upturned roots and stumps of large trees. The stumps were left standing in the ground where the soil was not very good; and where it was worth while to get rid of them, either burnt standing, or torn up with some machine. The houses, built mostly of wood, reminded one of Swiss châlets, with deep eaves: but without the picturesque decorations.

The slope of glowing trees, of every possible shade, from palest amber to deep carmine, mingled with gaunt bare pine stems, or deep black hemlocks, down to the river, was beautiful in the extreme; especially where at some bend in the track a further ridge came in sight, with intense blue shadows brought out by the brilliant foreground. But unluckily beautiful scenery will not satisfy the craving of hunger; and we were looking forward to seven o'clock for breakfast at Hornellsville with great delight, when, at a quarter to seven, outside the little station of Kenisteo, we came to a standstill. On inquiring, we found that "a freight car was off the track," a man observing coolly, "Run over a keaow, I guess!" which proved to be the case. So there we had to wait, let the down train pass us, get on the down track, and run up it for some distance, till we came to the next "switch" or siding. While we were waiting there, not over comfortable at our position, a train passed us to go to the switch at

Kenisteo, with several large open trucks full of blue barrels. These we were told were "oil tanks," otherwise petroleum cans,—pleasant neighbours on a jolting track. The tanks are now made of iron, an improvement on the old barrels: but, as a New York fellow-passenger remarked to us, "It's about as safe as gunpowder." At last the train moved on; and, passing the oil train, we got to Hornellsville, and our much-coveted and excellent breakfast, some of which we carried off, as we had hardly time to satisfy ourselves before the cry of "All aboard" from the conductor warned us that time was up.

In about two hours we came near Portage; and the conductor of our car took us out on the back platform to get the best view of the bridge, which is one of the wonders of the country. It is a "trestle bridge," built entirely of wood 800 feet long and 223 feet high, across the Genessee river, which here has eaten its way through the limestone rocks, and made a deep chasm. Below the bridge, the river falls into a deep basin of stone, then into a second, and then rushes away to the foot of a large conical rock, under which it turns sharply, another stream falling over the rock in a splendid waterfall, and joining the Genessee below; while all is softened, and yet brightened, by the vivid colouring of the trees on the crest of the cliffs.

After Portage came rather a different kind of country, as we were out of the Kenisteo valley. Forest close to the rail; sometimes a clearing in process of making; fallen trees, burning stumps, men with their axes hewing off the branches or loading the carts. Then upland fields, with here and there a vineyard. As we neared Buffalo it became still more open, with wide pastures, worm fences, wooded hill-tops, and at last a glimpse of distant blue flat-topped heights, on the further side of Lake Erie.

A boy had appeared in the cars after breakfast, dropping a tempting book on each seat, and returning just as the unwary had had time to feel a slight interest in the letterpress, for his book or his money. Now he came round with *Buffalo Morning Express;* and then again, offering us Isabella or Catauba grapes, with a tough inside and foxy flavour. Buffalo, where we stopped and changed engines, looked very uninteresting, on a dead flat. We saw nothing but six spires, a lot of shingle houses, and a great deal of smoke in the distance; with a fore-ground of large sheds, a good many cows, a boy and a dog. We now turned off on quite another line, and ran through a level country for some miles, with dikes on each side of the rail, filled with reeds, asters, œnothera, and golden rod; and our young friend the train-boy soon reappeared with apples, candy, and books of Niagara waterfalls, and the "Great Western Money Package." This packet, price one dollar, is said on its wrapper to contain

"Silver and gold in each package up to $2.50 (10s.).

"1 quire superfine quality paper.

"1 packet sup. envelopes.

"1 penholder and pen.

"1 sheet blotting-paper.

"1 photograph.

"5 views of Niagara Falls."

I saw a good many packages opened, chiefly by honeymoon couples, who abound on this line: but none of them contained the promised coin.

Then, running through some woods, we emerged beside what seemed a large and perfectly smooth lake about a mile and a half across, wooded down to the water: but on looking as far as one could beyond the train, a white cloud appeared, rising apparently from behind a wooded point; and in a moment we knew that our lake must be the Niagara river; the cloud was the column of spray from the Falls; and we gazed with all our eyes, till, plunging into the woods again, river and all was shut out.

After some consultation we decided to cross the lower

suspension bridge in the cars, and get our first view from thence; and when the time came, and the good-natured conductor took us out again on the back platform as we crept over the lofty bridge, we went rather in fear as to what our first impression would be. But in a moment there was no shadow of doubt on our minds. A dead silence; and then an irrepressible exclamation of wonder and delight. There, two miles up the gorge, at the head of a smooth green blue river, between high limestone cliffs, covered with blazing maples and black pines, was Niagara. When we had escaped the mob of yelling cab-drivers, who pounce on the luckless traveller almost before the train stops at the station, and had found our way in a comfortable carriage up to the Clifton House, our first thought was to rush out to the upper suspension bridge, and there to stand in silence trying to realize the whole thing. The extreme beauty struck us more than anything else. There was nothing horrible—hardly awful. The water as it fell looked so soft. I tried to think of what it reminded me most in substance, and all I could think of was whipped cream!—a sad bathos, but true. The sound of the water was soft, harmonious, musical, and, though strong, was never oppressive. The sun was bright, the air still; so that the spray rose straight up into the blue sky.

Sunday, 8th.—The sound of the Falls made sleep all but impossible. I was longing all night for day to dawn, that I might see them again; and when daylight came their aspect was completely changed. A strong wind was blowing, driving the spray down towards us, and covering all the view in a fine bluish white mist; the early sun caught half the Horse-shoe fall, leaving the rest in shadow; and lighted up the mass of blazing maples and Virginia creepers close to us.

The Rector, Mr. M'C., called for us at 10.30, and we had a glorious walk along the cliff over the river to his church at Clifton. We had a very nice service, the Dean preaching:

and it felt home-like hearing the prayers for the Queen so far away. The singing was good, but peculiar. A very pretty young lady played the harmonium, and three others and a gentleman sang. The fittings of the tiny church are good, though plain, made of the white pine of the country, topped with black walnut, which is very handsome. After service we walked back to the hotel, and then drove up to dinner at Mr. B.'s. There were several Englishmen there, and after dinner we all set out for a long walk. First we went to a high point directly over the Horse-shoe Fall, where we got the finest view we had yet seen, through a frame of maple and hickory. Then, turning up the railroad track, we walked along it for some distance, to my horror, till assured that there were no trains on Sunday, and that, if there were, it would not matter. Then a steep bit of road led us down to the level of the river. The water was quite quiet near the bank: but passing a small island we came suddenly upon a scene of fearful grandeur. We were within half a dozen feet of the rapids. Then for the first time we realized the awful force of the water. We sat on the bank throwing in pieces of wood; watching them whirled along; listening to the horrible stories of the accidents this year; till the place seemed haunted,—especially as the greatest tragedy took place close to where we sat. A man was crossing the river some way up. His boat by some means was swamped; and he was swept down towards the rapids. He swam the whole way, till he came close to the spot we were on, where at that time some workmen of Mr. S., who owns all this side of the river, were making a bridge. He made straight for them, swimming gallantly, thinking he was saved, and came within a few feet of the bank. They stretched a pole out to him to help him: but it was too short: they missed him! All hope was gone: and he just made straight for the Fall, still swimming, and, as he reached the edge, put his hands above his head, raised himself up, and dived clean over. His body was found torn limb from limb below the Falls.

We were glad to shake off such painful impressions, and wander on to Mr. S.'s beautiful place. His house is on the high ground, with woods and shrubberies down to the water, where a dozen little islands lie clustered, connected with pretty bridges, and fringed with a brilliant yellow-green reed about a foot high, which grows in all still creeks round this part of Canada.

Coming back, Mr. B., who is a good botanist, helped us out of some of our puzzles about the new trees and flowers we saw at every step. I got to know locust beans, button-wood nuts, a kind of plane, black walnuts—and learnt to my cost the difference between hickory and bitter hickory nuts, which look just alike, till you unwarily try, and tasting the wrong one seem to be eating a mixture of sloe-juice and tannin.

We walked home in the twilight, down a ravine in the cliff, half way between the Horse-shoe and the hotel; the American Fall, right before us, shut in the view like a huge white curtain; and when we got in it was quite dark.

Monday, 9th.—Out sketching on the piazza by 7.30; a splendid day: hot sun and strong breeze.

After breakfast the M'C.s called for us, and we went down three miles to Des Vaux College, on the American side. Mr. P., the head master, and his wife, took us all over it. There are about fifty boys, foundationers and term boys. They are nearly all gentlemen's sons. The College is conducted entirely on the military system, and seems most perfect in its arrangement. The dormitories were beautifully fresh and neat; each boy has his alcove, and has to keep it tidy, and make his own bed. Some of the rooms were gay with pictures and photographs. We went to the schoolroom, where the Dean spoke a few words to the boys; then into the armoury, where their muskets are kept; and on through dining-room, kitchen, and washing-room. Here Mrs. H. and I were much attracted by a capital kind of brush for cleaning boots, combining blacking and cleaning brush, with a nice handle into the bargain. Mrs. P. was so amused at our raptures that she dived into her store cupboard, and presented me with a new one on the spot.

The famous whirlpool belongs to the College, and is a large source of income, as visitors have to pay a slight toll for going to see it.

Above, looking up to the railroad bridge, the river is a mass of white foaming boiling rapids, leaping into the air, and ending in the angle of the cliffs in an apparently smooth round pool, which is in fact the whirlpool. At this point the river is completely shut in with high cliffs, covered with dark trees; and one thinks there can be no outlet: till, turning the point, you find that it makes a sudden bend at right angles, still between high wooded cliffs; then another bend, and it is lost behind the hills above Queenstown and Lake Ontario. There are rapids below the whirlpool: but they are not so dangerous. The 'Maid of the Mist' is the only boat that ever got safe through. There are always things floating in the whirlpool, sailing gently round and round till they touch the centre, when down they go in an instant, and do not emerge till they get a quarter of a mile down the river.

We "concluded" to spare ourselves the long climb down and up 300 steps to the river, as the sun was broiling, and we had a hard day before us; and so drove straight to the Falls city. If travellers get their first impressions from the road on the American side, I can better understand their being disgusted with the place.—Wooden shanties, desolate-looking trees, untidy little stores, German gasthaüser and wirthschaften, and horribly dusty roads. The Falls city, however, is a pleasant place, with good stores of photographs and Indian curiosities.

A visit to the drawing-room of the Cataract Hotel, which overhangs the rapids, only served to increase our satisfaction at being on the Canadian side; for the view of the Falls is entirely lost, and you are only impressed with the rush and turmoil of the rapids.

We explored Goat Island: but resisted all entreaties to risk our necks and get a ducking by going down to the "Cave of the Winds," below the American Fall, being quite content with its beauty from Luna Island, where the water, as it takes its great leap, looks like threads of spun glass, clear as crystal.

October 10*th*.—It was hard, after three days of such perfect enjoyment, to tear ourselves away from Niagara. Each hour that we stayed only brought out some fresh beauty, and made us long to spend weeks there instead of days. Were any one to take the whole journey from England and back again, and see nothing in America but Niagara, it would, I think, be well worth the trouble. But time was short; so on Tuesday morning we found ourselves on board the cars for Kingston, *via* Toronto. This part of our journey was not enjoyable; as, when one is once accustomed to the novelty of snake-fences, small farms, backwoods, clearings, and blackened trees, the constant repetition becomes rather tedious: and we were not sorry to reach Toronto, and spend some hours there in poking about the streets and making small investments in the fur trade, till it began to rain. About 6 P.M. we left by rail for Kingston, and most foolishly, in our ignorance, did not take places in the sleeping-car. Anything more uncomfortable than the six hours we passed in that train I have seldom felt: smothered with petroleum from the lamps—the lashing rain forcing us to keep the windows up—noisy fellow-passengers, and a road that nearly jolted one to pieces.

At 2 A.M. we reached Kingston, and as we drove up to the city in pitchy darkness, for the first time observed that the air was filled with the smell of burning wood. After a couple of hours' broken sleep in our clothes, we got up at five; the smell of fire was stronger; the air seemed full of smoke; and, embarking on the steamer 'Corinthian,' we were told that it was the smoke from Chicago, which was burning before we left Niagara, and from the great Wisconsin forest fires. It so filled the air, though it had travelled 500 miles, that it completely spoilt our views on the St. Lawrence; and we could only get any idea of the effect of the Thousand Islands covered with brilliant foliage, when we passed close between some of them. The rocks of which they are formed struck us as something quite new; and I have since learnt from Professor Dawson at Montreal that they are a spur of the Laurentian formation of Canada, through which the river has sawn its way with great difficulty, thereby forming this beautiful group of islands of every shape and size.

But a worse disappointment was in store for us. After we were clear of the islands the smoke grew so thick that, on coming to the head of the Grand Sault, our captain announced that he could not see ahead, and so dared not "shoot the rapids:" but was going down a canal by the side of the river at the rate of three miles per hour. This was intolerable, as we should be about twenty-four hours getting to Montreal: so we determined to "abandon the ship," and try our luck by land. The lock at which we were stopping was but three miles from a station on the Grand Trunk Railroad, where we found a train would arrive in two hours. Gathering up our bags and umbrellas—our luggage had happily been sent through by rail,—we prepared for a tramp, with the chance of losing our way in an unknown country. But a friend was at hand, in the shape of a respectable-looking man on the bank, who said he would "hitch up his waggon" and drive us to the station for a dollar with pleasure. The offer was too good to be refused; so we closed with him at once, and clambering up the steep canal bank, found ourselves in front of our friend's house, where his wife and daughter, both smartly dressed, made us welcome. In five minutes our host drove round from the little farm-yard in a light spring-waggon, with a gay pair of horses that would hardly stand still to let us clamber in, before they started at a furious pace along a perfectly break-neck road, full of rocks and ruts, with snake-fences on each side, and woods of hemlock, spruce, red cedar, and pine. Our driver was very communicative, and so delighted to hear about the "old country." His grand-father came from London; and he spoke with loving pride of England, as did every Canadian we met. They are far more loyal, alas! than many English people; and the Queen's birthday is a general holiday, and day of rejoicing all over the country. This man, who looked like a small farmer, and towed ships up and down the canal—a waggoner is the name of his class—said he "owned thirteen horses; and that his daughter drove a pair all about the country," adding, by way of encouragement, "not this pair, as these are apt to run away if they see a wheelbarrow or anything strange in the road." Happily for us they saw nothing "strange" before reaching the line; where we got out, thanking our friend—who seemed to think the obligation was entirely on his side—and walked up the track to the station in the casual way people do here, right in front of an engine with cars behind it full of gunpowder.

Montreal we reached late at night; and, owing to over-fatigue and a day's rain, we saw much less of it than we wished in our two days' visit. Then we crossed the St. Law-rence by the Victoria bridge, that marvel of engineering, two miles long; a night journey took us through Evangeline's country; and by daylight on Saturday we were running down the Hudson River Railroad.

October 14.—West Point.

We arrived at this paradise this morning; steamed across in the ferry-boat to the foot of a wooded cliff; and drove up a steep road to the Academy. It stands on a plateau about 100 feet above the river, on a point, as its name denotes, with views up and down the Highlands of the Hudson, wood-covered hills 3000 to 4000 feet high, while the river, which here makes a sharp bend, runs between them. The whole look of the mountains, but for the bright-coloured foliage, reminds one strongly of the best bits of Killarney. The hotel is in a perfect situation at the end of the point, looking up to Newburgh.

We started forth for a stroll before dinner, and went first to a pit on the parade-ground full of Michaelmas-daisy, growing so abundantly that it had just the same effect as a bed of blue-bells in spring at home. Then we tried a path leading down past the hotel, that looked as if it must take us to the river; as it did in course of time, after we had had a most delicious scramble over rocks and through trees, geologizing and botanizing to the best of our powers. We found three if not four new kinds of fern; one corresponding evidently to our Filix-mas, and a Polypodium so like *vulgare* that I could not tell them apart, save that their leaves might be a little longer and narrower than the English one. The rocks were covered with blueberry—the berries had gone—and Virginia creeper, which trails over rocks here as well as up trees. It seems to me quite a pity it should not be grown in this way in English gardens; the effect of the bright leaves on grey rock or dark soil is beautiful. The maple was dazzling; one bush we found with each leaf green in the centre, with a scarlet edge. Our path at last led down to the beach, where we sat on a huge ice-scratched rock, under a group of "white"—Weymouth—pines, looking up to the highlands, and feasting on the extreme beauty, which far surpasses anything we had been led to expect. We walked up to the hotel by a rather longer route, gathering leaves, nuts, and flowers. The arbor-vitæ grows magnificently in the rocky cliffs; juniper, covered with fruit, hickory, butternut, walnut, chestnut, birch, maple, white and purple oak, dogwood, guelder rose, all different shades of yellow, red, and purple; here and there the long scarlet and orange leaves of the sumach, like flames of fire; through the trees views of river and mountain; and all bathed in hot sunlight. When we got back, we soon set to work on an excellent dinner, which ended with ice-cream for dessert —a sign we were back in the neighbourhood of New York, where you seldom have dinner without it. At Mr. P.'s, in New York, we had ice in the shape of waffles, and cobs of Indian corn, the green leaves of Pistache, the pod of Vanille; and in the streets you get a wine-glassful for a cent, paying two cents if you have the luxury of a spoon.

After dinner, General R., the superintendent, kindly introduced us to his adjutant, who took us all over the Academy. The library is a fine room, where the students may come and read as much as they like. They have all sorts of books, from classics down to story-books. One table had a pigeon-hole devoted to each periodical magazine, British as well as American. There are a few very fine pictures of celebrated generals, more or less connected with the Academy —Washington, Monroe, Lafayette, General Totten, a noble-looking man—indeed, they are all fine heads, born to rule, such as it would be difficult to find here or in Europe now-a-days. We then went across to the gymnasium, out of which opens a room with models of guns and projectiles, in all stages of construction,—an admirable plan, as on the same board you have the bar of iron in every stage, up to the perfect barrel. Here I saw a Gatling gun for the first time, a beautiful weapon. It has, I think, ten barrels; a tin case containing twenty cartridges, with regulation musket bullets $\frac{55}{100}$ of an inch, fits into a slit on one side, and, as a crank is turned on the right by a handle, drops a cartridge from the left into the barrel, and fires instantly. Captain H. said he had fired one sixty times as fast as he could turn the handle, and found, on going up to the target, they were all in a space as wide as his own chest would cover. We then went up into the recitation and drawing rooms, and the engineering-room, with models of forts, pontoons, and maps; and, lastly, into a large room full of trophies and models, hung all round with the tattered colours which were through the Mexican war and the war with the South. But, of all the things in that room, the one that sent a thrill through one to one's very finger-ends was a small conical shot, not twelve inches long. It was "the shot" that opened the war, the one fired on April 12, 1861, on Fort Sumter. Opposite it was the return shot from the North, a round ball; and between the two a huge ball from the Northern iron-clads, thrown at Fort Sumter two years later, when it was in possession of the South.

It was a strange feeling: standing there with that terrible little shot in my hand, and the Stars and Stripes waving from the flagstaff outside.

In half an hour we went out to see a dress parade of the cadets. Just as we got opposite the flagstaff the gun fired, the flag dropped, and the band struck up a march. It was extremely pretty to watch the parade. Their drill was gone through like clock-work, and they doubled off the ground to perfection. There are 254 cadets at present. The discipline is Spartan; the course is four years, and for two years they have no vacation; then they have seventy days' leave of absence, and no more till they have done the other two years. They have no holidays in the week but Saturday afternoon; and then they may not go out of the Academy bounds.

Their uniform is a plain light grey: but the regular soldiers' full dress is most picturesque; light blue trousers, dark blue short jacket, and slouched beaver hat with a black ostrich feather at one side, looped up on the other side with a gold eagle.

Sunday, Oct. 15th.—This morning General R. called for

us to take us to service in the cadets' chapel. The chapel itself is not remarkable for beauty, being much like the buildings at Sandhurst; but inside, over the altar, there is a fine painting by Professor Weir, who teaches drawing here, and is considered one of the first American artists. Below the picture is a trophy of the American eagle with outspread wings, over a blue banner, with the national motto "God and our Country," under which are draped two ensigns crossed of the stars and stripes.

On the wall to the left, looking towards the altar, is a recess with glass before it, containing the flags captured in the Mexican war of '47, with two elaborately-chased guns let into the wall on each side, and the names of all the officers who fell inscribed in gold on small black tablets. On the wall too, right above where we sat with the General, are similar tablets, with the names of all the generals who served in the War of Independence, and have died since. Where Arnold's name should have been, a blank is left. In another recess were the five colours taken from us at Saratoga, and some guns and mortars captured at the same time, with the old G.R. upon them.

It gave one a strange feeling again: looking up at them, and hearing our first American service in the West Point Chapel. The service was very much shortened on account of the cadets; the singing, done by seven or eight of them in a gallery over the door by the organ, was exceedingly good, slow and reverent. Dr. F., the chaplain, preached a most impressive sermon upon Chicago, with a touching allusion to the sympathy of Britain and Germany. After the ascription he repeated the whole of the doxology

"Praise God from whom all blessings flow,"

and the whole congregation sung it slowly and solemnly to the dear "Old Hundredth." It was perfectly overpowering to our English ears. Then followed a short prayer for the army, navy, and the cadets, "that they might be made good men and good soldiers;" then the blessing, and we left the church. It was a very beautiful service :—so much reverence on the part of the young men, notwithstanding their different creeds.

General R. took us on the way to the hotel past Kosciusko's monument on the top of the old fortifications. There never was any fighting, he said, on this actual point: but at the old Fort Clinton, just below. At Constitution Island, just above, the army was disbanded after the War of Independence was over; and on the grass, at the end of the parade-ground, lie the old chains which were put across the river to prevent the Britishers getting up.

After dinner we walked to Fort Putnam on the hill above the point with Dr. F. The road winds up through rocky woods, and from the Fort we got a splendid view up and down the river, the Point and its buildings lying mapped out below. I caught a beautiful little tree toad, bright buff colour, with suckers on its feet; and near the top the Katydids —grasshoppers—were perfectly deafening. We came down just in time to hear Yankee Doodle played at the cadet Sunday parade, which we watched from the piazza of General A.'s house. He was in command of the Colorado district, which I hoped soon to visit. Here we met Professor Weir, the painter, who told me of a new way of preserving leaves and ferns, by dipping them in linseed oil, and pressing them between newspapers.

About 7.30 General and Mrs. A. called; evening visits being the custom in America. After they were gone we took a stroll. It was like a summer's evening, deliciously hot. The air was full of the sound of grasshoppers and frogs, and also, alas! of mosquitos, who are biting voraciously. This is our third Sunday in America. Each has been quite perfect in its own way; the first coming into New York harbour, the next at Niagara, and to-day at West Point.

CHAPTER II.

FROM EAST TO WEST.

Down the Hudson—Trains in the streets—Parlour cars—Baltimore—An American country-house—The Convention of 1871—Start for the West—St. Louis—"Arctic Soda"—Mustang fever—Kansas city—The Plains—Prairie dogs—An old "rattler"—Buffalos—United States forts—A railroad feat—Denver—The Rocky Mountains—The pioneer narrow-gauge railroad—Pike's Peak.

On Monday, 16th, we set off by train down the east bank of the Hudson, past pretty towns and villages of white houses, with a singular collection of names,—Indian, Dutch, Classic, and English, all mixed up together. For instance, you have Poughkeepsie, Hyde Park, Tivoli, Caatskill, Athens, Stockport, and Troy, all within some hundred miles of each other.

Close to New York we got a fine view of the Palisades, a curious line of basaltic cliffs 300 feet high, running for some miles along the western bank of the river. We came slowly into the city, down one of the streets, for three or four miles, a most alarming proceeding to our European nerves, as the street was crowded with children, horses, and carriages. Every moment we expected some one or some thing would get under the car wheels. But as the State affords no protections against accidents, people learn to protect themselves; and while the great train of cars steamed slowly on, the bell on the engine tolling funereally, the passers-by cleared off the track just in time to escape destruction. The apparent carelessness of human life struck us much when we first arrived in America.

The Dean asked the conductor of our car, as we crossed

the bridge at Portage, whether people were not forbidden to stand on the platform.

"Yes," he said, "there is a notice to that effect; but every one does it at his own risk, and if he is killed there is no one but himself to blame."

An American friend was greatly diverted at my horror as we ran into Baltimore, but confessed that he had once been thoroughly frightened. He was on an engine going over a flat stretch of road; and as it seemed perfectly clear for two or three miles, the engineer started full speed to show him the pace of the engine. Suddenly, as they rushed along, in the middle of their racing ground, they saw close before them a tiny child, of a year or so, sitting playing on the rails. They whistled and hooted and tried to stop. All in vain; the child did not move. But just as they thought in agony that in a moment more nothing could save it, a woman stepped leisurely from a cottage by the side of the track, picked the little thing up with one hand, and stepped back as the engine rushed past.

After breakfast in New York we started for Baltimore in a parlour car. The Bishop of New York and his daughter and several gentlemen, all on their way, like ourselves, to the Convention, joined us at the depot; so we were a party large enough to secure the whole central compartment of the car for ourselves. It was about 14 feet by 8, and 11 feet high, with five windows, and arm-chair seats for twelve, carpets, footstools, and bright lamps, as well as a tap of iced water. This really is the perfection of travelling. We walked about and talked to our friends, and had visitors in to see us from the other cars, all the afternoon; so that it did not matter to us that the New Jersey country through which we ran was flat and uninteresting, except for its extreme richness. Our chief external excitements were crossing the Raritan, Delaware, Schuylkill, and Susquehanna rivers, which are quite magnificent; and also in passing Philadelphia we got a fine view from the cars of the city, running past it through a part of Fairmount Park, one of the most beautiful, as well as one of the largest public parks in the world, being over 1600 acres, with the Schuylkill river flowing through.

At 8 P.M. we reached Baltimore, where our kind reception certainly went far to prove the truth of the popular belief, that it is the most hospitable city in the Union. And here I met Mr. S., who most kindly offered to be my escort to the West to join my brother next week, if I can find no one going sooner.

Thursday, 19th.—Mrs. H. and I took a little walk this afternoon to a railroad tunnel they are making near here, which is being lined with blocks of white marble. There were blocks of a finer kind, such as is used for building, in a yard close by. All the basements of the houses are built of this lovely marble, quarried about eight miles off, the upper floors being usually of red brick.

At four o'clock we went to dinner at Mr. D.'s, in Madison Avenue, where the Bishop of Minnesota was staying. He has given his whole life to the Sioux Indians, and has an extraordinary influence over them, which would not surprise any one who had the honour of knowing him.

Besides him we met Bishop Atkinson, and the Bishops of Rhode Island and Connecticut. The latter took me in to dinner, and was most agreeable. He told me much that was interesting about his diocese, where he said one could still find in the country districts that simple primitive New-England life one reads of in *Hitherto* and the *Gayworthies*, and which is becoming rarer every year, under the growth of large towns.

October 20.—Miss P. carried us off to luncheon at her father's country-house, five miles from town. We have had a lovely drive past pretty country places, with distant views of a rolling wooded country.

Mr. P.'s house was one's ideal of an American country place. A long road through purple oaks and yellow hickory led up to a rather low white house, its broad piazzas covered with luxurious rocking-chairs; and fragrant beds of roses either side of the steps. We went for a walk through the pleasure-ground, and passing a field of corn (maize) had the delight of picking off a large cob, as the corn was not yet cut. Luncheon was ready on our return; such a pretty meal: "Irish" and sweet potatoes, delicious rolls, thinnest wafer-biscuits; and in the middle of luncheon little old-fashioned glasses of "Confederate punch" were handed round by the negro man and maid. After tea and coffee, which are drunk at table, we sat in the piazza; and then took our leave, laden with boughs of scarlet maple, cobs of corn, Osage oranges we had picked up in the road, a glorious bunch of rosebuds and mignonette, promises of a collection of varnished leaves, and the kindest wishes for our speedy return.

During our stay we drove through the park just beyond the city. It had originally been a gentleman's place, and was given by him to Baltimore. The trees are beautiful; the winding roads up and down hill, with deer coming to stare at the carriage, the brilliant foliage, bright sun, and clear air, give one quite a new idea of a city park.

23*d*.—We went off to the city early, to the Convention at Emanuel Church, which of course the Dean attended every day; and we listened for some time to the debates, hearing some very good and some very bad speaking.

The General Convention meets every third year, the larger cities of the Union being taken in rotation. It met once before at Baltimore in 1808, when a small parlour was large enough for the Upper House, consisting of two Bishops out of a total number of six. In 1871 there met 50 Bishops in the Upper House; while in the Lower House were the Delegates, lay and clerical, four and four from each diocese, making a total, theoretically, of 400, practically of about 300. The Upper House, after the opening service, retired to a smaller church close by, where they met with closed doors. The Lower House continued their meetings at Emanuel, a very large church. The platform of the apsidal chancel was turned into a place of business, with a chair and table in the centre for the President, and others for the secretaries and reporters. The floor of the church was systematically mapped out, according to the dioceses. The name of each State or territory was printed in large letters on a standard, above the respective pews; so that one had the whole of the United States, from Massachusetts to California, from Alabama to Minnesota, brought before one in that little space.

24*th*.—Went into the Convention again, and arranged everything with my kind escort to the West; finished my packing; telegraphed to my brother in Colorado to say when I should arrive at Denver; and we then went to dine at the Bishop of Maryland's. We met there Bishop Wilmer of Alabama, and his cousin Bishop Wilmer of Louisiana, the Bishop of Albany, and various other people. Many were the questions I had to answer about my journey in prospect; and I was soon so tired as to be glad, in spite of all the pleasant acquaintances I made, and friends I met, to go quietly home to rest with Mrs. B., our kind hostess, till it was time to start.

Mr. B. drove me down to the depot about 10 P.M., and put me into Mr. S.'s hands; and in pitchy darkness and lashing rain I bade farewell to Baltimore, its charming inhabitants, and my dear English friends, and was fairly launched on my way to the unknown West.

My berth was extremely comfortable; and I had a good night, notwithstanding many stoppages and bumping to and fro, little dreaming of what an escape we had. In the morning it leaked out that during the night a train in front of us had broken down, and been unable to signal us; and had it not been for the powerful air-brakes they use on this line, we should have run right into it, as we were only able to stop just as we got up to it; while to add to the possible horror, another train was close behind us.

In the morning of Wednesday we were woke up at five by the conductor; when we discovered to our surprise that during the night we had climbed up about 2000 feet, and were now at Altoona, near the top of the Alleghanies. It was a misty morning, so that the views were rather

Horse-shoe Bend, Alleghany Mountains.

spoilt: but over the summit we caught glimpses through the mist and clouds of grand scenery as we wound round the mountain sides. On either hand were pine forests, some black from recent fires, others with a brilliant undergrowth of sumach and dogwood.

About eleven miles below Cresson Springs on the summit of the mountains, having run all that distance without steam, we came to the Horse-shoe Bend, where the curve is so great that, looking out of the windows of the last car, you see the three engines of the train running parallel with you, only the other way.

The rain cleared off, and the scenery became more and more distinct as we came down the side of the mountain trout-streams, their banks shaded with tall hemlocks, and a thick undergrowth of rhododendrons and ferns among the rocks.

At a thriving-looking city, called Johnston, we came to the first coal-mines, and they increased in number as we went on. They are mainly adits—galleries run into the hill-side horizontally. From Johnston we followed the Connemaugh river which joins the Alleghany above Pittsburgh, through the Packsaddle Gap, reaching the Wolverhampton of the States about 11 A.M. Here we changed cars; and with great difficulty found places in the sleeping-cars of the New York train we joined, as it was crowded with passengers. As soon as we were clear of the smoke and dirt of Pittsburg, the journey till dark was quite lovely. We crossed the Ohio, where we first saw stern-wheel steamers for shallow water; then ran along a stream for miles and miles, following its windings till the sharp curves made me feel almost giddy. So the night came on: and on the 26th we woke up to find ourselves among the rolling hills and plains of Indiana; and had breakfast at Terre Haut, of coffee, roast quail, and corn bread.

The country grew more level as we neared St. Louis; and about ten miles from the city we passed some bluffs standing out of a dead flat of alluvial ground running away to the river, which are supposed to mark what have been at one time the old banks of the river itself. In one part of this flat rose half-a-dozen mounds, believed to be Indian burying-places of immense antiquity. At last we reached the river, and all turned out of the cars into six huge omnibuses, with four magnificent horses to each, and drove down to a ferry-boat, where they were all drawn up side by side, the horses standing like statues; and so we crossed the Mississippi. Like every European, I was prepared to be greatly impressed by my first view of the "Father of Waters:" but I must confess to a feeling of blank disappointment. I saw nothing but a wide river— but not as wide as I expected, of a horrible pea-soup colour, covered with steamers; a huge unfinished bridge; and the city, on the other side, looking rather dingy, with its broad wharves or "levees," and long rows of tall warehouses.

Landing on the further bank, an incident occurred which gave one a glimpse of the rough and ready fashion of the West. The gangway of the ferry-boat was a good foot and a half below the levee or pier on which we had to land; and one naturally expected that they would either raise it in some way, or put down something to smooth the joining. No such thing. The horses were set off full trot; and they dragged us up with a bump that would have broken any ordinary carriage to pieces, sending the passengers all flying in a mass against each other in the middle of the omnibus.

This over, we went at a great pace up the muddy streets, away from the river to the hotel, where we stopped for a few hours. As the parlour was very hot, and full of crying children, we escaped and took a short stroll about the city. We went first to a German bakery, and then refreshed ourselves with an "Arctic Soda," flavoured with strawberry, 10 cents. These soda fountains are found at every "Drugstore" in the large cities, with taps of different flavours, and generally one marked "Tonic," which produces something considerably stronger than the innocent raspberry and pineapple syrups. Chemists are not allowed to sell spirituous liquors, except for medicinal purposes; and the police are supposed to search their stores at intervals. But when the officer comes in and asks if they have any spirits on the premises, he is occasionally silenced by a glass of "Tonic and Soda," and leaves the chemist alone till the next time he feels thirsty.

After laying in a small stock of provisions against our journey across the plains, we made our way down to the Missouri Pacific depot; and were soon steaming away towards the setting sun.

Now began the really novel part of the journey. I was west of the Mississippi; on that enchanted ground to which, if you have once set foot upon it, you must sooner or later return. "Mustang fever" is the name which Westerners give to that wholly inexplicable feeling, which is said to allure people back into the wilderness, almost against their own wills, when they try to cure themselves of their roving tastes, by living in the cities of the Eastern States, or even in Europe. Ere I went thither it was easy enough for me in my ignorance to laugh at this theory: but now I am not quite sure that I have wholly escaped the contagion. Certainly the journey of the first evening, as we left St. Louis, was most attractive. The moon was so bright that I was tempted to sit up looking at the country till nearly every one else had gone to bed. We ran for some hours alongside of the Missouri river, the trees on its banks reflected clear and sharp in the smooth water, reminding one of some charming old steel engraving. Then we crossed the river, and ran for some way with it on our right, and with broken ground on the left, in some parts cultivated, in others forest, with deep gullies worn by water through the light sandy soil.

At last I packed up for the night; and woke about six on the 27th to find the train at a stand-still at some bit of a place, a perfect specimen of a mushroom town. It consisted of a few wooden houses, a saloon, a boot-store, a dry goods store, and directly opposite our car a wooden shanty, with a plate on the door, stating that this was "Dr. Miller's Office;" while above the door the public were informed, in large letters, that H. C. Miller sold "drugs, medicines, paints, oils, glass, putty, books, stationery, and perfumery."

The ground was white with hoar-frost; and the sun rose crimson over an open country rolling away to the blue distance. With joy I thought,—" Only one night more, and we shall be at Denver:" but then, to our dismay, came the news that by some unlucky chance we had started in the wrong train, and must wait fourteen hours at Kansas City to catch the through train. My heart sank;

for of all places to wait at, a more unpleasant one on a hot day than Kansas City, which we reached about 8 A.M., can hardly be found. But in a new country one has to put up with many little annoyances; so we determined to make the best of a bad matter, and drove up to the Lindell Hotel. After breakfast in a very hot room, we explored the town a little. It stands on a sandy bluff over the river; a strange situation to choose, as the foundations for all the houses on the slope of the hill have to be cut out of the sand at great expense and inconvenience. There were two or three good streets, partly finished; several hotels; and scattered stores, some wooden and some brick, standing alone or in small clusters; little wooden saloons, with glass fronts, and various titles in English or German—" Colorado Saloon," " Denver Saloon," " Deutsches Gasthaus," etc.; and candy or fruit stores at the corners of what are in the future to be streets, but are now only masses of mud and stone with a boarded side-walk. One of these small booths bore a device painted in the very roughest style of art,—a large shoe, a green and red fly, and the word "syrup" written below them. After some reflection I found that it signified that "Shoofly syrups" were to be procured from the owner.

Higher up the hill there are churches, schools, and many good residences: but the day was so hot that I put off my further explorations to some future visit. Along the river below the city are lines of warehouses, and one of the huge elevators for raising and shipping loads of grain. Of this curious process an excellent description may be found in Mr. Macrae's account of Chicago in *The Americans at Home*.

After dinner we went down to the depot of the Kansas Pacific Railroad, to secure our tickets and places in the sleeping-cars. The heat was intense, the road being cut through sandbanks, which reflected the blazing sun overhead. The day wore away slowly, and I was rejoiced to hear about 10.30 P.M. the rattle of the four-horse omnibus outside the hotel, to take us to the train, and decided that I had seen enough of Kansas City to satisfy me: though I doubt not, from what I know since, I should have liked it better had it been less hot, and I less impatient to get on.

28*th*.—At daybreak I found we were on the prairies in good earnest; and in a couple of hours we stopped at Salina for breakfast.

This was the point from which, in 1867, the Trans-Continental Survey started, described by Dr. W. A. Bell, in his *New Tracks in North America*. It was then a place of importance as the temporary terminus of a line, where all goods were transferred from the freight cars to the ox trains, destined to carry them through the dangers of a hostile Indian country to Denver and the towns of New Mexico.

Directly we left Salina we came upon the regular plains; short grass in tufts on a sandy soil, and long stretches of brown, rolling away wave upon wave, like some great ocean turned into land in the midst of a heavy ground swell after a storm. Here and there was a prairie ranche or farm, with

Prairie Ranche near Salina.

its corral for horses and cattle, and the great heap of grass which represents the civilized haystack of eastern or European farms.

It is a lonely life, that of a rancheman. Settled out upon the prairie with his herd of horses and cattle, often without another house within a dozen or twenty miles, the only human beings whom he sees are the passengers on the daily train, or some passing emigrants, wearily crawling over the plains with their white-covered ox-waggons; except when he drives his beasts for sale to the nearest market. In the winter the snowstorms are terrible; and in December

1871, hardly more than a month after I crossed the plains, twenty-seven men were brought in on the Kansas Pacific Railroad frozen to death while tending their herds. One man, a large cattle-owner, was found dead thirty yards from his own door, with $5000 in his pockets; having evidently wandered round and round, bewildered in the blinding snow, and dropped at last from exhaustion, not knowing he was close to his home.

But that people can live out on the borders of civilisation and prosper is a fact proved by the very existence of such States as Indiana, Illinois, Missouri, etc. Fifty—certainly seventy—years ago they were quite as wild and much more inaccessible than Kansas and the Territories are now.

I could not take my eyes off the country, so strange and new it seemed; and suddenly my attention was attracted by a small brown post, about a foot high, planted in a sandy ring, with a little round pit in the centre. I looked again, thinking it a strange place for a post, and there was another, and a dozen more. All at once one of the posts threw itself flat down and disappeared into the pit, displaying four short legs and a twinkling tail; and I saw it was a prairie dog (*Arctomys Ludocicianus*). We were going through a dog-town, and there they sat by scores on their hind legs praying at the train and rubbing their noses with their forepaws. They are the quaintest little animals; and make charming pets, as they are very easily tamed. They are very falsely called dogs, their only claim to such a name being their cry, a short bark: but are really more nearly allied to marmots. They are usually supposed to live in the strange company of a small owl and a rattlesnake; and I have heard people assert that in each hole these three most uncongenial friends are found. This fact, however, I have been unable to prove satisfactorily, never having myself seen either snake or bird with the prairie dogs. Those who have had much experience in the West, tell me they have often seen the rattlesnake come out of holes in a dog-town, but have never seen any prairie dogs come out of the same hole. They are very difficult to catch, as their movements are very rapid. The best plan is to pour water down the hole, and so drown out the poor little beast, who comes up choking and spluttering, and is then easily made prisoner. The peculiar shake they give their short tails as they bolt down the hole has given rise to a Western phrase, denoting great rapidity,—"in the twinkling of a tail."

Prairie Dogs.

My brother M. had a narrow escape one day in drowning out prairie dogs. His party was surveying in New Mexico, near Maxwells; and being camped near a dog-town they determined, one stormy evening, having nothing better to do, to catch prairie dogs. So accordingly, taking off shoes and stockings, and armed with tin pan, pail, and shovel, four of them sallied forth. Turning a stream of water from the neighbouring irrigating ditch over the town, they waited over the holes with their hands down all ready to catch the unlucky little half-drowned dogs as they came up sneezing and snorting. Two or three were caught and deposited in the tin pan with the lid down; but one large hole tempted them to further endeavours; and the water being properly directed down it, M. was all readiness to grip his prey, when suddenly, instead of the furry head of a dog, appeared the flat skull and glittering eyes of an old rattlesnake. In an instant the valiant hunters were scattered, with the old rattler after them; and for some minutes a lively game was carried on, the rattler making darts at their bare shins as the four heroes hurled bucket, shovel, and volleys of stones against him. At last one lucky shot disabled him, and after he was despatched they "concluded" not to hunt prairie dogs any more that day.

Near Brookville, a little station some way beyond Salina, we passed through a range of the bluffs, which one hears of so often as a feature of prairie scenery. They seem to be entirely water-worn. A smooth grass-covered slope rises up in a gentle wave from the prairie, and ends abruptly in a steep rocky face. Sometimes, nearer the foot of the Rocky Mountains, a few pines or scrub oaks find shelter on the rocky side of the bluff; but out here on the plains no twig was to be seen. Among these bluffs large herds of horses and cattle were grazing; and we passed an occasional ranche till about mid-day, when every sign of civilisation was left behind, and we reached the edge of the buffalo plains.

Now began great excitement in our car, which was the last on the train; and some of us went out on the back platform to watch for the appearance of the buffalo. This is not a very safe proceeding, as there is only a rail just across the end, and the sides are open. Still there is something pleasantly exciting in sitting there as one whirls along the single track, over dry water-courses on fragile-looking trestle bridges; or between sandy banks, with high snow-fences to keep the snow in the winter from drifting and filling up the cuts; or over a wide smooth expanse, disfigured in many places by the long tongues of black running out on either side the track, where a spark from the "smoke stack," or chimney, has set the short buffalo grass on fire during the droughts of summer. In some places these fires had run for two or three miles over the country; and it was very likely owing to their pasture being so burnt that for a long while we saw no buffaloes alive, though endless skeletons lay on each side of the track, and we passed several dead bodies in various stages of decomposition. A most cruel and foolish fashion prevails on these trains, of shooting the poor animals from the cars as they go along, for the mere pleasure of killing. Of course, many more are missed than hit: but when they are wounded there is no means of stopping to despatch them; so they die in misery along the line.

However, for some time it seemed as if the passengers on our train were not to have any opportunity of showing their skill; for we reached Fort Parker without seeing a buffalo. But suddenly I caught sight of two about a mile to the north. Then the excitement among the passengers redoubled; in half-an-hour we heard the crack of a pistol from the front of the train; and as it sped on we came in sight of three huge beasts, not more than 200 yards from the track. They had been startled by the pistol-shot, and were galloping along in their clumsy way, parallel with the cars, as they always do when frightened. One wondered how such awkward-looking beasts could keep up such a pace; for long after we had passed them they kept in sight, still galloping after us, with their heads down. They are most hideous animals, with heavy heads and shaggy shoulders quite out of proportion with their small hind-quarters.

The buffalo, or more properly bison, ranges over the great plains of Texas, Kansas, Colorado, and Nebraska, in enormous herds; sometimes, in the summer, getting as far north as the 50th parallel. They seem very little disturbed at the invasion of their territories by railroads; and take kindly to the telegraph posts, evidently considering them put up for their special convenience to rub against. This, as may be imagined, does not improve the insulation of the wires; and so many posts were rubbed down at first, along the Kansas Pacific Railroad, that orders were given to stick the new ones full of large and sharp nails. This, however, only made matters worse, as the buffalos found the nails most charming combs for their shaggy coats, and the posts were knocked down more frequently than ever. So now the authorities have been obliged to give up in despair, and let the line take its chance.

At Ellice we stopped for dinner: but preferring our own provisions to a nasty meal of tough and almost uncooked buffalo-steak, I took advantage of the train waiting to get a little walk on the prairie, coming back into the cars with a handful of common weeds which were all new to me. Most of them were in seed, as the season for flowers, alas! was over; and some of my fellow-travellers were not a little puzzled at any one taking an interest in such rubbish.

Then away we went again over endless plains, through blinding sun and dust: when, to my amazement, I saw here and there, to the south, beautiful lakes and rivers, with trees along their banks reflected in the clear water. I had been assured that there was hardly any water, and not a single tree all across these plains; however, here they were most certainly, and I called my friends to look too. But as we approached one of the lakes it gradually faded away into the air, and we found it was nothing but mirage.

The utter desolation and monotony was only varied here and there by a herd of prong-horn antelopes (*Dicranoceros furcifera*), bounding away from the train, or a wolf skulking round some skeleton, or a great owl sitting blinking in the sun, or a group of soldiers or hunters drying buffalo meat, and curing hides at some "dug out" station.

These dug-outs were more used a year or two ago than they are now, as the Indians are quieter: but when the Kansas Pacific was building, and in the earlier days of stage-driving across the plains, they were absolutely necessary.

The following description of Pond Creek Station, from *New Tracks in North America*, will give a good idea of a fortified stage station:—"Standing side by side, and built of wood and stone, are the stables and the ranche in which the drivers and the ostlers live. Behind is a coralle or yard, divided off from the plain by a wall of stones. In this is kept the hay, etc., belonging to the station. A little subterranean passage, about five feet by three, leads from the stables to the house. Another one leads from the stables to a pit dug in the ground, about ten yards distant. This pit is about eight to ten feet square, is roofed with stone supported on wood, and just on a level with the ground, port-holes open on all sides. The roof is raised but little above the general level of the ground. Another narrow subterranean passage leads from the house to a second pit commanding the other side of the station, while a third passage from the coralle to a larger pit commands the rear. In both houses many repeating Spencer and Henry breech-loading rifles—the former carrying seven and the latter eighteen charges—lie loaded ready to hand: while over each little fort a black flag waves, which the red men know well means 'no quarter' for them. When attacked the men creep into these pits, and thus protected, keep up a tremendous fire through the port-holes. Two or three men, with a couple of breech-loaders each, are a match for almost any number of assailants. I cannot say how many times these little forts have been used since their construction, but during the three weeks (1867) we were in the neighbourhood, the station was attacked twice. The Indians are beginning to understand these covered rifle-pits, and the more they know of them the more careful they are to keep at a respectful distance."

About 4.30 we came across the buffalos again. This time they quite fulfilled all one's expectations as to number; and till sunset we were never out of sight of them. In one place we saw 200 or more a mile away, and in another the plain was literally alive with a vast herd, three or four miles off, which I was told must have numbered some thousands. The groups near the track varied from four to twenty, of all sizes; and once I saw a little calf, with its father and mother galloping on either side of it, to protect it from the black smoking monster that disturbed their evening's grazing.

As the sun set in crimson glory over the plains, we reached the station for Fort Wallace. The depot there was full of United States officers, who had driven in to get the mail and newspapers. The Fort was too far off for us to see it in the twilight: but those we had passed in the day had given one a good idea of these little centres of civilisation, with their neat white quarters, and the welcome Stars and Stripes waving from the tall flagstaff, as guarantees of order and protection out on the desolate prairie.

I could hardly divest my mind of the idea that we should be attacked by Redskins; for the name of Fort Wallace is associated with such horrors: but we met with no worse a misfortune than a very bad supper; and sped on towards Denver. During the night we passed Kit Carson, the scene of a terrible Indian raid in May 1870; and Elko, from whence, in the day-time, Pike's Peak may be seen, 100 miles away south-west. Kit Carson is the point from which began one of the most marvellous feats in the annals of railroading. 150 miles of road were wanting to complete the Kansas Pacific Railroad to Denver; and these 150 were graded and built in a hundred days. The last day twenty miles remained unfinished. Double gangs were put on, working towards each other from both ends; and before evening they met and put in the last rivet, one laying 8½, the other 11¼ miles.

On the morning of the 30th I was up before daylight. As the sun rose, ahead of us, pink in the dawn appeared range on range of hills; and I knew they were the Rocky Mountains at last. At 6 A.M. we steamed into Denver, where my brother M. was waiting for me on the platform. I fear my adieux to my travelling companions were sadly wanting in length and courtesy: and I have no very distinct recollection of how we

Street in Denver.

got up to the hotel. But ere long I recovered my lost wits as we sat down to a seven o'clock breakfast of delicious mountain trout, eggs, and good coffee, to which I did ample justice, as the food along the Kansas Pacific had not been very tempting, and Mons. Charpiot's cooking was not to be despised.

Denver stands at the junction of the South Platte and Cherry Creek, about fifteen miles from the mountains. It is certainly one of the most successful of all the new cities of the West, and is growing at a perfectly prodigious rate. The streets are wide, and laid out in straight lines, crossing at right angles. There are very few "mean" or badly-built houses, such as one is too apt to see in a new western town; most of the business blocks are of brick or stone, and in the residence streets pretty wooden villas stand each in their own little garden plot. Cottonwood (white poplar) trees are planted along most of the streets, and seem to thrive. The stores are excellent; and if one does not object to paying four times as much as one would in England, all the necessaries, and most of the luxuries, of life can be easily procured in Denver.

Later in the day, M. and I went to dine with Colonel and Mrs. G.; and after dinner they took us for a drive round the city. The day was bitterly cold and grey, with shattering of sleet from time to time; and I was thankful to put on sealskin and cloud and fur gloves—rather a contrast to our sufferings from heat on the plains only the day before. We drove across the Platte to a sandy hill, which is to be in future the public park of Denver. It is called the Boulevard, and has a fine riding and driving road laid out, with four rows of cottonwood trees and irrigating ditches. This, however, must be seen, like many other things in the West, by the eye of faith; as at present the road is a rough, sandy track, and when the Ute Indians visit Denver they make the park their camping ground. We got a very good idea of the city from the Boulevard. It looks just if it had been dropped out of the clouds accidentally, by some one who meant to carry it further on, but got tired, and let it fall anywhere.

To the east one sees nothing but brown barren plain, away and away. But on the west the view is superb. The prairie rolls up in great brown waves to the foot-hills of the Rocky Mountains, which bound the western horizon as far as eye can see, north and south. At first I confess I was disappointed as to their height; but I soon discovered to my consolation that I had not seen the real mountains. For just before sunset the clouds cleared off; and there, behind the foot-hills which lay in deep purple shadow, gleamed the white peaks of the Snowy Range, illumined by golden glory; and down South, Pike's Peak rose clear pink and white, seventy-five miles away.

Monday, November 1.—At 7.30 A.M. we were down at the depot of the Denver and Rio Grande Railroad, and found a quantity of new acquaintances, friends of M., going down with us,—among others, Mr. N., the chief engineer to the Fountain Colony, one of the very kindest of our many kind friends.

They were all, of course, full of talk about the railroad, the first division of which, as far as Colorado Springs, had only been open a week; and I was soon imbued with a proper enthusiasm at its complete success. It is the pioneer narrow gauge (three feet wide) railroad of the States, as well as the pioneer north and south road.

For some miles out of Denver the road follows the course of the Platte, till it turns to the mountains, and is lost to sight in the dark abysses of the Platte Cañon. Then, after leaving the Platte, the line follows one of its tributaries, Plum Creek, for about thirty miles, bordered with willows and cotton woods. Here I may as well explain that a "creek" in the West means any small river or stream. The land on either side of Plum Creek is taken up by settlers, and fenced off into ranches for sheep, cattle, and agriculture.

Every mile took us nearer to the mountains; and at last the train began climbing up the Divide, or watershed of the Platte and Arkansas. Here we first got among the Pineries, a great source of wealth all along the Rocky Mountains; and at Larkspur passed a large steam saw-mill in full work. Up the Eight Mile, a little creek which runs north from the top of the Divide,—where we passed an old man washing for gold,—the grade was very steep, seventy-five feet to the mile; and in a few moments we stopped at the summit, beside the lake, which from its north end feeds the Platte, and from its south the Arkansas. It was the highest point of ground I had ever been on, being 7554 feet above the sea; only second in height as a railway pass to Sherman, on the Union Pacific Railroad, which is 8370 feet.

We got out of the car while some telegrams were despatched, and walked about a little to warm ourselves; for the place bore out its reputation of being the coldest spot in Colorado; and then began the run down to the Springs, about thirty miles. The road now was picturesque in the extreme, winding along the banks of the Monument Creek, past fantastic sandstone rocks, water-worn into pillars and arches, and great castles with battlemented walls, on the top of every hill. Through the pine trees we now and then caught glimpses of the mountains, pink and purple, towering up ridge over ridge, till, about Husteds, the whole panorama south of the Divide lay stretched beneath us.

To the right the foot-hills rose, crowned by the grand snow-covered head of Pike's Peak, 14,336 feet high. To the south, the horizon was bounded by Cheyenne Mountain, standing right out into the plain; and from it to the eastward stretched the boundless prairie.

CHAPTER III.

LIFE IN A NEW TOWN.

A series of surprises—The young town—Our shanty and its fittings—How we live—Glen Eyrie—Tea in a loft—Bird-cage making—A "scare"—House-warming—The Soda Springs—A trapper—Walk to Mount Washington—School—Move to our new quarters—Staging and stage-drivers.

"Colorado Springs, Colorado, *Nov.* 1871.

"Dear * * *,—Here I am 'located' at last, and the best thing I can do is to describe our arrival here, and my first impressions, which, to say the least, are novel.

"We pulled up at a log cabin by the side of the track, and from the door-way came a voice, saying, 'Dinner's on table.' Out we all got, and I thought—Surely we can't be going to dine in this place: but M. took me round to the back door and into the parlour, where he told me to wait while he saw to the luggage. In a few minutes he returned, and took me into the dining-room, where I found, to my amazement, two large tables on one side, and four small on the other, with clean linen, smart waiters, and a first-rate dinner; far better than any we had had on the Kansas Pacific. I was in a state of complete bewilderment: but hunger soon got the better of surprise, and we were doing ample justice to oyster-soup and roast antelope when in came General and Mrs. P. It was pleasant to find well-known faces among so many new ones.

"You may imagine Colorado Springs, as I did, to be a sequestered valley, with bubbling fountains, green grass, and shady trees: but not a bit of it. Picture to yourself a level elevated plateau of greenish-brown, without a single tree or plant larger than a Spanish bayonet (Yucca) two feet high, sloping down about a quarter of a mile to the railroad track and Monument Creek (the Soda Springs being six miles off), and you have a pretty good idea of the town-site as it appears in November 1871.

"The streets and blocks are only marked out by a furrow turned with the plough, and indicated faintly by a wooden house, finished, or in process of building, here and there, scattered over half a mile of prairie. About twelve houses and shanties are inhabited, most of them being unfinished, or run up for temporary occupation; and there are several tents dotted about also.

"On the corner of Tejon and Huerfano Streets stands the office of the Denver and Rio Grande Railway, a small wooden building of three rooms, in which all the colony work is done till the new office is finished. It is used, besides, as post-office, doctor's shop, and general lounge for the whole town. My house stands next to it; a wooden shanty, 16 feet by 12, with a door in front, and a small window on each side—they are glass, though they do not open. It is lined with brown paper, so it is perfectly wind-proof, and really quite comfortable, though it was ordered on Thursday and finished on Saturday. M. has now put his tent up over the front of the shanty, with a rough board floor, and it serves for our sitting-room by day and his bedroom at night; so we can warm both tent and room with a stove in the former: but on Monday we forgot to bring the stove down from Denver, and I had to do without it as well as I could. In one corner of the shanty we put my little camp-bed; my trunks in the others. Our furniture had not arrived from Denver; so M. found an old wooden stool, which had been used for mixing paints upon, tacked a bit of coloured calico over it, deposited upon it a tin basin, and there was an impromptu washhand-stand. A few feet of half-inch board were soon converted into corner shelves, and, with warm yellow and red California blankets on my bed, and a buffalo-robe on the floor, my room looked quite habitable. In the tent we have put the stove, a couple of wooden kitchen chairs from the office, and a deal table; M.'s bed makes a comfortable sofa by day; and over the door into the shanty hang two bright curtains Dr. B. has brought me from Denver, as a contribution to our housekeeping. In the corner by the stove stands a pail of water; and over it hangs an invaluable tin dipper, which serves for saucepan, glass, jug, cup, and every use imaginable.

Our Shanty.

"Monday night, after paying one or two visits, we went to the office and had a game of whist with Mr. N. and Dr. G., who has been burnt out of Chicago and come down here to settle. Then I locked myself into my strange new abode, with M.'s revolver as protection against imaginary foes; and by dint of buffalo-robes and blankets, and heaps of flannel, managed to keep tolerably warm, though my breath condensed on the sheets, and when I got up the bucket had a quarter of an inch of ice on it.

"This is how our day goes, now that we have got

everything 'fixed' properly:—Get up at 7 A.M. in the cold frosty air. M. comes in and lights the stove; heats some water; and by eight we are ready for a walk of nearly half a mile down to the restaurant (the log cabin), with a fine appetite for breakfast. The food is good and plentiful. Beefsteak or venison; biscuit—as they call hot rolls out here; hot buckwheat cakes eaten with butter and molasses or honey; and the whole washed down with bad tea or excellent rich milk. Then if there is time we take a stroll and look for seeds and stones. There are all sorts of stones and crystals to be found here; and I hear of amethysts up the Monument. On Monday Dr. G. brought me a lump of rock-crystal as large as a man's fist, which he picked up close to our tent; and it serves me for a paper weight.

"At nine work begins, and I attend to my household duties, sweeping the room, etc., and then am ready to help M. in writing out agreements for lots and memberships. At 12.30 the train comes in, and we go down to dinner. At 5.30 it is almost dark; supper is at six, and then we shut up our tent and spend a cosy evening."

Wednesday, Nov. 2.—Drove up to Glen Eyrie with Mrs. P., and General P. and M. followed us up to tea. Glen Eyrie lies about five miles north-west of town, between the Garden of the Gods and Monument Park. It is a valley in the foothills, about half a mile long and a little less broad, shut in from the plains by a rock wall, which runs almost from Cheyenne Mountain to Monument Park, some fourteen miles, varying in height from fifty feet to some hundred, with here and there a gateway through to some valley or cañon. Into Glen Eyrie debouches one of the finest cañons in the neighbourhood; it has been explored for ten miles into the mountains, and goes on no one knows how much farther. At the very mouth of the cañon, close to a beautiful group of Douglassii pine, and just above the little rushing

mountain torrent, which used to be known to trappers as
"Camp Creek," the P.s are building a most charming large
house : but till it is finished they live in a sort of picnic
way, in rooms 10 × 10, partitioned off from the loft over the
stable ! There was just room for us all four to sit at tea,
and we had great fun. There were four cups, but no

The Cañon in Glen Eyrie.

saucers; and we had borrowed two forks from the restaurant,
so that we each had one. Their coloured servant had cooked
some excellent venison and "flapjacks" for us; and we had
Californian honey, blackberry preserve, first-rate coffee, and
baked potatoes.

M. and I drove home in the buggy, at 9 P.M., with two

mules that "scared" continually; and as the road down to Colorado City, three miles, seemed a series of hills, pits, gulches, banks, streams, etc., the drive was more exciting than agreeable. Just as we were crossing a little creek a huge owl flapped out of a tree right before us; and the mules, I thought, would have thrown themselves flat down: then, as we came to the Company's irrigating ditch outside Colorado City, they scared again, and nearly went over the side of the bridge. Through the city we heard what we thought at first were coyotes (prairie wolves), but it turned out to be a stray foal, which came after us full gallop, whinnying all the way, and caught us up close to the restaurant, where, of course, we had a splendid "scare." It was a glorious night; the moon almost as bright as day, and the air so mild that we felt oppressed in all our fur wrappings.

The first few days passed quickly in learning the ways of the country, and settling down in our new life. Up to that time I had seen nothing at all alarming in the way of Indians or wild beasts; but there came a day when M. was obliged to go up to Denver on business, leaving me under Mr. N.'s care. The day was busy enough. I had to manufacture a cage for some snow-birds (*Eremophila cornuta*, a sort of lark) which the French nursery-gardener had caught for me; and when one has nothing handy to make a cage of, it naturally takes some time. Leroy caught the cock first, late one evening; and I kept it all night in a little pen on the top of my trunk, made of *Martin Chuzzlewit*, a candy-box, my travelling-bag, and two blocks of firewood; the whole covered with a bit of flannel. But next day came the hen; and, of course, must have a cage, and the cage required much thought. First I begged an old candle-box from the grocery store, and over the front of it I twisted some wire which the negro from the office got for me off an old broom-handle. As there was not enough to finish it, and none was to be bought for love or money nearer than Denver, I had to put a board over the rest of the opening. In the evening, however, when I secured the tent-flap, and set to work to make up my fire, I began to feel the "creepy" sensation of our nursery days stealing over me. My only living companion was a very dirty black-and-white kitten called "Tucker:" but M. had left me his revolver, so that I felt pretty secure, and when I was well warmed I locked myself into my room, and with the pistol close to my side, and the kitten on my feet, was fast asleep in a minute. How long I had slept I knew not; but I was awoke by a sound I had never heard before. Peal upon peal of demoniac laughter, mingled with shrieks and screams, seemed sweeping past the shanty—now loud, now softer, till they died away in the distance. I flew up, and with the revolver across my knee, listened in a perfect agony of terror: but the sound, whatever it was, had gone by, and by the time I had struck a match, and found it was four A.M., I knew what it must be—a band of Coyotes (prairie wolves) had come through town on a raid after stray sheep. And small blame to me if I was frightened; for many a stout Westerner has told me how, camping out on the plains in hourly expectation of an Indian attack, a band of Coyotes have made every man spring to his feet with rifle or revolver cocked, thinking the wolfish chorus was an Indian war-whoop.

November 7.—The P.s came back from Denver, bringing me a splendid silver-back bear robe as a birthday present, which makes our tent look luxurious. We invited Dr. B. and Mr. ——— to tea in honour of my birthday, and M. and I had great fun preparing for our house-warming. He went out and got a white teapot and milk-jug, six tin mugs, six forks, knives, tea-spoons, and plates: a tin basin for washing the dishes, a packet of tea and sugar, a bag of crackers (biscuits), and two boxes of sardines. We laid the table in English style, and felt quite "high-toned"— to use a Westernism—when our guests came in. We had previously insisted on Dr. B. going down to the restaurant and eating a large supper, for fear of making too large an inroad on our tea, which was exactly like boiled hay. We thoroughly enjoyed being four Britishers together so far away from the old country; and, after our sumptuous tea, sat chatting and singing songs round the stove till eight, when our party dispersed, as the haunting demon of America—business—called for their services again, and M. got out his office books, and I answered home-letters.

November 8.—Having all my dishes to wash after our party the night before, I spent some time in "searching around" for a dish-cloth; and at last by good luck hit on half a towel in the office, and was boasting of my treasure at dinner to Dr. G., when he mildly informed me it was his, but, with a pioneer's proverbial generosity, allowed me to keep possession of it. After the dish-washing was accomplished, we went to see Mr. ——'s start for Wet Mountain, as small events are very great in the life of a young colony. He had an ambulance, packed with every kind of thing for setting up a ranche, drawn by a team of four mules, his own pony being tied behind. The waggon was drawn up close to the side of a shanty where some of the colony officers sleep; and when at last the mules were harnessed, and Mr. —— and his companion, a young Dutch master-carpenter, were getting in, the wheelers started forward, the leaders stopped dead, and crack, crack went the wheel against the shanty, carrying off half-a-dozen of the shingles. M. seized the mules' heads and stopped them after twenty yards; half the things fell out of the waggon, the whip flew one way, the oats another, and the bystanders looked on in perfect convulsions of laughter. After four false starts they got off at last, the pony hanging back and acting as a brake to the frantic mules: but how they have sped who can tell? Neither of them know the road, now deep in snow; and Wet Mountain Valley is 100 miles from here.

Two more English friends came down by the train; so we determined to pay a visit to the Soda Springs at Manitou, six miles off, where there is a temporary hotel kept by English people; and we set off about 5 P.M. It was dark, except for the light from four inches of snow, against which the road showed quite black; while an icy north wind was blowing down from the Divide, and whistled round and through us.

The road up to Colorado City, a gambling and drinking den two miles from the railroad, seemed to me decidedly bad, especially as it was two or three inches deep in stiff mud: but it was beautiful, compared to that from the city up to Manitou. We had to cross the Colony irrigating ditch two or three times, besides Camp Creek, and various other creeks, on bridges made of planks laid loose crosswise over supports without any fastening or any railing at the side. But worst of all was the ford over the Fountain Creek, close to the Soda Springs.

We drove straight down the bank into the river, which boiled and foamed over a rocky bed; and the descent was so steep that when the horses were in the water the hind wheels were as high as their backs. We plunged and struggled through, and up the other bank, and then breathed freely. Next day, when I complained of the road, I was seriously reproved by some stanch Coloradan, who said it was as good a road as any one could want.

The creek passed, in a minute more we were at the temporary inn, a long one-storied wooden shed of single boards, divided off into a double set of rooms on either side of a passage, excepting in the entry and dining-room, where it is open.

The night was cool, to say the least; and in spite of five blankets and a bear-robe, whose weight was suffocating, my face was nearly frost-bitten. For, as the hotel was only run up for summer visitors, the boards had large spaces between them; and when I woke in the morning I was surprised to find how much daylight showed through the walls.

On looking out of the window, I found we were in an exquisite valley, with pine-covered mountains rising 5000 feet up from the Fontaine qui bouille, as it used to be called in old trapping days. In these more prosaic times it is merely Fountain Creek. The sun shone bright over the snow, and blue jays, with crest erect and screaming voices, flashed through the scrub oak round the creek.

The Soda Springs lie in a group along the stream; some on the bank, and others in its actual bed. There are four principal ones; the first you reach is the "Manitou," close to the road, the basin of which is some five or six feet across. The largest spring, "the Navajo," has formed a large basin, six or eight feet across, in the centre of which the water boils up in a violent current. One would suppose there was water enough to make a good-sized trout-stream: yet not more than five or six gallons a minute issue from it. The overflow is carried off to the creek by a channel four inches wide and one inch deep, through the thick incrustation of soda deposit which spreads all over the surrounding rocks. Fifteen feet higher up the creek lies the third, a chalybeate spring, which deposits no sediment.

On the opposite side of the creek lies the "Galen Spring." It is the smallest of the four, but much the strongest; and is used chiefly for drinking. The cavity is about 12 inches in diameter, and the water $1\frac{1}{2}$ feet deep. The bubbles rise ceaselessly, but not more than half a gallon of water per minute passes off. There is a constant deposit of whitish substance from the spring, which extends down to the margin of the creek, twenty feet off, on each side of the tiny stream which trickles from the "Galen."

Professor Hayden, in the U. S. Geological Survey, says, "The water issues from the ground very near the junction of the sedimentary and metamorphic rocks, close by the base of Pike's Peak. . . . These springs must necessarily have their origin in the metamorphic rocks, although the waters may pass up through a considerable thickness of the older sedimentary. On both sides of Fountain Creek there is a considerable thickness of the carboniferous beds; but the creek seems to run through a sort of monoclinal rift, though at the falls above the stream cuts through the ridges nearly at right angles. At any rate, there cannot be a very great thickness of the unchanged rocks below the surface of the springs."

The water seems to maintain the same temperature, about 65°, all the year round, being pleasantly cool in summer, and never freezing in winter. About half a mile from the creek lies the "Iron Ute" spring, up a splendid gorge, called Ingleman's cañon, with *Pinus Douglassii* and silver fir springing up between every rock. This spring is the finest and strongest of all; the water containing, in addition to the salts of soda and potash of the lower springs, a large proportion of iron.

From the Soda Springs, a trail through pine woods, and up rocky mountain sides, leads to the summit of Pike's Peak. This expedition may be made in two days by sleeping at the half-way house just below "timber line;" that is to say, 11,000 feet above the sea; and, though rather a rough trip, is quite practicable for ladies.

It would be difficult, in any part of the world, to find such a series of mineral springs in finer scenery. And there can be no doubt that the prophecies of Ruxton and Fremont will be fulfilled; and that the "Fountain Colony" will answer all the expectations of its promoters, and become a dangerous rival to Saratoga and the Sulphur Springs of the East.

From the upper end of the Manitou valley a road leads up to South Park and the mountains over the famous old "Ute Pass," where the Ute Indians of the mountains lay in wait for the mountain buffalo coming down to feed in winter on the plains, when driven out of their summer haunts in South Park by the snow. All this little valley and the town site of Colorado Springs have witnessed terrible fights between the Utes and the Cheyennes. It was a kind of neutral ground; and when one tribe dared to set foot upon it, their enemies were all ready to pounce upon them. So late as 1869 the Cheyennes scalped and killed six white people between the present railroad track and Colorado City.

Sunday, November 12.—A splendid morning: but we were rather late, and just as we were starting for breakfast in the restaurant, the wind changed, blowing all the smoke and fire down into the tent; so I had to rush to the office, which is always my refuge when the stove goes wrong, which it does once a day, while M. fought the chimney. When it was brought to reason by the united genius of M., Mr. B. the contractor, and Butler the office-negro, it was too late for breakfast; so we cooked some coffee and "Ramornie" extract of meat, had some bread, butter, and potted meat, doing well on the whole for an extempore breakfast. Then M. was called away to the office, and I made my bed, "fixed up" my room, fed the kitten and the remaining snow-bird (the other having been frozen to death in my room on Tuesday night), washed all the breakfast things, and put them away; and by that time M. came back, and we settled down to write home.

Then the tent flap is pushed back; a head comes in; M. jumps up crying "Why, Ike! how goes?" and rushes out.

It is Ike, the hunter from Cheyenne Maniton; and they stand outside talking for ten minutes, while I make notes of the first real hunter I have seen, for the benefit of the home-letters. A tall young fellow in his Sunday clothes, which of course are not half as picturesque as his week-day ones would be. A soft black hat, rough pilot coat, dark trousers, tucked into long boots up to the knee, and a pair of beaver gloves peeping out of his pocket. He and M. make a good group; with his chestnut horse, and its queer bridle and Mexican saddle with broad stirrup straps and high peak in front; and the glorious mountains as a background. Off he canters one way, M. goes another, and I curl up on my bear-robe and begin to read; when I hear a clatter, and look out in time to see the Santa Fé stage with its four bay horses swing past the tent. I begin to read again, and the flap is slowly pushed aside, and in walks "Bruce," the deerhound, to grin lovingly at me, and retire to his wife "Lady" outside. Then comes a knock; a strange man appears to ask where B., the livery-man whom the company employs, lives; and by the time I have sent him off about his business it is dinner-time, and we go down to the restaurant.

We had settled to go up to Manitou for the afternoon: but at twelve the sun, which had been intensely hot all the morning, clouded over; a snow-storm swept over the mountains, coming down within a mile of us; and when at two it cleared off, we found that one of the mules had strayed last night, and that Butler the negro had taken the other to go and look for it. So we contented ourselves with a walk to Mount Washington with the two dogs: for as there is neither church nor service here yet, the only way Sunday can be kept is by making it a day of rest from the incessant business of the week.

We struck across the prairie-rise on which the town stands, passing bones of cattle and antelope strewn here and there, to a deep gulch, almost dry now; and climbed up the brown slope of sandy soil, to find the other side covered with gramma, buffalo, and bunch grasses—the three kinds which form the pasturage on the plains—mixed with the dry stalks and seed-pods of fifty varieties of flowers. What would I give to see them in flower! I gathered a few seeds, and passed a fine lupin, whose pods were not ripe. As we got higher up the vegetation changed a little, and the ground was strewn with blocks of stone, red granitic hornblende, and any quantity of quartzose stones, some pink, some white.

When we came to Mount Washington itself, a solitary hill about 2½ miles south-east of the town, rising some 300 or 400 feet above the plain, we passed a few Rocky Mountain pines (*Pinus ponderosa*) with their large cones and fine long foliage. We scrambled up the little mount over the red rocks, covered with bunches of blue gentian, now dry and withered, but, owing to the excessive dryness of the air, keeping their colour quite brightly; Spanish bayonet (*Yucca filifera*), the only green thing which shows now on the plains; and prickly cactus; and at last we stood panting on the top. The air is so rarified that it makes going up the slightest hill quite an effort.

It was a glorious view. North lay the Divide, shining with snow; west, the mountains in purple shade with snow clouds sweeping over the higher peaks; south, flat land with mesas—long table-lands rising out of the plain. East lay the Bluffs, a continuation of Mount Washington, shutting out the great plains from our view. These plains run east to Kansas, without a single tree, for 400 miles.

Talking of Kansas: the Kansas Pacific Railroad has been entirely blocked with snow for some three days. A train got into Denver the day before yesterday; and one tried to get in yesterday, but failed. It is a great pity, on account of our letters, which all come by that line. But on the other hand it makes us rather rejoice down here at the contrast between the broad and narrow gauges, as the little Denver and Rio Grande has never been stopped yet by the snow, and was only 2½ hours behind time on the worst day.

We walked back from Mount Washington as the sun went down behind Cheyenne Mountain, without seeing any game; which was disappointing to the dogs, who were looking out for a jack rabbit (*Lepus campestris* of Waterhouse), or a coyote, and got no reward for their long walk save innumerable cactus spines which stuck in their feet, and made them come limping to us every half-mile to have them extracted.

Last night, or rather about 7 P.M., we had a pack of coyotes through the town. We were sitting in the hut after tea; Lady was lying in the corner; Bruce was out; when the pack rushed past, yelling and laughing as if Bedlam were let loose. Bruce gave tongue outside; Lady dashed at the tent door, M. after her, catching her by her back; the cat jumped up spitting and growling; and I thought the world was gone mad. The whole thing took less time than it does to write it, and then all was quiet. These little excitements are very strange, and make one realize that one actually is in the Far West, among the wolves and trappers and the fantastic life which one reads of at home, and which it is sometimes difficult to conceive.

November 13.—A lovely morning, clear and hot, with a wisp of cloud hovering round the highest peaks.

Last night it was bitterly cold, and I had to go to bed without a fire, as no power which we could bring to bear would make the stove light.

Field and Hill's rooms, for the new office above their store, were ready; so we decided to move over in the afternoon; and I went out, and sitting on a log of firewood, did a sketch of our old shanty. I am really sorry to leave it: we have had such fun there: but it is getting too late in the year for tent-life, and it will be pleasant to get into a good plastered room.

Mrs. P. has undertaken to begin a school for the colonists' children, and opened it this morning. I went up before she arrived, and found seven children all in great excitement about their teacher. The school is some way up the town side; a pretty three-roomed house which Mrs. P. has rented till a regular school-house can be built.

I returned to the dear old shanty to pack up and move. What work it was: and how I hate moving! Leroy, the

French gardener, was invaluable, and kept running backwards and forwards between the shanty and the new office all the afternoon;—first with a teapot and lamp, then a bundle of rugs, then odds and ends of every kind, from sardine boxes down to fossils, which he stuffed into a big basket.

My room is delightful. The Company has taken the three rooms over Field and Hill's dry goods and grocery store, with an outside staircase leading up to them. The front room is the office, the middle M. and Mr. N. share, and the back one has been allotted to me. I have a splendid stove in the middle, which keeps me quite warm; and have two windows looking over the town east away to the plains, with the white bluffs at Jimmey's Camp showing twenty miles away. From the office windows we look on the whole range, with Pike's Peak as a central point, and have the amusement of seeing all that goes on at the depot and on the line a quarter of a mile below us.

The store is also the temporary Stage Office till the real one is built, and one of our daily excitements is the arrival and departure of the coach, coming up from the south to "connect" here with the up train, and taking the new arrivals on to Pueblo, Maxwells, or Santa Fé in New Mexico.

It is a sight I am never tired of watching: the coach with its four splendid bays, standing in front of the office; the horses held by two men, a third with the reins ready; the "messenger" stowing his mail-bags safely away; the passengers bundling in for a period of misery of varying length. When all is ready, and not till then, out walks the great man, in yellow blanket coat, and hat securely tied down with a great comforter. He mounts the box, arranges himself leisurely; the messenger is beside him, wrapped in buffalo robes; then the reins are put in his hand, and as he tightens them, away go the horses with a rush that takes one's breath away.

The Western stage-driver, on his box, with the "lines," as they call the reins, in his hand, is inferior to no one in the Republic. Even the President, were he on board, must submit to his higher authority.

Among many and varied accomplishments, these stage-drivers have the credit of being able to consume a prodigious amount of whisky. The following story is the most remarkable illustration of this trait in their character; the incident occurring, I was assured by the narrator, on the mail that runs south from Denver to Santa Fé.

"As the coach drove up to the door of the hotel in Denver, out stepped a jolly-looking Englishman, and asked for the box-seat. The stage-driver eyed him from head to foot dubiously, till he saw in his baggage a keg of whisky, when, with a slight change of countenance, he told him, 'he guessed he could fix it.' And when the messenger cried 'All aboard,' the Englishman and his whisky took the box-seat.

"The first twelve-mile stage was monotonous, the Englishman probably meditating on 450 miles by coach; and the stage-driver, who seemed desperately taken up with his horses, on 'that thar whisky barrel.'

"The station is reached at last; and the Englishman, feeling cold, announced that he was going inside for the next stage: but wishing to do the right thing asked the stage-driver first whether he would have a drink.

"'Waal,' says he, 'guess I will,' and catching hold of the barrel uncorks it with a masterly hand, and for the space of some twenty seconds goes through an elaborate process of "star-gazing" through a wooden keg.

"'Waal,' he remarks, 'that's rale good:' setting it down.

"'Oh, if you like it,' says the Englishman, 'just keep it up there, I shan't want any for the next stage,' and jumping in dozes off in a troubled sleep, or at least the nearest approach to one which the bumps and jerks of the old Concord coach will allow, till they change horses at the next stage.

"Feeling thoroughly chilled he jumps out and asks the driver for the keg, which is handed down to him, and through which he proceeds to "star-gaze" in the most approved Western fashion. To his surprise and horror not a drop oozes out.

"'Why,' he says, 'what's gone with the whisky?'

"'Why,' says the stage-driver, 'ain't there none thar?'

"'No,' said the Englishman; 'what's happened to it?'

"'I guess it leaked out.'

"'But that's impossible; where can it have leaked to?'

"'Waal,' says the stage-driver, 'guessed it's leaked down my throat.'

"'Down your throat! why, man, you don't mean to say you've drank it all?'

"'Why not? thar warn't much whisky nither.'

"'Why, my good man, you don't mean to say that in a twelve-mile stage you drank the whole of that keg of whisky?'

"'Yes. But then, ye know, what's one keg of whisky amongst one stage-driver?'"

CHAPTER IV.

LIFE IN A NEW TOWN—*continued*.

The weather—Washing and cooking—The penalties of a free country—Visitors from Denver—A snowy pillow—The cold " snap "—A presentiment—Sunshine again—The Falls of the Fountain—Starting a reading-room—Colonist-catching—The Garden of the Gods—Pete shows his wisdom.

November 14.—Swept out my new room and " fixed up " a little; but I have no shelves at present, which is distracting. Then I made six copies of school circulars for M. to send round to the outlying colonists. In the afternoon drove up to Manitou with Mrs. P. I had no idea how lovely the drive was; as when we went up last week it was quite dark, and coming down towards the town we miss the best view looking up the Fountain to Pike's Peak and the Lete Pass. We drove with a very slow pair of mules, so we had no time to go round by the Garden of the Gods, as we intended at first.

We are having glorious weather during the day, hot and sunny with a fresh wind, though the nights are very cold. Coming home we stopped at one of the Soda Springs; and an old man they call The Hermit, who has lived here for years in a shanty, and drinks the water all day to cure his rheumatism, brought us a tin cup to get some soda-water.

November 15.—Went over to Mrs. C.'s, and did a quantity of washing; it was hard work; and I am to iron the things to-morrow. When I first arrived I found that washing, done very badly, at $2.50 (10s.) a dozen, would not at all suit my ideas. So my kind neighbour, Mrs. C., offered me the weekly use of her wash-tubs and irons; and after scorching a few collars, getting into a state of black despair with the starch, rubbing the skin off my knuckles with the rubber, and burning my hands with the irons, I have turned into quite a good laundress. Many are the pleasant mornings we spend over our wash-tubs, while she tells me stories of her life in beautiful California and Oregon, which she left two years ago. The C.'s insisted on my stopping to dinner, and we had an excellent one of roast-beef and tapioca-pudding, which I helped Mrs. C. to cook in the intervals of washing.

This afternoon a man and his wife came up to the office to speak to M.; and, to my delight, I found they were English from Lincolnshire. They have been out seventeen years, most of the time in Canada; and have been down here rather more than a year keeping a dairy-farm over the Creek. I took Mrs. ——— to my room, and we made friends in a moment over our English sympathies. It was really delightful once again to hear a genuine English misplacement of "h's," in the way she talked of the "hair" of Colorado being very different from the "hold" country.

M. and I went for a walk down to see the "boarding train," in which the men at work on the line live; but it had gone up to the Divide, and we came home past the graveyard. It is right out in the open, so desolate, with railings round each grave, sadly suggestive of wolves.[1]

The school is flourishing, and every one is pleased. I went up to see it yesterday. It was just recess-time, and the children were getting their luncheon. A daughter of M.'s washerwoman came, and said "Good-morning" to me,

[1] Since writing the above, the graveyard has been moved to the southern slope of Mount Washington, where a pretty cemetery has been laid out.

with a kiss, which I did not receive with due gratitude, as
she had evidently breakfasted off garlic. But this is a free
country, where the washerwoman is as good as I; and
consequently I must submit, with smiling submission, to
being kissed by her daughter.

M. has made the two deerhounds a charming wooden
house under my window, into which "Lady" rushed last
night with yells of delight, took possession of the warmest
corner, and made a nice bed in the hay; but tiresome
"Bruce" refused to be caught, or to come when he was
called, and was only secured to-day, after he had been fighting another dog; whereupon M. tied him up to his house,
and he has been howling ever since, to our utter distraction.

The surveying and planting out of the Manitou valley
into villa sites began yesterday. Messrs. N. and Von M.
have begun mapping it out.

November 15.—Went up to my friend Mrs. C.'s, and
ironed my clothes. I am able to do it quite quickly now.

Mr. J., treasurer of the D. and R. G., with his sister
from Philadelphia, came down on the train from Denver.
I offered Miss J. half my room for the night, which she
accepted gladly, as there was no place for a lady to sleep in
nearer than Manitou.

About 4 P.M. M. had "Baby" and "Mouse"—two of the
mules—put into the ambulance, and took us for a drive to
the north side of the town, through a large prairie-dog town.
It covers some acres in that direction, and makes the road
at night rather unsafe; for the little dogs are fond of making a hole right in the middle of the road, quite undisturbed
by the traffic.

After supper, it was such a lovely evening, bright and
warm, with a new moon, that I proposed a walk; so the J.'s,
Dr. B., Captain de C., and we, walked off southwards across
the town-side, to the Santa Fé road. When we got home,
I made tea in my room, and we spent a most pleasant even-

ing, talking round the stove of England and America, and books, etc. When Mr. J. and M. left us, about ten, we found, to our amazement, it was snowing. We could hardly believe it after our delicious walk; but Miss J. and I made ourselves up as warm as we could, and went to bed. I covered her up with the buffalo-robe, as she was sleeping on a camp-bed, with her head towards the door, and went to sleep in a moment myself under my bear-robe. But in the middle of the night we were woke by a terrific windstorm, which made the house shake and rock as if the roof were coming off every minute. Finding, however, that we did not fly away in our beds, we "concluded" to go to sleep again: but about 4 A.M. I was woke by Miss J. saying, "I don't know what it is: but my head is getting very wet."

Up I jumped, lit a candle, and found that the snow was drifting right in through the cracks on each side of the door and the key-hole on to Miss J.'s head, and that there was a little drift on the floor nearly two inches thick. It did not take a minute to turn her bed round, put two chairs by the door, with my waterproof cloak over them as a screen, and fly into bed again. I slept till six, when I got up and lit the stove; but as I had nothing but "kindling," it did not burn long: M. having taken our one coal-scuttle into the office the night before, and forgotten to bring it back. There was nothing for it but to huddle ourselves up in blankets till about 7.30, when M. knocked at the door with some hot water he had heated for me in the office. The snow had ceased: but the wind was blowing a perfect hurricane against our door, and the house was rocking and shaking frightfully. At 8.30 we made a rush into the office, where M. and Mr. J. were waiting for their two half-frozen sisters. The wind was so strong I could hardly shut my door as we came out, and the cold, as we ran down a quarter of a mile to breakfast, was really fearful. I put on a fur muffler, and wrapt my cloud round and round my head, and yet my right ear, which was on the windy side, was in such torture I thought it must be frost-bitten; but I was consoled for the pain by learning that when it hurts you are all safe, and that only when a comfortable sensation of warmth comes on is one in danger of being "frosted." How good breakfast was after that bitter walk! but the struggle home against the wind was far less pleasant.

After we got back, Miss J. and I made our beds, put the room straight, and sat reading and writing all the morning, till it was time for dinner, when we made another rush for the restaurant.

The snow was drifting tremendously, the strong wind lifting the dry powdery particles off the ground, and blowing it across the plain in clouds of white dust. The thermometer outside our house registered 13° above zero,—19° of frost. The train, we thought, would of course be stopped by drifts on the Divide: but it was only one hour late; and, in the middle of dinner, in it steamed. It was really a fine sight. The little 'Cortez' had been through the snow-drifts, up to the top of the lamp in front of the chimney. The wheels, and every ledge and corner, were a mass of snow, and the icicles hung in a crystal fringe all along the boiler.

W., the engineer, came in to dinner, looking, as they said, "pretty wild, as if he had had a struggle for it," and said he thought they would not get back to Denver before morning, as the wind would be against them. So Miss J. decided to stay with me another day: while her brother and another official determined to risk it, and go back to Denver by the afternoon train.

W. is a fine fellow, and one of the best engineers in the West. He saved a train on the Kansas Pacific last summer, by his care and prudence, in a strange way. It was a very dark wet night, the rails very slippery, and he had a kind of presentiment that if he tried to make up time he would have an accident; so he went slowly down a long grade before coming to one of the longest trestle-bridges on the line, over a deep gully. When he got to it he felt certain something would go wrong if he crossed it; so he shut off all steam and jammed the breaks down: but by this time he was so close that the engine and some of the front cars were on the bridge before he could pull up. He sent a man on to see if all was right, and found that two of the trestles in the middle of the bridge were gone! Had he run on, the whole train would have gone right through to the bottom of the gully, a depth of forty feet.

The afternoon was as bad as the morning, driving snow-dust and bitter wind: but towards evening the snow began to disappear, evaporating into the dry air, though the thermometer never rose above 29° all day outside the house.

18*th*.—Woke at 6.30 to find the sun blazing through my red curtains, and not a breath of wind stirring. The snow is almost gone here; but we hear that the train had a rough time last night. They got up with great difficulty to within five miles of the top of the Divide: but, being short of water, had to run back ten miles; and at 2 A.M. this morning they had not reached the top, although forty men from the construction train had turned out to help them. However, they got into Denver at eight this morning, and the down-train started at 9.25.

After making the beds and sweeping the room, Miss J. and I went down for a walk to the creek. It looked very pretty, half-covered with ice, in the bright sunshine, the ice cracking and snapping like little pistols every moment. The bushes were bare, except here and there a plant of prairie-rose with its leaves still flame-colour; and I got two curious kinds of cones off a willow by the water.

Miss J. went off to Denver by the afternoon train; and Mr. M., an Englishman from Maxwells in New Mexico, who has been here for a day or two, left also; so we expected to be quite alone again. But the down train brought a very agreeable young German-Russian engineer, who has been sent out by the Russian Government to inspect American railroads and bridges. M. and I drove with him up to Manitou in the afternoon, and as he could speak hardly any English, I at once began talking French, and we had a very pleasant drive.

When we got to Manitou we three walked up to the Falls of the Fountain with Mr. B. and Mr. von M., about half a mile above the hotel. It is the most exquisite valley, or rather cañon, I have ever seen, just wide enough for a narrow road, while the foaming stream dashes down over red rocks and fallen trees, and barriers of frozen snow, with huge Douglassii pines, red cedars, and piñons, shading it on either side. We walked over the crisp snow, frozen so hard that it did not wet one's boots, and crossed the Fountain by a single log, not more than twelve inches in diameter, and slippery with ice. M. gave me his hand, and though I was in a great fright for fear of a cold bath, I got over all right. Then up we climbed a long narrow path along the face of the cliff, and saw a beaver dam down in the stream below. Up again, past a hut where the men who are blasting the road were cooking their supper, while two black-tailed deer's heads and skins were drying on a bush outside; and at last we came to the end of the present road, and climbed along a track in the rocks about sixty feet above the stream, where the road is to go, and M. gave me a helping hand again till we came to a point opposite the Falls. They are not very grand : but the cañon down which the Fountain comes is splendid, winding up into the mountains, which rise several thousand feet above the stream, their black pines standing out sharp against the gleaming snow. It was enchanting; the rush of falling water, the ice and snow, the pines, the crimson rocks, the noble mountains, and the fading light, made up a picture I shall never forget.

We turned homewards, and reaching the temporary inn found that Dr. B. and Captain de C., who walked up, had just arrived, to pretty Mrs. de C.'s delight, who had been all alone for three days, with nobody to speak to, and both her babies sick. We had a pleasant tea all together, and M. von W., Mr. von M., and I kept up a jargon of mingled French and German all the time, to the great diversion of the rest of the party. We had to finish tea quickly in order to be back at Colorado Springs in time for a meeting about the reading-room and Scientific Society; and Dr. B., M., and I drove home in the bright moonlight with Pete and Baby, who, unlike most mules, never require a whip; and got in just at 7.30.

As the population is increasing every day, we and some of the colonists have been trying to devise some plan to get up a reading-room, where the young men may spend their evenings, instead of lounging about the town, or going up to drink in the saloons at Colorado City. So we sent out to invite the colonists to meet together and discuss the subject this evening. We carried chairs, lamps, and benches over to the railroad office, and had a capital meeting of thirteen.

Mr. F. made a very good speech; and when M. and Mr. M. F. were appointed to frame the constitution and bye-laws, and some one raised the question of what would happen if they did not agree, Mr. F., in the most gallant manner, said of course M. "would do nothing without his sister's advice, so there could be no difficulty,"—a sentiment which caused much laughter. $143 were subscribed on the spot, and I had the honour of naming the Society the "Fountain Society of Natural Science."

November 19*th*.—M. and I drove up to Manitou after breakfast, and took the De C.'s to the Garden of the Gods, one of the great sights here.

Half way between the Springs and Colorado City we overtook a man, who M. thought might be a new-comer; and having the interest of the colony always in view, asked him if he would like a lift; and in he got behind. He was a New-Yorker, he said, and had been out three weeks in Colorado, having come for his health.

"He liked the place so well," he said, "that he had concluded to remain, and being a lawyer had stepped right into business." I happened to make some remark to M.: whereupon he said—

"Madam, I presume you are an English lady."

I laughed and said, "Yes, that I supposed he had found me out by my speech."

"Yes," he replied, "I could tell at once. I think it extremely pleasant to hear the language spoken by an English person, when they speak well."

M. said, "I suppose you would hardly take me for English."

"No, sir!" said the gentleman, "you are not English surely?"

"I ought to be," replied M., "considering we are brother and sister."

That was quite too much for our friend; however, we made him such pretty speeches, that when he got out at the very unattractive hotel at Colorado City, he nearly vowed eternal friendship, and gave us such pressing invitations to call upon him that we hope he will settle at Colorado Springs, in order to cultivate our society; so by a little civility we trust we have caught a fine large colonist.

When we got to Manitou we took up the De C.'s, and started back for the Garden of the Gods. We turned off the road half way between Manitou and Colorado City, across a sowed field, and over frightful ups and downs till we came to a bridge across the Fountain. It was just wide enough for the waggon—here all kinds of carriages are called waggons—

and was quite rotten. How we got over I know not, for
Pete, who had been turned out for some time, and was not
on his best behaviour, shied violently in the middle. However, we did get over in safety, and drove along what was
dignified by the name of a road: though it more resembled
newly-dug celery trenches, varied by gravel-pits, and a deep
ditch right across every few hundred feet. At last we got

The Gate of the Garden of the Gods.

into the Outer Garden, a great open space of grass under the
foot-hills, with scattered pines, and here and there fantastic
sandstone rocks; and further on, to our right, lay the great
rocks, the real wonder of the Garden. We passed many
weird-like figures praying, with their heads all bent towards
Cheyenne Mountains; then a red sandstone nun, with a
white cowl over her head, looking at a seal who stood

on his tail, and made faces at her. There, I was told, two cherubs were fondly kissing, though to my eyes I confess they looked more like a pair of sheep's heads; and so finding new absurdities every moment, we came to the great gateway; drove between the huge red rocks, 250 feet high; and turned to see the view. It surpasses everything I have yet seen.

The great rocks were of a warm salmon colour, with green pines growing in their crevices, bringing out the richness of their colouring; and between them, as if set in a glowing

Crossing a Trestle Bridge (p. 76).

frame, shone Pike's Peak, covered with snow, as a centre to the picture, with Cameron's Cone and the foot-hills, all blue, white, and pink, three or four miles off.

I wish every one at home could see this view. No descriptions or photographs can do it justice; and as for drawing it—who can do that?

We had come into the Garden "the back way;" the best plan being to come first through the great gateway, and drive out at the other end. Driving back the way we came, we got along without misfortune, till we came to the unfortunate bridge again; and this time Pete positively refused to cross. Twice M. got him to the middle, and Pete tried to push poor Baby over the side and then backed side-ways. At last M. told us to get out, and he took them at it four times: but a mule's mind, when once made up, is not to be moved, and we had at last to drive round another way. On the whole, perhaps Pete was right: for he had twice been through a bridge,—the last time having been lame for a month; and the chances were considerably in favour of his going through this one.

CHAPTER V.

CAÑONS AND COLD.

My first Cañon—Wild beasts—Pleasant society—A spelling match—Camp Creek Cañon—Exploring by moonlight—Mountain air—Snow drifts—Triumph of the Narrow Gauge—The Fountain ditch—A Westerner—Antelope-shooting—A grand view—A change in our plans.

"COLORADO SPRINGS, *Tuesday, Nov.* 23.

"DEAR * * *,—I have been up a cañon. Anything so wonderful I never saw in my life.

"It was on last Sunday when we went up to Manitou, the Soda Springs; and, fortified by a good English dinner, Dr. B. proposed a walk up a little cañon at the back of the temporary inn. We turned off the road about fifty yards below the hotel, up a path through scrub oak, wild rose, gooseberry, raspberry, and spiræa bushes, besides many other shrubs, which, as they are leafless, I cannot identify, with clematis festooning every bush. The valley for a quarter of a mile was an ordinary wooded mountain gorge; but it suddenly closed in, and we found ourselves in front of a narrow gateway of rocks, a hundred feet high or more; and in a moment were in the cañon.

The trail led up the bed of a little stream, then dry, which had sawn its way through walls of sandstone of every imaginable colour, from rich purple and crimson, to salmon-colour and white. The rocks were worn into the most fantastic shapes, battlements, castles, and pillars, hundreds of feet high, sometimes almost closing in the path; then opening out on one side or the other into almost perpendicular hill-sides, covered with piñon, red and white cedar, rocky mountain pine, and *Pinus Douglassii*. We went under several of the latter growing in the cañon. One I measured, which was eleven feet round, four feet from the ground; and I am told that is a mere sapling to some higher up in the mountains. One had fallen, and we had to walk its whole length; rather a slippery path, as it was covered with frozen snow several inches thick. Then came a sudden twist; the rocks almost met over our heads, sandstone on one side, limestone on the other; and I touched both sides of the cañon at once, without stretching my arms to full length.

"It was the wildest scene—the towering rocks, black pines, and white snow. We looked such impertinent atomies, daring to venture into the heart of the mountains. I never heard such stillness before; it was quite oppressive; not a breath of wind, not a leaf stirring; no sound or sign of life, save ourselves, and a solitary hawk wheeling round against the streak of blue sky we could see from our prison walls. For about a mile we went up, twisting and turning every twenty yards; so that, looking back, one could not imagine how one had got in, or would ever get out again.

"This cañon has never yet been thoroughly explored: but it runs on for miles and miles into the mountains, getting grander and wilder the further it goes.

"This is certainly a most uncanny country. Every stream saws out a cañon. Every rock takes the likeness of some fantastic building or creature.

"Tell G. I have seen plenty of beaver dams; the streams are full of them all round; and deer (black-tailed) are very plentiful, coming right down to Manitou. There are no bears very near, and no wolves, except coyotes, who very often come through the town at night, and scare us all, for their cry is just like the Indian war-whoop.

"We are getting quite a pleasant society here; and, besides those who are settled here, like ourselves, there is a constant stream of Englishmen coming in from the ranches, or up from Maxwells; and a good many visitors already come down from Denver. This morning I met Gov. H. at breakfast, and with him Mr. Bowles of "The Springfield (Mass.) Republican," who, with his very charming wife and daughter, has come out to see how Colorado is getting on. We walked together up to Gov. H.'s new house, which is nearly finished, and I took them to see our dogs, who are considered curiosities out here. Mr. Bowles asked me to join his party in an expedition down to the Indian Reservation in Kansas next week; and much I wish we could do it.

"If the weather is fine, M. and I hope to take a trip this week or next up to Bergun's Park, twenty miles from here in the mountains. I hear it is a lovely place. It will be a three days' trip, and we shall stop at a ranche half way.

"So you see, after all, though we are in 'the wilds,' we are tolerably civilized; and do not go about clothed in skins, or armed with revolvers, or meet a bear if we take an afternoon walk."

23*d*.—At dinner-time M. rushed in to say he must go up to Denver with Dr. B. on business; so I was left alone again, and went over to the school to see Mrs. P., who is going on most perseveringly with her self-imposed occupation. I heard the children's spelling-match, and the length of the words and the correctness of the spelling quite alarmed me. A spelling-match is a regular American institution, and is capitally described in that most remarkable book, *The Hoosier Schoolmaster*.

Friday, 25th.—It has been a glorious day, bright sun, and quite warm, and I have never yet seen the mountains look so beautiful. Went up to the De C.'s after breakfast, and on the way back called in to see Mrs. G., who has moved into her new store on Tejon Street to-day. It looks resplendent. The front is painted in black and white checquers, and a huge scarlet boot is hung out as a sign. It is one of the best buildings we have got in the town. On coming home, feeling in a very energetic frame of mind owing to the change of weather, I pulled all my small amount of furniture into the middle of the room, covered the floor with tea-leaves, which I had saved from our last tea-party, and swept out my room on the most approved English method.

Sat. 26.—Mrs. P. asked me to drive up to Glen Eyrie with her, and explore the Camp Creek Cañon, above the house. Anything more lovely I never saw. At the entrance of the cañon the coloured rock-walls are about a stone's-throw apart; and the ravine on either side of the clear foaming stream is filled with a rich growth of trees and shrubs, festooned with Virginia creeper and wild clematis. Further up the walls close in; and we scrambled up, crossing and recrossing the stream every few yards, by fallen timber and boulders under lofty pines and cotton woods, till we came to the "Punch Bowl." The stream has scooped itself out a round path in the red and white streaked rocks, which rise high above the bed of the stream. The basin is about twenty feet across, and fills up the whole cañon. The water falls into it over steps of rock; and above it the cañon winds up into the mountains, no one knows how far, as only a few miles of it have been as yet explored. About two miles up are some beautiful falls, which M. discovered last year: but as the only way across the Punch Bowl was by a single log of pine, very thin and covered with ice, and as I was wet through from wading through the snow, which was quite deep in some places, I did not feel inclined to risk the chance of an icy bath, but determined to see the Falls some other time, and we turned back to Glen Eyrie for dinner and dry shoes.

General P. and Professor H. of Madison, Wisconsin,

came up, and we started, as the sun set and the moon rose, to explore the upper end of Glen Eyrie. The moon looked so tempting over the crest of the hill that we set off on a track that leads up the high ridge dividing Glen Eyrie from the Upper Garden. After we had passed the great Echo Rocks, and made them sing two or three songs a couple of bars behind us, a narrow track led us to the top with a scramble; and once there, the view was really superb. To the right, on the crest of the hill, was a group of pines, through which the moon shone so brightly, it was like white daylight. Behind us lay the Glen, with its strange red rocks, and the hills rising up to old Pike all covered with snow; and in front of us another deep valley, shut in with another wall of rock, widening out into a park above, and below narrowing into a cañon which apparently had no exit. None of us had ever been there before: but we plunged down the hill through deep snow, with here and there a Spanish bayonet sticking up to prick the unwary, down to the bed of the cañon. It was so narrow that only one person at a time could squeeze along between the rocks; and I began seriously to fear it would soon get too narrow for us to escape, and that we should have to stay there for the rest of our days. Suddenly, however, out of the intense black shade, we came into a streak of brilliant moonlight, which streamed through a cleft in the rocks before us not more than three feet wide; and we saw we were at the gate of the cañon with the outer valley in dazzling light beyond.

We sat still for a few minutes to gaze in delight through the rocks; then squeezed between them with some little difficulty, and looking back, could not see the passage by which we had emerged. It seemed as if we had broken through the lower panes of a Gothic window, which had been partly filled up with stone.

Turning to the right we went up a high snow-covered hill to the foot of the outer wall of the Garden, more than 7000 feet above the sea. This wall is a mass of rock from fifty to three hundred feet high, and in some places not more than eighteen feet thick, running along the top of a line of hills made apparently of débris of old rocks, and extending from near Cheyenne Mountain to Monument Park, with here and there an opening into one or other of the gardens or parks, where some creek has sawn its way through.

It was a stiff climb through the snow, in the intensely rarefied air, which completely takes one breath away going up hill; and for five minutes after we reached the top I felt as if my chest had been scraped raw: but after a little rest this sensation went off. Going down was much pleasanter than getting up, and in a little while we were wading through the snow and mud up to the stable, where the P.'s are still living, as their house is not finished.

After supper and a very pleasant evening, Professor H. drove me home, and we found M. waiting to receive us.

He had had a rough journey down from Denver; but was more fortunate than the hapless people who started the day before him, for they broke down three miles north of Sloan's Mill on the Divide, and were twenty-four hours getting those three miles. The Saturday train caught them up at Sloan's Mill, and they joined company, every man turning out and digging in the snow for four hours; by which means, and by driving the engine against the snow full speed, they got through at last.

This fall of snow is exceptionally heavy; and unlike what we usually have here, being soft and wet, like Eastern States or English snow, instead of dry and powdery. With the high wind we have had it drifts badly, and packs into a much closer mass than our usual Western snow.

The narrow gauge still holds its own against the broad gauge, and a freight train got through behind the passenger-cars yesterday; while on the Union and Kansas Pacific Railroads no freight has got through for two weeks, and all the passenger trains have come into Denver one to four days late. There have been two feet of snow for the last week at Denver, and every one is sleighing who can afford it; while the sleigh-owners are making small fortunes by charging eight to ten dollars an hour.

28*th*.—Yesterday was bright, but horribly cold. The trees by the creek had each twig covered with rime half an inch thick, from a dense fog which had frozen upon them the night before. It was an important day to us; as the Fountain Ditch, *i.e.* the irrigating ditch by which the water from the Fountain above Colorado Springs, is to be brought down to irrigate the town site at Colorado Springs, was finished.

Yesterday the water was turned in, and so we hoped that it was slowly making its way down the ditch last night towards us: though, as the ditch is $11\frac{1}{2}$ miles long, having to be carried round hill-sides and over gullies, it will take some time to fill it thoroughly. Just now, however, one of the engineers came in to say that the water had broken through the bank close to one of the flumes (wooden troughs, in which the water is carried over gullies), just by Colorado City, and had run away and made a great lake.

M. has sent him up with planks and men to fill in the hole; so we hope all will be right. How it can have happened we cannot tell. It may be that the frost has shrunk the earth at the joining with the flume; but some fear that it may have been done out of spite.

November 30.—Thanksgiving Day.

The snow is gone, and the sun blazing in a cloudless sky. I watched the avalanches falling on Pike's Peak all the morning, and, after each, the cloud of snow-smoke rising, and blowing round the top of the mountain.

To-day is such a contrast to the last three days, which have been so bitter we have only left the house for our meals, and then rushed down muffled up in every wrap we possessed to keep out the wind.

Yesterday afternoon, as M. and I were sitting in the office, the door opened, and in walked a man followed by a large saffron-coloured bull-dog, called Rattler. This man, whom M. knew very well, is the most thorough specimen of a Western man I have yet seen to speak to. He was dressed in apparently five or six flannel shirts, two undercoats, thick trousers tucked into long boots, a light-blue soldier's great-coat with capes, under which knife, pistol, and powder-flask peeped out, and a slouched felt-hat completed the costume. As I sat listening to his yarns to M., I could have fancied myself reading a chapter of *Catlin*. Here was the real thing. A fine-made young fellow about twenty-eight, with bright blue eyes and brown hair and beard, up to anything, from shooting a wolf to riding 240 miles in thirty-six hours to catch a prisoner; yet civil and courteous to me in the extreme. All the time he was here I never heard a single bad word from him, though I saw that he caught himself up short two or three times. It was strange, seeing and hearing with one's own eyes and ears what one has read of since childhood.

P. has just been in to get the surveying things. He said it was so cold he could not get the men to go out early this morning. At 8 A.M. it was 9° above zero, and at 10 only 15°. There was a grand dinner at the restaurant in honour of Thanksgiving Day; but we missed it, M. having to go up to Glen Eyrie on business. I went with him, and as no one was at home at the stable, Mrs. S., who is cooking at a log cabin for the men working on the house, gave us a capital dinner, off tin plates; and taught me how to make biscuit, which means hot rolls, and slap-jacks, a kind of pancakes which one eats at breakfast and tea, in a little pile, covered with butter and syrup, or honey.

December 2.—The "cold snap" has driven large herds of antelopes in from the plains to the shelter of the bluffs, and yesterday, hearing there were some near town, M. and I had out the ambulance with the mules, and drove off in search of them, armed with a revolver. We had not gone more than a mile and a half west of the town site when we saw a herd in a hollow to the right of the road. M. got out and crept away after the antelope, telling me to drive slowly after him. There were about twenty-three, and when we had crossed the hollow and got to the top of the next rise, we saw an immense herd of some hundreds a mile west. I watched M. along the crest of the hill, the antelope meanwhile running round below him out of sight, when suddenly he stopped. Piff, piff, piff went the pistol, and I drove on to him. No luck, alas! as Butler, the negro at the office, had loaded the revolver, and carefully put in half charges; so every shot fell short. We drove after them, and M. got three more long shots from the waggon, but to no purpose.

In the evening we drew up a sketch of the constitution and bye-laws for the "Fountain Society of Natural Science." We keep the list of members in the office, and the number is increasing every day, as every one who comes in is immediately attacked for a subscription, $3 giving a yearly membership, or $20 a life membership.

This morning I got up at 5.30, just as the eastern horizon grew crimson over the plains before sunrise, lit the stove, heated some water, and cooked two cups of "Ramornie;" by seven o'clock we were off with Mr. de C. in the waggon to try after antelope again; and I tried to cure my uncontrollable dislike of fire-arms by keeping one of the rifles on my knee till it was wanted.

We fell in with two herds in the same place as yesterday: but our luck was as bad as ever, for so many parties of shooters were out after them, that we could not get within range. We drove on the bluffs in hope of smaller game, and Mr. de C. got a "cotton tail" rabbit (*Lepus Artemisiæ*), and we looked in vain in the bushes for prairie chicken. But we got what quite repaid us for the want of sport—a magnificent view of the mountains to the south, which at the town are hidden by Cheyenne Mountain. Across long stretches of plain we saw the Greenhorn jutting out from the main chain, with the Spanish Peaks sticking up blue and golden beyond it, and in the furthest distance the Raton Mountains, over Maxwells, two hundred miles away.

The antelopes are so starved this winter that they are coming in by thousands off the plains all along the base of the mountains. At Greeley, the colony town north of Denver, they come among the houses and get shot from the windows. A herd of forty was crowded in a field, and the Greeleyites went out and surrounding it shot them all down, poor little things! They are so pretty, it seems cruel to kill them in this unsportsmanlike manner.

On the 5th a large party of railroad officials and visitors came down to the Springs, and we spent two days showing them the sights of the country, the Garden of the Gods, Glen Eyrie, Manitou, etc. The weather was perfect for sight-seeing, and the evening so mild that we sat at Manitou with doors open to the porch, and walked up and down outside without hats or jackets.

While our visitors were down our plans for the winter underwent a considerable change. Important business requiring General P.'s presence in Mexico, he and Mrs. P. asked me to join them in January or February, in a journey *via* San Francisco and the Pacific to the city of Mexico; thence to Vera Cruz and New Orleans, and so to New York; while M. and some engineers received orders at the same time to be ready at any moment to start for the same point overland.

CHAPTER VI.

MONUMENT PARK.

Expedition to Monument Park—A cheap dinner—The monuments—A rough road—School-keeping a failure—Locating the skating-pond—Snow-birds—A second Monument Park—The southern mountains—"Over the Ratons."

December 10.—All the time I have been here, I have never yet seen one of the strangest of the many strange sights in Colorado. So this morning, the weather being fine, with hot sun and no wind, my brother M. got a "buggy" and a good horse, and we started for "Monument Park."

About twelve miles north of the town are a set of bluffs, the beginning of the Divide, running out eastward from the mountains some twenty miles into the plains; and forming a series of grass valleys, or "parks," as they are called in the West. The largest of these has all along its northern side innumerable groups of sandstone rock, worn by weather and water into the strangest forms, and not inappropriately called monuments. The lower part of the monuments is of light yellow sandstone conglomerate, capped with a harder sandstone, coloured dark brown by the presence of a good deal of iron.

A wave of upheaval seems to have run from south to north and cracked the hard sandstone pan, letting in the influences of weather to the softer conglomerate below, till the whole has been eaten away, save these isolated pillars.

A similar wave seems to have formed the bluffs among

which they lie. The northern sides slope smoothly down, covered with grass, into the Parks; while their southern sides are rocky, with pines growing on them, and the strata seem turned back and set on edge.

We crossed the Monument creek about four miles above town. How we did cross I do not know, as the bed of the creek had changed, and the wooden levee at the ford was now of no use. The stream was also covered with ice, all but a couple of yards in the centre. With some persuasion the horse plunged into the ice, and dragged us up a perpendicular bank on the other side. But this was a trifle to what was coming. We followed up a newly made trail

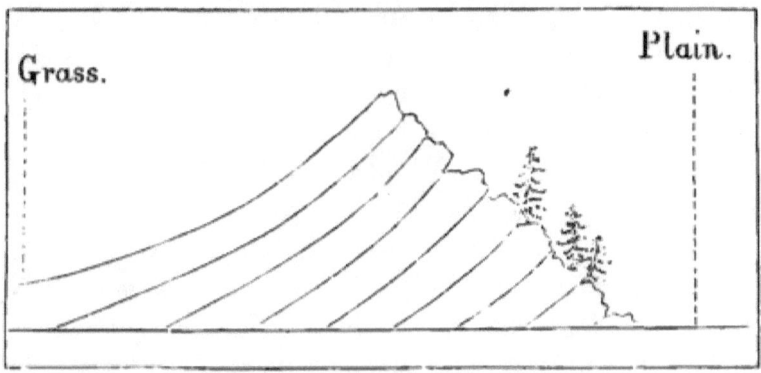

through the brushwood, not cut, but only run through by the passage of a waggon or two, which led us at last up a gulch under the railway. It was a horrid place; just room to squeeze under the trestle bridge, with the wheel on one side three feet higher than the other; a careless driver could not have got through without an upset.

We then came to a good road, and trotted away across plains between the bluffs, covered with Spanish bayonet and burrowed with prairie-dog towns. We drove along, skirting the bluffs for eight miles or so, with the mountains on our left; till turning in through a sort of pass, through rocks which seemed full of iron, we found ourselves in a " park."

Through this we drove on three or four miles, till we came

to the railway-crossing at Monument creek, and there stopped at a very nice roadside boarding-house called "Teachouts," where we put up the horse, and went in for dinner. It is kept by a charming old lady and her son. She looks thoroughly English; though she is, I believe, an American; like an ideal farmer's wife, in neat dress, snowy cap, and apron, and with that indescribable air of comfort about her which belongs to an old-fashioned farm-house kitchen. Two ladies were staying there, who had come out with their sick husbands in search of health in this pure mountain air. One of them had made a really fine collection of minerals and crystals during the months she had spent out here. She took me up to her room to show me her treasure, and gave me several specimens of smoky quartz, satin spar, and white chalcedony. One crystal of smoky quartz which she found not far from here was one of the finest I have ever seen; nearly a foot long, and quite perfect. We had a capital dinner, cooked by a German maid,—a kind of meat pie with a bread-crust, potatoes, bread, pickled cabbage or "cold slaw" as it is called here, and apple tart. The whole cost of our dinner and the feed for our horse was 1 dollar 25 cents—quite astonishing in this land of high prices. After saying good-bye to our new friends, and begging them to call on us at Colorado Springs, we turned up towards the park.

Monument Park is a large glade about two miles long, running from east to west; the end of the glade being filled up with the blue and red walls of the foot-hills covered with pine-trees, which rise about 3000 feet above the valley. The south-western slopes of the bluffs are covered with the Monument rocks, which, at first sight, strike one as irresistibly absurd.

They are of every height and size, from the great giant thirty feet high, to the pigmy of twelve inches; sometimes they stand alone; sometimes in groups of twenty or more. No two are alike, and each year they change their shape; as wind, snow, frost, and rain go on with the work of destruction, with which for ages they have been moulding this group, as if over some set of Titanic graves.

We drove along to the end of the Park, and turned up over the southern bluffs, which, as far as I can see, have few if any monuments on them. The road or track was so bad here that M. made me walk up, as he expected the buggy to upset. The sun was so intensely hot that I was nearly

The Monument Rocks.

smothered going up-hill in my sealskin, though we were at least 7000 feet above the sea. At the top I looked in vain for a road down. There was positively none; and to my amazement I saw M. deliberately turn the horse right down the hillside, which was at an angle, I should think, of 35°, and covered with stones. I could hardly keep my feet in some places, and how the horse got down I cannot tell : but he crept along with the straight shafts of the buggy right over his ears, and by dint of careful driving and patience arrived safely at the bottom. We saved nearly four miles, and drove home by Glen Eyrie, stopping to "prospect" on a little creek, where we found good indications of coal, plenty of what is here called "kidney iron," some imbedded in sandstone, some lying loose, and M. found some fossil shells.

"COLORADO SPRINGS, *December* 20, 1871.

"DEAR * * *,—Since I last wrote I have been trying a new occupation, and have made a great failure in it. I have been keeping school for two days!

"I got a telegram last Monday from the P.'s, who are in Denver, to say they were detained; so I went up to the school, intending to send the children home. But when I got there I found more than twenty children assembled outside in the snow; and they were so anxious to have school that at last I consented to stop and teach them myself. The door was locked: so I made two of the bigger boys get in through a window, and following them in unfastened the door; and we soon lit the stove and set to work. They were of all ages, from five to fifteen, so that it was rather a difficult matter to keep them all at work at once. However, as I was a novelty, and as we only worked till twelve, they were very good, and got on capitally. Next day, however, was a very different matter. I went up again; but found that some of the boys were evidently determined to try how naughty they could be. They threw things at the girls; refused to do their work; and when I found one pretty little girl in floods of tears, and asked what was the matter, she sobbed out, 'They call my hair *beaver tails*.' I could hardly help laughing at such a thoroughly Western form of insult: but I found that 'young America' was a good deal too strong for the 'English school-marm;' and after shutting one of the chief offenders in a room by himself for an hour, which a little quelled the disturbance, I was delighted when twelve o'clock came; and sent my young tormentors home with a tremendous scolding.

"We went out on Thursday to the great gully behind the town, with the chief engineer, to 'locate' a skating-pond for the use of the colonists. We found a capital place, where, with very little trouble in making a dam, we can get 700 feet by 130. The water will be turned into it from the Fountain Ditch, which we hope will soon be full: but the heavy frosts which came just as it was finished have cracked the banks in so many places, that there have been constant leaks all along; and the engineers have been up nearly every day stopping them.

"I have got seven snow-birds and a bunting (*Junco cani-ceps*) in my room now. They fly against the telegraph-wires in the strong wind; or some of the numberless hawks and buzzards which abound here hurt them; and we find them lying dead on the ground in hundreds. All that I have got have been hurt or benumbed; and are now quite tame, and will feed from my hand.

"When it snows, they come in immense flocks of many thousands; and disappear again as soon as the snow melts. They must be quite tired, poor little things, of these constant changes. One week it is so hot one cannot bear a jacket in the daytime, and the next week it is freezing. But it is a glorious climate; and I am gaining weight and strength every week. I never was in a place where one so enjoys the mere fact of living.

"We had a glorious ride last week over the plains, in search of antelope, to the bluffs about five miles from town; and riding up between two bluffs found ourselves in a valley full of monuments, like those in Monument Park. It was quite a discovery, as no one had heard of their existence before. If there is any water there it will be a charming site for a house some day, as the glade is much prettier than Monument Park itself; and the views between the bluffs, of mountain and plain, are magnificent.

"Whenever I get out on the plains and look southward to those endless mountain-ranges which stretch away into New Mexico till they are hidden by the roundness of the earth, I am seized with a longing to go south and see them. But the stage-journey is enough to deter any one from going who is not absolutely forced to go. My desire, however, was not thoroughly cured till M. gave me an account of a night-journey he made across the Ratons. I have since got him to write it down for your amusement at home; and I think it will give you as good an idea of the difficulties of winter travel out here, without railroads, as you could have, unless you came and tried it.

OVER THE RATONS.

"We're going to have rough work over the mountain to-night," I said to Dutch Sam, the messenger of the S. O. M. (Southern Overland Mail), at the Red River Station, where we stopped for supper on a night in the end of December 1870. "Who takes us over?"

"Frank Blue's turn to-night, I think.—Supper's ready."

In I bundle, and find Frank stretching himself, after a three hours' snooze, preparatory to driving forty miles on a bitter winter night over the roughest piece of road in Western America.

"Hullo, where are you coming from? Who's aboard?"

"Nobody but me."

"Bully for you! Where's your bottle?"

A "square drink" opens his eyes a little, and as we discuss some steaming beef-steaks he gives us the pleasant news that "the other side" (the north side of the mountain) was sloppy with half-melted snow as he came over in the morning, and that it is probably now a sheet of ice.

"However," he adds, "as there's nobody but you aboard, don't much matter if we do go over."

On which I thanked him, and asked him how long ago it was since he had overturned, so as to calculate the chances against his doing so to-night.

"Well," he said, "Old —— went up with me last night, and I told him the mules wanted roughing. He said they didn't, so just to show him they did, I piled the leaders into a heap just above Dick Wooten's there, and I guess from the row the insides, Old —— among 'em—kicked up, he'll believe me the next time."

"But where on earth did you go?" I asked.

"Oh," he said, "I waited till I got a snow-bank kinder handy, pulled on my near leader, slipped my brake, bucked myself into the snow-bank, and let the old shandrydan rip."

"Well," said I, "thank goodness *I* am not one of the Company's officers!"

After another long drink we muffle up, and I jump on to the box-seat beside Frank, while Sam turns inside for a snooze.

In five seconds more the helpers swing the leaders into their place, and with a tremendous plunge that threatens to burst every piece of tackle about them, the four mules "lay themselves down" and race away, their ears laid back along their necks, their tails tight down to their quarter, bucking and squealing along the only piece of level this side of the mountains. We are over it in a minute, and in and out of the dry watercourse with a lurch that makes me grip the handrail, the mules steadying on the further side, where begins the steady pull up the first ascent.

What a gorgeous wild scene it is! In front the range rises in a black weird wall, and the full moon streams down on the white broken crags, making them look like the battlements of old ruined castles; and across the road the pines shed a ghastly shadow, setting off still more brightly the moonlight on beyond. And now we are in the cañon itself, and the crags beetle a thousand feet high on either side, save where here and there a long steep slope runs up far into some snow-covered glen.

I express a hope that the other side is as clear as this one, as up to the present the road has been perfectly clear of snow; and Frank says that all is dry up to the summit, but from that down we shall catch it.

We trot on in silence for the next half-mile, crossing and re-crossing the stream several times, till we open a little glade, at the further side of which we see the camp-fires of a Mexican bullock-train, whose ten waggons are drawn up in a semicircle against the rock, forming an enclosure to keep the cattle from roaming. The fires shed a warm kindly blaze round, lighting up the dark pine stems, and playing on the little white points of rock at the opposite side of the cañon. The team object strongly to passing them: but Frank's heavy whip soon reassures Kitty, one of the leaders, who squeals and bucks each time the thong cracks across her quarter. As we lose the fire we plunge again into the darkness of the cañon, and steady the team as we near the Devil's Gate, so called from two enormous rocks through which the water-course has worn a channel only just wide enough for a waggon to get through, and which tower over our heads to some 200 or 300 feet high. It is a wild place, and was famed in old times for desperate Indian encounters.

From this up to the summit we have better going, and the mules, well warmed to their work, take us up quickly and steadily; and almost before I am aware a piercing cold blast warns me that we have reached the summit, and that there is nothing to shield us from the north wind, which I see swirling the snow in wreaths on the top of Fisher's Peak, ten miles away. Anxiously we strain our eyes down the northern slope, only to find deep snow over everything.

The road turns sharp at right angles along the crest of

the hill for the next quarter of a mile past the old tree which marks the boundary-line of the territories of Colorado and New Mexico, and on which ten years ago a famous highwayman was lynched. As we reach the turn in the road where the descent begins we pull up and begin to prepare for it.

Sam and I get out and tie the front and hind wheels together with ropes so as to block the coach entirely, and prevent the hind-wheels from swinging round, as if they did so it must upset the coach. This done, Sam goes forward a little way to reconnoitre. Not five steps has he gone when his heels fly up into the air, and down he comes on the broad of his back, with a crash that re-echoes through the still night; and it is some seconds before he can find breath to reply to our questions of what had happened, and how did it look. All that we get, however, is a confused sentence, out of which I catch, "The darn'dest meanest road this side of ——," which we receive with shouts of laughter, and Frank tells him to jump on board.

This time I get inside, as Frank says he's "going to run 'em down."

Sam follows my example; and we each station ourselves at a window. Frank gets the team's heads straight, and in another second we are sliding over a sheet of ice at twelve miles an hour, on a gradient of one foot in ten. A sudden jar, a grunt, and a half-choked groan from one of the mules, while a half-smothered curse from Frank tells that something has happened. I crane out, and see the off-wheeler down flat on her side, fortunately with her legs outward, as, had they fallen inwards, she would have thrown the other wheel mule, and then nothing could have saved us. As it is, how we get down the next 400 yards goodness only knows; but at the end of it we find a big snow-drift; and into it Frank unhesitatingly shoots us, thus enabling him to stop the team. I run to the leaders' heads, while

Sam gets hold of the fallen mule, and now the question is, how to get her on to her feet. Frank tells me to swing the leaders across the road from the mule so as to give her room to struggle; and then applying the whip as hard as he can across her loins she struggles up, only to fall again, as the leaders, frightened at the crack of the whip, make a wild plunge forward. My feet slip from under me, and for a second I think that the whole team and the coach beside are over me: but thanks to the rough lock of the wheels they could not move the coach, and I struggle up, only to have the same thing happen again. But this time the old mule keeps her feet; and after cutting away the snow a little round the wheels we jump in, and off we start again. The worst part is over; and the next half-mile we sail along grandly, when down goes the same wheeler again, and we drag her thirty or forty yards before we can stop. We get her up again: but she is so much hurt and cowed by the fright, that she falls again three or four times before we reach the station about a mile ahead. Here we find that the poor brute has not got a single hair on her left side from the point of her ear to the root of her tail, and on the shoulder, ribs, and hip-bone a good deal of skin has come off as well. 'But any way,' Frank says, 'she's only a mule;' and sure enough a year afterwards, I sat behind her over the very same piece of mountain, looking as if she had never skated down the Ratons."

"You will easily imagine that after hearing this story I felt somewhat like the man who said, 'I *kin* eat biled crow, but I don't hanker arter it:' and did not 'hanker' any more after a journey across the mountains."

CHAPTER VII.

CHRISTMAS AND NEW YEAR.

A Christmas treat—Stock-farmers' troubles—The western metropolis—Parlour skates—The fall of the Ulsters—Sleighing—A warm Christmas day—Christmas tree—God save the Queen—My first Indian—A wind storm—New-Year's Day—Our new hotel—Ute Indians—A "surprise party"—Cow-catching a dangerous amusement.

"DENVER, COLORADO, *Dec.* 27, /71.

"DEAR * * *,—As Christmas comes but once a year, and it is many a long day since we spent it together, we determined to give ourselves a treat. So on the 20th of December M. shut up his books and papers; I wound up my affairs by taking my collection of snow-birds, now numbering eight, to a neighbour; locking up my valuables, and putting on a clean dress, and at 12.30 we were in the cars *en route* for a week in Denver.

"When we crossed the Divide the difference in climate showed strangely. With us at Colorado Springs, the snow has never lain more than four days at the longest. Northward, the country is covered with a solid cake of frozen snow, two to twelve inches deep; and our Scotch friends on Plum Creek are in sad trouble about their cattle, most of them having run off before the storms to the rich pastures of the Arkansas river, a hundred miles south; while those that remain are grubbing about in the snow for patches of buffalo or bunch grass, under shelter of the bluffs. To be sure, it is an exceptional winter: but it is a serious matter for the stock-raiser to be liable to such a winter, if it only comes once in seven years.

"Denver looks wintry enough, under six inches to a foot of snow: but it is full of life and bustle. The toy-shops are gay with preparations for Christmas-trees; the candy stores filled with the most attractive sweetmeats; the furriers display beaver coats, and mink, ermine, and sable, to tempt the cold passer-by; and in the butchers' shops hang, besides the ordinary beef and mutton, buffalo, black-tailed deer, antelope, Rocky Mountain sheep, quails, partridges, and prairie-chicken.

"The streets are full of sleighs, each horse with its collar of bells; and all the little boys have manufactured or bought little sleds, which they tie to the back of any passing cart or carriage; and get whisked along the streets till some sharp turn or unusual roughness in the road upsets them.

"The first night I spent here I could hardly sleep from the heat. I had been looking forward with delight to having a carpeted room again: but when I came to try one, it seemed so stuffy after the bare floor and innumerable draughts of air from windows and door in my 'sky parlour' at the Springs, that I was nearly stifled, and had to throw the windows open, with the thermometer down in the neighbourhood of zero outside.

"We found plenty of old friends up here, and have made many more since we came. In the frank unconventional state of society which exists in the West, friendships are made much more easily than even in the Eastern States, or still more, in our English society; and, if one wants to have, as the Americans express it, 'a good time,' one must expand a little out of one's insularity, and meet the hearty good-will shown one with some adequate response.

"There is unluckily no out-door skating to be had here, as the snow has spoiled all the ice: but we have discovered a capital substitute in the roller-skating rink, where, in a large hall on a board-floor, with four-wheeled parlour skates, you can do every figure that is possible on ice. Every day a large party of us, both Americans and English, go down to the rink, and great is the fun we have. The fact of being a first-rate skater on ice does not help a bit on roller skates; and after shuffling about helplessly myself, envying one young lady, who was skimming round with perfect ease, it was, I confess, very comforting to see two distinguished performers, both over six feet high, skate hand in hand to the end of the hall, and, losing all control over their feet, rush violently against the wall, and fall flat on their backs side by side.

"Talking of falls, M. and two other large Englishmen, all three in Ulsters, which create much mirth out here among the small boys, were walking along one of the streets here the other day:—you must understand that in a new city the wooden side-walk is often only made in front of each house; and where there is a gap in the buildings there is a corresponding gap in the pavement. As the street was covered in snow, our friends did not see one of these sudden precipices before them, and walked calmly on, and over the end of the side-walk, which was nearly two feet above the ground, all three falling flat in the snow side by side, to the intense delight of the passers-by. On Friday evening, after two hours' skating at the rink, we went out for a sleigh-drive, the first I have ever had; and most delightful it was. We were muffled up in blankets and buffalo robes and all our furs. The thermometer was 2° below zero; the moon as clear as day; and, with a capital pair of horses, we flew over the smooth sparkling snow, our sleigh-bells jingling in the frosty air. When we got home, about 11 P.M., M. looked just like Santa Claus, with his moustache and hair all snowy white from his frozen breath.

"Christmas Day was bright, and even hot in the sun; and we had to pick our way to church through rivers of melted snow. The Episcopal church looks rather like a wooden coach-house outside: but inside it is very nice, and was prettily decorated. The excellent Bishop of Colorado, Dr. Randall, is still in the East, getting together a number of clergy to come out to the Territory; or we should have had the pleasure of hearing our Christmas sermon from him. But even his absence mattered little to any one who had had no chance of getting to church for two months; the dear familiar service alone was quite enough to satisfy one. The singing, by an amateur quartett choir, of two ladies and two gentlemen, was very good, but florid.

"I was asked to eat my Christmas dinner at Colonel M.'s, where Miss J. boarded; and, simply because I was her friend, every one in the house made me welcome. Dinner of the orthodox turkey and mince-pie over, we were summoned to the Christmas-tree in the parlour, which was decorated, in place of our holly-berries, with strings of raw cranberries and snowy popcorns, pretty to look at, and nice to eat.

"There were several children in the house; and I hardly know whether they or their black nurses were most delighted. One little negro girl, who had charge of Mrs. M.'s lovely baby, was nearly crazy, as every one in the house had put something on the tree for her; and when a large brown paper parcel was given her, down went the poor baby on the floor, as she tore the parcel open and found a pair of new boots inside. I shall never forget the child's ecstasy, capering about like a black puppy, and showing her white teeth from ear to ear.

"The evening passed with games and music, and constant refreshments in the shape of candy and hickory-nuts; and suddenly our host turned round to me and said, 'Now, I'll sing something for you;' and began the first verse of 'God save the Queen.' It sent a thrill over me, hearing it a thousand miles west of the Mississippi for the first time since leaving England. And then I was made to sing it all through; for, though the tune is familiar enough in America, no one present knew the right words. It was a pleasant ending to a pleasant evening.

"To-morrow we go home to Colorado Springs, so farewell."

On the 28th we started for home, dropping half-a-dozen of our English friends at Plum Creek; and, on the Divide, I had a new experience, for there I saw my first Indian. At first he looked to me like the most ugly of all old Hampshire gipsy hags; but as we got nearer to him, his hideousness was amazing. A smooth copper-coloured face, with a very long nose; straight black hair, the two front locks (the scalp locks) braided with beads; buckskin moccassins and shirt; a buffalo robe, inside out, wrapped round him, and fastened at the waist by a belt; and a bow and arrows in his hand—altogether the most revolting specimen of humanity I had ever seen.

M. and Dr. L. went and spoke to him in a jargon of Spanish and Indian; and he asked where Washington was. At first they thought he meant the city, but he said,—"No, no; he is somewhere near;" and M. found he meant Washington, the old chief of the Northern Utes; and that Ulay, the new Mexican chief, was on his way up to have a "big talky-talky."

The day before we came home the most terrific windstorm began at the Springs, and people were sitting up all night expecting their houses to be blown down. The only harm, however, that it did was to blow down or unroof a few shanties; and when we got down, it was quite calm again, and no snow to be seen. It was very pleasant getting home again, and having such a warm welcome from every one; and I had graphic accounts of their Christmas gaieties, which had consisted of a ball in Foote's Hall, a large building just finished, where, I believe, as many as twenty couples mustered; and a most successful school-treat, which

Mrs. P. had arranged for her school children and their parents.

December 29.—The day began in perfect calm. I went up to Mrs. C.'s to do some ironing, and the morning was so hot that we were obliged to keep both window and door open while we did our work. The thermometer was $52°$; hot sun, and not a breath of air stirring: but over the top of Pike's Peak hung a small white cloud, a certain sign of mischief; and so it proved, for about 3 P.M., as I was making a sketch on Tejon Street, suddenly, without any warning, down rushed the wind from the mountains in a moment, and nearly blew the pencils and paper out of my hands. I packed up as quick as possible, and, running to Mrs. de C.'s, borrowed her thickest gauze veil, tied it tight over my face, and, walking sideways like a crab, started the half mile for home. The wind was from west, and my road lay north-west; so, by taking advantage of every lull between the gusts, and making a dash up-wind, the next gust did not blow me quite out of my course. I could just keep my feet along the open: but coming to the business block where the houses stand, I saw the dust-storm coming too, and right in my face. I tried to cross the street, one hundred feet, to a boarding-house where I could get shelter; but midway the whirlwind caught me, bringing with it sand, bits of wood, and pebbles as large as a sparrow's egg. These missiles cut so, even through the thick veil, that I could only cover my face with both hands and stand still. Staggering to the wall of the house, and hoping for shelter, I found it was rather worse than in the open; so I managed at last to creep round to the back-door, and came plump upon a terrified cow, who had gone there too for safety. My sudden appearance caused much astonishment to the inmates of the house: but they forgave my unceremonious entry, and gave me house-room till the gust was over, and I could get home. All that day the storm raged: but abated towards evening; and the day ended with a splendid lunar rainbow between us and the mountains.

Dec. 31.—M. and I went a long walk up the Monument specimen-hunting, and found some pretty bits of crystal and fossil wood. About two miles above the town, on the banks of the creek, is a large bed of fossil shells.

January 1, 1872.—The new year has come in with bright sun, no wind, and cloudless blue sky. It is a marked day in the life of our little colony; for after two months of delays, the Colorado Springs Hotel was opened at 2 P.M., and we went to our first meal there, and ate with English knives and forks, off English china, a first-rate dinner.

But this was not the only event of the day; for in the morning a swarm of Indians came into town. They were Utes from New Mexico, and M. recognised many old acquaintances among them. One of the young braves was, he said, the greatest thief unhung in New Mexico. He has five squaws, and makes them all steal for him. He had on a scarlet blanket over buckskins; a kind of breastplate of beads, mostly white; and a row of silver beads down the parting of his hair, ending on his forehead with a silver crescent. There were several squaws of the party, whose ugly faces we were glad to see, as their presence is a sure sign of peace; and for a few weeks rumours had been flying about of an intended outbreak among the Utes on the other side of the foot-hills. The men and women were dressed very much alike; except that the women's hair was cut straight round just below the ears, and the men wore their long scalp locks with little cases of beads, like a bouquet-holder, surrounding them. Some of their faces were painted with red stripes; and one had red and yellow stripes on the cheeks, yellow being the second mourning for a near relation. When an Indian dies, the nearest of kin paint themselves entirely white, and retire to their lodges for ten days, during which time no one sees them. They then come out and paint themselves red and yellow till the end of the month or moon, when the days of mourning are over. The Ute war-paint, which I happily did not see, is black and white. The Indians were intensely interested in the railroad track—the first they had ever seen ; and squatted down, rubbing the metals with their

Indians.

fingers. They hung about all the morning, on the look-out for a little pilfering; and when the train started, some went up to Denver by train, and the rest camped up the Fountain, about a mile below Manitou, to hunt in the mountains.

In the evening we determined to get up a "surprise party" for Mrs. F., one of our neighbours, and this is how it was managed. During the day we went to all our friends, and asked them to meet us at seven o'clock, and in a body, and without giving our hostess that was to be any warning, we knocked at her door. The surprise was on her side, not ours, when she opened the door and found a dozen people outside wishing her a happy new year, and come to spend the evening. Of course she had been able to make no preparations for us: but that makes just the fun of a "surprise party:" one goes merely for the sake of a pleasant evening, and does not expect anything more than the hearty welcome one is sure to get.

January 3d.—Dr. B. asked me to drive the L.'s, who arrived from England three days ago, up to Manitou with Governor H.'s ponies. Half way up we passed the Indians' camp, and saw their lodges, tents of dark brown skin, supported by poles tied together in the middle. As we went by, one of the Indians was kind enough to stand in the bushes close by the road, with bow and arrow ready drawn. The ponies were almost frantic with terror; and one of our party was somewhat alarmed too, thinking our last hour had surely come. Horses, and still more mules, cannot bear the smell of an Indian, and will often "scare" at them—as the phrase is—when their driver cannot see one within a quarter of a mile.

5th.—M. went up to Denver, and the L.'s, Dr. B., and I went up with him as far as Teachouts, and spent a couple of hours in Monument Park. I was invited to go on the cow-catcher, with which every American engine is armed. It is a kind of nose of iron bars sharply pointed, which sweeps any obstacle from the track; and on the top there is just room for three people to sit with their feet hanging down close to the rails. But though in my secret heart I wished just to feel what it was like for once, M. told me that it was really such a risk that I resisted the temptation, and we settled ourselves comfortably on the back platform. If you do run over a cow, which very often cannot be avoided with one of these stupid Texan beasts—for they will seem to be moving off when the engineer "toots" at them, and then, as he starts again, turn right round, and walk into the train,—it is thrown up on the top of any one who sits on the cow-catcher. A man could raise himself up: but a woman must either be thrown off, or receive the cow, in a mashed state, in her lap. Then, again, the "eccentrics" may get out of order, and a dozen bumps will come, which must throw one off. And, in addition, this particular engine "throws fire," unless there is a very strong head wind; so, altogether, it was much more comfortable to be sitting in the sun on the hind platform, than getting holes burnt in my clothes, as our cow-catching friends did before the trip was over.

It is curious how soon one gets accustomed to the seemingly reckless way people go on here. There we stood or sat on the platform, with our feet hanging down almost touching the rails. It was perfectly safe, because we knew the risk of a slip, and guarded against it: and we thought no more of there being real danger than if we had been sitting on a coach-box at home.

CHAPTER VIII.

MOUNTAIN EXPLORATIONS.

Bronco manners—Mountain appetites—The Rainbow Fall—A scramble—The new road—Trailing Arbutus—Glenwood Mills—Beavers—A cold bath—Arkansas hospitality—The Ute pass—A scare—A "washing bee"—Our first Episcopal service—The ditch full at last—Growth of the town—A ride over the mesa—An exploring expedition—The "Pike's Peak gold fever"—A "cold snap"—Our concert.

In the beginning of January we had a spell of perfect weather; and we took advantage of it to carry out our long-talked-of plan, of driving up into the mountains to see Bergun's Park, which belongs to Dr. B. So, early on the 7th we started in a buggy, with Governor H.'s two brown ponies, celebrated all through Colorado as the most enduring pair of animals in the Far West. It was a bright cold morning, but we were well wrapped up in buffalo robes and blankets, with our luggage in two small travelling-bags stowed under the seat. Our first excitement was on crossing the Monument Bridge, beyond the railroad track. An old man was just harnessing a pair of broncos, or tame wild horses, to his waggon, preparatory to his day's journey; for he had been camping in the bushes by the creek for the night. Either our buggy or a herd of cows which came over the bridge startled them, and after the manner of broncos, they reared, kicked, jumped over the traces, knocked the old man down, and were just making off when he got on his feet, and with the help of the cow-herd stopped them. We stayed to see no more, for fear our ponies should do likewise, as they usually run away on starting. We saw nothing more of interest till we passed Colorado City, and arrived at the Indian camp, where a small child in a red jacket appeared, running about among the rocks like a brown monkey; and a little further on we fell in with a squaw, dressed in buckskin and a red blanket, trying to lasso three run-away ponies.

At Manitou we stopped for breakfast with General and Mrs. P., and must have considerably astonished their New York cook by our mountain appetites, for a second supply of broiled venison was sent for in five minutes, and George, the negro servant, was running in continually with fresh dishes of hot biscuit. Mr. B., who was staying there, volunteered, after breakfast, to go with us up the new road through the cañon of the Fountain, while Dr. B. took the buggy over the Ute Pass, to meet us where the old and new roads join. So we walked up the cañon as far as the place where the workmen are blasting for the road, and then climbed down to the top of the Lower Fall, a dangerous bit of rock work, as a slip would have dropped us into the stream below; however, we got down safe, and then crept along the right bank of the stream, sometimes on ice, sometimes swinging ourselves round the stem of a tree, and soon found ourselves at the "Upper or Rainbow Fall." The stream comes over a rock wall about a hundred feet high, which shuts in the whole valley. The cañon is not more than twenty feet wide, and the effect of the white stream falling into this narrow chasm, whose walls tower up hundreds of feet, is most beautiful.

Then we turned up the mountain side to the right, as it is impossible to scale the rocks on each side of the fall. It was a hard climb; sheets of rock and pulverized granite, with here and there a tuft of grass, a scraggy oak or pine tree, or a creeping cactus; and woe to the unwary one who laid hold of the latter for help! The sun was intensely hot, and beat down on us unmercifully; and the slope was so steep, we had to use our hands and knees in many places. When we got to the top, about 500 feet above the stream, we were rather out of breath, and not at all sorry to rest, as going up hill in this rarefied air is no easy matter. The way down to the creek again was rough, through bushes burnt by some mountain fire, and over big boulders; and in one place we had to swing by a little tree over a rock, alighting on a sheet of ice. We were quickly down, however; struck the trail for the new road by the creek about a quarter of a mile above the Rainbow Fall, and soon came to a place where we had to cross the creek. Boughs had been thrown in to make a crossing-place: but the stream had risen from the melting snow; so we got fresh saplings of cotton-wood, and some logs which were lying about, and tossing them in on the top of the old boughs, crossed dry-foot. But what was our disgust when, thirty yards on, round a corner of rock, we came upon a second ford, which had to be bridged back again. Above this the road had all been graded and bridged, and we got along at a good pace. Here the cañon narrowed, with rock walls on either side of pink granitic hornblende, several hundred feet high. Huge Douglassii pines grew along the creek, arching overhead, with spruces and pines, or felled across it, their feathery branches cased in a delicate coating of ice, taking the exact form of each twig. Great boulders lay in the stream; the water rushed past them or under sheets of ice; and overhead, on the topmost rocks, and sometimes coming down to the road, was brilliant hot sunshine. It was the most beautiful road one could see or imagine.

We followed it for about a mile and a half, and as the rock walls grew lower, came upon the shanties of the workmen who were making the road. The men all came out and stared at us in speechless amazement; for we were the first passengers who had ever come up the road, and it was some time before they could collect their senses to speak to us.

But at last the contractor, being persuaded that we had not dropped from the sky, recovered himself sufficiently to say that we were only a quarter of a mile from the junction of the old and new road. We hurried on, and found Dr. B. and the ponies waiting for us beside a spring, at which we slaked our thirst with the clearest water imaginable; and bidding farewell to our guides, drove off again.

The road now followed the Fountain up a fine valley, with rocky pine-covered hills rising to an immense height on either side. In some places we were a good deal delayed by ice on the road, having to get out, scrape up earth with our hands to strew over it, and then lead the ponies over: but we got safely, about 1.30, to Sale's Sawmill. Here the valley widened out a good deal, with grass slopes up to the edge of the pines, and occasional prairie-dog towns; and four miles above Sale's we came to the fork of the roads, the left leading into South Park, to Fair Play, and the great mining districts, the right to Bergun's Park. The rise here began to be steep, and we got into snow, and soon reached the pineries of the Divide, between the Platte and Arkanzes. The quaking aspen, showing that we were near snow-line, grew among the pines at the top of the Divide, which was just 8000 feet above the sea. The ground under the pines was covered with trailing Arbutus, which Dr. Hooker pronounces to be exactly the same species as that of the Scotch Highlands—*Arctostaphylos Uva ursi*—it is called by the Indians "*kinikinick*," and is used by them as tobacco. Immense quantities of trees had been felled for timber on the Divide, and we drove down through the pineries for a mile or more, till we reached a little grass park or opening where Dr. D. has established a fine sawmill, just seventeen miles from Colorado Springs. Here we were to stay for the night. So we pulled up at a new wooden shanty near the mill, and were taken into a nice large sitting-room, with open hearth and roaring pitch-pine fire, where the ladies of the family made us welcome. They were horrified, however, at our instantly setting out, as supper was not ready, to see a fine beaver-dam up the valley.

We waded through frozen snow about a mile and a half up a side-stream, now sinking into a drift over our boots, now getting out of the way of stray cattle, now being flown at by a fierce dog from some solitary shanty; finally, after crossing two streams, we came, in a narrow valley, to the dam, which amply repaid our rough walk. As it was covered in ice and snow we could walk all over it. It formed an irregular semicircle about 100 yards wide, thrown right across the flat part of the valley. The bank in front was about five feet high, thrown up like a fortification—a breastwork of earth gently sloped back, and beaten quite smooth by the beavers' tails as with a spade, with a wattle of sticks from half-an-inch to an inch thick along the top. Willow and oak bushes grew in the water behind the dam; and a dozen yards back from the edge was the beavers' house, a round heap, three feet above the ice, of sticks and logs, with a little mud in the interstices.

All the streams in the mountains round here are full of beavers; and though one never sees them, their work is only too visible. Two families of beavers last December took possession of the Fountain Creek, close to Manitou, and in a fortnight had felled most of the largest cotton-wood trees, some of them two feet thick, which we were watching with pride and delight as one of the ornaments of the valley. The families must have been cousins; for when the upper dam was finished, its makers came down and helped those at the lower one, who were slower at their work; and unless they are kinsfolk, beavers never help each other.

The sun had set ere we finished our exploration, and we hurried back to Glenwood Mills, to find supper ready for us in the kitchen. We had stewed oysters, smoked beef, mountain raspberries of Mrs. D.'s own gathering and preserving, bread and potatoes. There was neither butter nor milk in the house; but a few hours' fast makes the best sauce in the world, and we ate our dry bread and drank our tea with great enjoyment. We sat round the fire in the sitting-room chatting and looking at specimens; and Dr. D., who is a Yorkshireman by birth, told us a good deal about the country, which he knows thoroughly, especially about South Park, where he lived for eight years. One winter, he said, the snow was eight feet deep all over the Park, and they had to get in and out of the houses by the upper windows. One of the ladies kindly gave me up her room, the sleeping-rooms being divided from the sitting-room by an eight-foot partition, which had the advantage of letting in the warmth of the roaring fire; and about 9.30 our party broke up, and I was not sorry to get a few hours' sleep after our long day.

Toward morning the cold was intense, and a little after 6 A.M. we were glad to roast ourselves by the fire, after washing our hands and faces in a tin basin of water from the pond outside, to get which ice a foot thick had to be broken. While we were at breakfast at seven, the sun rose; lighting up Pike's Peak, which we could see from the house towering up over the pineries; and by eight o'clock we had bidden farewell to our kind hosts, and were once more in the waggon and off to Bergun's Park. The ponies, refreshed as much as we were by the good cheer at Glenwood Mills, testified their joy by making a bolt from the door as we were just gathering up the reins, and running away for half a mile over ditches and through pine-stumps before we could pull them up.

We followed the valley about two miles through the snow, then up a hill into the pine woods, and through the boundary fence of the Park. We now kept in the forest for a mile and a half, and then down a steep pitch nearly two feet deep in snow, to a pretty grass-glade with a stream in the middle, and woods of huge pine, spruce, Douglassii, and silver fir round it. The latter is, I think, the most beautiful of all the fir tribe, when it is self-sown, and not crowded by other trees; a black and silver pyramid without a twist, or a single branch out of place. Then came another belt of wood, and we emerged into the Park itself. It is about eight miles long, and in some places a mile wide; a fork of the South Platte runs through it, on each side of which the grass

Pike's Peak.

slopes up to the pineries, and they again to the mountains, both scattered with a few huge red sandstone monuments. Looking north, the park is shut in by a strangely jagged mountain, known as the Devil's Nose. South, you get a magnificent view of Pike's Peak, which looks much grander from this side than from the east.

The stream is full of excellent trout, and we tried to get some from a family of Germans who have taken up a claim right in the middle of the Park: but being surly, disagreeable people, and possibly feeling they had no right to be there, they would give us neither fish, milk, or butter, though their cows were feeding on Dr. B.'s hay. We felt rather like the man Governor H. tells of, who, travelling in Arkansas, rides up late one day to a lonely ranche. The sole occupant is a woman, who comes to the door hearing a traveller arrive; and the following dialogue ensues:—

Man.—" Good day, ma'am, how goes? Can you give my horse a feed?"

Woman.—" Wa'al, I hain't got *much*."

Man.—" Can you give him some corn and hay?"

Woman.—" Wa'al, I hain't got no corn, and I hain't got no hay."

Man (inquisitively).—" Can you give him some fodder?"

Woman (reflectively).—" Wa'al—no; I hain't got no fodder."

The horse must take care of himself evidently; so the traveller begins again persuasively:—

" Well, can you give *me* something to eat?"

Woman (doubtfully).—" Wa'al, neaow, I guess I hain't got much."

Man (impatiently).—" Can you give me some bread and beans?"

Woman.—" Wa'al, I hain't got no bread, and I hain't got no beans."

Man (furiously).—" Why, how *do* you people do down here?"

Woman (cheerfully).—" Oh, pretty well, thank you; heaow do *you* do?"

So after resting the ponies and making a sketch, we turned homeward, reaching Glenwood at 1 P.M.

We got a warming by the fire for ten minutes, but no

food, as our visit had completely cleared out the larder, with the exception of one slice of dry bread, which kind Mrs. D. bestowed upon us. So we divided it into three portions, and satisfied our hunger for a little while. When we started again, the snow on the Divide had melted somewhat in the hot sun, and balled a good deal, so that our progress was slow for some miles, till we got clear of it. Then the road being down-hill, we went along well, and reached the foot of the Ute Pass at 3.15 P.M. There of course we all got out, and clambered up the hill, which was hard work, as in many places there were sheets of glaze-ice, from ten to twenty yards long, on a steep slope, which had to be strewn with earth before the poor ponies could be dragged over. It is by no means a pleasant task, when one's own fingers are half-frozen, to have to use them like terrier's paws in scratching earth out of the frozen ground, and then running the risk of slipping down one's-self and dragging the ponies over one, or being knocked down in their slips and struggles. The Pass winds over two hills with a deep gorge between them. At the top of the first hill we got into the waggon, and drove for a little way, being rather tired: but just before the dip into the gorge we met an ox-team. In most places you cannot pass anything on this road; here, however, a dry stream-course enabled us to turn out of the way, and stand to let it pass: but just as it got by, the ponies smelt some raw beef which was at the back of the ox-waggon, and reared and plunged, dragging us straight up the bank of the stream. I thought we must go over; however, strange to say, we got by in safety.

These ponies have a peculiarly delicate sense of smell, and will "scare," as the phrase here is, at anything with a game scent; so much so indeed, that we are always obliged, on starting for a drive with them, to have any bear or buffalo robe thrown into the back of the waggon at the last minute, or they become almost unmanageable.

From the actual summit of the Pass we got a magnificent view of the Plains, stretching away like a ripe harvest-field in the light of the setting sun, yellow and purple; while the mountains between which we saw them, and the cañon of the Fountain, were all in deep shadow. It was a frightful road, steep as a house-roof, with stones, rocks, and ice to improve it; and as our front axle was sprung, and our break did not act properly, we had to walk all the way down the Pass to Manitou. Here the P.'s wanted us to stay and refresh ourselves, but we were such objects, and so tired, that we preferred going straight home, and reached Colorado Springs at 7 P.M., as starved, burnt, ragged, and footsore a set of travellers as could well be seen.

Jan. 8.—So stiff after our mountain-trip I could hardly move. However, I went up to Mrs. C.'s, where we had agreed to have a "washing bee," and initiated Mrs. L., who was fresh from England, into the mysteries of soaping, boiling, rinsing, starching, and ironing.

10*th.*—Dr. B. started for California to see General R., and arrange about the Mexican expedition, and as soon as he comes back we shall all start west and south.

Saturday, 12*th.*—As M. was away at Pueblo, Mrs. P. brought me up to Manitou yesterday; and this morning we have been roaming up the cañons, collecting seeds and stones. A white spiræa grows here in great quantities, and when it is in flower I am told it looks like powdered snow among the green leaves. The day was so hot that we could not bear jackets over our gowns. After luncheon we walked down to the beaver dam, on the Fountain, and got some chips from the trees the beavers have felled. They are exactly the shape of ordinary chips cut with a hatchet, from an inch to three inches across.

To-morrow we are going to have our first Episcopal service in the town; Mr. E., the clergyman from Pueblo, having offered to come for a Sunday; and we hope that till a church is built here, the Bishop will be able to send us a clergyman once a month. We are determined to begin with as good a service as possible; we have had several practices this week for it, and had our final one this afternoon. Mr. E. arrived on the coach; and I found that he was not only an Englishman, but came from Marlowe, so we had a pleasant talk over all our Berkshire friends.

Sunday, 13th.—A lovely day. A little before 11 A.M. we went over to Foote's Hall, where the service was to be held. I had Mrs. P.'s harmonium over from the school, and we managed the Canticles and two hymns very creditably, most of the congregation joining in. There were sixty-five people present, a good many of whom were Methodists, etc., but the larger proportion Episcopalians. As no one else seemed inclined to lead the responses, I did; and was much laughed at afterwards for my emphatic "Amen" to the prayer for the President; but I explained that I had my English Prayer-book with our dear Queen's name open before me, and it was for her and not for the President that my Amen was said.

After service we took a stroll to the Fountain ditch, which the engineers reported would be full to-day at last: but the water had not yet come down. After dinner at the hotel, we sat down on the piazza or in the parlour, with all the doors and windows open. The sun was so strong that we were quite glad to get into the shade.

Later in the afternoon we took a walk, and as we neared the great gulch at the back of the town we heard a curious and most unusual sound for this part of the country, like a large waterfall, and on getting up to the edge, found, to our great delight, that the ditch was full, and was pouring a strong stream of muddy water down into the gulch below, where the reservoir is to be made. Now that it is full, the colony authorities are going to cut small ditches down each street, and plant trees by them, which will soon improve the look of the town; and the colonists are already talking of planting gardens and fencing in their residence lots.

The town certainly is growing prodigiously. I find it quite difficult to keep pace with all the new arrivals, or the new buildings which spring up as if by magic.

The hotel is a great success, and is pronounced to be the "best house west of the Mississippi." It is full of visitors already from Denver and the east, who come in search of health or to enjoy our beautiful scenery; and the Denver and Rio Grande Railroad is just moving its offices down here from Denver, which will bring down a most pleasant set of people to add to our little society.

15*th*.—We went out riding a little after seven along the Colorado City Road, and then turned up the Mesa which lies between the plains and the foot-hills. A Mesa here means a huge bank or down of earth, sometimes 200 feet high, and seemingly the deposit of ancient glaciers. I had never been on the mesa before. It is quite flat on the top, covered with buffalo and gramma grass, Spanish bayonet, and cactus, with low thorns, scrub oak, and here and there an old cedar growing down the steep sides into the valleys, which run up into the mesa in all directions. We rode along the top for a mile or two, and it was some time before we could find a place to get down, the slopes to the flats below being almost perpendicular and covered with stones: but at last we managed it, crossing the ditch a second time, and then the Monument Creek at a ford.

Temporary Inn, Manitou, Jan. 19.—I came up here a week ago to pay a visit to General and Mrs. P., who are living here till Glen Eyrie is finished, and we are very busy preparing for a concert. The reading-room is in want of funds, so we have determined to give a concert for its benefit; and have enlisted all the musical talent in the neighbourhood to help us.

20th.—M. came up, and we started on a great "exploring expedition" to find, if possible, a direct road across the mountains from Manitou to Glen Eyrie, about four miles, prospecting by the way for silver and coal leads. Our first discovery, on the first hill we climbed, was a quantity of galena, which seemed tolerably rich with silver: but, as we expected, we did not find anything worth working, as all this neighbourhood has been thoroughly prospected for silver and gold mines already since the days of the great "Pike's Peak gold fever," when Colorado City had for one brief year 4000 inhabitants, and all this country was swarming with miners and emigrants from the East, who thought, poor creatures, that a second California was discovered. Thousands poured out here across the plains, of whom hardly a tenth ever got home again. Some were killed by Indians; some died of the hardships of the journey; or ended still more sadly when their dream of prosperity faded; or crawled home broken-hearted, like the poor fellow who was seen starting across the plains from Kansas with a good team of horses and smart waggon, with this inscription painted in gaudy colours on the tilt—" Pike's Peak or Bust," and who, a few months later, came creeping wearily home, ragged and ruined, with a lame mule, supposed to be stolen, in place of the horses, and on what remained of his waggon-top the one word scrawled—" Busted." But those who survived, and who braved all the risks and difficulties of the new country, are the people to whom Colorado owes her present and future prosperity. The Fiftyniners, as they proudly call themselves, are looked on with a kind of respectful admiration by the younger Coloradans, as the little pioneer aristocracy of the territory; and they still keep up the old bond of friendships made in the midst of unheard-of dangers fifteen years ago; and have a gathering once a year in Denver of " The pioneers of 1859."

But to return to our scramble—for a scramble it was, as

we were the whole time going up or down hill. From the top of the hill, about 500 feet high, we descended through cactus and yucca, white cedar and piñons, into a deep cañon, the first of three we had to cross at right angles. The sides were so steep that M. had to slide down to the bottom, and catch me in his arms as I came down after him. In this cañon we found three distinct coal banks; one of them seemed exceedingly good coal, and close to the surface; the only difficulty in working them would be the distance to haul the coal by waggons, which would make it more expensive than coal brought a much greater distance by rail.

Then we turned up a rising plateau of good grass; and down into a second cañon, a very large one, with huge blocks of stone lying along it, shaded by cedars and Douglassii firs. We jumped from rock to rock, followed the cañon up for about a mile, and then came to the grassy Divide, between the slope we were following up from the Fountain river, and Glen Eyrie. That was a hard bit of walking, the keen air taking away one's breath, and making a rest every quarter of a mile really necessary. Pushing up a steep rise, through scrub oak and a thorny bush which caught and tore our clothes, we reached the top at last, and got a glorious view. We were considerably over 7000 feet above the sea. To the south-west was Pike's Peak, just enough veiled in an incipient snow-storm to look majestic; and to the north, beyond the salmon-coloured rocks of Glen Eyrie below us, lay the plains and the pineries, fifty miles away, all purple in the setting sun.

As soon as we were rested, down we went to the Glen by a little cañon—such a scramble! but I only got one fall the whole way, which was fortunate, considering the places we had to go down; and we reached the house, where the carriage was waiting for us, at sunset, having gone four and a half miles in two and a half hours, crossed three cañons, and never been on half a dozen yards of level ground the whole way.

In this air it is almost impossible to feel fatigue. At the end of the day one is wholesomely tired: but in the morning one gets up as fresh after a long walk as if one had been doing nothing out of the way.

Jan. 28th, Manitou.—Our concert is over, and has been a great success, in spite of the cold. After a month of perfect weather we have had a " cold snap," and the thermometer was down last night 22° below zero. I went down three days before the concert to stay at Colorado Springs with the F.'s, to be on the spot ready to practise at any time of day.

On the 24th there was a dense snowy fog, and the thermometer never rose above zero all day, and when we met in the evening at the L.'s for a practice, it was 19° below. We were nearly frozen. We put the piano close to the stove, and between each verse of the songs which I was accompanying, I had to jump up and put my fingers into the open stove door to thaw them; for they were quite numb from touching the keys.

My warm room with a hot stove in the F.'s well-plastered house, and two "comforts" (quilted cotton-wool covers) on my bed, was delightful, after the cold struggle home through the snow. The luxury of being in a well-built house after the temporary inn at Manitou was very great; for the latter was only built to accommodate summer visitors, and is about as warm to sleep in as an ordinary cow-shed. I heap clothes on my bed—seven blankets and a bear robe—and keep quite warm all night; but as there is no stove in my room, getting up and washing in the morning is a great trial.

On Thursday, the day of the concert, the weather was a little less severe. Practices of one kind or other were going on from early morning; and we had a full rehearsal in the afternoon as soon as the southern stage came in; for it brought a bass viol and its owner from fifteen miles down the Fountain. He made a most imposing foundation to the "concerted pieces," which were valses and écossaises played by the owners of the livery stables on two violins, Mrs. H. on M.'s guitar, and Miss B. at the piano.

It was a new and pleasant sensation making a toilet— though a very plain one—for the concert. We colonists hitherto have not been able to indulge much in evening dress, though doubtless that will come soon with our rapidly growing civilisation; and a thick tweed gown has served me for morning and evening, Sunday and week-day alike, ever since I came here three months ago.

The tenor from Colorado City came to tea at the F.'s; and so did M., and we had some really pleasant musical talk in the intervals of writing out programmes for the evening.

The concert was advertised for 7.30: but we did not all get together till nearly eight; and by that time Foote's hall, which at present is used for every sort of public gathering, was crowded with an orderly audience of about 150, of all classes, down to "bull-whackers" who dropped in after their day's work with the ox and mule teams.

At last all was ready. Captain de C. appeared with a jug of egg-nogg under his coat, which was cunningly deposited under the piano, so that as the performers went up to the very shaky platform they could stoop down and refresh themselves unseen; and the concert opened with a chorus. Everything went well. The bass viol, who I found had only tried his instrument a fortnight before, scraped away and tuned his strings, which insisted on getting out of tune every six bars. Our prima donna Mrs. P., and M., got rapturous applause. Mrs. P. sang a scena of Verdi's and two or three popular ballads; and M. began with "The Fox went out on a Moonlight Night," which was so successful that he had to sing two other songs as encores. We wound up with the "Men of Harlech;" after which loud cries for M. began; and he was obliged to sing again.

All went home delighted with their evening. The result to the reading-room was most satisfactory, as after all expenses were paid we netted $60 (£12 sterling), a creditable amount for a town only five months old.

CHAPTER IX.

LAST DAYS IN COLORADO.

Valentine's day—The "Iron Ute"—Move to Glen Eyrie—The Servant question—Snow blockade on the Union Pacific—A perilous path—The land of surprises—Cheyenne cañon—A distant view—Prospecting on Pike's Peak—Colonists—The irate market-gardeners—Indians and their doings—Farewell to Colorado.

"GLEN EYRIE, *Valentine's Day* 1872.

" DEAR * * *,—Here is indeed the 'erster Frühlingstag.' Oh for a poet or a musician to put it into word or sound!

"I am sitting writing in the cañon, under a grove of cotton-wood, Douglassii fir, and silver spruce. My chair is a lump of red granite, with a wall of the same rising behind me reflecting the hot sun, so that I begin to feel like your idea of perfect bliss—a lizard on a hot wall. The creek frozen solid, gleams white, at my feet; and opposite rises the south wall of the cañon, 800 to 1000 feet high; red, pink, and salmon rocks show through the pine and piñons, which cover them; and all is in black shade, save the streaks of snow which lies here and there still unmelted.

"There is not a sound except the sighing of a breeze in the pines, or the scream of a blue jay as he flashes past in the sunlight, and scolds at finding me intruding on his solitude; or when a solitary half-tame sheep that haunts this valley comes rustling down through the scrub-oak off the mountains to drink at the creek. The air is full of the scent from the cotton-wood, which is beginning to bud; and a fly settles on my paper to rest after his first flight in the spring sunshine. How strange to think I am in the Rocky Mountains; all alone with my books, writing and drawing; out of all sound of human voices, and yet as much at home as if I were in England.

"But I must have done with sentimentalities, and tell you how I have been spending the last fortnight.

"For the last week at Manitou, before we moved over here, we were nearly frozen, and I spent most of my time in-doors trying to keep warm, and talking French and German with charming Miss S., while we worked at cotton gowns for the Mexican trip, which looked excessively out of place in such weather.

"On Sunday week we walked through a dense fog to the 'Iron Ute Spring,' which lies nearly half a mile from the Soda Springs, up a beautiful gorge. The water tastes just like ink: but its effect on me was perfectly magical. I drank again and again, and walked home feeling a different being—for I have been quite ill from the cold,—and since then have been perfectly well.

"The following day we moved over here to Glen Eyrie, General P.'s lovely house, which has been building for the last six months, and is at last finished enough for us to get into it, though it is still haunted by armies of painters, etc. It is built close to the mouth of the cañon I am writing in, on the slope of the hill, with the glen stretched out before it dotted with tall pines and fantastic rocks of every colour except bright blue, shutting it in from the outer world.

"I have been very busy since we came, helping my kind hostess to settle in—no easy matter in this servantless land—where one has to do most things for one's-self. The want of servants in the West is a very serious difficulty, and one it seems almost impossible to overcome. They are simply not to be had, whatever you pay them. One of our neighbours has been trying the whole of this winter to get a servant, sending to Denver, Georgetown, Central—everywhere, in fact. After doing all her own house-work, and cooking for her own family and several boarders for two months, she got a girl at last from a ranche in the mountains, who thought she would like a change. To this creature, who could not cook or make herself useful in any way, except in actual scrubbing, she paid $25 (£5) a month, board, lodging, and all found; and before the month was out the young lady found Colorado Springs was 'too dull for her,' and went off to Denver, leaving my friend servantless again. I remember finding this advertisement in the *New York Times* one day:—'102 East 36th Street, between 3d and 4th Avenues.—A respectable young lady as cook; willing to assist at washing and ironing. Call for one day' Imagine the condescending way in which the 'respectable young lady' would cook one's dinner *if* it suited her to do so; and then how she would dress herself up and walk out in French gown and bonnet after the cooking was over! This gives one some idea of the 'servant' difficulty in the eastern States. How much greater must it be out here!

"In the case of having good servants out from the east or from England, their passage-money, some $80 to $100, has of course to be paid in advance; and though it could easily be refunded to their mistresses out of the first year's wages, the chances are so strongly in favour of their marrying or wishing to change their place before the year is out, that it makes the risk too serious for the plan to succeed often. The only hope I see of getting any good servants is by importations of Chinese from California. Already all the washing is done by them in Denver, and one blue-coated and pig-tailed gentleman with some outlandish name, has made his appearance down here; and will soon, I suppose, be followed by more.

"We are hoping every day for Dr. B.'s return. He has been nearly a month on his journey from San Francisco, which usually takes four days; and the line is now so badly blocked on this side of the Salt Lake that large provision trains on sleighs are being sent to snowed-up passengers, who are actually suffering for want of food—at least so say the papers. It is a bad look-out for our journey west. Nevertheless we are getting very impatient to be off; for now that I find you approve of my going to Mexico, I am so afraid lest anything should prevent our trip. We are working away at Spanish, and reading up all we can find about the country, which seems really a land of enchantment.

. . . . .

"The other day M. drove up from the Springs, bringing a Hollander to see General P. After a late breakfast, we wandered out, and as we had much to talk over, we lay down on the grass in a sunny place, and then climbed up the great red rocks, to the top of a hill, where we sketched the most beautiful view I have seen yet. The great rocks for foreground, then the Garden of the Gods a mile and a half away, and the mesas and mountains and purple plains behind them.

"Yesterday I went up there again to colour my sketch, and thought I would try going home by a new way; so I carefully clambered down some sheets of red sandstone rock, till I came to such an awful place, that I confess I was fairly frightened. It was a cleft between two rocks, and thinking I could get down it, I made for a pine tree which overhung it a little, and of which I caught hold, and looked. I found I was on the edge of a kind of step about twenty feet high; below it was another; and below this second I could see nothing, but there must have been an overhanging ridge any height from twenty to two hundred feet from the ground. I held fast to my tree, for one false step would have sent me over. Luckily my head is perfectly steady; but every time I moved, a pebble rolled down, and jumped from ledge to ledge, and then disappeared with a last skip into the unknown depths. I stayed to pick a bit of creeping juniper which grew at the foot of the tree, pretending to myself that I was not a bit frightened; and climbing up on hands and knees along the path I had come down, was thankful, in spite of all my assumed bravery, to find myself on the safe side of the hill again.

"I fear my admiration and wonderment at this strange country must be growing too wearisome to you. But every day I find some fresh puzzle or curiosity that I have not seen before, and long for you to see it too, and explain it to me. For instance, I found a hill of gypsum, 500 feet high, within a quarter of a mile of this house the other day; and borrowing a pickaxe from one of the workmen, toiled up to the top of it, and spent an hour in clumsily picking out specimens, some white, some satin spar, some a faint pink, of which I have since made you a paper weight. We had no notion that there was any gypsum in the glen before this week: but it is a land of surprises, and there is always the delightful possibility, if one goes out for a walk, of making some new discovery in geology or botany, or of finding some fresh view or way over the mountains which no one has ever thought of. One of the great charms of a new country is the feeling that one is looking on places which probably have never been seen before, save by some stray trapper or savage Indian. So you must have patience with me if I grow prosy over our wonderful mountains and rocks.

"As I was writing this, I heard voices coming up the cañon; and soon Mrs. P. appeared, bringing several of our Denver friends who are down at the hotel. We all scrambled up the cañon, along the ice-covered stream, with birds singing among the pine tops in the sunshine overhead. We made our way above the Punch Bowl, which is now, with the waterfall, a mass of solid ice, to Daphne's Leap, a beautiful bubbling spring under a group of pines; and as we stood there, a noble eagle flew over our heads, so close that we could see his yellow gleaming eye looking down on us as we held our breath in surprise and delight."

. . . .

Colorado Springs, Feb. 21.—All the railroad officials have moved down here at last from Denver, and I am staying with Mrs. W., who is settled in two comfortable home-like rooms at the Hunt House.

The last few days at Glen Eyrie have been lovely—quite summer weather; and we have been panting for summer garments. After dinner to-day Captain S. and I started for a long ride to Cheyenne Cañon. It is close to Cheyenne Mountain, about six miles from here; and the huge blue cleft in the hills has looked so mysterious and awful that I have always longed to explore it ever since I first came.

We went across the railway track south of the town, inspecting the track layers' work on our way; over the Fountain, through ploughed land, and past alkali springs, up a long flat valley to the mouth of the cañon. We tried to ride up it a little way: but found the horses could not keep their feet, the sides were so steep. So dismounting, we led them back; tied them by the reins to two pine trees; and then walked up along a side-hill on one side of the little stream, pushing our way through bushes and trees, on such a steep slope of pulverized granite that I could not keep my feet without a hand to help me. We scrambled along till we reached a side cañon, and here sat down to rest.

The rocks are magnificent; far finer than any I have seen before—of red granite straight up many hundred feet in smooth rock walls, so worn by water that they look quite polished. Wherever there is a crack, fine pines grow in it, if there is place for a root.

We sat some while enjoying the grandeur and solitude, the silence only broken by the stream below tumbling over the great boulders, and then turned back, as further progress up the valley was impossible without a hatchet to clear a way through the brushwood; to find our horses safe by their respective trees. Then mounting, we turned up to the right over a mesa into a second valley, which would make the most perfect site in the world for a house, with a wall to the west of red and green rocks considerably over 1000 feet in height, crowned with pines, over which circled a huge pair of bar-tailed eagles.

We forded a stream, with a scramble over fallen logs and boulders, which made me respect my horse's power of keeping her feet, and toiled up the great mesa which stretches down from the foot-hills into the plains. At the top we stopped to breathe the poor horses, who seemed to feel climbing up 1000 feet as much as human beings do, and there we got a fine view. The mountains rose behind us in rugged masses to the very sky. The plains east and south stretched away and away like a purple ocean in the sunset. To the north-east we saw over the Divide, which rises nearly 2000 feet above the plains, to Cedar Point on the Kansas Pacific Railroad, ninety miles off. We kept along the mesa for some two miles, and then up and down rolling hills and valleys of short buffalo grass, full of prairie-dog holes, which made careful riding necessary, till we struck the Fountain again, and got into the town just at sunset.

Feb. 22.—M. returned in the afternoon from Pike's Peak, where he and Captain D. have been for three days prospecting for water for the ditch. Their object was to find a place on the Peak where water could be stored in large quantities, and let out to supply the ditch at the time of year when it is wanted for irrigating the crops, without diminishing the stream, so as to interfere with the rights of mill-owners and farmers below, who are not on the Company's lands, and who, crying out before they were hurt, have been raising a violent opposition to the colony for taking any water at all from the Fountain.

Our poor prospecters, on the second day of their expedition, walked sixteen miles to the lakes, just below timber line (11,000 feet), across fallen trees, with snow from two to five feet deep. When they camped at night they had a little excitement in the shape of a mountain lion (puma); who, coming close up to their camp-fire, scared the donkey who carried their camp outfit to such a degree that he jumped on the top of Captain D., who lay asleep on the ground; and there was a regular mêlée of men, donkey, and fire, while the puma trotted off before any one had time to get out a rifle.

23*d.*—Dr. B. at last arrived from San Francisco, having spent twenty-four days on the road, thanks to the snow. He, however, has not suffered from starvation, and we have received most encouraging reports as to the probability of the line being open in a fortnight, which is the time actually fixed for our start westward.

25*th.*—Cold and sleety, after a week of spring weather.

26*th.*—In the afternoon, while I was waiting for M. in the office, some colonists—a man, his wife, and three children—came in, having come down by the train. They were English, from Southampton, and utterly disgusted and disheartened, of course, by the place at first sight. They expected a large town, with fine farming lands, ready ploughed and fenced, all round. They had no bedding, nor any necessaries for life in a shanty. The baby was ill, the little girl crying with fatigue and bewilderment, the father cross, and the mother dirty. M. put them for the night into our old shanty, which happened to be vacant; and gave them his own bed, as they were from the old country, though they were disagreeable enough, goodness knows.

But never will I persuade people to emigrate after seeing

these and other colonists arrive, utterly unprepared for the sort of life they will have to lead. Thinking that a town here means what it does in England; that farming lands—which, in truth, are good enough when they are irrigated and properly farmed—are to be like a rich bit of Hertfordshire or the Vale of Thames; and finding what it is in reality, they turn round and accuse those who have advised them to leave the struggle for existence in the old country, of sending them to their death and ruin in the new.

Two men—nursery-gardeners from Long Island—came in the other day. M. was out; so they attacked the chief engineer, who was in the office.

"Where are General ——, and ——, and the people who wrote that circular; because, if we catch them, we'll *shoot* them."

Mr. N. tried to pacify them.

"Where are the farming lands?"

"There, outside, by the creek."

"That's nothing but a gravel patch."

"You can feed your cattle on it all winter nevertheless," replies Mr. N. But still they rave; when in comes Mr. ——.

"N., can you help me to some hands for the new road over the mesa? I can't get enough men to work on it."

The enraged colonists prick up their ears.

"Here are two already to hand," says Mr. N.

"What may you happen to give for work in this country of yours?" sneers one.

"The usual wages for day-labourers—$2½ a day."

Thereupon a wonderful calm comes over the irate nurserymen, who consider that a place where you can get 10s. a day for common labour cannot be such a very bad place; and in a week they come in, like most other emigrants, vowing it is the finest country in the world.

Feb. 27th.—A cold sleety morning. I drove down alone to Colorado Springs from Glen Eyrie. Two Indians were outside one of the stores, indulging in such extraordinary antics that I was really afraid to drive past. They ran along like beasts on all-fours; then they tumbled down and rolled over; and then they crouched and pulled their bows. One of the men from the store seeing me, kindly ran and held them till I had passed.

Yesterday, as we were at dinner, a quantity of Indians rode past the hotel, trailing their tent-poles; the squaws with the papooses on their backs, laden, besides, with all the belongings of the tribe, while the *braves* rode on in front with no load save their guns and bows. To-day the town is swarming with them; and I was called into one store to see two men and two papooses about ten and twelve. The men had brought in buckskins and buffalo robes to trade for cartridges for their revolvers, and "papoose boots." Some unwary new-comers traded for buffalo robes; but when the purchases were made found they had bought a good deal more than they bargained for, as the robes were so filthy that they had to undergo some weeks of cleaning before being admissible to any civilized house. These Indians are disgusting people; and my terror of them grows greater the more I know of them. The bravest men, who would go into battle with as little concern as they would walk down the street, have told me that they feel perfectly paralysed at the idea of an Indian fight. Their cruelties to women are as bad, or worse, than to men; and friends of my own, who crossed the plains in the days before railroads, when they were liable to attacks any moment from the Cheyennes and Arapahoes who then haunted the stage route along which the Kansas Pacific Railroad runs, have told me of Indian attacks and almost miraculous escapes which, if put on paper, would beat, for tragedy and horror, the most sensational novel that ever was written.

A trustworthy informant vouches for the truth of the following, which happened to a lady now living in the territory:—

She was crossing the plains some years ago in a waggon train. The Indians attacked the party. The horses of the waggon she was in happened to be particularly strong; so she managed to escape from the general massacre which ensued, with her baby in her arms. A servant with her, and the driver, were the only ones who got away, the whole of the rest of the party being killed.

The Indians pursued her. The driver at last, thinking escape impossible, was about to cut the horses loose and save himself by riding one of them off. She, however, drew her revolver, which she held at his head, telling him she would shoot him dead if he did not drive for life. There she sat, with the baby clutched in one hand, the revolver in the other, and the arrows whistling around. At last the Indians stopped to pick up some things which had fallen out of the waggon, and she was saved: but in her agony of terror she had squeezed the baby to death, and had to drive for three days and nights with the dead child in her arms, expecting another attack every moment, till Denver was reached, where her husband awaited her.

March 4.—To-morrow we start. All our preparations are made; M. and the five others of the engineering party leave by the overland stage; and the P.'s and I go north on our way to San Francisco.

Before we meet in the city of Mexico, the overland party will have no easy trip southwards; and some people have been kind enough to suggest, in Western phraseology, that " ha'ar is riz down south;" signifying that, as they have to pass through the Apache Indian country, they run a chance of getting scalped.

It is sad to leave so many dear and kind friends, whom I seem to have known for years instead of months: not knowing whether most of us may ever meet again.

If anything had been needed to make me believe in the kindness, generosity, and warm-hearted friendship of Americans, the four months I have spent here would have proved to me—what I knew already—that in no country on earth can one find better and truer friends than in the United States.

CHAPTER X.

COLORADO—ITS RESOURCES AND PROGRESS.

Surface features—Climate—Irrigation—Timber—The mining interest—Coal beds—Attractions to settlers—The snowy range—Population—Denver—The Denver and Rio Grande Railway—Colorado Springs: its foundation and growth—The Soda Springs—Pueblo—Cañon City—Difference between the Old and New Worlds.

THE territory of Colorado forms, so to speak, a saddle upon the great Continental backbone. "Lying between 37° and 41° of north latitude, and 102° and 109° of west longitude, it extends east and west about 390 miles, and north and south about 275 miles, forming a rectangle, containing an area of 106,500 square miles, or 68,144,000 acres. Reaching from near the middle of the great trans-Mississippi plain up the mountain-slope, it laps over the summit of the continental Divide (watershed), and rests its western border on the Colorado basin. It includes within its bounds the system of mountain-parks, and the sources of the four great rivers, the Rio Colorado, the Rio Grande del Norte, the Arkansas, and the Platte.

"Of the large area contained within its boundary lines, about four-sevenths are embraced in the true mountain region, whose snowy summits form the watershed of the Continent. The remaining three-sevenths, situated chiefly east of 105° west longitude, and extending the whole length of the territory north and south, consist in great part of broad plains furrowed by shallow valleys, widening and fading away as they extend eastward, and, with the exception of the parks and some valleys of the mountains, contain all the arable lands of the territory."[1]

[1] U. S. Geological Survey of Colorado, 1869.

These arable lands may be divided into three distinct districts, to each of which belong one of the three great rivers on the east of the mountains. The northern of these divisions extends along the course of the South Platte river and its tributaries, from near the north-east corner of the Territory, bounded by the eastern slope of the Rocky Mountains, till it is shut in on the south by a high, broken, irregular ridge, called the Divide. This ridge starts from the base of the mountains opposite South Park, running far eastward covered with pines, till lost in the plains; and forms the Divide or watershed between the waters of the South Platte and Arkansas rivers.

The second district extends from the Divide southwards to the Raton Mountains, on the borders of New Mexico, and is watered by the Arkansas river and its tributaries.

The third and smallest district consists of the San Luis Park, and its tributary valleys, some of which extend over the Colorado boundary into New Mexico. It cannot, therefore, be divided by the arbitrary line of division between these two territories. Its waters find an outlet into the Rio Grande del Norte.

This belt of arable lands along the mountains is becoming daily more thickly settled by farmers, who find that wheat and oats can be raised along the courses of the three great rivers, with as much ease and less risk than gold and silver can be mined in the mountains of the Territory.

The climate of this agricultural region, whose elevation varies from 4000 to 7000 feet above the sea, is remarkably dry, bracing, and healthy. Snow generally begins to fall in October, and ceases in April or the beginning of May, in the northern districts. North of the Divide it sometimes attains a depth of one to two feet for a time: but south of the Divide, in the second or Arkansas river division, it seldom, except in the valleys, lies more than twenty-four hours, evaporating and leaving the ground below quite dry. In winter the sun is usually brilliant, and powerful during the day-time; while the nights are excessively cold, the thermometer falling occasionally 20° and 30° below zero. In summer, though the heat by day is extreme, the nights are always cool—the air rarefied on the plains, rising, while a refreshing breeze sweeps down from the mountains to take its place.

The rainfall at Colorado Springs for the year ending November 30, 1872, was 28·30 inches. The mean temperature for the same period was,—winter, 29·84; spring, 46·78; summer, 67·29; autumn, 45·85; for the year, 47·44.

Besides the agricultural interests, which are yearly taking a larger and more important part in the industries of the territory, these arable lands are largely devoted to stock-raising. In consequence of the dryness of the climate, cattle and sheep are herded out all the winter, feeding upon the brown grass: but owing to this same dryness the pasturage is very thin; so that, acre per acre, this section is capable of sustaining much fewer cattle than is the case in a well-watered country.

Water is the great want in the territory. The soil, though good, is light, and except in the "bottom lands," *i.e.* directly along the courses of the rivers or streams, is incapable of cultivation without irrigation. Every year, however, more attention is being given to this subject; and if the Coloradans will, as they seem inclined to do, learn a lesson from their neighbours the Mormons in Utah, whose system of irrigation is the most perfect and successful in the New World, there seems no reason why millions of acres now covered with buffalo grass and prairie flowers, should not be used for raising wheat and oats instead of antelopes and prairie-dogs.

Leaving the plains and ascending the foot-hills we find up to "timber line," 11,000 feet, vast tracts of mountain slope covered with pine forests, chiefly composed of Rocky Mountain pine (*Pinus ponderosa*). Of these forests the one most worked at present is that which covers the Divide, and which is chiefly manufactured into "lumber" at Larkspur, a station of the Denver and Rio Grande, near the summit of the Divide, where there is a large steam saw-mill. The supply of lumber on the Divide convenient for transportation is, however, already beginning to be comparatively small; and the mountains west of it in the region of Bergun's Park are sending large supplies. About 16,000,000 feet of lumber are sent from the Divide each year, and from 30,000,000 to 35,000,000 of feet are cut annually in the territory. Colorado lumber now fetches about $25·00 per 1000, and it takes on an average about five trees to make 1000 feet; that is to say, a thousand square feet one inch thick. In the fourteen months from September 1871 to November 1872, the Sloan Saw-mill Company at Larkspur turned out 3,052,036 feet of manufactured lumber, that is, floor boards, scantlings, etc.; 75,000 railway ties (sleepers); 3000 telegraph poles; 2100 cords of wood, or bales four feet thick each way, of odds and ends suitable for firewood and such purposes.

This lumber is a great source of wealth at present: but the supply is not inexhaustible; and people seem apt to forget that, though it takes but an hour to cut down a tree, it has taken that tree many years to grow, and will take as many to replace it.

Scarcity of timber, however, is not the only evil that will arise. By destroying the forests the already small rainfall will be yet further diminished.

In Nebraska this is felt so strongly that a "Timber Bill" has been framed by Senator Hitchcock and passed, allowing 160 acres of the public land to every person who will plant forty acres of trees and keep them in good order for ten years. The State law of Nebraska also exempts all lands from State taxes for five years when the owner or farmer will plant a few acres of timber on them. This good example might easily be followed in Colorado. Trees are largely planted in all the new cities which are springing up along the mountain base: but this is not sufficient; and those who take the deepest interest in the welfare of this noble territory, will do well to restore as speedily as possible the forests which are now being destroyed.

Having reached the mountains we now come to an entirely distinct source of wealth from any before named: I mean the mines of Colorado.

The counties in which mining has been chiefly carried on, are six: Gilpin, Clear Creek, Park, Summit, Lake, and Boulder counties, though minerals of more or less value are found throughout the length and breadth of the territory. It would be impossible to attempt any description of the number and value of the mines which are now being worked. Suffice it to say, that the discoveries daily made in these regions, are helping to make this one of the most important mining districts in the United States. Large towns, such as Georgetown, Central, Golden, Blackhawk, Idaho, are coming into existence round the mines; reduction works are being built; and railways for the transportation of the rich ores, are being pushed into the heart of the mountains. As an instance of the rapid growth of the South Park section, the assessed value of Fairplay, its principal town, in May 1872 was $36,000; in May 1873, $196,000. Its population in May 1872, 350; in May 1873, 1500.

"The shipments of ore from Colorado east and to Europe amounted during 1872 to 160 car-loads; the quarterly returns showing a steady increase, thus: 26, 37, 45, and 52. The value of this ore was $560,000, and the total bullion product of the year was $2,295,040."

Besides the precious metals, that is to say, silver and gold, which are found "native" as well as in galena and quartz, the mountains contain vast quantities of iron; and as the foot-hills are full of coal, there seems no doubt that in a few years ironworks will be started which may rival those of Pennsylvania.

Near Cañon City, in the Arkansas Valley, large and valuable coal mines have been opened close to the Grape Creek Iron Mountain. This coal (a lignite), which is already largely mined, is of a better quality than any yet found in the territory, and is capable of being successfully used for smelting purposes.

The following table, drawn up by Professor Raymond, showing the relative values of some of the most important of the Western coals, is taken from a paper read before the American Institute of Mining Engineers at Philadelphia, May 21, 1873:—

No.	Carbon.	Hydrogen.	Nitrogen.	Oxygen.	Sulphur.	Moisture.	Ash.	Combined Water.	Calorific Power. I.	Calorific Power. II.	Calorific Power. III.	Temperature. Degree C.
1	59·72	5·08	1·01	15·69	3·92	8·91	5·64	17·65	5800	6172	5757	2529
2	61·84	4·34	1·29	15·52	1·60	9·41	3·00	17·46	6056	6685	5912	2536
3	65·81	3·90	1·93	10·99	0·77	9·17	3·40	12·36	6515	7172	6400	2605
4	61·39	3·76	1·74	15·20	1·07	11·56	1·68	17·10	5892	6462	5738	2512
5	68·14	4·36	1·25	9·51	1·03	8·06	6·62	10·73	6679	7264	6578	2630
6	56·79	3·26	0·42	21·82	0·81	13·28	4·05	24·55	4768	5498	4565	2313
7	67·05	4·06	0·61	19·01	0·63	16·52	4·18	21·38	4814	5766	4610	2373
8	67·58	7·42	1·58	12·80	2·92	3·08	9·28	14·40	6522	6729	6428	2532
9	60·72	4·30	...	13·42	0·43	5·18	5·77	15·10	7430	7845	7330	2683
10	60·72	4·30	...	14·42	0·08	14·68	3·80	16·22	5768	6560	5602	2497
11	72·91	4·50	1·79	11·77	...	4·50	4·50	13·24	6938	7208	6843	2654

No. 1. Monte Diablo coal,—*Analyst*, H. S. Munro.
2. Weber Cañon, Utah, „ „
3. Echo Cañon, „ „ „
4. Carbon Station, Wyoming, „ „
5. „ „ „ „ „
6. Coos Bay, Oregon, „ „
No. 7. Alaska,—*Analyst*, H. S. Munro.
8. „ „ „
9. Cañon City, Colorado,—*Analyst*, Dr. T. M. Drown.
10. Baker Co., Oregon, „ „
11. Block Coal, Sand Creek, Ind., Prof. E. T. Cox.

Enough has been said to show that the territory of Colorado has no lack of natural attractions for those who go "out West" with a view to making money. For the ordinary traveller, searching either for health or amusement, it is no less attractive.

The climate, as I have already said, is bracing and healthy, and so dry, that, even in winter, one does not feel the cold nearly so severely as at a higher temperature and lower altitude. For invalids suffering from asthma or consumption, if the latter disease is not too far advanced, the air works wonders; and they are ordered now to Colorado from the Eastern States, and even from Canada, as English people are sent to Cannes or Madeira.

One invalid whom I happened to know, came out in the summer of 1871 apparently dying of consumption, obliged to be moved in an invalid carriage. In the spring of 1872 we wished him good sport as he started on foot for a week's shooting and camping in the mountains!

To the botanist and geologist there is an endless field of interest in the flowers on the plains and the rocks in the hills; while even a member of the Alpine Club could hardly despise the scarcely-explored wonders of the Snowy Range.

One of the members of Professor Hayden's Survey thus describes the view from the summit of Mount Lincoln, in the spring of 1873 :—

"We reckoned carefully, and estimated that we had in view more than one hundred peaks, which would not fall below 13,000 feet, and at least fifty of 14,000. The two great connected ranges which were most conspicuous were the Sierra Madre to the west, beyond the Arkansas Valley, and the Blue River range to the north, a continuation of that upon which we were, but bending around westward enough to bring a great line of rugged peaks against the sky. In the Sierra Madre lie two prominent summits, named Yale and Harvard by Professor J. D. Whitney, in his explorations here four years ago; and the ridge finishes abruptly at the north with the highest peak of all, estimated by us at 15,000 feet, and named the Holy Cross, from the two immense snow banks intersecting each other conspicuously on its side, as seen from Grey and Evans, farther north than this. . . .

"Rumours of surpassing heights attach themselves to the name of the Holy Cross and to Sopris Peak; the explorations of this summer will go far toward settling what is after all the highest summit in Colorado, and in the whole United States. As viewed from Grey, Evans, and Lincoln, the palm belongs to the great mountains far beyond the Sierra Madre, and near to one another; one a ridge with a hump upon it, and the whole covered with unbroken snow, like an Alp; the other a mass ending in a perfectly conical black peak. By levelling and estimate of distance, we believe those summits to rise above 16,000 feet. We are making off in that direction.

"But to return to Mount Lincoln. Almost below it lies the Hoosier Pass, a low ridge across the valley up which we had come, perhaps of moraine origin, separating the affluents of the two great oceans, the Platte, leading to the Gulf of Mexico, the Blue, to the Gulf of California. Indeed, on the next mountain are head branches of the Platte, the Blue, and the Arkansas, and it has been thence very suitably named *Trecuique*. We see the Platte tumbling down the precipice just opposite, out of an always frozen lake. On this side, the famous mountains Grey and Evans are hardly conspicuous among a host of their equals; Long's is almost hidden by the narrow ridge. South-eastward the Park makes a marked and welcome variety in the scene, and beyond it the great isolated mountain of Pike's Peak is very distinct and striking. On the whole this mountain summit commands points in a region of country nearly or quite 25,000 square miles in extent."

And now let us see what sort of population is springing up in this vast Territory, larger than all Great Britain. Some foreigners, and a good many strangers from the Eastern States, cause no small amusement to the inhabitants of Colorado by the stupendous preparations they make before coming West to insure their personal safety. "Among their last acts," says an indignant Westerner, "before leaving the States, is the purchase of a pair of Colt's navies, and at least one of Bowie's brightest blades. A Sharp's carbine further contributes towards the completion of the military outfit, while their trunks and valises fairly groan with multitudinous packages of cartridges and fixed ammunition. . . . . The people who thus make walking arsenals of themselves and infernal machines of their luggage, in view of a Western trip, only succeed in making themselves ridiculous, and in putting themselves to a vast amount of expense and anxiety, without rhyme or reason."

"Ah! but," says some one, "there are the Indians!"

True, there are Indians; but there are many more white men; and the Indians are quite wise enough to know by this time, that the less trouble they give the better for themselves. The Utes, who are the Indians most largely spread over Colorado, are now perfectly peaceable; and the Cheyennes dare not venture into the thickly settled belt along the base of the Rocky Mountains.

But let us take this same thickly-settled belt, from Denver southwards, and mark its progress in the last fifteen years.

In 1858, a little knot of some half-dozen enterprising men arrived at the mouth of Cherry Creek, attracted across the plains by the news of the gold discoveries at the base of Pike's Peak. Here they decided to "locate" themselves; and Mr. A. J. Williams, now one of the leading citizens of Denver, built the first store in Auraria, now West Denver. He, with General Larimer and a few others, soon afterwards

K

crossed Cherry Creek, and surveyed and laid out a new town, which they named after the then Governor of Kansas, —General Denver.

On the 1st of January 1871 the Census returns for this city gave 5000 inhabitants; and on the 1st of January 1872, 10,000 inhabitants; showing that in one year the population had doubled. Now in 1873 its population is between 15,000 and 20,000.

In the beginning of 1870 the whistle of an engine had never been heard in Denver. In March 1872 five railroads were running out of it, and several more were projected.

And this is no mushroom growth. The progress of Denver, though rapid, is substantial; and it has already taken its place as the most important commercial city between Kansas and Utah.

In 1870, the Kansas Pacific Railroad being finished to Denver, some of its most influential officers and promoters, struck with the future importance of the belt of country down the eastern base of the Rocky Mountains, conceived a scheme for developing it by making a line of railroad, which, running from north to south, should connect all the great Transcontinental lines, to wit, the Kansas Pacific, the Atlantic and Pacific, and the Texas Pacific, and also tap the vast resources of the mountain chain along which it should run.

This line was incorporated under the name of the Denver and Rio Grande Railway; to commence at Denver, having as its ultimate point El Paso del Norte, on the frontier of Mexico. Besides being the first north and south road in this section, it possessed an extreme interest for all railroad men, being the first narrow-gauge road in the States, its projectors having decided upon a 3 feet gauge in place of the usual 4 feet $8\frac{1}{2}$ inches of the other railways. The grading of the road was begun in March 1871; and the first division, from Denver to Colorado Springs, a distance of seventy-six miles, was completed on the 27th of October 1871, when the first train ran through. The grading of the second division, from Colorado Springs to Pueblo, a distance of forty-two miles, was begun January 1st, and completed June 15th, 1872. The Arkansas Valley branch was opened in November of the same year. The total length of line now in operation is 156 miles—118 of main line; a branch, known as the Arkansas Valley branch, of 38 miles; and construction is being rapidly pushed on to Trinidad, on the borders of Colorado and New Mexico.

A bare comparison of the amount of passenger and freight traffic along this route, before and after the railway came into operation, will serve to show how great the development of the country has been, and how fully justified were the original promoters in their anticipations. Before the railway replaced the stage-coach, the latter ran tri-weekly, and carried an average of five passengers per trip, or thirty, both ways, weekly. During the year 1872, the railway, being still partly under construction, carried on the same route, 25,168 passengers, or an average of 484 weekly, being an increase on the stage-coach of 1500 per cent. As regards freight, Mexican teams, and a few others, carried all there was. The freight hauled by the railroad in 1872, an average distance of sixty-one miles, was 46,212 tons. The earnings for transportation during the year 1872, exclusive of construction materials, was $281,400.29; operating expenses for the same, $175,206.32; leaving a net balance of $106,193.97. The business for the first three months of 1873 was 45.5 per cent. over that of the same quarter in 1872; while the net earnings for July 1873 showed an increase of 94 per cent. over the corresponding month in 1872.

Southward from Denver, along the line of the Denver and Rio Grande Railroad, the lands on each side of the Platte river are now nearly all taken up; and farmers are bringing them under cultivation, wherever it is possible to get water upon them. In the same way the "Divide" country, before the advent of the railroad, was almost entirely open to settlement. Now, besides the timber cut from its forests, it is being settled rapidly, and producing good crops of potatoes, oats, barley, and hay.

Seventy-six miles from Denver we reach Colorado Springs, the first town of any importance south of the Divide. Before the construction of the railway this place had no existence, the town-site being then bare prairie. Many reasons influenced the promoters of the Denver and Rio Grande Railway to fix upon this as the spot for establishing the "Fountain colony;" and, as the event has proved, they were not mistaken.

In the first place, this is the very best point for many miles, for entering the mountains, both for the transportation of ores from South Park down to the railway by the Ute pass, and for tourists who wish to see more of the range than its eastern face. At the foot of Pike's Peak, five miles off, are the famous Soda Springs of the Fontaine qui bouille, described by Ruxton, Fremont, etc., and this was thought to be another and important reason for building a town within easy reach.

The first sod of the temperance colony town of Colorado Springs was turned on the 4th of August 1871. Now (November 1873) its population numbers between 2000 and 2500. There are between 400 and 500 buildings; and the "frame" is now giving place to stone and brick as building materials; the mountains close by supplying excellent stone, which is dressed in the town, while the bricks are manufactured on the spot. Schools abound; there are two public schools; three or four private ones; and the new public school-house, a handsome building of brick and stone, to cost $15,000, is in course of building. Two churches, Presbyterian and Methodist, are already finished; the Baptist is in course of construction; and the Episcopalians are now building a stone church of Gothic architecture, which is acknowledged already to be the best built and prettiest church west of the Mississippi.

Of course, the usual lodges of Masons, Oddfellows, Good Templars, and so forth, are to be found; besides a Fire Company and Military Company. At the Stores every want may be supplied. There are banks, admirable hotels, planing-mills, telegraph offices, and a steam printing-office, where a first-rate weekly newspaper and monthly magazine, called *Out West*, bearing chiefly on the Rocky Mountain section, are published. These are conducted by an able English editor, whose enterprise and perseverance have succeeded in producing the most trustworthy, and at the same time most readable magazine, that ever appeared in a town barely two years old.

Residence lots in the town are worth from $100 to $300. The farming lands belonging to the colony round the town are worth from $20 to $50 per acre, and to irrigate these, twenty miles of irrigating ditches have been constructed by the Fountain Colony.

At Manitou—the Soda Springs—which also belongs to the colony, hotels have been built; and thousands of tourists from the Eastern States and Europe have visited these mineral springs in the last two years; while all round, the villa lots worth $500 and $1000 are being rapidly bought up by people who wish to make their homes in this lovely spot. I have just heard that six villa lots have been sold to English people of good means in the last three months. Indeed, the English and Canadian incomers are now making a marked portion of the population. During the past summer (1873), a Government signal-station has been established on the summit of Pike's Peak; and a trail has been made to it from Colorado Springs, which is now the head-quarters of the Territorial Geological Survey, Dr. Hayden, its distinguished chief, being well enough satisfied with this spot, for scientific as well as social reasons, to propose making his home in the town.

Following the Denver and Rio Grande farther south we come to Pueblo, about forty-two miles from Colorado Springs. The land along the Fontaine qui bouille between these two towns was fairly settled before the railroad was built.

Pueblo, the present terminus of the main line, made good its claim a few months ago to the title of "city." It was, before the railroad came, a sort of border land, between American civilisation and enterprise pushing its way down from the north, and the remnants of Mexican semi-barbarism of the south, struggling to keep possession of its old haunts. The northern race has won, as usual, and now the old adobe Spanish houses are giving place to "iron front brick stores." Not content with the old town, on the north bank of the Arkansas, which now has a population of 3000, a new town in connexion with the railroad company, known as South Pueblo, has been started on the southern bank; and, though only a few months old, 100 buildings have been put up, and some 500 inhabitants settled there. From Pueblo, the Arkansas Valley branch line of thirty-eight miles leads up to Cañon City, close to which, at Labran, the coal mines, mentioned before, have been opened. This city is growing no less rapidly than the others along the railroad; and, besides its commercial importance, is likely to be attractive to all classes of travellers, as it lies within easy reach of the great cañon of the Arkansas, the finest cañon north of the "Big Cañon of the Colorado," where the whole Arkansas river has sawn itself for miles a narrow channel many hundred feet deep through the solid rock.

Farther south than Pueblo we need not go, as we are at the end of the railway: but when the tiny track is carried on—which it will be in the course of the coming year—to Trinidad, on the borders of Colorado and New Mexico; and later down to the very gate of Mexico, at El Paso del Norte, the same phenomenon, which I have tried to describe, will be seen. For the new world differs essentially from the old world in this point. Its inhabitants do not say, "Let us make a railroad from this town to that:" but, "Let us make a railroad; and then, when it is done, let us make the towns along it."

CHAPTER XI.

THE PACIFIC RAILROAD.

Denver Pacific Railroad—A pigs' paradise—The highest railroad point in the world—Snowbucking—How to keep well—Sage-brush and sandstones—The Mormon Railroad—Great Salt Lake City—Angelic architects—Commerce and holiness—Shoshonee Indians—A lofty breakfast-room—Miners—Flowers—Poison-oak—California—The Pacific at last.

March 6, Wednesday.—At 8.30 A.M. General and Mrs. P. and I steamed out of Denver on the Denver and Pacific Railroad, bidding farewell to the last of our Colorado friends at the depot, excepting Colonel G., who came with us as far as Cheyenne. I sat on the back platform, which was preferable to the car, as one got a much better view; though for some distance there was nothing to be seen but prairie, with a dead antelope lying here and there, and the Platte running parallel with us, between low banks covered with red-stemmed willow. The morning at first was grey and cloudy; but as the sun rose higher it caught the points of the snowy range, and brightened the northern slope of dear old Pike with pink and opal, as I took my last look of his familiar rounded head 150 miles south of us.

On our left ran the foot-hills; and as we went on a series of fine snow mountains came in view, one after another. Mount Rosalie; Long's Peak, or rather twin peaks, 14,000 feet high; and finally, Grey's Peak, 14,300 feet, towered above the rest of the snowy range.

Close to Evans, a small colony town, named in honour of Governor Evans of Colorado, we crossed the Platte on a long trestle-bridge, the barometer falling to 4800 feet, a difference of nearly 1000 feet in little more than an hour. The river was very wide, but not deep, with great shoals of gravel and débris washed down from the mountains, and forming barren islands in the stream. On the further side we soon came to Greeley, the rival colony to Colorado Springs. "The location" of the town site is not nearly so good as ours, as it is rather in a hollow, which with all the snow this winter has become a perfect mudhole. But the Greeleyites have the advantage of an unlimited quantity of water, the Platte lying on the south and east of the town, the Cache la Poudre on the north; and certainly the ground, which had been irrigated, looked excellent wherever we could see it through the snow, which still covered most of the country north of Evans.

At Carr station we got once more into a Mesa country, showing we were approaching the Black Hills, with prairie-dog towns and sandstone bluffs; and the train rattled across trestle-bridges, over dry arroyos, and climbed up a rather steep grade, the only hard piece on the whole road. The pace was fair: their average speed is twenty miles an hour: but between Denver and Johnstone, the second station out, we had been going forty miles an hour, which is very fast for a Western road. Then a second line of telegraph-wires came in sight, and at noon we ran into Cheyenne, the junction of the Denver, Pacific, and Union Pacific Railroad.

As the hotel was burnt down this winter, we had to pick our way along a plank path to a nasty eating-house, for we did not think it prudent to begin upon the two well-stocked luncheon-baskets we had brought from Denver, before there was any need. In half-an-hour the Union Pacific train came in; we took our places, which had fortunately been reserved for us, in the crowded sleeping-car; and amused ourselves by watching the happy pigs which abound in the town. It is quite a pigs' paradise at this time of year, being a Slough of Despond to human beings. Even in walking from the depot to the eating-room, Mrs. P. got over her shoes in mud.

Leaving Cheyenne, where the elevation is 6072 feet, the road, in thirty-two miles, rises to Sherman, on the Laramie range. This is now the highest railroad point in the world, being 8242 feet above the sea, with an average grade of over sixty feet to the mile up to it.

"From Cheyenne to Granite Cañon," says Professor Hayden, in the U. S. Geological Survey of Wyoming, "near the summit of the first range"—a distance of about nineteen miles—"the recent tertiary beds lie close up to the flanks of the mountains over a belt of several miles, affording comparatively easy transitions from the newer formations to the granite nucleus. For hundreds of miles, either north or south of this line, it would be difficult, or perhaps impossible, to build a railroad across the mountains; but here nature seems to have provided an easy inclined plane to the very margin of the mountain summit. The ridges are very nearly concealed, while on either side they can be seen as formidable as anywhere along the eastern base."

As we climbed up through the foot-hills, we got into a sub-alpine flora, and strangely rounded red granite castles, with scattered pines.

Sherman itself, at this time of year, was not impressive. Nothing to be seen but a few wretched wooden houses, a bar, a bakery, and an erection dignified by the name of "Summit House," with great snow-heaps piled all round them; a few pigs, and here and there a red rock sticking up on the bare hill behind the station. When we left Sherman for the run down to the Laramie plains, we plunged at once into snow-sheds; and once, where there was no shedding, we plunged right into a snow-drift, as high as the top of the cars. This caused a good deal of unpleasant excitement; and, for a moment, we thought we had stuck fast, and should have to be dug out by the swarm of workmen who were clearing the track: but, just as we were preparing to look our misfortune boldly in the face, the engine "bucked" right through, and we were free.

"Snow-bucking" is a most exciting amusement on these Western roads. If a train get into a drift through which there seems any chance of forcing it, the cars are taken off and left in safety behind; the engines are backed about fifty yards; and then run full speed right at the drift, forcing their way in—thanks to the sharp-nosed "cowcatcher,"—and sending the snow flying in clouds round them. This process is repeated many times, getting a little further each run; till at last a passage is made by sheer force.

Down we went a tremendous grade, crossing the head of Dale Creek, three miles west of Sherman, by a bridge 650 feet long and 126 feet above the little stream which runs in summer at the bottom of the valley, but which was now buried in snow. Then past the City of the rocks, a curious collection of natural houses, castles, churches, and monuments, all in red granite, relieved here and there by a green pine. South in the sunset lay the snowy range, shutting in North Park; north were the Black Hills we had just crawled over, and at which we looked with extra interest, as in the morning a telegram had appeared in the papers stating that "the richest mines in the continent" had just been discovered in them up north. Passing Fort Saunders, a large and important U. S. Fort, we reached Laramie, 7400 feet, in the midst of the Laramie plains, about 6.30, and the train stopped half-an-hour for supper: but, warned by our dinner at Cheyenne, we had had an early supper from our own stores, and spent the time we waited in walking up and down the platform and round the hotel, to get a little exercise before the night's journey. If any travellers across the continent wish to keep in perfect health during the journey, let them, in the first place, take their own provisions, so as to be perfectly independent of the food at the ordinary railroad restaurant,— to wit, half raw beef-steaks and hot bread; and let them also, whenever the train stops, and while the rest of the passengers are laying in the seeds of indigestion and dyspepsia, take a brisk walk, circulating their blood, and getting plenty of fresh air into their lungs, instead of the heated atmosphere of the restaurant dining-room. And, above all things, let them never drink water on the plains without mixing even a teaspoonful of wine or spirits with it; as the water with which the car is supplied is often taken from tanks in which it has been standing for days, and is consequently exceedingly unwholesome.

But to return to Laramie. The town seems a tidy-looking place, the streets wide, and the houses built of wood. They consist, however, for the most part, of eating-houses and saloons, which latter look as if a good deal of shooting might go on in them.

On the 7th, morning broke over the desert, covered with snow and sage-brush (*Artemisia tridentata*). We were now fairly over the Continental Divide, on the Pacific watershed; and at breakfast-time we reached Bitter Creek, a tributary of Green River, which joins the Rio Colorado above the "Big Cañon," and flows into the Pacific, the rivers on the eastern side of the Sierra Madre joining the north and south Platte, and flowing by way of the Mississippi into the Atlantic. All day we ran through the alkali and soft sandstone formation which extends from here right down to Arizona, between the Sierra Madre and the Wahsatch Mountains;—mesas of light yellow soil, with flat cakes of sandstone sticking out in straight lines near the top, each layer marking some ancient sea-beach; and again, sandstone rocks honeycombed into the strangest forms, or left standing like huge castles, as in the case of the two well-known rocks near Green River, which stand out alone, masses of sandstone forty feet high by twenty or thirty feet wide, on a bare hill over the river.

At Rock Springs we passed the coal mines, which produce some of the best coal yet worked in the Rocky Mountains, and supply this whole line of road. The delays with snow of the night before had made our train so late that it was too dark, when we reached the Wahsatch Mountains to see anything of Echo and Weber cañons,—the only pass through the whole range,—except high bare rocks tower-

The Rocks near Green River.

ing up on either side in the gloom. At Ogden, which we reached late at night, we found the hotel was crowded; so, as the sleeping-car of our train was left at the station, being the end of the Union Pacific division and beginning of the Central Pacific, we remained all night in it; and were up betimes on the 8th for a day at Salt Lake City.

At 8.30 we left Ogden in the Mormon Railroad, with a Mormon conductor, who did not object, however, to giving his "Gentile" passengers plenty of information about his railroad and his country. We crossed the Weber river, a large stream of sweet water which flows into the Salt Lake, and ran south parallel with the Wahsatch range, which lay on our left. There had been a fall of snow during the night: but now the sun was shining brightly, and we got exquisite views of the snowy mountains all round the great basin glistening in the sunshine, with deep blue shadows. The plain was covered with sage-brush: but between the bushes grass was growing, and innumerable cattle, in very good condition, were feeding round the little white farms. From the blue-green waters of the great lake rose high islands, each the property of some elder, for it is the mark of Mormon aristocracy to own an island; and behind them towered purple mountains, with the snowy peaks of the Oquoh range showing over them again. About Kaysville, a neat town, with straight streets of brick and wooden houses, orchards and shade trees, the farms became very numerous, especially along the base of the mountains. The houses were substantial, with good wattle fences or ditches round the land, which in some places grows corn without irrigation. The meadow larks were singing on every fence, and the lake was covered with wild-fowl.

As we neared Salt Lake City, we were half-choked by the fumes of the hot sulphur springs, which lie close to the track. The city stands just below the slope up to the Wahsatch Mountains, with the great lake stretching to the north and west, while south a broad plain leads the eye away between ranges of mountains, till the horizon of shadowy hills melts into the blue sky.

We spent the morning in seeing all the wonders; first walking up town past the theatre to Brigham Young's house, or rather houses,—for he has a perfect nest of buildings, inside a high stone wall; and storehouses, in which to receive the enormous tithes he claims from "the Saints" for doing them the favour of governing them. We went next to the Temple and Tabernacle, which stand on the

Temple Block, 666 feet square, enclosed by a high wall. A portly Mormon took us into the Tabernacle—an immense oval building, 150 feet by 250, and 80 feet high, with a huge domed roof, supported by forty or fifty stone pillars, 20 feet high, the spaces between being filled with masonry and innumerable doors. We asked our guide how many it held, and he replied, " 13,000 by measurement; but I have seen 14,300 leave this building in three minutes, less six seconds." The fittings are perfectly plain; the only ornamental thing in the whole building being the organ, the second largest in the States; built, with the exception of the keyboard and a few pipes, in the city, and under the superintendence, I am sorry to say, of an Englishman from one of the large London firms, who has turned Mormon.

The Temple close by, " for church purposes only," our guide said, is only four feet above the ground as yet. Brigham Young, who is the architect, claims that the designs for it are revealed to him by angelic visions: but as the foundations have been altered several times already, the angels do not seem infallible. The building is made of fine grey granite, from the Little Cottonwood cañon, with a freestone moulding; and as all the material till lately has had to be hauled down by ox-teams, the progress of building has been slow and expensive, as it is now several years since it was begun, and the foundations, so far as they have gone, have cost $4,000,000. Now, however, a narrow-gauge railway runs up to the cañon, so that there is some chance of the Temple being finished ere " the Saints" have ceased to exist.

There is a museum in the city, where we saw specimens of the natural products of the country, such as ore from the famous " Emma Mine;" selenite from the Southern Utah; a fine white encrinitic marble of exquisite texture from near the city; and a variety of curiosities, among which the most remarkable was a shawl made by a Mormon lady from the hair of her favourite dog!

There are also capital shops; and the Mormon women are famous for the manufacture of excellent buckskin gloves, prettily embroidered with silk, for which, however, they ask an exorbitant price, the plainest pair being four or five dollars. The Saints also make very good "candy," as we proved to our entire satisfaction. The store at which we bought it bore, like all the other Mormon shops, this extraordinary inscription—above a golden eye with rays from it, is written "Holiness to the Lord," and below, "Zion Co-operative Mercantile Institution," a most characteristic combination. The streets are 130 feet wide, with an irrigating ditch down each side, and a row of trees shading the side walk. Each house stands in its own garden plot, with fruit-trees around it, and the water from the ditches is let into each garden for a certain time every day. The air was soft and balmy from the melted snow; and the peaches and almonds just coming into blossom, and grass beginning to show along the ditches, were a pleasant sight to our eyes, accustomed for so many months to the barren brown plains, or black pines in the mountains.

We got a capital dinner at the Townshend House, which was crowded with Englishmen, come out, we supposed, to look after their interests in the Emma Mine; and at 4.15 we were back again at Ogden, with an hour for writing home-letters before the Western train started at 5.30 P.M.

The train from the East was delayed by a "wash" on the track; so as it was telegraphed several hours behind time, our westward train started without it, with only our three selves and two other passengers as occupants of the whole sleeping car. For eight and a half hours we ran along the northern shore of the Great Salt Lake; and woke on the 9th on the Sage Brush Desert, close to the Humboldt river, along which we kept all day. At Elko, where we stopped for breakfast, the first of the Shoshonee Indians made their appearance, idling about the station; dressed as usual in buckskin, coloured blankets, and felt hats; and at Carlin quantities of squaws, with papooses on their backs strapped up like mummies with a wicker covering to their back-board to protect their ugly little heads, crowded round the cars like hungry dogs, thankful for any scraps left from our breakfast. Nothing has ever given me an idea of more thorough degradation than the way those Indian women clawed bits of bone and skin, and either gnawed them like wild beasts, or thrust them into their pouches, to feast on at their leisure. The mixture of races at all the stations was most striking—Indians in their blankets, and Chinese in their blue tunics, standing side by side; rivalling each other in ugliness: but with one very marked difference,—that whereas the Indians were always lounging about doing nothing, Johnny was sure to be hard at work, turning an honest, or it may be dishonest, penny.

At the Palisades Station, where the rail follows the course of the Humboldt river through a narrow cañon of strangely distorted strata, we saw immense waggon trains, which had brought ore down from the celebrated White Pine mining district, and were now camped close to the track; the white-covered waggons drawn up side by side, and herds of mules and oxen feeding in all directions. Following down the cañon for some distance, round sharp curves, we got once more on the alkali flats, and ran on all day between endless purple hills with snow-covered mountains beyond, while red willow and cottonwood grew along the river banks; a grateful relief to the wearisome glaucous green of the sage-brush; till at dusk we came to the "Sink of the Humboldt," a lake thirty miles long, into which the river—like almost all in the Salt Lake basin—flows and disappears.

During the night we climbed up 3000 feet; and by daylight on the 10th were at Summit, the top of the Sierra Nevada, 7017 feet above the sea, breakfasting by lamplight in the dining-room of the station, under sixteen feet of snow.

When we started again General P. wrapped us up in rugs and blankets, for it was bitterly cold, and we sat on the back platform of the car, running through forty miles of snow-sheds, and from time to time catching glimpses of magnificent scenery through the gaps between the sheds— snowy mountains piled up to the sky, and black pines. At Emigrant Gap we were almost out of the snow-sheds, and were running down a steep grade, with the steam shut off and every break screwed down tight. Near Blue Cañon, over the American river, we bade farewell to the snow, and looked down into the gorges, sometimes 2000 feet and more below us, as at Cape Horn, where the track is cut in the solid rock, round a precipice 3000 feet above the river, which winds among blue shadowed pine-clad hills, with silver threads of mining streams gleaming down their sides. At Dutch Flat we were in the midst of the great gold-mining district of Placer County. In some places whole hills had been entirely washed away by years of gold-washing, leaving ghastly hollows to puzzle the geologists of the future; and two or three streams, one above the other, were carried round the hill-sides under the giant pine-trees, in iron pipes, or ditches, and flumes, like the one poor little Mliss ran over in Mr. Bret Harte's story.

A coach was waiting at Dutch Flat to take passengers to Little York and " *You Bet* Bridge;" a most convincing proof, if we wanted any, that we were in very truth among the miners. They stood about the stations, some clothed in blue or red shirts, their trousers tucked into high boots, seeing off their friends, dressed in irreproachable Sunday suits of black by the train. They were tall, strong, bearded men, capable of much evil, but of much good too under all their roughness, as surely is shown in Bret Harte's descriptions of that Californian life.

As we passed not far from Virginia City, I read his poem

"In the Tunnel," so exquisite in its rough pathos that I cannot help transcribing it in full:—

"Didn't know Flynn—
　Flynn, of Virginia,—
　Long as he's been 'yar?
　Look'ee here, stranger,
　Whar *hev* you been?

Here in this tunnel
　He was my pardner,
That same Tom Flynn—
　Working together,
　In wind and weather,
Day out and in.

Didn't know Flynn!
　Well, that *is* queer;
Why, it's a sin
To think of Tom Flynn,—
　Tom with his cheer,
　Tom without fear.—
Stranger, look 'yar!

Thar in the drift
　Back to the wall
He held the timbers
　Ready to fall;
　Then in the darkness
I heard him call:
　"Run for your life, Jake!
　Run for your wife's sake!
Don't wait for me."

And that was all
　Heard in the din
　Heard of Tom Flynn,—
Flynn of Virginia.

That's all about
　Flynn of Virginia.
That lets me out.
　Here in the damp,—
Out of the sun,—
　That 'ar derned lamp
Makes my eyes run.
Well, there,—I'm done!

> But, sir, when you'll
> Hear the next fool
>   Asking of Flynn,—
> Flynn of Virginia,—
>   Just you chip in,
>   Say you knew Flynn:
> Say that you've been 'yar."

Every half-hour, as we got lower down, brought us a week or two later in the year, till, in the four hours' run, we seemed to pass from winter to England in June. Delicate pines and shrubs covered the hill-sides; then came live oak; peach in flower, and a vineyard. Lower again, geraniums hanging in baskets outside the windows, green grass, well-kept gardens full of vegetables, oak-trees full of mistletoe. And round Auburn, only 1320 feet above the sea, the green glades and woods were glowing with crimson cyclamens, and the meadows blue and orange with Nemophila and Eschscholtzia. General P. and I stood on the platform; and, if the train stopped for a moment, we jumped off and gathered up whatever growing thing we could lay hands on. After our first raid, we came back in triumph with young red shoots from what we supposed to be a dwarf oak, when one of the black-coated miners in the car walked up to us, and, with a bow, said—

"I suppose you are strangers, and are not aware that that is poison-oak; and I advise you to throw it away as soon as possible."

We lost not a moment in following his advice, and, with a sigh, cast our beautiful red shoots out of the window: but not before they had done some mischief; for the General and Mrs. P., having touched them with bare hands (I luckily had on gloves), were quite badly poisoned; a red irritating rash coming out wherever the plant had touched their skin, which lasted for a fortnight. I met a man in Colorado who was still suffering from the effects of poison-oak, with which he had accidentally rubbed his head three years before.

The children at each station came into the cars with bunches of wild-flowers; and at Rocklin, instead of getting out to dinner like the rest of our fellow-passengers, we ran off to an oak-grove hard by, and soon had our hands full of Nemophila, Cyclamen, and the "long-stalked golden violet" (*Viola pedunculata*), a brilliant yellow pansy with an almost black eye.

Truly, Californians may be justly proud of their country. It seems a veritable land of promise, with its rich pastures just like English parks, dotted with groves of live oak, and full of the finest stock; its noble wheat fields; and the white saw-like line of the great Sierras, towering up behind into the sky, full of precious metals.

In the afternoon we reached Sacramento, half under water, as the American river was all in flood. Then a few hours, through green meadows and corn-flats, across the San Joaquin, and over the coast range, took us to Oakland; and we ended our journey with a quarter of an hour's steam across Pacific waters, in one of the huge ferry-boats, to San Francisco, with its rows of lamps, like festoons of light, up the hill-side, on which it is mostly built.

CHAPTER XII.

CALIFORNIA.

Californian oysters—The Seal Rocks—A Western play—Chinese opium-eaters and temple—An opera "buffa"—Earthquakes—Sacramento Bay—San Raphael—A council of war—Seal and salmon—Preparations for journey—Yo Semite photographs—The San José Valley—A Californian country-house—The successful millionnaire—Chinese servants—*Adios California*.

"Lick House, San Francisco,
March 13, 1872.

"Dear * * *,—If you were only here to share the 'good time' I am having! On Monday we began the day by the treat of a late breakfast at ten o'clock, General and Mrs. R. calling on us before we began. Such a good breakfast it was; such delicate little fried oysters, no bigger than a shilling, so different from those great Eastern ones, of which you have to take three or four bites!

"Then we went out for a drive round the town, with its quaint streets up and down hill, and green gardens round the houses, planted with Eucalyptus (Australian blue gum), geraniums, roses, Calla lilies, and fuchsias, all in flower. Our driver, after he had taken us all about the city, proposed to drive us out to Point Lobos, seven miles, to see the 'Seal Rocks.' We did not know in the least what the Seal Rocks might be, but consented. So away we went over Telegraph Hill, past the old Mission Dolores, with its cemeteries spreading over acres, along a good road, over sand dunes covered with blue lupin brush, till we got our first view of the Pacific stretching away green and rainy to the west, with the famous 'Golden Gate' leading from it into Sacramento Bay to our right, and huge hills of blown sand to the left.

"At the point there is a large hotel; and as it was raining when we arrived there we had some thoughts of driving straight home again: but on second thoughts we 'concluded' to get out and see what was to be seen, as we had come so far; and it was lucky we did so. We went through the hotel, which is built on the cliff, about fifty feet above the sea, to a broad gallery with rocking chairs and telescopes; and below us rose out of the water a group of brown rocks.

"Presently, as we were looking about, a strange sound greeted our ears; a hoarse bark; and looking more closely at the rocks, we discovered to our amazement that they were literally alive with huge seals. There were hundreds of them crawling up and down, barking, catching fish, and fighting like a set of animated caterpillars. It was the strangest sight I ever saw; and we stood there watching them for nearly an hour. The chief of the herd, a gigantic old fellow, is called General Butler. He lay at the top of a rock waiting till some unfortunate young one had crawled up on his flippers with infinite difficulty, and just as the poor little beast arrived safely at the top, the General rushed upon him open-mouthed, and sent him spinning into the water again. They are usually called 'sea-lions' (*Otaria*), species undetermined; and I hear that on the Farrallone Islands, some sixty miles out to sea, they swarm in even greater numbers than at Point Lobos. It is immensely to the credit of the San Franciscans that these seals are preserved, and so jealously do they guard them that if anybody shot one I do not think his life would be worth much.

"Then we drove home, and had a walk about the streets till dinner at 5.30, and after dinner we went to the theatre. Here people only put on evening dress for the opera, so we went in morning gowns and hats. We saw a capital translation from the French, thoroughly well acted throughout; and then a local sketch, 'by one who knows how it is himself,' called 'Stocks, or Up and Down.' It was extremely interesting, though not pleasant, being an *exposé* of one of the bubble mining companies; and as every character in it was some well-known Californian the excitement in the house was intense.

"On Tuesday we went off by the street-cars to the Chinese quarter; and at last found our way down an alley to the Chinese temple, a red brick house, with gold, red, and blue tablets on the gate-posts. There was no one to show us the way; so General P. opened the first door we saw, and we looked into a large dark room, where on beds, covered with sheets like corpses, with a tiny lamp burning at each bedhead, lay a dozen or more opium-eaters. It was horrid: and the General shut the door a good deal quicker than he had opened it, while we made our way up the stairs. On the next floor we found a number of old Chinamen sitting round a table writing with big reed-pens, which they hold quite upright; and smoking. They pointed up another flight of stairs, and there at last we reached the temple.

"There were three altars, one behind the other, the first with silver monsters on it, and artificial flowers and joss-sticks in a carved stand. The second had a carved frame over it, with more tinsel flowers; and on the third, at the end of the room, was a great image of a red man with three black beards, surrounded by cut paper-ornaments and peacocks' feathers.

"The Chinese names sound very absurd. Sam Yek sells fruit; Wing Hing takes in washing. I longed for you yesterday to draw a splendid Chinese lady whom I saw, with her skewered chignon, and purple-silk jacket and trousers, and jade bracelets. She looked just as if she had walked off a fan.

"Last night we went to the opera to hear the 'Ballo in Maschera,' and have been ill from laughing ever since. The real prima donna was a pretty pert little Italian girl dressed as a page, who sang charmingly. The other lady who considered herself the prima donna was first dressed in black, then in green satin. She had a face like a living skeleton, with the most enormous teeth I ever saw. She wore a long train, which was very much in her way, and she kicked it vigorously from time to time. She also had a white veil, which was a source of great trouble to her, and to the baritone, who had to put it on her several times after she, in her excitement, had unveiled, rolled it carefully up, and put it in a corner. The baritone was the best of the troupe, and sang very well when he was not acting lady's-maid. Then there was Signor Catalani, 'the silver-voiced tenor from Milan.' I daresay his voice was very silvery, but we could not hear very much of it; also, he did not know his part; and he looked so painfully 'like bursting' when he held a high note and grew impassioned that I felt quite anxious. Ulrica, the witch, sang rather well; and looked imposingly ugly in black and gold, surrounded by a chorus of ten girls, who knew no more of their parts than I did. The men's chorus sang well: but the villain, in a costume which had evidently been used for a cavalier's part for many years, would come in at the wrong time with a roaring bass, which had a most melodious effect, and set the gallery (which was full of miners and that class) yelling and cat-calling, till we thought they would 'bring the house down' in earnest. I believe there is sometimes a very good opera in the city; but certainly Covent Garden would not have given us half the amusement we had last night.

"By the bye, we had a lively little earthquake this morning. It came up with a little grumbling roar at ten minutes to seven; shook my bed backwards and forwards about four times; and then passed on: and as nothing more happened I turned round and went to sleep again. I could not conceive at first what it was, as I have never felt one before. They are very common here, and sometimes are rather strong; indeed once the whole of the population rushed out into the street, thinking the city was going to be swallowed up like Lisbon.

"It is so hot to-day I am writing with open windows in a spring gown, having left off nearly all my winter things, with a bouquet of rosebuds, heliotrope, and stocks beside me.

"Do not expect to hear for some time after we leave this. We shall be at the city of Mexico in a month if we are lucky; but we may be delayed by a hundred things, so do not be uneasy if you do not hear soon."

Thursday, March 14.—San Raphael. Left the city for a visit to General R. at San Raphael. The bay is certainly one of the loveliest things I have ever seen; the city built upon the hill-side, with a veil of smoky mist hanging over it in the bright sunshine. Then to the left, as we steamed out, the Golden Gate away to the open sea, with a few vessels coming in, or starting out. Angel Island in front, with Tamalpais (the head of the range), 2300 feet high, as a background. Far away on the right the beautiful coast range, stretching south like a string of opals, till it fills up the circle by fading away behind San Francisco itself.

The sea-water from the Pacific was blue and green, in marked contrast to that of the Sacramento river, which flowed out muddy brown, and met the inflowing tide near Angel Island. The hills and islands were brilliant green, with acres of buttercups growing on the grass in the open, and groves of live oak and bay down to the water's edge. Wild ducks and sea-fowl of all kinds were innumerable; and dolphins played all round the steamer.

Our trajet took about an hour; and we landed at a point

called St. Quentin, and went across a long marsh in a small railroad, to San Raphael. It is a lovely village, in a valley of green hills at the head of the marsh, with Tamalpais towering over the foot-hills to the west. There are 800 inhabitants; and many of the houses are pretty villas with gardens full of flowers, belonging to gentlemen who have business in the city. Most of the wealthy San Franciscans live out in the country, going in daily for their business by rail or steamer, or like one of our acquaintances at San Mateo, driving in twenty-five miles with fast trotters at fifteen miles an hour.

We were received by General R. with true American hospitality; and after a light luncheon, at which we made acquaintance with dried Californian figs, one of the most excellent of preserved fruits, we rushed out into the garden. There we found quantities of flowers wild in the grass, which in England we cultivate in the gardens as annuals; roses, heliotropes, verbenas, and our hardy hothouse flowers, and all Australian shrubs, grow out here all the winter. Frost is very rare, and the thickest ice they have had for two years has been one-eighth of an inch thick: but it is never very hot in the summer near San Francisco, the thermometer seldom rising above 70°.

After dinner, the plans for our Mexican journey were thoroughly discussed. There are three routes by which to go, but all have some disadvantages. The first is from Manzanillo, by way of Colima, Guadalajara, etc. This is of course the best, being a stage route nearly all the way; and for various reasons it must be reconnoitred at some time or other. But the only fear for this route is, that as the rebels have been defeated and disorganized in front of San Luis Potosi, we may be troubled by bands of them as robbers on the road.

The second is from Acapulco across to the city of Mexico; about a ten days' journey, but no roads; so it would be a case of riding on horseback, and camping at night the whole way. Also it is not the line of country we wish to see, and would leave all the northern line still to be reconnoitred.

The third is to Panama, and then to St. Thomas, Havanna, and Vera Cruz: but that would take too long; longer indeed than if we went by rail back to New York, and down to Vera Cruz by sea.

The telegrams from Mexico all declare that the revolution is at end, and that Porfirrio Diaz, the chief of the rebels, is killed, so that there is no risk in our undertaking the journey; and as the first route is so much the best in many ways, it is almost decided that we are to take it in preference to any other.

Friday, 15th.—A day of sunshine and flowers. Mrs. R., Mrs. P., and I went out for a drive in a charming low phaeton, with a splendid pair of Californian horses, across the marsh by a frightful road to the point where we landed from the steamer. We went round the point past the Penitentiary, and up a green hill covered with flowers. Then down no road at all to a second marsh, and round to a beautiful valley, green hills shutting out all the bay save a little corner, which looked like a lovely fresh-water lake, with Tamalpais rising right above us. Then we turned up to the right, over a hill covered with trees, which divided us from the San Raphael valley, and down through groves of red wood and bay, with a luxuriant undergrowth of grass, ferns, and flowers,—fritillary, lupins, vetches, and cyclamen, besides a dozen others that I did not know.

March 16.—Another lovely day. Mr. O'C., a neighbour, drove us down to the station, and we had a charming steam across to the city. Half-way across we saw a curious battle between a seal and two sea-gulls for a large salmon. The seal had caught it, and was trying to bite it in two, jumping half out of water, flinging it away, then catching it again, and worrying it like a terrier with a rat, till his splashings attracted two sea-gulls, who swooped screaming down upon him, and all three fought together for the fish till we passed out of sight of them.

At the wharf Mr. Y. and Señor A., a young Mexican, who with General R. are to make up our travelling party to Mexico, met us; and the gentlemen all went off together for blankets, carbines, and "six-shooters" for the journey. Mrs. P. and I went out later to complete our part of the outfit, and replenish the medicine-chest with large stores of quinine pills.

Then I went to see Mr. Watkins, the celebrated photographer of the Yo Semite Valley, to whom I had a letter from the C.'s of Colorado Springs. His photographs and his descriptions of the Valley made me wish more than ever that our time had been long enough in California to allow us to get down there: but at this time of year it is impossible, as there are forty feet of snow in the valley. However, if anything could give one an idea of its grandeur, these photographs would; and when next morning I found a collection of six dozen on my table, which, with Californian generosity, Mr. Watkins had sent to me, simply from my being a friend of his friends, I was quite content to wait till some future day to see the Yo Semite.

March 17.—Started this morning at 8.45 for B——, twenty-five miles down the San José Railroad. Mr. R., its hospitable owner, and Captain O. and his pretty daughter, joined us at the depot. The road runs down the long peninsula at the northern point of which San Francisco stands. At no point of our route was it more than ten miles wide, the bay lying on the east, and the Pacific shut out by green hills about 400 feet high on the west. The day was perfection; and the views across the blue waters of the bay, with its white-sailed ships, to the pearly pink and blue coast range beyond, were exquisite. Monte Diabolo stands up in the centre of the range, proud of his little 4000 feet height, which looked low enough after our Colorado giants. The marshes on the edge of the track were brown now: but when the hills get dried up in the summer, then a plant which grows all over the marshes gets bright green as a compensation. The meadows were ablaze with flowers, yellow, purple, and lilac; the orchards full of peach-trees in flower. The whole scene appeared so English, that I had to look at the vegetation to persuade myself I had not swooped down on the dear old country in June. It is most provoking that we happen to be here the only month in the year that the strawberries are not ripe. One gentleman told me that he had several acres of strawberries; and that after he has used all that he wants for his house and preserving, the remainder are left to rot upon the ground, as they are so common here they do not pay the labour of picking for sale.

We drove from the depot up to the house with a pair of fast trotters, and sat down to a sumptuous *déjeuner à la fourchette*, at eleven. The house is built on no exact plan: but a block has been added here and a room there, and the result has been charming; a wide gallery, enclosed with glass, runs round all the lower rooms, which are fitted with Californian woods, pine, cedar, redwood, walnut, and laurel, or, as it should be called, bay. It is the most beautiful wood I have ever seen, like a rather dark orange wood, and taking the finest polish. I saw a pianoforte made of it by a San Francisco maker, which was as beautiful outside as its tone was good when opened. After breakfast we went all over the house, and afterwards went off to the stables to see the horses, and a marvellous collection of Californian carriages, of which there were sixteen, of all shapes and sizes.

Then we went to the ten-pin alley and had a game of bowls, till a team of four fine Californian horses came round in one of the sixteen carriages, and I and some of the rest of the party drove up about eight miles to San Mateo to see Mr. ——'s pretty place.

The stables there are unique, all in polished woods of the country, with silver fittings. On one side of the entrance is the coachman's room, with luxurious sofas and chairs; and on the other the harness-room, in which the harness is kept in glass cupboards lined with velvet. There is a broad passage from end to end, and we drove right through, with our high carriage and four horses, between the stalls, which were full of magnificent thoroughbreds.

Mr. ——'s story is a strange one; and I hope I may be forgiven if I put it down as it was told me, as one of the most remarkable instances of persistence and industry one has ever heard.

He came out here not many years ago, and took up a claim for a quartz mine—that is to say, a mine where the gold has to be crushed out of the solid quartz rock, instead of washed from the loose red soil, as in hydraulic mining. He worked at it, feeling sure it would pay, till he had exhausted all his money and all his credit, and found no gold. Then a friend came out and joined him, who had \$3000 or \$4000. They worked on till the friend's money and credit were also exhausted; but still no gold. The friend now got discouraged: but Mr. —— insisted on his keeping on, and three days after they struck the vein. He now took out \$1,000,000 a year, finally sold the mine for an immense sum, and his income now averages \$60,000 (£12,000) a month.

We found him most kind and agreeable, and he took us all round his grounds. The shrubberies of Australian mimosas and Peru pepper were full of the pretty crested Californian quail, quite tame, and by the door were a tiny Japanese cock and hen, and when Mr. —— took the cock in his arms, fondling it as if it were a kitten, the little creature was as pleased as could be.

We drove home through San Mateo, a pretty village, with fine trees round the houses. The old live oaks were just coming out with fresh green shoots.

After our drive Mrs. R. took us into her kitchen, with its four Chinese cooks in white aprons. She gave me a most attractive account of the merits of Chinese as servants, saying that she had never known comfort till she had every servant in her house a Chinaman, except the butler. They require explicit orders at first: but when once they know what you want, they go on doing it day after day just like machines.

There is a story told of some San Franciscan who wanted to see how far his Chinese servant used his reason in serving him. So one day he called John into his garden, and taking up a brick, carried it about twenty yards, laid it down, took it up again, and carried it back to the starting-point.

"Now," said he, "John, you are to do what you see me do."

Off he went, leaving John hard at work; and coming back several hours after, he found poor John, with his hopeless yellow face, going on taking up the brick, carrying it the twenty yards, and bringing it back again, as regularly as clockwork. His master had told him to do it, and he got his money for it; so it was no business of his to question the sense of the proceeding.

About 5 P.M. we bade farewell to B——, and drove down to the station in two carriages, our host driving the first himself, and when we reached a turn in the road about half a mile from the depot, we saw the train was in. On shot our host and his fast trotters, leaving us behind; and just as he was nearing, the train started; so the groom made our horses gallop down a steep hill. Mr. —— managed to stop the train for a minute, and into the station we swung full gallop, jumped out on the platform, and got into the cars as they started for the second time.

We are all prepared for our start to-morrow. Our luggage is compressed into the smallest possible compass. My cabin-trunk and a small valise contain all my worldly goods that are to go to Mexico. I have laid in a stock of paper and ink here, and all that I have to do to-morrow is to get a Spanish Grammar. Our medicine-chest is well stocked, and we have each private stores of quinine pills in case of "chills and fever;" so now we have nothing to do but bid farewell to all our San Franciscan friends, and beautiful California, hoping that it may not be the last time we shall see its hospitable shores.

CHAPTER XIII.

DOWN THE PACIFIC.

The "peaceful ocean"—A tumble—Sea-gulls and Spanish lessons—An odious child—Orchilla—The new "Earthly Paradise"—A narrow escape—Sunday—An addition to our party—Gloomy forebodings.

On board the 'Alaska,' March 20, 1872.—The Pacific Ocean was well named. On the 18th of March, as we steamed out of the Golden Gate, there lay before us a glassy sea, unruffled by a single breaker, and so it remained during the eight days of our voyage. The sun blazed overhead; the shores of California rose green and red on our left; crowds of sea-gulls flew screaming in our wake; the Chinese sailors glided noiselessly about the deck in their blue dresses; and the "walking beam" of the great engine moved up and down with a relentless regularity, carrying us away from civilisation, comfort, safety, to we knew not what.

All the first day we ran down a few miles from the coast in sight of the soft green hills, which looked just like the southern coast of Ireland on a summer's day, save where in one place they were covered with acres of wild oats, and at nightfall we passed Monterey Bay, with the lights gleaming from its old town, the oldest settlement in California.

I slept soundly in my pleasant roomy cabin on deck, till about 3.30 A.M., when the Chinamen began washing the decks just outside. Still sleepy, I thought it was raining, and jumped up to shut the port; knocked my head violently against the top berth, and then, forgetting that I was in the land of "Saratoga trunks," and that berths were made high in proportion, I finished my misfortunes by tumbling right out on the floor, and lay there for some time, feeling myself all over to see which bones were broken. Finding nothing worse than a few scratches and bruises, I went to bed again in a humbled frame of mind.

Yesterday (Tuesday) was as beautiful as the day before. The sea was so calm, that one could not be sea-sick. Señor A. gave me two Spanish lessons, and I did nothing all day but learn Spanish, till I gave myself a headache: but an hour's sleep set me all right, and after dinner we walked up and down the deck, the two Generals discussing railroads and finance, etc., till I felt quite learned on the subject.

To-day we have been out of sight of land. The crowd of white sea-gulls which have followed us from San Francisco have left us during the night, and their place has been taken by a few larger brown ones, with smaller bodies and longer wings. This morning we saw a great shoal of dolphins; as far as I could judge it was a quarter of a mile long, and rushing from the ship, they skipped away to the west, leaping right out of water in their haste.

Thursday, 21*st*.—All day we have been steaming along under blazing sun on the blue sea. The hours go very slowly between the doses of Spanish, and Cooper's novels, to which I have been reduced, as I have read the few other books in the ship's library. We have plenty of time to watch our fellow-passengers, a few of whom are very pleasant: but one woman with a particularly odious child is our *bête noire*, as she is always turning up and coming exactly where one does not want her. As soon as we got on board the child insisted on running out in the sun bareheaded; so the woman screamed to her, "Now, you shall come in. Is you the boss of me, or is I the boss of you?"—enough to show us she was to be avoided.

Sunday, 24th.—On Friday night we ran into Magdalena Bay, to take in a cargo of Orchilla, too late to see anything but the bare outline of the hills.

Saturday morning we got up early, as we could not sleep much, the ship being still, and moreover full of Mexicans, who came on board as soon as we dropped anchor, and laughed, shouted, danced, and sang the livelong night. After breakfast General P., Señor A., and I rowed off to land in a boat belonging to the Captain of the port, with two other Mexicans to row us. As soon as we started I was initiated into one of the Mexican customs. The Captain took out of his pocket a bundle of cigarettes, and drawing one half out, offered it to me with a bow. I refused in the best Spanish I could muster, and got Señor A. to explain that "Americanas" do not smoke, to prevent hurting the good man's feelings: but even then he looked rather dismal, and greatly puzzled at my want of taste.

Overhead flew numbers of the "Tijeras"—Scissor-kite (*Nauclerus furcatus*).

The hills are quite bare of everything except low bushes, on which the orchilla grows—the only article of commerce this forsaken place produces. It is a long grey lichen, which only grows in a very dry climate, close to the sea, in this and the corresponding southern latitude. It is worth twenty-five cents per lb., and is sent entirely to England for dyeing, producing a fine crimson colour.

This place was called "Paradise" by some Eastern speculators, who got up and sent out a colony of some 500 people a year or two ago, after the method of Martin Chuzzlewit's "Eden." This is the Paradise they found awaiting them. A narrow peninsula of perfectly bare red hills about 1000 feet high, between the ocean and the bay, ending at the water's edge in a strip of sandy beach, on which stands a warehouse and a store for the orchillas and the people engaged in picking it. Here we landed, and Mrs. R., the Mexican wife of the American representative, made us welcome, and we sat in the store, which was pleasantly cool. She told us that there was no water nearer than eight miles off, along a spit of sand we saw on the eastern side of the bay, and that was from a laguna where the water is brackish: so, she said, she had most of the drinking water from San Francisco by the steamer once a fortnight. She offered us some pale ale: but being curious we were foolish enough to refuse, and ask for a glass of laguna water. One mouthful was enough, and too much; and our politeness was put to a hard proof in swallowing that one.

After a few minutes' rest we went out along the burning beach. It is made of shell-sand; and just above tide-mark was a curious ledge about five feet high, formed of recent fossil shells. They seemed so fresh—in some pink Balani the colours were as bright as in those on the beach—that I fancied they must be merely a huge shell-heap lying loosely: but on trying to pick a shell out I found they were firmly imbedded in a hard sandy clay. I managed, however, with some difficulty, to knock off some good specimens. We picked up quantities of shells, alive and dead, and disturbed hundreds of sea-gulls who were wading about at the water's edge, feasting on shell-fish, and quite tame. I ventured on to the top of the shell-ledge, and found the orchilla growing on scrubby bushes. One prickly plant was in leaf—the only green thing to be seen: and besides this there was a euphorbia with tiny red flowers and no leaves, and cactus of four kinds: one of the other passengers higher up the beach found a fine Mesembryanthemum in flower. But I was so horribly afraid of meeting a rattlesnake that my scientific search was a very hurried one, and as it was it very nearly came to an untimely end.

General P. had gone back to the ship to fetch his wife,

and as we had been told the cargo would be several hours coming on board, I was wandering on half a mile from the landing-place, when suddenly the whistle blew from the steamer. I was for getting back as fast as possible: but Señor A. would not hurry, and said it was all a mistake—he *knew* they were not to sail till 4 P.M. "Any way," I said, "we will go towards the boat," and having gained that point with some difficulty, we waded through the burning sand, under a scorching sun, I scolding and Señor A. grumbling, till, horror of horrors! the whistle blew again; there appeared the Capitano of the port, waving his arms and yelling to us to hurry; and the boat seemed just shoving off. I began to run, with Señor A. after me, and what with heat and anger, and the sand in which I sank deeper and deeper at each step, and the fear of being left for a fortnight with nothing but the laguna water to drink, I felt as if I were in a hideous nightmare, and that the boat was going farther and farther instead of my getting nearer. However, we did reach it at last; and in half an hour more, when we were displaying our treasures on deck, and under way, I made a solemn resolution never to put my faith in any one's judgment but my own where a steamer's sailing was concerned.

This morning we stopped at Cape San Lucas, the southernmost point of Lower California, and took on board several Mexicans. One plays the piano quite beautifully. We have had a good deal of music every evening, after it is too dark to read. Mr. —— from San Francisco has been reading aloud to some of us Joaquin Miller's Songs of the Sierras, some of the most perfect descriptions of western and tropic scenery, we all agreed, that have ever been written.

To-day the heat has been suffocating, not a breath of air to be had, and the sun driving down through the awning.

We had service on deck at 10.30 A.M. Mr. W., the U.S. Navy Chaplain from San Francisco, conducted the service, and we had two hymns, which Mrs. P. and I led, and a good and attentive congregation.

Monday, 25th.—Steaming across the Gulf of California, or *Mar de Cortes*. More motion, and there are a good many vacant places at table. At luncheon-time we sighted the coast of Sinaloa. The air is deliciously cool: but our cabins last night were unbearable, as they are on the ocean-side of the ship, and the breeze comes from the land.

Two Mexican gentlemen,[1] who say they are merchants travelling for a house in Guadalajara, have been talking to Mr. Y., and have asked leave to join us as far as Colima. The General has consented, as two more armed men may be an advantage to our little party; and though we do not expect to have much trouble, it is always best to be as strong as possible.

To-morrow morning we land, and then our journey begins in earnest. This has only been a preliminary. We have been holding a council of war as to where to hide the few valuables we did not send back from San Francisco. My trinkets, and an English bank-note, with one or two valuable papers, are stowed in a tiny oilskin case inside my dress. General P. has been instructing Mrs. P. and me in the mysteries of pistol practice, and we can go through our drill pretty creditably now. All on board shake their heads, and beg us to come on to Acapulco or Panama: but the lot is cast, and the country must be seen, and so we must make the best of it.

---

[1] One of these gentlemen proved afterwards to be Don Porfirio Diaz, the leader of the Revolution, who, so far from being killed—as was generally believed at the time of our leaving San Francisco—had escaped from Mexico somewhere on the east coast; thence to New York; crossed the Continent by the Pacific Railroad; and come down to Manzanillo on board the 'Alaska.' On his return the Revolution, which had dwindled into comparative insignificance during his absence, flamed up more fiercely than ever.

CHAPTER XIV.

FROM THE COAST TO COLIMA.

The Puerto de Manzanillo—*Frijoles* and *tortillas*—Mexican meals—The exports of the port—Our start for the interior—The Laguna de Cuyutlan—The delights of a night journey—Guadalupe—Salt collecting—Don Ignacio Lagos—Lace and embroidery—Tropic woods—Rumours of the Revolution—Tecolapa—A rough road—The volcano of Colima—Colima—Feast-day sights—Martial music—Easter decorations—A *huerto*—The Alameda—Hacienda de San Cayetano—The eruption of February 26th—More news of the Revolutionists.

Colima, March 28, 1872.—Thus far on our way in safety, and amid new sights and sounds in this pretty town, I must try and write the history of the last two days.

On the 26th, I was woke by the gun at 5.30 A.M., and by 6 was dressed, as the sun rose and we steamed slowly into the "Puerto de Manzanillo," on the western coast of Mexico.

The harbour of Manzanillo, though small, is very good and safe, with water twenty feet deep close to the beach. It consists of two bays; the inner is almost landlocked, the entrance to it being between two lofty rocks, covered with scrub and cactus. To the north of the bay is a belt of low thickly-wooded land, from which rise the feathery heads of the coquito palm, backed by blue mountain-ranges one above the other till the last is half lost in the clouds.

Facing the west lies the little town, consisting of two large warehouses with deep verandahs and red roof, and a few dozen small houses and huts, mostly thatched with palm leaves, along a narrow strip of sand. Behind the houses rise wooded hills between the sea and the Laguna de

Cuyutlan, which lies two hundred yards behind the town, and is reached by a narrow gap in the hills. The said hills look quite brown now, as it is nearly the end of the dry season, and the leaves will not be out till the rain comes in six weeks more.

We landed at 7 A.M., and were made welcome at the house of some German merchants, where we spent the hot hours of the day, most hospitably entertained by our hosts and the French Consul.

Our first quest was to get a "*sombrero*" for General P.; as a felt hat was unbearable under such blazing sun. So off we set, with a Mexican guide who professed to speak English. We soon, however, found that his English was, if possible, worse than our Spanish; I therefore plucked up courage, put my lessons from Señor A. to the proof, and found to my great delight that the half-dozen words I attempted, helped out with violent gesticulations and a loud and impressive delivery, were understood, whether they were correct or not.

In the little market-place half-a-dozen men and women were sitting in picturesque attitudes on the ground, under a tree, selling fruit, peppers, beans, and queer pottery of all shapes and sizes, from blue and red dogs and images up to large water-jars.

The beach was gay with groups of pretty black-eyed children, in bright-coloured cotton clothes, playing in the sand; women passing along with earthen water-jars in their hands, their "*rebosos*" (a long dark cotton scarf, which all Mexican women wear) drawn gracefully over their heads, the right end thrown over the left shoulder; and men dawdling about, as if such a low thing as work were unknown, dressed in pink or white cotton shirts, white trousers, the universal broad-brimmed palm-leaf "*sombrero*," and a "*serape*" or blanket, of various colours thrown over one shoulder.

The water of the bay looked bright under the tropic sun; and made us long for a sea-bath after the heat of our voyage; till we saw an ominous black fin appear above water within thirty yards of shore, and then learned that the bay was full of sharks.

"There has been no accident with them, however, for years," said our informant reassuringly: but we thought the time for a disaster might be just recurring, and that we would rather not be the victims.

When we got back to the house, we went into a large upstairs room, with an outside staircase from the court at the back of the house, where a young coco-nut palm and a *Ciruela* hog-plum (*Spondias*) tree hung with birds in cages, made me feel I was really in the tropics again. A barefooted Mexican boy brought us up cups of chocolate and "*pan de huevos*," literally, egg-bread, light sweet cakes, something like French brioches. But one must taste Mexican chocolate to know its charms; it is thick, yet light, and each tiny cup—for a little goes a long way—is crowned with the most delicious brown foam, which melts in the mouth as you drink it.

The morning passed very pleasantly. The room we were in looked right over the bay, and away to the mountains on the north; and the new sights on the beach were enough to keep one amused for a week. Once we heard fearful yells; and, rushing to the window, saw two stalwart men dragging a large pig along the sand by his hind legs. Their object was to get him into a boat, and take him off to a ship hard by: but to this he strongly objected, and emitted the most unearthly sounds; the whole process, which, in England, would have taken three minutes, lasting about half-an-hour, as the men found it necessary to rest every two or three yards, have a gossip with passers-by, and smoke a cigarette.

Besides these outside diversions, we had several visitors; among others the Commandante of the Custom-house, who brought Mrs. P. and me each a pretty little calabash, stained and carved by the Indians, and full of beautiful shells. There was a piano in the room—old and of the tin-kettle order, it is true: but we managed some music nevertheless. M. G., the Consul, gave us a capital song in Spanish and Apache Indian, and some absurd little Mexican things; and then I started a Volkslied, and our German hosts went on with one after another till dinner, at 12.30.

Woman making Tortillas.

At dinner we were introduced to Herr D.'s pretty Mexican wife: but unluckily she could speak nothing but her own tongue, so that we ladies could only make eyes at each other. Dinner was excellent; and we had the two standing dishes of the country, "*frijoles*" and "*tortillas.*" The first are a small brown bean, which forms the chief food of the lower orders throughout Mexico, and without which, in one form or another, no meal is considered perfect. They are very nourishing, and pleasant occasionally : but, as one of the overland party expressed it, " They are very good for 365 days : but when you get them oftener than that they become wearisome." "*Tortillas*" are very thin cakes of maize. They are made by boiling the maize and then rubbing it into a fine paste on a Lava stand, called a "*metate*." When the paste is perfectly smooth, a piece is taken in the two hands, and patted and slapped till it is as thin as a half-crown, the size of a breakfast plate, and about as tough as an ordinary sheepskin. It is then baked for a moment on a griddle and served hot, but quite limp. It is used as a spoon and fork with which to eat the frijoles; you tear off a corner, and divide it in two, doubling up one half as a receptacle for the beans, which you push in with the other bit, and eat spoon and all together. A common joke takes its rise from this—" That the Mexicans are so proud and so rich that they never use the same spoon twice."

In Mexico the day begins early with a light meal about 6 A.M., called "*Desayuno*," when you take a cup of chocolate, and "*pan dulce*." Then about twelve comes "*Almuerzo*," breakfast, a heavy meal with several dishes of meat. About 5 P.M. comes "*la Comida*," dinner, a lengthy proceeding, with endless courses of meat, which are all served alone, excepting the "*Puchero*," boiled beef with a mixture of every imaginable vegetable in the same dish; and dinner ends with small cups of excellent Café noir.

Manzanillo, though such a small place, does a large trade. It exports coffee, rice, indigo, various kinds of wood, such as cedar, rosewood, and primavera (a hard yellow wood used for the bodies of railway cars), and coquitos; these are small brown nuts, about the size of a pigeon's egg, from the coquito palm, and are used for making palm-oil and candles; 500,000 lbs. are exported annually from this port. In the outer bay of Santiago large quantities of pearl oysters are found; the pearls are very fine, and fabulously cheap. There are also good eating oysters in the bay and all along the coast: but hardly any attention is paid to them, the difficulty of transportation being so great. If a railroad ever comes here, oysters will be an important item in its freight; as with a Roman Catholic population the demand for them inland would be immense. Now everything has to be carried to and from the interior on pack-mules, which is a serious obstacle to trade of all kinds.—Ah for a railroad!

Our baggage was sent on by this same means of transportation early in the day; and much I trembled as I saw my poor old cabin-trunk, a faithful companion for so many thousand miles, tied with cords on one side of a thin, dirty, vicious mule, with one of the valises on the other side to balance it, and delivered over to the tender mercies of an "*Arriero*," or mule-driver, who looked quite incapable of taking care of anything, and quite capable of any amount of robberies, and worse.

We expected all day that our two fellow-passengers from the 'Alaska' would make their appearance: but no one had seen them land; so it was decided that we would wait no longer, but go on without them; and at 4 P.M. our cavalcade started, creating no small excitement.

General P., General R., Mr. Y., and Señor A., with two officers of the Custom-house, who joined us as far as Colima, were mounted on pretty little Spanish ponies, which looked half-buried in their trappings; Mrs. P. and I set off in a dilapidated old phaeton drawn by two mules; and were, oddly enough, the first people who had ever driven out of Manzanillo. It was only three days before, that enough of the road by the laguna was finished to enable a carriage to get to the Puerto. Usually passengers go by a small steamer, or in canoes, up the laguna to Cuyutlan Sillo: but this year, owing to the extreme dryness of the season, it was too shallow for navigation.

Passing through the single street of the town, we came suddenly on a magnificent view across the laguna, which is forty miles long, by one to ten miles wide, with a belt of brilliant green fringing the water, and a background of blue mountains. The lake, bathed in evening sunlight, was literally covered with wild fowl and white cranes; while here and there a black log turned slowly over in the water, and as it disappeared we found we had been watching an alligator. Our road wound along the shore of the lake, bordered with mangrove trees, raising themselves from the poisonous swamp on stilted roots, three to six feet high. On the right rose the rocky hills of the *Puenta de Ventanas* (the Cape of the Winds), covered with huge *Organo* Cactus forty feet high, with single stems three feet in diameter, standing like giant candelabra among the bush. They are thus named from their straight branches, resembling the pipes of an organ.

The road itself baffles description, being still in process of making; suffice it to say that we were bumped and jolted over rocks, stones, and hills till we came to what was, if possible, rather worse—deep sand on the narrow strip of land dividing the sea and the laguna. Then, for two leagues (about six miles), we had to go at a foot's pace smothered in blinding dust. But wherever the road was good we enjoyed the drive, as the vegetation was much greener than on the hills at Manzanillo, and we soon had our hands full of lovely flowers. The air was rich and heavy with that peculiar scent which you find nowhere but in the tropics; parrots flew screaming and chattering overhead; and from time to time we heard the roar of the surf on the shore to our right.

At Campos, a picturesque village of a few palm-thatched huts, we halted at sunset. As the mules were unharnessed, we sat in the carriage, and had our supper of coffee, *pan de huevos*, tortillas, and boiled eggs. It was cooked on a primitive kind of stove—a table covered with clay, and the fire built on a few stones; the eggs were brought us in a hat for want of a dish: but everything was excellent, and, as we all agreed, far above any meal one would get at an ordinary railroad restaurant in the States.

After supper we changed into a three-seated ambulance with no springs to speak of; a wooden roof just too low for my head, so that I had to lean forward all the time; four mules; and an intensely stupid driver, called Guadalupe. We went on at a good pace in the darkness, through the woods, along a road which had just been cleared; having to keep the curtains down tight to avoid scratches from the frightful thorns every tree seems to bear in the tropics. For the first hour we pretended that we were very happy; sang songs, told stories, and kept up a spasmodic conversation with our two outriders, Mr. Y. and Señor A., who preferred their ponies to the jolting of the carriages: but gradually the songs grew flat, the stories lost their points, the riders relapsed into silence; and we had to acknowledge that a night-journey was not a pleasant experience.

One or two of the party managed to get snatches of sleep: but I was a little too tall to curl myself up on the floor as Mrs. P. did, and never closed my eyes, in spite of the comfortable beds of blankets that General P. made for us. The hours went by slowly, as we now crept through sand, now jolted through a clearing over all the stumps—Guadalupe took special pleasure in driving over stumps,—then dashed full gallop across an open bit of dry swamp. Here and there we passed an ox or mule train halting for the night, beside a bright fire. Then came an interchange of compliments between the drivers, and with a "*buenas noches, Señores*," on we rattled, Guadalupe making the night hideous with grunts, groans, and yells of "*hecha mula, ar-r-r-hé*," and cracks of his long whip like a series of pistol-shots. Mr. Y.'s white pony was always to be seen as he rode by our side, keeping Guadalupe in order; which was needed, for he was as pig-headed as most stupid people are; and but for the white pony's rider, I believe we should never have found our way to Cuyutlan Sillo; but have lost ourselves as Señor A. contrived to do, not coming up with us till four hours later.

At 1 A.M. we reached Cuyutlan Sillo, the end of the laguna; and crossing a long dike, stopped to change mules. The ground was white with salt, by which the people round get their living, collecting and sending it inland. The beach near by is very fine, and as many as 5000 people come down here annually from Colima, Zapotlan, etc., for sea-bathing and salt-collecting, though there is no good road to the interior. If there only were a railroad, what an amount of passenger traffic would spring up! The annual produce of the salt-works here is 7,500,000 lbs. It was a malarious place, and we were glad, when the mules were harnessed, to leave it, and to make the best of our way to el Paso del Rio, where we were to have a few hours' rest.

The Rio de la Armeria, when we reached it at 3.30 A.M., was nearly dry, having only about a hundred and fifty yards of water at the ford: but though it was only three feet deep, the passage was sufficiently alarming, as the river-bed is nothing but huge stones, and of course in the worst place the mules refused to move. However, we got through somehow, and half a mile more took us to the house of Don Ignacio Lagos, where we halted for what remained of the night.

It did not look inviting; nothing does, I think, at 4 A.M., after twelve hours' travelling. But at last we roused up the inhabitants, and Mr. Y. went on a reconnaissance for clean beds, if such were to be had. His report was favourable; so we crawled out of the waggon with stiffened limbs, went through a deep verandah, with people sleeping in hammocks and on rugs; and found two rooms, bare of furniture, it is true, save sacking beds and a table, but tolerably clean. In a few minutes Señora Ramonsita Lagos, a comely lady, brought us clean sheets and pillow-cases; and with our own Californian blankets we made ourselves pretty comfortable. Sleep, however, I found, was out of the question; as an incessant noise was kept up by *burros* (donkeys), cocks, mules, cicadas, and human beings, who seemed to get up just as we went to bed.

By 8 A.M. we were ready for breakfast. It was prepared in the palm-thatched portico of the house, which was built round the farm-yard; so we had plenty of company in the way of fowls, dogs, and pigs. Our breakfast was delicious; we had "*pollos*" (chickens), eggs, tortillas, frijoles, chocolate, and coffee. The Colima coffee is the best I have ever tasted—equal to or excelling the finest Mocha; and as it is kept in the little husk which surrounds the two berries, and is husked and ground fresh each time it is wanted, loses none of its delicious aroma by keeping. It was the first time that most of us had eaten a meal, every item of which, down to the sugar and salt and the earthen cups we used, was produced in the country.

Don Ignacio gave us plenty of information about the country and its products. He owns a large tract of land; and grows sugar, coffee, and rice on it. His handsome wife, who is a good deal younger than he, showed us after breakfast some of her lacework and embroidery, for which the women in this State are famous. The lace is made by pulling out threads of coarse linen at different intervals, and working on the lattice-work left, much like Greek lace. It is used for trimming, and though coarse has a very good effect. In quite poor houses the pillow-cases are bordered with this lace, sometimes six inches deep. The embroidery is much prettier. The dress of the women of the country consists of a short full petticoat over a white shift coming high over the shoulders, and the *rebozo* over their heads. The sleeves and neck of this shift are beautifully worked with white or black cotton in delicate patterns. Señora Lagos had embroidered on the one she wore a wreath of black vine leaves and berries, worthy of French work.

A little before 10 A.M. we started again, sending back the saddle-horses and going on in the two carriages; a "*muchacho*" (boy) sitting on the front seat by the driver to help him to urge on the mules by means of showers of stones: but we soon got rid of him, and took the Commandante instead, to learn as much as we could from him of the country.

We drove for four miles over a grassy plateau about fifty feet above the river, with fine mountains on three sides and the ocean on the fourth, though we were not quite high enough to see it. When we left the plateau, which is many miles long, and good grazing land, the road took us without a turn for several miles through the woods. These were very disappointing after a former acquaintance with tropic woods in the West Indies. The timber was poor and crooked; the trees burnt and brown with the summer sun; and the only flowers to be seen were here and there a yellow acacia or a cactus flower like a ball of living flame. However, we were told that in the rainy season, which lasts from May or June till November, the country is completely transformed.

One halt we made at a hut beside a little stream, when the Commandante, with his usual good-nature, got us a big bunch of bananas, and some "*Agua de Coco*"—the fresh clear water from the green cocoa-nut, which was most refreshing after a dozen miles of heat and dust. While we were stopping, two exceedingly handsome young Spaniards, fully armed, rode up; one of whom we found was Señor C., nephew of General C., the Commander-in-chief of Guadalajara. They told us that the revolutionists had been giving some little trouble between Colima and Guadalajara, and the telegraph lines are all cut; so that we could not communicate with General C., who was going to protect us on our journey: but they did not think we should have much trouble from the rebels.

One A.M. brought us to Tecolapa, a pretty village with a grove of coco-palms, where we stopped to change mules; Señor P., the Commandante, went out to forage for provisions, and soon returned, followed by two señoras. One was old and ugly: but bore on her head a tray of excellent eggs and tortillas. The other was a lovely girl of seventeen, by name Catalina, dressed daintily in a white gown, little pink apron, red shoes on her tiny feet, and a blue cotton rebosa covering all her pretty face save her large brown eyes. She seemed as handy as she was lovely; for "*los frijoles con queso* (beans with grated cheese) *de Catalina*" were perfection; and what we left were carried off as a prize by our men.

We had been coming along the best road, though not through the most populous district, leaving most of the large sugar, maize, and cotton "*haciendas*" (estates) on the left, between us and the Rio Armeria. The uncleared land costs $4 or sixteen shillings per acre; and will always produce one crop of sugar or cotton in the year; but with irrigation it would produce two crops.

Leaving Tecolapa, which is about 450 feet above the sea we got our last view of the Pacific Ocean; and began a steep ascent through the forest to the mountain pass at Los Molos, where the descent into the Valley of Colima begins. The woods were much greener in the mountains, bamboos and palms (Chamædorea) growing among the hardwood trees. The summit of the pass is 1470 feet above the sea; and up the last part the Government has made a good graded road through a rocky bit, in which we found a fine vein of white marble, evidently quite unnoticed. We longed to "pre-empt" it at once, as it will be valuable some day.

The descent from Los Molos looked so uninviting that

most of us preferred walking down a mile, to trusting our necks to four mules at full gallop and an improvised brake, made by tying one of the hind wheels with rope to the front axle, over a road which was simply a pile of rocks on a slope as steep as a house-roof. Strange to say, the ambulance when we reached it had not upset, nor had the wheels come off, as we expected; so we drove on: but the road, though rather less steep, was quite as rough, and in one place General R. and I, who were sitting together on the back seat, were shot up against the hard wooden roof of the ambulance; and I got such a blow on my head that I subsided humbly on the floor, and did not say much for some time.

At about 5 P.M. we approached Las Mescales: and here, as we emerged from the mountains, burst upon us one of the most sublime sights I have ever seen. From a plain twenty miles broad, and less than a thousand feet above sea-level, rose the volcano of Colima, 13,396 feet high, with a crown of smoke pink in the setting sun against the clear blue sky, and wreaths of light clouds floating along its sides. Much as we had heard of the grandeur and beauty of the volcano, it far exceeded all our expectations; and its sudden appearance across the plain greatly increased the effect.

From Las Mescales, with a "*remuda*" or relay of three ponies and a mule, all with horribly sore backs, which seemed to make no difference to their owners or drivers, we started along a good though dusty road up the last rise before reaching Colima. The ground in one place was covered for acres with black volcanic stones, an unpleasant donation from the beautiful volcano we had so admired; and here we saw something else for the first time, quite as ominous as the black stones; a little wooden cross by the side of the road on a heap of stones, and an inscription scribbled below it to the effect that some Augustin or Juan or Domenique had here been killed by robbers.

From the rise we looked over the fertile valley, with its watercourses shaded with trees, its rows of coco-palms, and rich fields; and driving along sandy roads shaded by great fig-trees, with sweet black fruit the size and shape of sloes, we reached the town of Colima about 7 P.M.; and rattled through the streets, our "*cochero*" yelling and whipping the hapless ponies till they fairly galloped. Everything was dark, or at least as good as dark; for the only light was from a wretched lamp lit with coco-nut oil, hanging from a chain across the streets at very long intervals. We went through the Plaza Nueva and the Plaza des Armes, to the hotel, expecting to find tolerably uncomfortable quarters there: but as we drew up, out came the proprietor, and, with many bows and pretty speeches, explained that Señor Don Juan F. H. expected us at his house, which he had, with true Mexican hospitality, placed at our disposal. The street was too narrow for our ambulance to turn in it; so we had to make a long round to get back into the Plaza des Armes, which we had only passed by a dozen yards. However, we rattled back, and drew up before a grand house with a Moorish façade occupying the whole north side of the *plaza* (square). A muchacho took us through a passage and up a long stone stair, at the head of which, with a huge Newfoundland dog by his side, our host was awaiting us, and made us truly welcome.

"COLIMA, *Easter Day, March* 31, 1873.

"DEAREST * * *,—If verbal photography were invented, how gladly would I use it to describe the view from our windows, as it passes before us, like a series of strange pictures!

"We were fairly puzzled the morning after we arrived here to know where we could be; buildings, trees, and people are such a mixture of the old and new, eastern and western worlds.

"To-day being 'Fiesta' (Feast-day), as well as Sunday,

the place is swarming with life. From our sitting-room, with its fresco-painted walls, tiled floor, and large windows opening into the iron balcony, we look out upon the Plaza des Armes, a large square. On the east side is a church with picturesque stone belfry, and the State's prison; a

Bell Tower at Colina.

dozen soldiers lounging by the door in blue and red, with white kepis. On the south and west side run single-storied buildings with arches in front of them; and our host's house, with a fine Moorish front, takes up the whole of the north side. The rooms are on the first floor, above stables, offices, etc. Under the '*portale*' or arcade in front of it on the ground-floor are a series of shops; and on the pavement beneath the lofty arches stand '*cajons*' (boxes), as they call the booths where the common goods of the country are sold. In the centre of the Plaza is a fountain, with its group of idlers gossiping with the water-carriers; and round the carriage-road runs a tiled pavement, along which orange-trees in full flower and fruit are planted every eight or ten feet, each protected by a quaint double stone seat. Far away lie the blue mountains through which we came from Manzanillo; with a foreground of coco-nut palms tossing their leaves in the hot wind over the red-tiled roofs, while a score of *zopilotes* (black vultures) sail overhead in the cloudless blue sky. Below, in front of the window, sits a lazy fellow under the orange tree. He has on a white shirt, open at the neck; white loose trousers; a crimson *faja* or sash round his waist; a grey and red striped *scrape*; white boots; and a broad sombrero trimmed with black, shading his brown face: more Indian than Spanish.

"Now comes a procession round the carriage-way; three or four men with guitars, flute, and harp, strumming away an accompaniment to a pretty Spanish song which two women in front are singing; and before them trots a hideous old Indian in very scanty clothing, with a fire-stick in one hand and a bunch of little rockets in the other, which he lets off every few minutes with a fizz and bang that drives Ali, the Newfoundland dog, nearly wild with excitement, as he thinks it must be a revolution at least. They parade all round the Plaza, and disappear down a side-street, to have their place taken by a '*circo*,' three or four gaily-dressed men and boys on horses, with a distracting brass band before them, who also vanish in the same place. They are succeeded by an absurd procession of little boys, who have got entire possession of a clown hideously painted, three musicians with fiddles, and a drum; and in their midst a bit of white *manta* (cotton cloth) on two sticks, with five little dolls hung against it by the neck. What the meaning of this is, or whether it has any meaning, I cannot say; but it seems to give the muchachos infinite satisfaction. There goes a man calling '*Pastèles, pastèles*,' with a tray of sweet cakes on his head; or another, crying over his fruit in the most heartrending of all Gregorian tones, '*Buenas naranjas de Chi-i-na-a-a*' (fine China oranges), '*Sandias*' (water-melons), sweet limes, bananas, and zapotes. Patient little *burros* jog by, with loads of green maize fluttering in the breeze, or with four earthen water-jars in picturesque wooden panniers.

"Under the orange trees the sellers of *rebozos, serapes*, and *fajas* are chaffering with their customers; asking, after the manner of the country, three times as much as the article is worth, and coming gradually down to the lowest possible price.

"The '*Señores caballeros*' ride by with their broad felt sombreros heavy with silver trimmings, dainty short embroidered jackets, and buckskin silver-buttoned '*pantalones*,' open from the knee, over full white drawers. Their saddles are plated with heavy embossed silver; the stirrups are also silver; and besides the embroidered saddle-cloth, their horses' flanks are nearly covered with *chapaderos* of tiger or goat skin, which hang down nearly to the ground, with a serape rolled up and strapped behind the saddle.

"On Thursday we took a walk to the Alameda, the public garden or park. To our surprise we were told to come out without hats or gloves, and only a light shawl over our evening dresses. All along the streets ladies were sitting on the pavement at their doors, while black-eyed Señoritas looked out from the prison-like iron-latticed windows, and talked with the Señores caballeros, who lounged against the bars rolling their cigarettes. It was just like a series of Philip's Spanish pictures.

"In the Alameda the band of a battalion just arrived from Guadalajara was playing, and playing extremely well; but it had to stop while the retreat was beaten at the barracks close by. Of all hideous and indescribable noises Mexican martial music bears away the palm. Imagine two or three boys with no ear for music learning to play on cracked cavalry bugles of different keys; then add half-a-dozen other boys drumming on old tin trays and toy drums; and you will have a fair idea of what goes on four times a day in every Mexican garrison town.

"On our way home we went into two of the principal churches. Being the Thursday in Holy Week, they were crowded with people kneeling on the floor, and gorgeous with lights and ornaments. The high altar was a blaze of tinsel, gilt vases, flowers, and candles. One kind of decoration was really pretty, though rather absurd,—from long strings hung round green balls; and on examination, I found they were covered with live mustard and cress, growing on flannel, just as we used to grow it on bottles at home in the nursery. But in one church I saw what, to my unaccustomed eyes, seemed shocking. Close to the door lay, on a kind of bier, a life-size figure of the Saviour, with the head bound up, dressed in grave-clothes and strewn with flowers. Those who were used to that sort of thing seemed to think it all right: but I confess I was horrified, and glad to get out into the cool dark streets.

"On Good Friday, having no church, alas! to go to, we stayed in till the evening; when Don Juan took Mrs. P. and me out for a walk, across the bridge of the Rio de Colima. It was quite dark, save for the light of the coco-nut oil lamps, and the little fires of the women cooking and selling '*tamales con puerco*' (a horrid invention of bits of pork inside a little hot maize roll) on the pavement. We went into one church which was nearly empty. The altar and crucifix were shrouded with dark green boughs, against which the life-size figure hung ghastly pale; a frightful figure of the Virgin in black, with a kind of white cap, leant against the feet.

"Yesterday, Don Juan drove Mrs. P. and me out to his '*huerto*,' or fruit orchard. Colima is celebrated for these gardens, belonging to the different residents; and our host's is one of the finest. It is about a mile from the Plaza, and just outside the town, where the ill-paved streets and long rows of one-storied houses, looking with their barred windows, like successions of prisons, change to sandy lanes with a few miserable huts. In the high wall, a large gateway leads into the garden-house, with a great swimming-bath, and a cool tiled piazza, where Don Juan told us he sometimes gives dinners to his friends. Thence through a bower of roses, and the '*manta de la Vierge*,' a beautiful climber with pink flowers, a narrow walk hedged on either side by scarlet hibiscus, took us to the garden proper. This consists of rows of coffee, oranges, limes, mangos, bananas, and zapotes; and everywhere the slender stems of the coco-palms rise through the lower growth, their broad heads of leaves, with a zopilote roosting on each leaf, forming a dense green roof overhead. Returning to the garden-house, the gardener's pretty little barefooted boy had prepared for each of us a glass of '*agua de coco*,' the clear water from the green coco-nut, standing in a plate in the midst of a wreath of roses and hibiscus; and we drove home through the town with a glorious bouquet apiece. All the inhabitants were sitting out at their doors: so we had a good opportunity of judging of the good looks of the people; and were greatly disappointed. Some of the young girls were rather pretty; and one we saw who was perfectly beautiful; with very delicate sharp-cut features, fair skin, great black eyes, and the usual magnificent hair which is the glory of the women here; they wear it in two plaits down their backs, which often reach down to their feet. But the older women are perfectly hideous; the Indian blood showing strongly in all.

"I am getting on with my Spanish; and can now make the servants understand, and I follow most of a conversation: but for the first two or three days I did make the most absurd mistakes. However, now we are obliged to exert ourselves, and plunge along through a perfect quagmire of mistakes, as both Mr. Y. and Señor A. are off for two days on a reconnaissance, looking for a better pass through the mountains, for the way we came is too steep for a railroad, and we hear that there is a very good pass, keeping the course of the Rio Armeria all the way.

"I hope you will get this. Señor P. has 'thrown himself at my feet in kissing my hand,' as they say here, and offered to take a letter for me, and send it from Manzanillo by the Panama or San Francisco steamer."

Monday, April 1.—Yesterday, at about 5 P.M., after spending the afternoon drinking half liquid lemon-ice and eating Granadillas, we went to the Alameda of the Plaza Nueva; got out, and walked among crowds of people, who were listening to the band. I was really quite uncomfortable at the way the people all stared at me, and especially at my feet, of which I cannot say I felt at all ashamed, as I had on a particularly pretty pair of English shoes. At last it grew quite unbearable; and I was getting hotter and hotter every moment, when, to my intense delight, we met the American Consul's wife, and another lady. They soon explained the mystery; and told me that the Mexicans think it very improper to show one's feet. All the women have their gowns made as long or longer in front than at the back; and thus their astonishment and amusement at my very inoffensive short gown were accounted for.

This morning, at seven, Don Juan, who really seems to think no trouble too great if it adds to his guests' enjoyment, drove Mrs. P. and me out to the hacienda de San Cayetano to see the cotton-mills belonging to General de la V. and his brother. They are about two miles from the city, along a lovely lane between stone walls enclosing gardens of bananas and coco-palms. Figs and prima-vera trees, so valuable for their fine timber, with their glory of golden flowers, arch overhead; and the avenue leads you straight to the gate of the hacienda.

General de la V. received us at the door, and took us into a long low room, divided off by lattices five feet high, and serving for office, sitting-room, bed-room, and armoury. The gates of the hacienda are kept closed all night, and twenty men armed with rifles and muskets in case of robbers or revolutions. After coffee, ham, and dry bread—there was no butter, though all around is fine pasturage—we went over the mill. It is worked by a thirty-horse-power steam-engine, and a forty-horse-power water-wheel, the water coming from the river close by, in a stone dike one-fourth of a mile long. The looms and spindles are from Boston; the steam-engine from Brooklyn. Two hundred men, about thirty boys, and one hundred women, all Mexicans, are employed. Mr. B., the English chief engineer, told us that they work well when some one is by to keep an eye on them. We went through all the rooms, and saw the cotton in every stage, from the first, where, freed from the pod, it is put into the carding-machine and the seeds taken out, to the looms where the coarse white "*Manta*" (cotton cloth) is made. The engine-house was exquisitely clean; and the "governor" ornamented with a bunch of tropical flowers in honour of our visit.

We then went along the water-conduit to the two reservoirs, into which the water is let at night; and back to the hacienda, past a field of mulberry-trees for silk-worms, of which six thousand are raised on the estate every year. The *patio* (court) has a garden of fruit-trees at the northern end, and opposite the mill runs a long low building of separate tenements, two rooms deep, for the work-people and their families.

Mr. B. showed us a most interesting sketch, done on the

spot by Señor de la V., of the eruption of the Volcan de Colima on the 26th of February. Mr. B. said that the first he knew of it was hearing all the workpeople rushing out shrieking and praying into the patio; and he thought at first, from the disturbance, there must be a revolution. On going out, however, he found it was something much more awful than any work of man. From the nearest peak rose a huge tree of smoke, with showers of ashes falling back from the red-hot stones, which flew up a certain height, and then seemed to explode. It has been in almost constant eruption ever since; the last explosion was on the 26th of March, the day we landed: but since we came in sight of it, it has most provokingly chosen to be quite quiet. We live, however, in hopes of its going off again; and every time there is any sudden stir in the town, we rush to the stairs outside the sala, from whence we can see the mountain, in hopes that it has been considerate enough to begin its fireworks again for our benefit.

About 10 A.M., the sun being very hot, we drove home, laden with pomegranates and bouquets of orange flowers.

Tuesday, 2d.—Our start has been postponed, and we cannot get off till to-morrow. The Governor of Colima has been here this morning giving advice about our journey. We are to go to-morrow as far as San Marcos, a large hacienda just on this side of the famous *barrancas* or cañons, where we are to sleep, and cross the barrancas next day without an escort; so that we must trust to our own arms. The Governor says that if we meet the *pronunciados* (revolutionists) without an escort, they will not molest us: but should we have Government soldiers with us, and meet them, like Artemus Ward and the Indians in the happy hunting-grounds, "guess there will be a fight." He says also, that we are not likely to fall in with robbers on the first two days' march, till we get near Zapotlan; and there he has ordered a carriage and an escort to meet us. It sounds altogether "rather warlike." To-night, Incarnacion M., the owner of the horses we have hired, has been round to say that the revolution has broken out strong near Quesaria, and that he will not start till we give him security for his animals. This our people will not do, as these good Mexicans are quite capable of getting a friend, in the guise of a Pronunciado, to steal the horses, and then demand the value from us. However, at last, after an hour's talk and argument, he consents to go, if we take two extra armed men : so we go.

CHAPTER XV.

ROBBERS AND REVOLUTIONS.

Our start—An ill-broken team—La Quesaria—Chicken wine—Barrancas—San Marcos—Mule trains—An uncomfortable luncheon—The "*Pedregal*"—A break-down—Zapotlan—A revolution—The baffled bridegroom—Rough lodgings—Pulque—Severo—An early breakfast—A "scare"—Onions—"*Los bonitos rifles*"—Pronunciados—Alkali flats—A dry lake—"A friend indeed"—Our escort—La Coronilla—Robber towns—Guadalajara at last.

Wednesday, April 3.—At 3 A.M. our host woke us, and in half an hour all was bustle and confusion in the house. By 5 A.M. we were ready, and our start was one of the prettiest scenes possible. Pack-mules were kicking and twisting; saddle-horses held by armed servants; our party all armed with Henry rifles, carrying sixteen shots, and with revolvers; the crowd of lookers-on standing gaping round; Señor H. on his grey pony, with a huge umbrella strapped to the saddle; Ali, the Newfoundland dog, bustling about to see all was right; and the first crimson streaks of sunrise behind the old bell-tower.

Mrs. P. and I were both armed; it was a queer sensation buckling on a revolver for the first time: but our pistol-drill on board ship has taught us how to avoid shooting our companions; and notwithstanding the laughter that greeted my first appearance with a full-sized Smith and Wesson on my belt, I mean to stick to it; and am already beginning to look on it as my best friend.

For the first ten miles the order of march was this:—First, two armed men; then the five pack-mules, with their two drivers, also armed; then two of the gentlemen, Mrs. P., and I, in the same old phaeton that brought us from Manzanillo, with Mr. M.'s (the U. S. Consul) horses in it; the rest of our party, with Don Juan, another gentleman, and Mr. M. who is coming through to Guadalajara with us; and two more servants to bring up the rear.

I never remember a more lovely morning, the air was so cool and the sunrise over the mountains was glorious. We reached the rancho of the Cebana at about seven, and there Don Juan and his friend left us, much to our regret, for we had all got really fond of the dear old gentleman; and his kindness and hospitality were boundless. We also at this point changed Mr. M.'s horses for a pair which I am certain had never been driven before. To begin with, they would not start. Two of the servants then rode up, one on each side, and catching them by the heads, and flogging at the same time with the raw hide whips they use here, got them off with a bounce at last. They went for a little way full gallop, till our gentlemen were left far behind; when, coming to a slight rise, they stopped dead, and began backing. Then, the harness being perfectly rotten and tied together with bits of string, the near horse slipped under the traces, turned completely round, and stared at us with his head at the end of the pole. At last they were started again at a furious pace: but in a minute Mrs. P. and I discovered that the near horse had not got the bit in his mouth at all, but had slipped it out, and it was hanging on his throat. Scream as we would to the *cochero*, he would not or could not understand us: but drove solemnly on, flogging the horses to a wilder pace, till at last, much to his astonishment, we dragged the reins from his hands, and as we fortunately were going up hill, the animals at last stopped. The gentlemen then caught us up; the harness was "fixed up," and we set off once more, with Mr. Y. and Señor A. by our sides : but in about a mile the horses behaved so badly again that we could bear it no longer, and entreated to get on the mules. So we pulled up at a palm-thatched hut, where our steeds soon arrived.

Mine was a brown one, and very ugly : but a solemn and patient beast, who jogged along most comfortably if allowed to choose his own road. Mrs. P. rode a little black one, who, in memory of our Colorado pets, we called Baby. They paced about four miles an hour: and passing through fields of maize, frijoles, and sugar-cane, all irrigated and looking exquisitely green, we came at 11 A.M. to the La Quesaria, a large *hacienda* or estate, 3820 feet above the sea, seventeen miles from Colima.

Entering by a gateway in high thick walls, we passed through a large outer yard strewed with megass (the crushed sugar-cane), and surrounded by low houses for the workmen and their families, to the inner enclosure. We went through an archway of volcanic stone, and under a massive stone aqueduct on solid arches, to the house, where, beneath a double wooden piazza, our pack-mules were already unloading. On the wall dividing the two enclosures stood a quaint bell-tower with three handsome bells, which were rung at noon by three boys in white in the most primitive fashion. The two smaller bells had strings tied to the clappers, both of which one boy pulled at the same time ; while the two other acolytes were occupied in hoisting the third and largest bell mouth upwards, and then, having once set it off, turning it over and over as fast as possible, producing altogether about as deafening and inharmonious sounds as can well be imagined. Till breakfast was ready we wandered about the patio, saw the sugar-mill, and went into the quiet little church, just opposite the house. The hacienda employs 200 hands; and produces yearly 225 tons of clayed sugar, 78 tons of "*panela*," coarse brown sugar, 50 tons of rice, and 1200 barrels of rum. Señor A. came in when we had almost finished an excellent breakfast of eggs, chickens, and frijoles; and after giving the various items of manufacture of the estate, ended with the extraordinary statement, "And they make chicken wine."

Of course he was greeted with shouts of derision: but he stuck to his point, and soon, to convince us, a bottle was produced with "*Vino de pechuga*" (a chicken's breast) on the label. We tasted the decoction; and found it very bad rum, without any perceptible flavour of feathers. It is sent in large quantities to the interior. Three barrels are made daily, worth thirty-six dollars each; and two chickens are boiled in every four gallons of the wine. Such is the fact: but the reason why still remains a problem for future travellers to solve.

We were not much reassured by the accounts of the road, which a priest told us was "*muy peligroso*" from robbers, and that the league and a half between La Quesaria and Tonila was the worst part of all. So, when we started, at 1 P.M., three servants were sent ahead as videttes; we all came next, with the baggage-mules, and the four other servants behind us,—a party of fourteen in all. In about a quarter of a mile we passed the Barranca de la Quesaria, the first of any size we had yet come to; it was very steep, the road zigzagging down the side to the stream below. Then up the other side, and along a broad road between stone walls. Oh, what a sharp look-out we kept! but no robbers appeared. After half a mile we came to the Barranca del Muerte (of death), an ill-omened name. It was full of yellow Alamanda; and the stream was fringed with exquisite ferns, though higher up the rocks, which in the rainy season are alive with green, they were now all parched and dead.

Climbing up the further side, we rode into the little agricultural town of Tonila, and through its quaint streets of old houses, with crinkled Roman-tiled roofs and wooden corbels. An old church, with three bells in a belfry standing apart from the main building, in front of the door, was being rebuilt, bricks being mixed with volcanic stones.

Out of Tonila we took a short cut across the slopes of the Volcan de Colima, which now towered up above us, with its two peaks of "*fuego*" and "*nieve*," fire and snow. Smoke poured from a fissure low down on the side below the peak of "fire;" and near San Marcos the ground was quite grey with the dust which had fallen in clouds five weeks before, during the eruption of February 26. The country was open and bare of trees, except along the streams, which all cañon as they do in Colorado, each cañon taking a southerly direction towards the Tuxpan or Apiza river. We were also pleasantly reminded of our northern country by the re-appearance of the Spanish bayonet or yucca. In the north we know it from one to three feet high; here it grows to twenty feet, with many branches and fine heads of flowers; and is used as a hedge to the corn-fields.

Our only excitement during the march was just as we were turning up a hill, when two horsemen appeared at the top. They drew up. So did we: and the gentlemen all rode to the front. They hesitated, and seemed inclined to turn back: but finally reassured—every one declared—by my umbrella, which was unfurled in a most peaceable style, they came down the hill; and, as they passed, with a pleasant though rather trembling "*buenas tardes*" (good-evening), we saw it was only a poor fat old gentleman travelling with his servant, who had evidently been much more scared at us than we had been at them.

About 3.30 we caught the first sight of the hacienda of San Marcos, rising up white on a knoll of rock, over a mass of low buildings clustered together. What a view it was! The volcano, with its two peaks and its pine-covered slopes, was on our left; and far down to the right, across rich sugar-fields, ran the dark line of the great Barranca de Beltran, with the mountains of Morelia rising rugged behind it.

After half-an-hour more, over two small cañons and along an open plain, we jogged up to the hacienda, not at all sorry to ride in through the wide open, hospitable gates, and jump off under the orange-trees.

Don Mauricio G., the owner, was not in : but soon returned ; and his family being at Zapotlan, he placed the whole of his house " at our disposal," and we are to stay two nights to enable the gentlemen to examine the country. After an excellent dinner, we proceeded to " fix ourselves up." The P.'s and I had two immense rooms, with no windows,— theirs opening on to the street outside, and mine on the deep verandah which runs round two sides of the yard. The servants (there were about eight) were intensely stupid, and would not understand; so of course we had to call our constant helper Mr. Y. to the rescue ; and, thanks to his superintendence, we at last got some beds made up. Then we retired for the night : but no sleep came to me, for my bed was nothing but a flat table on low legs, instead of high ones, plus a mattress an inch thick entirely made of hard knots, and one sheet. The bedding, I suppose, is in Zapotlan with the family, judging by the scarcity here.

Thursday, 4th.—This morning I got up pretty early, aching rather more than when I went to bed, and went out in the piazza till breakfast.

It is just the middle of " crop time ;" so the whole place is in a state of the greatest bustle and animation. The "*Alto*" (high place), a small mound of rock about 100 feet high, is surmounted by a beautiful old Spanish castle, where the family live when they are at home. It is reached by a long flight of red earthen steps from the *patio* below. All round the *patio* are low buildings inside strong walls,— sugar-mills, stables, *corral* for mules, a small church, and the long suite of rooms where we are lodged.

All the day Mrs. P. and I have been spending in the greatest comfort, lying in hammocks in the verandah, writing, sketching, studying Spanish, and watching the endless life of one of these large haciendas; the mule-carts and pack-mules, with great loads of sugar-cane, coming in from the fields to the mill; men and women, in gay-coloured cotton dresses, coming and going all day long; a traveller, on a tired mule, arriving from time to time; our own men lounging about, waiting for the Señores caballeros to come in from their reconnaissance, and creeping round behind me with a "*mira!*" to each other of admiration at my wonderful genius in having put a dolefully bad likeness of Severo, our picturesque "master of the horse," into the foreground of a sketch;—and behind all these kaleidoscope groups rises the *Alto*, and the *Volcan de Fuego* as a background.

One of the women servants, with whom I made great friends, presented to me as a "*recuerdo*" (keepsake) a paper full of the grey dust which fell from the said volcano; and Don Mauricio, on my showing this to him, brought me some of the pumice which fell in quantities at the same time.

The following account by one of our party will give a good idea of one of these large haciendas :—

"San Marcos," he says, "is a sugar plantation covering 22,000 acres, whose lands extend to the summit of the Volcan de Colima. The slopes of the volcano are covered with pine. On the lands of San Marcos are 1600 souls. The hacienda employs 300 hands, and produces yearly 3000 barrels rum, 550,000 lbs. sugar, besides corn and frijoles. The hands employed in the sugar-works are paid ten dollars (£2) per month, besides rations. Those working in the field earn five dollars per month and rations. These wages may be considered average prices for labour on the haciendas in this region, of which San Marcos is a fair specimen."

From the same source came this account of the reconnaissance, which was very successful, considering how few hours they had for it :—

"We examined the Barranca de Tuxpan, the Platanillo, and that of Cuchipehuatl. From a projecting ridge we could see about seven miles east and five miles west. The general line is nearly straight. At its junction with the Barranca de Beltran, the top of the Tuxpan cañon is 3250 feet above the sea, the bottom 2570. As far as discernible, the bottom of the gulch is a succession of valleys sloping towards the bed of the river, averaging half a mile in width. Generally the river runs between a valley and a bluff, alternating according to the windings of the gulch. Most of these valleys are cultivated. The fall of the river is about fifty feet to the mile. The Barrancas of the Quesaria, Tonila, and El Muerto are described as uniting before their junction with the Tuxpan river."

On the 5th we had to get up at 3 A.M. for our start, but were amply repaid for the trouble by the picture which met our eyes as we came out into the piazza. The whole court was lit up by two huge fires in iron cressets to light the men at the mill; for they were grinding cane all night; and the red glow and dancing shadows played upon the walls and towers of the Alto. Close by, our servants were packing and saddling the mules and horses under the orange-trees. Our host, followed by a troop of dogs, was overseeing everything; servants ran about with cups of chocolate and plates of cakes; and some sleeper was still swinging in his hammock at the end of the piazza.

At 4 A.M. we set out to cross the famous "*barrancas*," or cañons, as they would be called in Colorado. A road between fields of sugar-cane hedged with bananas, led us in half a mile to the brink of the Barranca of Tuxpan. It is about 700 feet deep, and the paved road is zigzagged down the almost perpendicular sides. We preferred dismounting and walking, and even so could hardly keep our feet. At the stream which runs along the bottom we mounted, and Mrs. P. and I had each a *mozo* (servant) by our sides, in case our mules should slip going up the steep ascent. Old Salomi, my *mozo*, was also keeper of the ammunition—a very important person. At the top of the Tuxpan we struck a long barren plateau of volcanic ash, and then descended into the great Barranca of Beltran, and kept some way along its "bench," a flat valley a mile wide, 500 feet below the upper plateau, with the river in a yet deeper cleft on the right, and beyond it the impenetrable mountains of Michoacan, full of robbers and "mountain lions."

The trees were full of parrots, and of the *chachalapa*, a handsome game-bird, as large as a cock-pheasant, with a curious double larynx, which enables it to produce a hideous noise. Everywhere the Alamanda was in blossom, and Baby's black head was soon decorated with bunches of its lovely yellow flowers. Passing the little village of Platanar, with 500 inhabitants, we turned down through a stream, then up to the high land again; and at Agosto struck the first pinery, at an elevation of 3500 to 4200 feet above sea-level. They seemed to me much like the common Rocky Mountain pine; only the tufts of needles are larger and longer, and have a kind of debilitated droop, like those of the Sierra Nevada.

Soon we came to the regular pine barrens; and rode through them for some miles, passing two immense trains of mules. We met and passed during the day's journey 1000 animals, loaded with an average of 300 lbs. each, or a total of 150 tons. Some of these were carrying salt, sugar, dry goods, groceries, hardware, rum, coffee, rice, and timber, from the coast to Guadalajara, and other towns of the table-lands. Others were loaded with soap from Zapotlan, crockery from Guadalajara, cotton goods, potatoes, etc., bound for Colima and the coast.

These mule trains are continually robbed in passing the pine barrens; and whenever we came to a sandy *arroyo*, or gulch, we kept a sharp look-out. A band of robbers a week ago made this road almost impassable. They stopped every one who came along the road, and after robbing them, gagged them and bound them to the trees till night came; when they loosed one man, and, making off, left him to untie all his fellow-sufferers.

The heat and dust were unbearable; and, wearied out with climbing up and down the barrancas, we were truly thankful to reach the last of them, the barranca de Atenquique, at the bottom of which is a "*paradero*," or stopping-place. Here the mules and horses were unladen, and trotted off to the stream, where they stamped about in the cool water to escape the flies. We meanwhile rested outside a miserable palm-thatched hut, as the house was too filthy to enter; and tried to get something to eat for luncheon, as we were nearly starved. The mistress of the house, a great fat dirty woman, brought out some "*mole de guajulote*;" namely, turkey stewed till it is almost black, in a sauce of red pepper so intensely hot that one feels as if one were positively eating fire. Some of our party, whose throats were hardened to Mexican cookery, thought this excellent: but we wretched ladies wept involuntary tears after a bit the size of a six-pence; and as Atenquique produced nothing else, we set to work to forage in our own luncheon basket for anything that might be left therein. To our joy we discovered one tin of sardines remained; a few Albert biscuits of Mackenzie and Middlemass—a strange place for Scotch biscuits to get to!—and a bottle of Burgundy. It was quite sour: but that did not matter a bit. Then I plucked up courage, went into the filthy hut, and with Severo's help manufactured some tea in an earthen pipkin, which was very reviving; and thus we got our luncheon. The pigs grunted round our feet: the chickens, whom their fat mistress called "Jews of Pollos," flew over our cups and plates: a large dog jumped in and out of the low door away across our laps; and the picture of discomfort was completed when a horrible beggar woman came and joined the group.

This barranca joins the Tuxpan about a quarter of a mile below the road, and from that point the Tuxpan winds to the south and south-east. To any one accustomed to the magnificent cañons of Colorado, I must say that these barrancas, though very grand, are certainly disappointing. But we, perhaps, are hardly fair judges, as we passed them in the dry season; even from the flowers and ferns which we then saw we got a faint idea of the magnificent vegetation which covers their sides during the rainy season, when each little thread of water has turned into a foaming torrent, with tropical trees covered with flowering creepers growing down to the water's edge.

At the top of the barranca, 4030 feet above the sea, we found an old "mud waggon," with five mules, waiting for us; and, with a warning from the chief of our escort to have all arms in readiness, as the road was swarming with robbers, we set off for fifteen miles jolting into Zapotlan.

The road was indescribable, through sandy tracks in the pineries, creeping along at three miles an hour, for we took five hours to do that wretched fifteen miles. Then out of the forest and into a fresh misery, in the shape of our first "*pedregal*," or stony place. A pedregal is a series of lava screes, where the hot lava has run over the country from some one of the innumerable volcanos which, active or extinct, appear all over Mexico. This one, where the road crosses it thirteen miles from Atenquique, is 4970 feet above the sea, so that we had been rising steadily since leaving the Barrancas. It was a wild tract, a mile or more wide, of horrible lava rocks, among low scrub of mimosa and nopal (prickly pear), and in the very rocks themselves, where nothing else would grow, nestled the most exquisite cacti of endless variety. Our escort previously had all agreed in assuring us that the pedregal was the most likely place on the whole road for the robbers to attack us, so that our feelings were not exactly comfortable when we discovered that they and our mules had gone round by another road a quarter of a mile off, and just at that moment our wretched old coach, as the mules tried to drag it up a great step of rock, broke down utterly. The cochero got down; the muchacho got down; we all got out; everybody suggested something different; and I retired to a convenient rock near by with one of the rifles, and tried to imagine what I should do if the robbers pounced upon us. At last the escort came up, their mouths full of some sweet fruit, something like a yellow plum, which they found on a tree near by; and, after gallantly presenting us with some of their spoils, the united energies of the whole party succeeded in dragging the stage over the rock, tying up the broken part with cord, and on we went again, arriving at Zapotlan at 5 P.M.

Zapotlan, April 6.—In a town with Pronunciados all round us, advancing from all sides, expecting their arrival to-night, and not knowing how we shall get out—such is our state at 12 A.M.

When we arrived at the hotel yesterday at five, even before we could get out of the coach, a gentleman rushed to the door to ask if we had come from Colima, and if we knew anything of Don Julio Garcia and his movements. We of course knew nothing: but later in the evening came startling news.

The day after we left Colima it was attacked by the Pronunciados under Julio Garcia. The colonel of the Government troops was wounded.

This morning the news is confirmed: but Don Julio was "whipped," and is now retreating in this direction, to join forces, as they suppose, with La Bastida, another rebel chief who is coming down from Seyula. The telegraph line has been cut between here and Colima. The operator there managed to send the news through, and then Don Julio caught him, maltreated him, and destroyed the wires. They expect that he may arrive here this afternoon or evening. This morning, scouting parties are out all round the town, and the troops are all under arms: but they would not do much good in case of an attack, for their rule is to retreat to the barracks under such circumstances, and shutting themselves up securely, to leave the town in the hands of the revolutionists.

Nobody seems to mind much. There is no excitement, and things are going on much as usual. The women are sitting on the pavement selling fruit and flowers. The men are lounging about, gossiping over the fountain, or drinking "*pulque*" from carved calabashes in the *fondas*. The very soldiers are loitering at *posada* doors. And all this, with an enemy advancing from two sides: not to kill them, it is true, but to levy a heavy sum on their city, and take what they will.

All we can do is to wait quietly for the stage, in which we start to-morrow at 1 A.M.; pray that Don Julio may be detained; and eat water-melons.

We are advised to hide all our arms for fear of the Pronunciados, till we get to Zacoalco, where the danger of meeting them ceases, and the real danger from the robbers begins. The former, every one says, will not annoy us at all if we meet them: but would of course take our arms if they could get them, and search for Government mails or property. But the robbers between St. Ana Acatlan and Guadalajara are a very different matter. The stage is robbed by them nearly every day. Yesterday it came through safe: but the day before it was attacked by fourteen robbers, and the seven passengers were robbed of all they had. They did not make any resistance, and had no escort, both of which protections we shall have. That makes a great difference; and Don Ramon V., to whom kind Don Juan F. H. has given us introductions, and who is going to lend us the captain of his own private escort, says that he has no doubt that we shall get through perfectly safe.

I have discovered that the young man who greeted us so eagerly yesterday on our arrival, had good cause for his anxiety about Colima. He is the son of a wealthy "haciendado" near here; and accompanied with three servants splendidly armed and mounted, was on his way down to Colima to be married. This morning he got a message from his father, forbidding him under present circumstances to go on; so he has had to turn back and go home again, leaving his poor bride waiting disconsolately among the cotton bales with which they have fortified Colima, till Don Julio clears out, and her lover can travel in safety.

Our gentlemen intended to go off at five this morning on a reconnaissance down to Tuxpan, a fifty miles' ride: but as Don Julio is advancing just that way, they had of course to give it up: so we had a good sleep and breakfast at nine, an unheard-of luxury in this country of early rising. But our rooms—what would you at home think of them? They are just like prisons; very high, without a vestige of a window. Heavy wooden doors, barred like barn-doors, open into the courtyard, into which all the mules, horses, and stages come: the floors are brick, and the walls roughly painted. The furniture of my room consists of a chair and table of the very rudest kind, and three beds, which were all so dirty that it took me some time to settle which I would take possession of. But there were clean sheets; and with my own blankets to cover the filthy mattress, I soon forgot about everything, and had the soundest night's sleep I have had for a long while.

Some of the party, as they could not make the long expedition to Tuxpan, rode out about five miles to the hacienda of Huascalapa. "From this point," says one of them, "which is on the very verge of the Tierra Caliente, we obtained a good view of the country lying south, towards the Tuxpan river. It is a large plain, covered with plantations, producing all the fruits of the tropics; sugar, coffee, cotton, rice, bananas, etc. From this plain the country rises gradually to Huascalapa, a large stock farm, whose lands in the direction of the volcano are well timbered with pine, oak, cebano (a hard constructing wood), and roble, a kind of red oak. Huascalapa, and the country to the north, produces corn, wheat, barley, frijoles, and all fruits of the *Templadas*, or temperate zone."

This morning General P. and I took a walk round the town. It is a thriving place, of 25,000 inhabitants, standing at a height of 4900 feet, on the slope of some hills overlooking a magnificently rich plain, on the further side of which, to the east of south, rises the Volcan de Colima, or, as they call it here, " de Zapotlan." The streets are much wider and better than those of Colima, and the plazas are larger, though not so pretty. The Plaza Grande, on which our hotel is, has oleanders and oranges round it, and a few large shade trees, which seem to be a kind of ash. Low houses, with arcades painted white, pink, and blue, run round it; and the tower and walls of a splendid old church stand in one corner. They are building a new one of fine grey lava close to it. The city must be extremely old, judging by the pillars of lava one sees about the streets, and which look like what we should consider in England Roman work.

This is the first place where we have risen high enough into the Tierra Templada to meet with the maguey, or great American Agave, from which *Pulque*, the national beverage of the Mexicans, is manufactured.

We tasted some pulque: but I think it was sour, for it was a good deal thicker than it usually is. It was white, and felt in one's mouth like a crisp kind of cream: but tasted like yeast, with a flavour of pigskin; and I did not feel at all inclined to acquiesce in the Mexican song, in which some enthusiastic pulque-drinker says that "it is preferred by the angels to wine!"

Zapotlan has another trade, which supports a large number of its inhabitants; for it is the head-quarters of the soap manufacture, and supplies nearly the whole of the Western States of Mexico. The *Tequesquite* or impure carbonate of soda or potash used in this manufacture is found round the lagoons of Seyula and Zacoalco. As much as 100,000 *cargas* of 350 lbs. each are annually freighted from these lagoons to Zapotlan, Guadalajara, and a few intermediate places.

There are some very good shops; and a pretty market, with heaps of peppers, tomatos, limes, zapotes, etc., on the ground, shaded by a square of "*tule*" matting on a stick, something like a Chinese umbrella. This matting is made from the *tule* reed, which grows in all the fresh-water lagoons, and is plaited by the Indians into mats, which are called "*petates*," and also into "*tompiates*," baskets the shape of a bucket, and of every size from that of a tea-cup to a bushel, which are used throughout the Republic for holding and carrying all manner of stores. Under an arcade, Indian girls were selling flowers; and we took home to Mrs. P. a quantity of red and white frangipani (*Plumieria*) flowers, of which they had great saucers-full pulled off the stalks.

This morning at breakfast, Severo, the "master of the horse," brought in to Mrs. P. and me a great bunch of poppies and stocks. He had observed how eager we were for any flowers we saw, and the good-natured fellow had been out to the market to get these for us. He is a very fine-looking man—a fair Spaniard, six feet high, with blue eyes and light hair. His dress is a magenta shirt, with black in front; buckskin pantaloons, with rows of silver buttons and black embroidery down the leg; a short embroidered buckskin jacket; a rainbow-coloured scarf round his throat; a black belt, with silver-mounted pistol; and a sombrero, with silver embroidery—altogether one of the most effective costumes I ever saw.

Guadalajara, April 8.—Thank God, we are here safe at last! and I hope we may never have to go through another such day of anxiety, and perhaps danger, as yesterday.

After about four hours' sleep, the second night at Zapotlan, I was woke by sundry thumps on my prison-door, and the voice of a mozo calling, " *Las doce y media,*" half-past twelve. I jumped up, and, by the light of a miserable wax-candle dressed myself, and found my way through waggons and mules, and sleeping Indios in the patio, to the *sala*, where the sleepy "*amo*" (host) had prepared us chocolate and sweet bread.

By 2 A.M. all was ready, and with no feeling of regret we bade farewell to Zapotlan, and started in a regular American 'Concord' stage-coach. We were a party of nine ourselves, as Severo, and Galindo the captain of Don Ramon V.'s private escort, have come through with us. Our only other fellow-passenger was an old Señora, the mother of the Colonel of Zapotlan, who sat in a corner by me, and puffed cigarettes all the day long.

For the first part of the road we kept our arms out, as there are some bad places between Zapotlan and Seyula. There was no light for a couple of hours, except from the stars; but we could not sleep; every nerve seemed strained to catch some sight or sound which might denote robbers, and the Southern Cross shining down on us in its calm beauty seemed almost a mockery of our disturbed and anxious feelings. Where we stopped to change mules especially, we were on the look-out, as the "*ladrones*" are very fond of making a rush upon the coach as it stands still. A regular plan was arranged in case of an attack. We were all to fire at once, without giving them time to come near. "Fire low and keep cool" were the orders. Then we ladies, if the ruffians did not run at once, were to throw ourselves on the floor, and fire from under cover, while the gentlemen got out to fight.

Our road led us up and over a steep divide, some miles from Zapotlan; and just before dawn, as we were going down the further side, between high cactus hedges, we had a "scare;" for in the grey light we saw a man drop suddenly into the ditch behind us. He was evidently on the lookout for us, but not liking the muzzles of the rifles out of the windows, let us go by untouched. At sunrise we reached Seyula, a pretty old town, and changed mules. Here the news was worse and worse. The Government troops were marching south on the town; beyond them the Pronunciados were in force on the road; and beyond them again the country was swarming with robbers in bands of any number from two to two hundred.

Leaving Seyula, all the arms were hidden, in hopes of saving them should the Pronunciados catch us. The rifles were wrapped in a *serape*, and stowed under the back seat; but we kept our pistols on us, concealing them under our clothes.

A little way from the town we struck the Lago de Seyula, a salt lake, with soda flats all round. A few miles along the lake we met the Government troops, a fine body of cavalry, and their colonel confirmed the reports of the road we had heard. The alkali dust was perfectly choking, scorching the very skin; and we muffled our faces in handkerchiefs, and so jolted on hour after hour over rocks and gulleys, and in one place through half a mile of heaps of broken pottery, layer upon layer, several feet thick, imbedded in loose sandy soil, till at 11 A.M. we drove into the village of Cebollas (onions).

We pulled up in front of a poor-looking house, with a young fellow lolling on the window-seat, where breakfast was preparing, of which we were in need, as a cup of chocolate was all we had tasted since five o'clock the day before. Severo and Galindo were left to guard the coach, and we dragged our stiffened limbs across the patio and into the house, where two or three women received us with great *empressement*, and gave us Zapotlan soap and water to wash off a little of the dust from our scorched and blistering faces, and then sat down to a most uninviting meal of omelet and "*carne seca*" (dried beef). Just as we did so, however, we heard a clatter in the court-yard, and in rode two Pronunciados and dismounted. In a minute, two more and an officer appeared in front of the windows; and they then sent in word they wished " our permission " to search the coach for arms. Those of the gentlemen who were not out already went out instantly. Every possible argument was used: but Chavarin, the major, said he had orders to come and take the rifles. Expostulation was in vain; resistance out of the question; for, though we could easily have overpowered this party, they were but the outpost of another body. So, with dismay, Mrs. P. and I next saw the five rifles and two pistols handed in through the window, to be taken by the women who were serving us, and stowed away in an inner room. It was evidently a prearranged thing, and the whole pack were in league,—the women were so very reassuring to us in the way they hovered about us while all this was going on, begging the " Señoritas to fear nothing, there was no danger ;" and the young man in the window, who watched us so closely, and then disappeared, I cannot help fancying was in the secret also. In fact, we found out afterwards that our party and their precious repeating rifles had been watched and followed all the way from the coast.

After a long argument, " Major" Chavarin gave us back the two pistols—all the others were safe under our clothes— and promised to go with us and meet his colonel, who, he said, was about a mile up the road, and confer with him about giving us back the rifles. He came in to breakfast with us, and, as he sat by me, my feelings alternated strangely towards him, as he seemed so embarrassed that

I could not help being sorry for him; and then, thinking of the loss of our arms, I wished—well, some wishes are best unspoken. He was dressed in a linen jacket, and high embroidered boots over linen pantaloons; was well armed; and on his left wrist wore a suggestive bracelet—a leather strip about an inch wide, ornamented with a hundred or more copper caps. His men were a despicable set of ruffians, in any kind of dress over military trousers, wretchedly armed with old muzzle-loading carbines, and all drunk.

We set off again with heavy hearts, which were not lightened when we got to the place which Chavarin had spoken of as his colonel's post, and he rode up to say that his colonel had been obliged to go off to Zacoalco, and had left a scout to tell him; so there was an end of our rifles. He promised, however, to escort us through the worst bit of robber country near St. Ana Acatlan, and half promised that he would there give back two of the rifles. So on we drove in blazing sun over the alkali plains by the side of the lakes, choked and scorched with the dust, which seemed to blister the skin as it touched, and watched the lake on our left with reflections of the trees towards Zacoalco in its bright water, which rippled on the shore. Suddenly some one said—

"Why, there are clouds of dust blowing across the lake!"

And as he spoke the water began to fade away as we drew nearer, and we found it was nothing but a horrible waste of soda sand, and that our rippling lake was only mirage.

That mirage and the word *Cebollas* will always call up unpleasant associations in my mind as long as I live; for as we were looking out at this strange sight, up rode three of the Pronunciados, and said that the Major had been obliged to turn back, and that they must go too, being alarmed at a cloud of dust ahead, which they thought must be Government troops, and would like our ammunition.

That, of course, was refused; and fearing they might get a *recuerdo* from our revolvers, they sneaked off, leaving us comparatively defenceless at the very edge of the bad country. There was nothing for it but to get on as fast as possible. Three of the gentlemen got outside the coach; Mrs. P. gave her pistol to Galindo, and I mine to Señor A., as they were now unarmed. So each man had a pistol, thirty-six shots in all; and I kept the ammunition in my lap, to be ready to load again if need be.

We turned from the horrible alkali plains, with their dancing lakes of mirage, along a road between stone walls and bushes. On the hillside all the trees had been burnt or cut, to leave no shelter. How we strained our eyes at each gap, expecting to be pounced upon every instant! We soon stopped for a *remuda* at a village of three or four huts, and then saw a white rag on the hill. The people said, "Oh, it was only clothes washing:" but General R. went up and found it was tied on to a rail stuck upright—a rather curious way of washing clothes. Then we were made to barricade ourselves with cushions and valises, with orders if firing began, to throw ourselves flat down and heap the blankets over us. The gentlemen got out and went ahead in a skirmish line up the hill for a mile or so: but nothing befell us. When they stopped, the poor *cochero* entreated them to go inside, for he said, "If we are attacked, and you fire, and make me drive on instead of stopping, as Mexicans always do, to allow the coach to be robbed, then the robbers will certainly shoot me as I come back to-morrow." So Mr. M. came inside: but the two Generals still stayed out, thinking our safety was more important than that of the hapless *cochero*.

The road wound along the foot of the hills, with a rich plain below us; fields of sugar-cane, maize, wheat, and grass, and large herds of cattle grazing. But we were almost too anxious to take much interest in statistics; and it was with no slight feeling of relief that we saw in about two hours more the town of Sta. Ana Acatlan ahead of us, and rattled through its street and market crowded with people.

At the diligence office we halted, and—thanks to the great kindness of Don Ramon V. of Zapotlan, who gave us letters to the Gefe Politico, or chief man of the town—we were provided with an excellent escort. In an hour twenty-eight trusty men, haciendados and rancheros, mounted on little tough spirited horses, and well armed with musket, pistol, and *machete* (a strong short sword), under the command of an old army officer, were assembled in the street ready to take us the whole way to Guadalajara. While the escort were assembling we tried to refresh ourselves a little with water-melons, and I made sketches of little boys, who came and stared with round black eyes at the American *señoritas*. The doorway of the house was a perfect study, carved in grey stone in the most delicate and elaborate way. Meanwhile the old señora, our companion, was holding quite a levee of friends, who came crowding up to the coach window to talk with her, and congratulate her on escaping so far the dangers of the road. She behaved admirably, good old lady, throughout: only whispering to me from time to time in a tone of despair "*Ah los bonitos rifles!*"—"The beautiful rifles!"

When all was ready, and we had persuaded a drunken Zouave, who said he had been left behind by the French, that we could not possibly give him a place in the coach to Guadalajara, as he desired, we clattered off through the streets and up a hill towards the Coronilla Mountain. At every turn we met ox and mule trains, who had all been robbed that day, the drivers giving different accounts of the number of the *ladrones*, and looking at us with pity.

But our good escort kept up gallantly, forming front and rear guard in the bad places, and dodging along to cut off corners in the safe ones; and so we crossed the Divide under the Coronilla in safety, where Mr. M. had himself seen two sets of travellers robbed. This mountain was the scene of a desperate encounter between the Imperialists and General Ramon Corona, who was advancing from Sinaloa with the Republican army of the West. The Imperialists were defeated, Corona's troops carrying their position at the point of the bayonet; and he arrived before Queretaro, which was then being besieged, in time to frustrate the success of the Emperor Maximilian's desperate sortie, which was made with a view of cutting his way out, and escaping to the Pacific coast *via* Morelia.

Down in the valley below we were told to be on the look-out; a robbery had been committed in the morning; and the ground was strewn with papers left from the plunder. Our escort formed in single file on either side of us, and some skirmished along behind a high cactus hedge, till we came to a robber-town, Santa Cruz; a miserable place, with *adobe* houses, for the most part roofless, looking quite worthy of their owners' trade. On the top of the church we saw four men evidently watching us, and outside the town two or three more on horseback sneaking off into the distance, thinking us too strong to be meddled with.

We climbed up and over another Divide, as the sun set blood-red behind the mountains, and passed the old Casa Fuerte, which used to be a military post: but now, because there is more need than ever of protection on the road, all the troops have been withdrawn.

At Santa Augustin, another robber-den, we stopped an hour after sunset to change horses, thankful for even a few minutes' rest from the jolting of the coach; and got a cup of chocolate, our escort halting close round us to prevent a rush on the coach, as armed men were hanging about the doors, looking at us with longing eyes. Then, with six stout ponies, on we went, getting snatches of sleep between the bits of pedregal; and I think I had been dozing some quarter of an hour when we stopped, and up rode the Captain to say we were to be very watchful, as we were coming to a bad barranca. It was a wild scene, as I rubbed my sleepy eyes open and looked out. We were tearing on with our half-broken ponies over an open sandy rise; our escort, with carbines unslung and ready to fire in a moment, galloped alongside, with their serapes over their shoulders to keep off the cold air, and most of them were masked with handkerchiefs to keep off the dust. After this place was passed in safety, we dozed off again from time to time, till, on coming to the city outposts, six miles from Guadalajara, we were stopped, and a " passport of arms" demanded by the picket. This we had not got: but when it was explained who and what we were, the sergeant in command let us go by, as one of the worst places was still to come, and to have passed it without arms would have been mere folly. Nothing, however, occurred, and at 10 P.M. we rattled down the streets of the capital of Jalisco, our muchacho on the box carrying a flaming torch, which left a trail of sparks behind him, and our faithful escort keeping close around us.

We pulled up at the Diligence Hotel to leave the old Señora; and having got us there, the proprietor was determined to keep us, and positively refused to allow the coach to take us on to the rival Hotel Hidalgo, where we intended to stay. Neither threats nor persuasion availed, and the mozos began taking off the luggage. We had, perforce, to alight, and had some difficulty in getting even a chair for Mrs. P. to rest upon, who was quite exhausted. Leaving some of the gentlemen to see to the luggage, we set off to walk to the Hidalgo, as it was past ten o'clock, and no hack-carriages were to be had. But our troubles were now over, for on our way we met the Commandante, Colonel U.; and in a moment more General C. himself, who took us straight to the house of some German gentlemen, which in deed, as well as word, was placed at "our disposal." And, supper over, we were thankful to go to our comfortable home-like rooms after twenty-three and a half hours' travelling.

CHAPTER XVI.

GUADALAJARA.

The Paseo—Barricades—The Belen Cemetery—Attractive baths—A fortunate escape—The Cathedral—Confessionals—*El Hospicio*—Señor Menesses—A clean kitchen—Embroidery—The *Casa*—A wonderful contralto—*Helados*—A wicked bull—Pottery—The opera—The States Prison—An embarrassing present—Mexican troops—How to make a *pronunciamiento*.

Guadalajara, April 10.—We are in perfect Paradise here after "roughing it" for so many days. Our hosts are kinder than words can say; and one almost forgets that there are such things as robbers and revolutions till one sees all the gentlemen and the coachmen going about with revolvers, and barricades across the streets for fear of the rebels making an attack.

The 8th was spent by Mrs. P. and me in resting and enjoying our host's excellent German piano, while the gentlemen received all the authorities, who paid them a long and satisfactory visit. Everywhere as yet the idea of a railroad has been received with acclamation.

In the afternoon at five we took a drive in a comfortable carriage, with a pair of fine mules. We went along the Paseo, a boulevard planted with trees, which runs all round the town. There are now only two points of egress from the city to the Paseo, as all the streets are barricaded with strong *adobe* (sun-dried brick) walls, very well done.

We passed in one street a church built in old days by the Indians. The whole front is carved in the most elaborate and beautiful way in brown lava; and as a pillar for the corner is a gigantic figure of St. Christopher, sixteen or twenty feet high, carrying the Infant Christ on his shoulder. From thence we drove to the Belen Cemetery, a strange place. It is inside immensely high, with thick walls. In these walls are niches, into which the coffins are put headforemost, with the name on a glass or stone door. Each niche is leased out for the space of five years; and if at the end of the time the lease is not renewed by the survivors, the coffin is taken out and cast away, and the niche let to some fresh person. In the centre of the cemetery is a fine building, with four avenues of orange-trees leading up to it, in which all the bishops and priests are buried.

The sun had set; the new moon, a mere silver thread, rose in the crimson sky over the pinnacles of the gateway, as we turned to go home: while away on the hill-tops we saw a bright fire, and wondered if it were not a signal of the robbers.

This cemetery is connected with the Belen Hospital— a vast building, covering I know not how much ground, with wards for sick and insane, and schools for children, within its walls, managed by Sisters of Mercy. Its revenues at one time were immense. But becoming impoverished through endless revolutions, it had almost fallen into ruin, when Bishop Portugal, some dozen years ago, rebuilt and reendowed it. We went all over it during our stay in Guadalajara; and though, thanks to the climate, the wards were tolerably fresh, with roses and oleanders and plumbago peeping in at the ever open windows, yet from what little I could see in half an hour, both medical skill and nursing knowledge are at rather a low ebb in the State of Jalisco.

When we got home, General C. and his beautiful American wife came to call on us. She really is kindness itself: but one offer she made us is so thoroughly characteristic of the state of the country, that I was immensely amused at it.

We were talking of the baths which abound round the city, and she said—

"You ought to go to the baths three miles from town; they are much better than those nearer; and it would be quite safe for you to go with a guard of half a dozen troopers, which the General would give you any day."

We thought that on those terms "*le jeu n'en vaut pas la chandelle,*" and with much laughter declined. The more we hear, the more thankful we are at having come through so far safely. General C. telegraphed to us to say we positively must not come, as he could not spare us a sufficiently strong escort; a small one would have compromised us with the Pronunciados, and nothing under 300 or 400 men would have made us really safe. He never received any of our telegrams, as the lines were all cut, and we of course could not get his.

Then again, by staying that one extra day in Zapotlan, we were saved from what befell the people who came through the day before us. The stage between Zapotlan and Sta. Ana was attacked and robbed by a large body of robbers. Everything was taken, and the ladies and children were actually stripped of all the clothes they had on, and sent on in the coach in this state.

This is a fact, horrible as it may seem: and yet here everything goes on as usual; and the men, instead of rising and sweeping such wretches from the face of the earth, lounge on the Plaza, listen to the band, shrug their shoulders, and say, "What a pity!"

Yesterday morning we took a walk about the city, Mrs. P. and I being stared at in the most disagreeable way, I suppose on account of our wearing hats, instead of mantillas or rebozos. Some one remarked that it is just the way the Chinese are stared at in New York,—a flattering comparison! The cathedral, to which we went first, was, I must confess, disappointing. It is a magnificent building, standing on the

Plaza: but, being built of adobe, which is much used here on account of its being safer, because more elastic than stone in case of earthquakes, the authorities have seen fit to paint it skyblue and yellow. So, like the houses, which are painted in the same way, it has a kind of gingerbread look.

Inside the cathedral there are altars to different saints or virgins along the sides, with life-size figures of the special

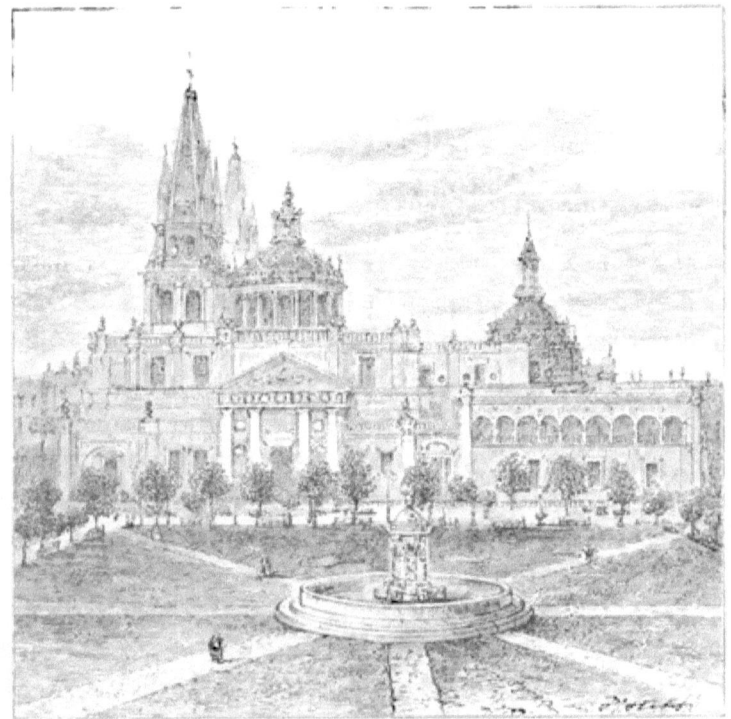

The Cathedral, Guadalajara.

saint by the side of each altar; they were really very fine; all coloured to imitate life, in perfect proportion and well executed.

By each altar also was its confessional-chair,—a carved wooden sentry-box, shaped like a chair; and in one sat an ill-looking priest, listening to a woman who was kneeling, her head completely covered in a black shawl. She made her confession through the side of the box; and the priest sat there, paying, it seemed, very little attention to her, but staring about and watching our movements with great interest. It was the most revolting form altogether of the Roman Catholic religion,—all its beauty gone, and nothing but the worst features left.

One priest actually came lounging into the choir, with a cigar in his mouth.

In the afternoon one of our hosts and Señor H., General C.'s A.D.C., drove with us to the *Hospicio de Guadalajara*, which was founded a hundred years ago by Bishop Juan Cruz Ruiz Cabanas; and is the most perfect institution of the kind I have seen in any country. It stands on a rise in the suburbs of the city, the other side of the little river, at the end of a long street. In the centre rises a magnificent dome over the chapel, round which all the buildings cluster. It covers between six and eight acres of ground; and there are twenty-five different gardens of flowers, each with a deep corridor running between the flower-beds and the rooms, which are built all round. Within its walls are 700 children of all ages, from the little foundling of a few days to the young workman of twenty. The Sisters of Charity who manage it received us at the door, and took us to the parlour, where we were joined by Señor Menesses, the maestro of the Opera and music-master of the Hospicio. He is a genius of whom the Guadalajarans are justly proud. At seventeen he wrote an opera, and sent it to Verdi for corrections, who returned it without altering a single note. He was good enough to play to us some marvellous variations of his own on Lucrezia Borgia, which were a triumph of execution. After this most pleasant prelude we went all over the institution, going first into the children's schools. Of these there are three degrees; one for the infants, mixed, from three to six years old; the next, also under two Sisters, for girls and boys, separate, to ground them; and the third for elder children, the boys of about eleven being passed on to a master.

Among the infants I was shown one jolly little English boy, whose father, a workman, had died out here, leaving this mite. He seemed perfectly happy, and had forgotten every word of English. In the department of the "*niños*," the boys were carpentering, making shoes, and weaving. All the clothes they wear they make themselves; and the cotton cloth and blue rebozos for the girls were perfectly woven.

The kitchen is a splendid room forty or fifty feet long, with a high dome in the centre, and two enormous ranges standing out in the middle of the floor covered with coloured tiles. They looked pleasantly familiar to me when I saw they came from "Leamington, England." The elder girls in turn do all the cooking, and anything so spotlessly clean as the kitchen I never saw. One might have literally eaten one's dinner with much greater comfort off the glazed red-tiled floor than off many of the tables we had had to be contented with in the last few weeks.

Everything and everybody looked happy. Flowers and birds were in all directions, and pets of all kinds, from a little chestnut-coloured pig to dogs and babies, roamed about wherever they pleased.

We had not time to go into the infirmary and the old people's department—an almshouse on a large scale—but went on to the girls' school. Here they were saying lessons, drawing, and embroidering. The drawing was very fair, but the embroidery in gold and silver thread on velvet was most beautiful. This is one of the Mexican specialities, and a pair of blue velvet slippers embroidered with the Mexican arms in fine gold thread would have held its own against most Indian embroidery. The maiden of fourteen or fifteen who was working it blushingly uncovered it to show us, and was perfectly enchanted at our admiration.

Through this department we went to the "*Cuna*" or nursery. Here there were thirty little foundlings, each with its own nurse. One was dressed up in white, just going to be baptized. It was found on the doorsteps six days ago by one of the Sisters as she opened the gates in the early morning. Poor little things! it was the saddest sight: but perhaps it is the best fate that could befall them, for they will be happy and well taken care of, and then started in a good position in life. All the foundlings save two or three were white. The poor Indios, low as they are, hardly ever abandon their children.

From the *Cuna* we went to the music-room, to hear Señor Menesses give his lesson to the girls. There were about twenty, from fourteen to nineteen years old. They sang first a chorus from the "Elisir d'Amor" with two soprano and one contralto solos, and then another from "Semiramide"—both perfectly rendered. Then the contralto sang us a scena from "Semiramide" quite splendidly. She has the finest contralto I have ever heard for depth, evenness, and quality; and with age—for she is not quite sixteen,—and the good teaching she is sure of, it will be something wonderful. These girls, as soon as their education is finished, if they do not marry, which many do at once, get first-rate situations as governesses; indeed, Señor H. told us the demand was much larger than the supply.

The last part we went to was the Collegio, where the "paying class" is taught. It is a large boarding-school for the sons and daughters of gentlemen from all the Western States of the Republic. Our dear old friend Don Juan F. H.'s son and two daughters are here. The son, a pretty little gentleman-like fellow, came to see us: but the daughters were away with the Superior at a watering-place on Lake Chapala, where the Guadalajarans go for bathing. We went away at six, after a two hours' visit, thoroughly delighted, and very much astonished by all we had seen.

In the evening, as two fine bands were playing on the Plaza, we all went out and walked round with hundreds of other people, or sat under the orange-trees, listening in a delicious, lazy, dreamy way to the music till near ten, when we adjourned to the saloon for "*helados*" (ices). The ice comes from Cuyuitlan, only two leagues from here, a place about 5000 feet above the sea-level. It is made by putting the water in little pits at night; and by the excessive radiation of heat it becomes ice by morning.

Wednesday morning.—General P., Mrs. P., and I drove out at eight to "*los Banos del Agua Azul*,"—the blue water.

They are a quarter of a mile from town; and in the bath-house, outside which climb Banksia roses and heliotrope, are five large swimming baths of spring water, which bubbles up from the pebbly floor. The water, about four feet deep, is never cold, and myriads of little fish swim in the baths, and nibble one most unmercifully.

As were we going to drive away after a delightful swim, we heard shouts and galloping, and towards us, over the green meadows and gardens, came a big bull, pursued by two or three men riding with lazzos. The bull was determined not to be caught, and made for a deep dike close to the baths, through which he got in some unaccountable way. It was much too deep and wide for the horsemen to follow him; and he was trotting away tail erect, and looking as wild and wicked as only a triumphant bull can, when one of the lads threw himself from his horse, tore off most of his clothes, and, lazzo in hand, cast himself into the muddy dike. He emerged on the other side, as black as the wicked boys after St. Nicholas's ink-pot: away he ran after the bull; and the last we saw was the pursued and pursuer disappearing in the far distance among the rolling meadows: but we never heard whether the bull was caught.

After breakfast I went out with Mr. M. to do some commissions for his wife under the Portales. There are excellent shops, full of American and European goods; while at the *cajons*, on the pavement under the Portales, goods of the country are sold, as in Colima. But here they have one manufacture which neither Colima or any other city in Mexico can boast of to a like degree. I mean pottery. It is made in every shape and for every use, and is so cheap one can hardly understand how it pays to make it. I got at one of the *cajons* two or three handfuls of the tiny models of the larger pots and jugs and basins which are made as toys for the children, and a perfect Noah's ark collection of tarantulas, *alacrans* (scorpions), ducks, cocks, cranes, and nameless birds and beasts, painted the colour of life, except, I think, one monkey, half an inch high, who rejoiced in a red and blue coat and a yellow head. All these, delicately painted and finished, I got for the enormous sum of 16 cents, or 8d. English. We went to one Plaza, where a regular crockery market is held, and there laid in an immense store of the different wares. I bought a large black water-bottle, beautifully painted, with gold and silver patterns, and quantities of smaller jugs, pots, and tazzas of endless varieties, some in the same black and gold, others grey with gold tracery. One water-jar which seemed in great favour was in the shape of a grey pig with golden snout and tail, and a hole in his back through which the water was poured.

But my greatest treasure I got quite by accident. One morning one of our hosts came and said, "Here is an old Indio who is famous for painting pottery, and he has brought the only things he has by him at present."

Out I flew to see, and there found a pair of exquisite jars about fifteen inches high, with quaint covers. The ground was a delicate pinky grey, on which were painted patterns of eagles, deer, trees, and buildings in black, gold, and silver. I thought, of course, they would be quite ruinously expensive, and asked the price in fear and trembling. What was my amazement, therefore, when the old man humbly asked 6 *reales* (3s.)! The bargain was concluded without hesitation, and the old fellow went off delighted with his miserable payment. Mr. S., who had been standing by, thought me wildly extravagant, and said it was preposterous, and that I ought to have got them for half the sum: but I was far too pleased with my treasures to grudge the old Indio a farthing, and indeed they would have been well worth ten times the money.

The Guadalajarans also make very good figures of their pottery; and, thanks again to the kindness of our hosts, we carried away a very good collection of "*Typos del Pais*"—types of the native costumes. They are six to ten inches high, and very well made; dressed exactly like the different classes of the people, who each have their distinguishing dress. One which I got was a portrait of a well-known "*Alcalde*" (chief man) of a village a few miles from Guadalajara; and it is, so said those who knew him, an excellent portrait, as he stands with his cigarette in his mouth just ready to light it with the slow match in his hand.

This pottery is sent from Guadalajara all over the Republic.

On Wednesday evening our whole party with General and Mrs. C. went to the opera. An Italian troupe are staying in the city, who gave "Rigoletto" very well indeed. La Visconti as Gilda was charming. She has a pretty sweet voice, though it is not very strong, and her singing and acting are excellent. Verati, the Duke, has a nice voice, and sang "La Donna é mobile" well; and the quartett with Grossi as Rigoletto could hardly have been better rendered anywhere.

Between the acts we went out into the corridor, where a good many of the ladies were smoking cigarettes, as a matter of course. We however only refreshed ourselves with ices brought round by little barefooted black-eyed boys. The opera-house is a huge building, and when finished will hold

4000 people; at present it only seats 1600. Last night it was miserably empty, and the empty boxes looked all the worse from the fact that there are no seats in them, as every one who comes has to bring his own chair, like a snail with his house. There are five rows of boxes, one above the other, and the original plan was to make the columns between each box of crystal. However, as one political party or another has come into power from time to time they have appropriated the building funds for their own uses; and so the idea of crystal columns has had to be given up, white marble ones being now put in their stead.

Friday we went to pay a visit to the States Prison, in hopes of finding some lace which we had been told was made there. However, there was no lace to be got in the women's quarters, where we went first, and Mrs. P. so little liked the looks of the men who appeared on the other side of the double iron gate through which our guide wished to take us, that she went back to the carriage. But I was curious to see the prison, and so went on with Señor A. and the turnkey. The prison is built on a peculiar principle: long streets of cells radiating from a common centre, so that the priest standing in the middle can preach to all the prisoners at once. I confess when the heavy bolts turned, and I found myself the only European among such an assemblage, I rather repented not having followed Mrs. P.'s example. The prisoners were making hats and baskets of palm-leaf, and crowded round me in such a way that I was rather alarmed. However, poor fellows, they were very civil, though their curiosity at the white-faced Señorita knew no bounds. They wanted to load me with their little manufactures, and it was only by desperate exertions on Señor A.'s part, and assurances that I was going across the sea, that I was not forced to carry off a cardboard house covered with powdered stone, besides various other equally trying inventions. One man, however, would take no refusal, and insisted on giving me a pair of pretty little fine baskets of his own making; and when Señor A. told me in English I must take them, and I accepted the gift, the poor fellow's delight and triumph knew no bounds. But I was not at all sorry to get out of the double gates, between which some prisoner was receiving a visit from his wife and child, and regain fresh air and liberty.

At dinner we were startled by a military band striking up outside, in the Calle San Francisco, and found that as it was the last day of our stay at Guadalajara, it had been sent to play under the windows by kind General C. Later in the afternoon he sent the troops round, and we all went out in the balcony, and watched them march past the house. They were short and small, slouching along with heads hanging down, and muskets all criss-cross anyhow, as thoroughly unsoldierlike a body of men as I ever saw. But the reason is, I believe, that they are all Indios, who, by fair means or foul, are pressed into the service. Hardly any enlist of their own free-will, much preferring the promises of the chief of any revolutionary party, of large pay and plunder, to the small pay and hard work of the Government. ———— made us laugh by an account he gave us of how he could raise a body of Pronunciados :—

"I have only to go out on market or *fiesta* day, and call the people round me, and say, 'Now you shall have as much *pulque* as you like, and I will give you four reals a day if you will pronounce for me;' and then I give them *pulque*, and they all get drunk, and then I draw my sword and I make them a speech about '*la Patria*' and '*Libertad*,' and they all pronounce, and then there is a revolution."

CHAPTER XVII.

UP THE VALLEY OF THE LERMA.

The Rio Grande de Santiago—Ocotlan—Ordering dinner—The robbers—La Barca—An escape—A luxurious bed—Dug-out canoes—Buena Vista—A dead robber—Wine-growing and pedregal—"*Una Señorita tan grande*"—The faithless negro—Farms and farming—The Padre's "boys"—An indigestible meal—Hanging a robber—Irapuato—Molasses candy—Swape wells—Cereus and nopals—Salamanca—Singing birds—The churches of Celaya—Indian music—A story of the "*Plagiarios*"—Peru pepper—Jumping cactus—A pretty leap—Approach to Queretaro.

April 13.—Guadalajara to Ocotlan.

At 6.15 A.M. we left hospitable Guadalajara, carrying away none but the pleasantest reminiscences of our stay of six days.

Pablo, a pleasant young fellow, who had been our *cochero* in Guadalajara, came with us as *mozo*, and was in a state of supreme delight at being armed with a Henry rifle and revolver. Mr. M. also came with us as far as La Barca.

The usual route from Guadalajara to the capital is by La Venta, Lagos, Leon, and Guanaguato; but for two reasons we chose the more southern route, past Lake Chapala and up the Rio Lerma. First, because the engineer's party from the north (of whom we had heard nothing as yet, which made us very anxious) must pass along that route, and so be able to give a report on it. Secondly, because we were told the Chapala route was shorter and better, if there can be anything "better" in one Mexican road than another. Certainly, after the first few miles it was bad enough—rough and stony, and in the softer places there were clouds of dust.

At San Pedro we stopped and got three men as escort, and at 9.30 came to San Antonio, a hacienda where we changed mules, and had breakfast in a hut by the roadside. The women in the hut, which was only made of sticks and thatch, gave us eggs, frijoles, tortillas, and *carne seca*, in *chilli colorado* sauce, which for hotness almost beat the *mole de guajalote* at Atenquique. But besides these native viands we got capital chocolate, made from some cakes we had brought with us. So, on the whole, we fared well.

At 12.15 we came to the summit of a small pass (4850 feet), and there before us lay a splendid valley, rich with golden wheat-fields, with a fine river flowing through it on our left to the north-west; and we knew we had struck the great central valley of Mexico, commonly known as the Valley of the Lerma.

This valley is one of the richest portions of the Republic. Its length, between Guadalajara and Queretaro, is about 230 miles, and its greatest width (between Leon and the mountains of Michoacan), 60 miles. About one-tenth of the available land in it is under cultivation. Wheat, maize, and beans grow freely without irrigation, yielding good crops year after year without the slightest pains being taken to improve the soil. With irrigation and better farming two crops might be obtained; and when a market for the produce, and easy means of transportation are supplied, this tract will become one of the most important wheat-growing districts of the world. The amount of wheat which could be raised in this valley alone has been variously estimated from 500,000 to 1,000,000 tons yearly, equal to or surpassing the whole yearly yield of California.

The river rises in the Lago de Lerma, near Toluca, outside the western rise of the Valley of Mexico; and from its source, till it flows into the eastern side of Lake Chapala at La Barca, is known as the Rio Lerma. It passes out of the northern side of Chapala at Ocotlan, and from thence to San Blas, where it falls into the Pacific, is called the Rio Grande de Santiago. North of Chapala the Santiago flows through a very deep cañon; and there are also two fine falls on it— one a horse-shoe fall; and another about twenty miles from Guadalajara, of which I saw a photograph, which the Guadalajarans consider only second to Niagara.

The valley, as we jolted along it, seemed one vast cornfield. High mountains lay on the north, and our road ran along a southern ridge which divided the valley from Lake Chapala. There was very little timber on the mountains, and in what little there was many fires were burning, for everything is as dry as tinder.

At 4.30 P.M. we left the hills; crossing a bridge over a branch of the Santiago, where the Indian women were filling their water-jars, and swimming about in the water like a shoal of fish; and reached Ocotlan, a large hacienda two miles from Lake Chapala.

We stopped here, intending only to get a relay and go on the last stage to La Barca: but Mrs. P. was ill, so we decided upon staying there for the night. The owner in Guadalajara had given our party letters to his Administrador, so we were most kindly received, and rooms instantly prepared for us. The hacienda was the prettiest we had seen. The centre of the patio was filled with a garden of the loveliest flowers and shrubs imaginable; roses, carnations, plumbago, oleanders, oranges, and bananas growing together in wild luxuriance; and on one side was a high tower, with shaky steps and shakier ladders leading to the top, up which I followed the rest, after seeing to our invalid, and was rewarded by a glorious view.

North and west were the mountains, with the forest fires flickering up and down their slopes. South we got a glimpse of the lake, beyond a rich flat with various branches of the river winding down round the little town. East stretched away a valley through endless hills. A thunderstorm was raging over the mountains of Michoacan, on the further side of the lake. The sun was setting behind the mountains we had passed, in a perfect glory of crimson and gold; and over our heads, so close we stretched our hands to catch them, flew flocks of black rice-birds, thousands upon thousands, in a ceaseless stream, to the eastward.

But we were hungry, and supper seemed as if it never would come; and when it did come at last, though excellent for strong people, yet there was nothing fit for our invalid; so Pablo and I went off to the kitchen, to see what could be done. I gave him orders, in abominable Spanish, interlarded with signs. These he, in turn, translated as he thought best, to the half dozen women who were scuttling about the kitchen, making as much fuss as if they were preparing dinner for a regiment; and at last, strange to say, I succeeded in getting some eggs properly boiled, which I carried off in triumph.

The Administrador came in to supper, and gave us the latest "*novedades*," which here means robber stories. The Pronunciados have been giving him a good deal of trouble lately. About two weeks ago they came down on the hacienda, made a levy of thirty dollars; and as he did not pay fast enough, they carried off his corn and sold it.

As to the robbers, they are getting the worst of it thereabouts. There was a family of robbers near by, who attacked the neighbouring rancheros (small farmers), carrying off their flocks and produce; and about fifteen days ago, the rancheros, unable to stand it any longer, got together in force, attacked the robbers, and killed the whole family, father, sons, and cousins, save one, who was badly wounded. Next day, as the victors were carrying off their prisoner, other robbers appeared to the rescue; so the rancheros killed the wounded man, and a few of the fresh robbers; the rest ran away: and they got off all safe themselves.

After supper came a delicious lazy lounge in the corridor while the gentlemen smoked, with the air full of the scent of roses and orange-blossom, and then I went off to my room in intense heavy heat, and tried to sleep on a bed which almost rivalled those at San Marcos for hardness.

April 14.—Ocotlan, 4875 feet, to Piedad, 5400 feet.

At 6.15 A.M. we started, with the Administrador and four of his men, well armed and mounted, as escort. In about two miles, after crossing various bridges, we struck the lake (its level is 4850), and drove eastward along its shore for nearly two hours. Here it is between twenty and thirty miles wide, and on the further side the mountains of Michoacan rise in grand rugged masses to a considerable height. Between the water and the road runs a narrow stony strip, which the Indians have irrigated thoroughly, and where they raise fine crops of chilli, tomatos, sweet potatoes, and cucumbers.

At 7.30 we passed Tamein, a town of 3000 inhabitants, who get their living chiefly by fishing and gardening; raising, besides cattle, corn and wheat.

Soon after this we turned away from the lake, which here makes a southerly bend; cut off a corner of some miles; and reached La Barca, on the Rio Lerma, just above where it flows into the lake, at 9.30.

It was market-day, and the Plaza was densely crowded with a noisy mass of buyers and sellers. We stayed there for breakfast. The food was very good at a dirty little *Fonda* (restaurant) close to the stage-office; all the walls of which were decorated with little bits of Guadalajara pottery, hung in patterns round some larger bowl or plate. We heard here of a most fortunate escape we had had the night before. When we stopped at Ocotlan, a courier from a house of business in Guadalajara, who had ridden beside us all day, went on, thinking we had only halted to change mules. A few miles on he fell into an ambush of robbers, who robbed him; beat him within an inch of his life; and asked where the stage was. He declared it was but three or four miles behind. "Well," they said, "we will keep you here; and if it doesn't come we will kill you." In the night, however, he got to his horse, and managed to escape to La Barca; where some of our party heard his story.

Our stage had to be conveyed across the river in two dug-out canoes, a difficult operation, as the canoes are made of a single log, scooped out into the semblance of a boat. Two of these had to be put side by side, and the stage run into them, two wheels in each boat, and so ferried over. This took some time; so, after breakfast, I had time for a sleep, and found that, under some circumstances, two chairs, with a couple of loaded rifles across them, make a tolerable bed; and I got a comfortable nap, with my hand on my revolver, though the door was crowded with beggars and muchachos, and the floor was so alive with creeping things that I had perforce to keep my feet off it.

We walked down to the river through the Plaza, laying in on our way a good store of splendid water-melons, and crossed in one of the dug-outs to the further bank, where the stage was in readiness. The river level was 4900 feet, a rise of fifty feet from Ocotlan.

Mr. M. left us here, to our great regret, to return to Colima; going back across the lake by a little steamer belonging to Mr. C., an enterprising American, who runs it once a week from Chapala, at the western end, to La Barca. Just across the lake at this point is La Palma or Tequiqui, a place to which great part of the goods for the Western States are brought by a mule route from the city of Mexico *via* Morelia.

Bidding farewell to Mr. M. we started from the river bank at 12.30, and in half an hour reached the Hacienda de

Buena Vista, where we stopped for an escort. This hacienda stands on a little rise above the river; and the *casa* is really a very fine building, with deep portales, fresco-painted walls, and a high and picturesque bell-tower rising at one end. It occupies one side of the Plaza, which is in the centre of a town of 5000 inhabitants, all belonging to the estate.

While some of the gentlemen went off to the casa to see about the escort, Mrs. P. and I sat in the stage regaling ourselves on water-melons and sweet limes; watching the people coming and going, and the mules laden with *maguey* rope from the *pulque*-growing districts of the eastern plateau. We were much puzzled as to the use of a large round building with a thatched roof, like an unfinished theatre, and found out at last that it was a cockpit!

General R. succeeded in getting a capital escort of eight private soldiers belonging to the hacienda, all armed with pistols, carbines, and lances. These latter are the same strong spears which are used in the bull-fights, and are considered the best weapon against robbers.

Our next halt was to change mules at Tanguato, a pretty town twenty miles from La Barca, with a population of 5000. All the land round was irrigated, and brilliantly green with fields of *garabances* (horse-beans) and tobacco. Just outside this pretty, peaceful little town, we passed a dozen men carrying something on a litter covered with a serape, and found out afterwards that it was a dead robber, who had just been killed.

For the first time for many months we felt the first drops of rain. A delicious thunder-shower cooled the air and laid the dust, and made our escort wrap their serapes round them as if it were the depth of winter. How we rejoiced in it, though it lasted only a few minutes!

At 5 P.M. we got a relay at Yurecuaro, and half an hour after stopped at Salitrillo, a small village on the borders of the Nacimiento lake, to make some Liebig soup for Mrs. P., who was tired out. The villagers get their living by making *petate* mats from the *tule* reed, which grows all along the lake. We set off again at a quarter to six, and on our left saw a long low hill of volcanic ash, which would make splendid grape soil. We all agreed how in the future we would establish a great wine-making place there, and what the wine should be called, and how we would send samples to all our friends, and rival the trade of Xeres; when to our dismay we turned right up the said hill, and in a moment wine and railways and all thoughts of anything save present misery took their flight. Never have I felt the equal of that shaking; it was not mere stones or screes, but a real *pedregal*; downright rocks, between which the wheels would stick, and the mules stop short; and then came a perfect hurricane of bad words, blows, and stones, till up we went with a jerk that sent us all flying.

The last bit of the ascent we had to walk, as the jolting grew unbearable; and a sorry procession we looked, wearily dragging ourselves and the rifles up the rocks, the bushes cut on each side of the track for fear of robbers lurking in them, and our wretched team coming slowly behind with the heavy coach. Five hundred feet did we climb up that *pedregal*, and by the time we reached the summit, 5500 feet, there was barely light to read the barometer.

When we began the descent the scene was wild in the extreme. Our escort, with their long lances pointing upwards, and their serapes thrown over their heads, to keep off the rain, which was falling again; a thunderstorm raging in the mountains; the fireflies flickering in the damp pastures; the mules struggling along the horrible road; and the pleasant possibility of robbers any minute. Our poor beasts were completely used up, and it seemed once or twice as if we never should reach our journey's end. But at 10 P.M. we drove into Piedad, wearied to death, and Don R. V., to whom we had letters of introduction, being ill, we were passed on to a friend of his, Don Ignacio ———, who placed his house at our disposal, and late though it was, had beds made up, and an impromptu supper prepared.

April 15.—Piedad, population 10,000.

Mrs. P. and I shared a small room, without windows, opening into the patio, with large wooden doors. I could not sleep much, as the fleas were maddening, so got up about 6 A.M., and dressing in the dark, after a cold bath on the plan which Miss Nightingale so much approves, *i.e.* a pint of water and a wet towel, I went out into the patio. There I found the daughters of Don Ignacio smoking cigarettes, and we soon made friends, they, in their good-natured fashion, excusing and understanding my halting Spanish in a marvellous way. They were very nice girls, though quite uneducated. Señorita Cresencia, the youngest, was very handsome, with heavy but well-formed features, and beautiful eyes and teeth. The patio had bananas and fruit-trees growing in it. One by one our party appeared, and we at last got our *desayuno* of chocolate and *biscoches*, for which I had been longing for some hours.

After we had a little satisfied our hunger, General R. and I, being in an inquiring frame of mind, set out for a walk, and first went to the church on the Plaza, where our appearance sadly disturbed the devotions of the worshippers. For, when we paused for five minutes in a side-chapel to examine a fine old carved altar into which were let some good paintings, numbers of the people who had been praying in the body of the church followed us in, and, kneeling down close to us, pretended to go on with their prayers, but really stared at us from behind their hands.

We walked on through the town, which is mostly built of *cantera*, a light volcanic stone, grey or pink. This stone is very easily carved, and is found all over the central plateau. We got some specimens of it from a heap of stone lying ready for use, and found that a thin slip of it broke and crumbled easily in one's fingers.

We then strolled on to the Purissima, a very old church standing close to the river. It was a most picturesque building, and I tried to begin a sketch of it: but by this time a swarm of about forty muchachos of all ages, from two to twenty, had collected, who calmly followed our every step and motion, and at last we had to beat a retreat. We longed to put them to flight, but though General R. appealed touchingly to their feelings in the best Spanish he could muster, nothing had the slightest effect, and they followed us to the very door. There, however, they got their reward; for Don Ignacio, happening to see our triumphal entry, pounced out on them and soon dispersed them. He apologized to me afterwards for his fellow-citizens, saying that besides my *hat*, which was a sight in itself, as all ladies wear rebozos or go bareheaded, they had never seen "*una señorita tan grande*" (such a tall lady). How unlucky for me that the Mexicans are small!

We found that while we had been out walking those who stayed at home had discovered an old white-headed American negro, who kept a restaurant in Piedad for the stage passengers, and who professed himself capable of cooking a "reel elegant brekfass, sah. I cook for Gen'ral Scott, sah, when he come to Mexico." So, out of sheer joy at hearing the familiar dialect again, we were delivered over into the old fellow's hands; and there we sat, trying to while away the time till the "reel elegant brekfass" should appear. But hour after hour went by, and we felt more and more starved, and still no food came. At last, after various messages had been sent, and endless excuses returned about the difficulties of getting what was fit for "'Merican ladies and gen'lemen to eat," we discovered that just as everything was ready, the stage for the West had come in, and the faithless old wretch had given the passengers *our* breakfast, and was slowly preparing number two for us. However, we got it at last, two or three hours past the appointed time, and whether it was our hunger, or the real excellence of the meal, we found it very good.

We were all desperately tired, and spent most of the day pretending to read and work up the notes: but every few minutes one or other would give a desperate nod and subside into silent contemplation of a map or note-book, with his head on the table.

We are all getting so statistical we have agreed, that when we return to civilized society we shall be unendurable. My special department is to keep notes at each rise or halting-place of the elevation from the two barometers; besides general notes, as all the others do, of the produce and trade of each place we pass.

April 16.—Piedad to Irapuato, 5500 feet.

Left at 6.15 and crossed the Rio Lerma, which here is 100 feet wide and fordable at this time of year above and below, by a fine bridge. It was made of cantera, with eight arches, carved balustrades, and a tablet at each end stating when and by whom the bridge was built, and that it cost 7265 dollars (£1453). A mile from town we came to the hacienda Santa Ana, belonging to a rich widow. It stands on a little rise above a fertile plain, where ploughing and sowing and harvesting were all going on at once. In one large field we counted fourteen ox-ploughs at work. The plain is a continuous wheat and corn field for miles and miles, varied by a stretch of mesquite trees, with good grazing beneath them. All the valley seems to have been covered at some period with this mesquite, a beautiful tree of the acacia tribe, with delicate fern-like leaves, and pods of edible beans. In many places trees of it are left standing here and there in the corn-fields, and used as growing granaries for the corn stocks, which are stored in the branches. Goats are particularly fond of the mesquite beans; and near St. Ana we saw a large flock of them actually clambering up into the lower mesquite bushes, after stripping the branches within reach from the ground.

At the hacienda de la Laguna Largo, garabances were being threshed by a man driving a mob of horses round and round an enclosure over the beans. They are used for fatting hogs, of which immense numbers are raised on the hacienda, and driven all the way to the city of Mexico, at the rate of three leagues (between eight and nine miles) a day.

Food here is very cheap; a fat sheep costs $1; chickens thirty-one cents (fifteenpence); eggs nine cents a dozen.

At 12.23 we stopped for breakfast at Penjamo, a robber-town of 6000 inhabitants. Of this town we heard many uncomfortable anecdotes in Guadalajara, and were quite surprised to see it look neat and civilized outwardly. Among other little tales, one gentleman told us that the priest of Penjamo was a kind of chief among the robbers, and that he (our informant), being obliged to stop for a night in the town, had taken the precaution of getting a letter to the priest, who took him in and treated him most hospitably. Emboldened by the pacific look of his host, he ventured to touch on the subject of the robbers, and the priest's supposed authority over them.

"Oh," said the Padre, "would you like to see my boys?" and opening a door he ushered his astonished guest into a patio where twenty or thirty villanous-looking fellows were assembled in readiness at a moment's warning, to go out "on the road" and rob or murder to any extent. Our friend was thankful enough, he said, to be under the Padre's protecting care: but not at all sorry to make the best of his way next day out of reach of such a formidable family.

How true this might be we had no opportunity of judging, I am thankful to say: as it was, the breakfast we got in a horrid little *fonda* was misfortune enough for one day. I never saw such a filthy place. In England one would hesitate to put pigs into such an abode. Breakfast, which was cooked and served by two disgusting women, consisted of eggs, rice, and chillé, with a little sour bread. As ill luck would have it, I came in late, when all the boiled eggs were gone, and had to swallow two fried eggs, which, though excessively nasty at the time, satisfied my hunger completely, and I did not discover till afterwards that they had been fried in tallow-candle grease. The consequences may be imagined; and the rest of the day's journey, which luckily was over by 5.30, is a doleful blank in my mind, as I lay on a bed of rugs in the coach in helpless hopeless misery, except just as we were entering Irapuato. I was then roused effectually by some one calling from the outside of the coach, "They are hanging a robber!" General P. made Mrs. P. and me cover our eyes (not that we had the slightest wish to look out), and told us afterwards that a robber captain who had first been shot, was, according to the custom of the country, being hung to a tree outside the town, to make quite sure of his being dead.

April 17.—Irapuato, population 14,000.

We had intended staying till 3 P.M., and then going on four leagues to Salamanca to sleep; but owing to some trouble about relays of mules, we had to stay at Irapuato all day. This was no hardship, as the hotel, the San Francisco, was good and clean; and I, being still rather the worse for the tallow-candles, was glad to spend the day lazily resting. In the hotel were delicious baths of hard water, which could hardly be called cold, and yet was not warm, and in each of them floated a little ball of maguey fibre, serving for sponge or flannel for soaping.

The "Gefe Politico," Señor ——, gave our gentlemen a great deal of information, and in the course of the day took them out for a ride round the neighbourhood of the town. He is a determined and go-ahead man, a great enemy of the robbers. We found it was he who had ordered the execution of the robber captain the day before; and he says he means to hang every one he can catch, without mercy.

Towards evening we went out for a walk to the Plaza, which is prettily laid out with quantities of flowers, shrubs, orange trees, and adobe seats. As we came into the town the night before, General P. counted seventeen towers and domes. They were venerable-looking, being built of grey *cantera*; while the buildings to which they belong, and the houses, are all of *adobe* (sun-dried brick).

As we came home through the market, Mrs. P. and I, to our great joy, discovered a woman selling long sticks of real molasses candy, just like what we used to get in the States. It was the first really home-like thing we had seen; so we invested in a great bundle, and carried it back to the hotel in triumph.

18*th*.—Irapuato, 5500 feet, to Celaya, 5710 feet.

A delightful day's journey, leaving Irapuato at 8.30 A.M. The town is buried in flower gardens. Outside, on the eastern side, the road goes along a causeway to a stone bridge of five arches over the Silao river; and a little farther on reaches a second bridge over the Guanajuato river. One of the arches of this last one, however, is not safe, and sooner than take the trouble of mending it, the townsfolk have made a crossing over both rivers, which certainly at this time of year are nearly dry: but in the rainy season it cannot be at all easy to ford.

The valley of the Lerma, up which we travelled all day, is here about fifteen miles wide. The mountains of Guanajuato, with their countless wealth of mines, lay to the north, and those of Morelia and Michoacan to the south. The plain between was beautiful, covered with mesquite, and white-walled haciendas, on little knolls, every few miles; a thick line of trees marking the river course, and hundreds of acres of wheat, green or golden; in some places the reapers were cutting it, and in others the land was being ploughed up again for a second crop. In only two places did we see any dressing put on the land.

Round all the villages swape wells, like those of Egypt, are largely used for irrigation; and in some places there is an absurd invention. A great wooden spoon is fastened on to a crossbar between two posts; and as a man pulls down one end with a rope, up flies the spoon and empties its spoonful of water into the little irrigating ditch.

The road was plentifully ornamented with little wooden crosses, showing that, peaceful as everything seemed now, robbers had plied their unholy trade here at some time. And to prove this still further, a mound was pointed out to us by the roadside where but a few months ago some famous robbers were caught and hung.

The "Gefe Politico" of Salamanca, a Spaniard, was still lame from a spear-wound he got in the leg a fortnight ago, in a hand-to-hand encounter with some of these "gentlemen of the road," in which, I am happy to say, he came off victorious, in spite of his wound.

We reached Salamanca at 10.30. The approach was very pretty, through long straight streets of organo cactus (*Cereus gemmatus*), mixed with mesquite, for a mile or more before we reached the city. This cereus is most useful for hedges. Joints of it, a few inches high, are planted side by side, and in a very short time they grow into an impenetrable green wall, sometimes eight to twelve feet high. In other parts hedges are made of the nopal or tuna (*Opuntia stricta*). Single leaves are stuck into a little trench, laid alternately to and from the road, and when they grow into large plants they are useful, not only as a hedge, but for their fruit and young leaves. The fruit of one kind of nopal is yellowish green inside; but the best is a variety with bright canary-coloured flowers, and a deep blood-red flesh to the fruit, which on the hottest day is always cold and crisp, almost like a water-ice.[1]

But to return to Salamanca. It is such a bright clean place that we quite wished to stop there for a longer time than was needed to eat an excellent breakfast. The Diligence Hotel was charming, with a patio full of roses and oranges, and singing birds in cages, and after breakfast Mrs. P. and I were taken into a little sitting-room with rocking-chairs and sofas, which was most luxurious after the wretched places we had lodged in before.

Salamanca is a thriving town of 10,000 inhabitants, who get their living by hand-manufactures of shawls and *rebozos*. There is also a porcelain-manufactory near by. General P. got an exceedingly good pair of goatskin-gloves, made in the town, thoroughly well cut and sewed, for 12 *reales*, 6s., which in Denver would have cost four or five dollars.

We left at 12.20, and our next halt was in $7\frac{1}{2}$ miles, to change mules, at the hacienda del Molino de Zaralia. There is at this hacienda a large olive-yard, and a mill where a good deal of olive-oil is made. How much exactly we could not ascertain; for after General R. and Señor A. had both tried to find out how much an olive-tree yielded, and had both failed signally, Mr. Y. "went for" the man, who completely shut him up by replying, "Oh, as much as God pleases." We tried no more statistical questions after that!

While we were waiting, Mrs. P. and I were attracted by the brilliant note of a bird, and going into the piazza round the house, found a dozen birds, most of them new to us, in cages. Of course there were several mocking-birds, "*Sen Sontile*," as the Indians call it, meaning "a hundred sounds," and a

---

[1] "I saw also another fruit called carreau—the 'Nuchtli' of the Mexicans. The skin is very tender, and of an orange colour; the inside is red as blood, and the flesh like that of plums; it stains where it touches like mulberries; the taste is very good, and it is said to be excellent for curing the bite of venomous creatures."—Champlain's *Voyage to the West Indies and Mexico*, 1599-1602.

pretty blue bird, "*Gouroullone Azul.*" But our songster was a quiet-looking dark grey bird, a little smaller than a blackbird, whose song was like a series of metallic notes from a loud and clear musical box. The Mexicans call it "Clarin," and it comes, so said the woman at the hacienda, from the Tierra Caliente, near Vera Cruz.

We walked in the *huerta*, where they grow olives, figs, and grapes: and besides the more useful trees, the walks are lined with roses, pinks, and sweet peas, like a garden at home; which so delighted us that, to tell the truth, Mrs. P. and I tempted the gentlemen to steal some for us. Leaving the hacienda we drove for some distance down a water-lane from the Celaya river, and at 2.30 passed through an Indian town, whose inhabitants can speak no Spanish at all, and cannot make themselves understood; so it has been called the "*Puebla de los huajes,*" the Town of Fools. Close by is another puebla, where all the people are robbers. They come out with clubs and daggers, and rob the poor foot-passengers: but never attack an armed force; so they did not trouble us.

At five we got to Celaya, the prettiest town I have seen in Mexico. The approach is up a long straight causeway, with running water on each side, and hedges of cereus, mesquite, reed, and Peru pepper-trees, round small fields and gardens of alfalfa or "Chilli-clover" (*Lucerne*), used as food for horses, lettuce, onions, and barley; and at the end, rising over thick banks of trees, the white and painted domes and spires of the town.

The Plaza is beautiful—a perfect tropic green-house; with a fine white column of cantera in the centre, surmounted by the arms of the republic carved in stone, and painted of their proper colours. Round the foot of the column is a fountain of excellent water from an Artesian well, which also supplies "*los delicios baños termales,*" tepid baths opposite the hotel. We felt quite civilized again, the hotel being two stories high; and from the balconies of our rooms we got a splendid view of the innumerable churches of Celaya. There are twelve, to a population of 30,000. Two had large domes, covered with coloured tiles of a yellowish green, with patterns in the centre of each division of the dome in darker colours. The effect is exceedingly good, as they look like fine mosaic. One thing which has struck us all through the journey, is the amount of magnificent churches all over the country. Every day we have passed from ten to twenty, and as often as not, the village round the church is nothing more than a collection of two or three dozen huts, more fit for pigs than human beings; the whole wealth of the neighbourhood having gone into the hands of the priests, and produced this great useless building, leaving the Indios round sunk one step lower in poverty, superstition, and ignorance.

I tried to make a sketch of one of the churches from my window, which was on the second floor, and attracted thereby a crowd of idlers, who quietly took up their position in the street below, watching all I did, and making remarks on me and my occupation, which seemed to puzzle them greatly. In the evening we went out on the Plaza, which was crammed with people, to hear a band of Indian musicians with native instruments, who were playing under the column. The music was unlike anything I have ever heard before, save perhaps the crooning of an Irish bagpipe. I could not see exactly what instruments they had; some were wind: but besides these there were little drums and stringed instruments. The music was wild and soft, but very barbaric.

At last we have heard of the overland party from Colorado. One telegram arrived from Zaccatecas this morning, saying they were well and safe, and another after dinner asking for an escort to Guanajuato, as the pronunciados had taken their arms: so they have had troubles as well as we.

A few weeks after we had listened to the musicians on

the Plaza of Celaya, not dreaming of dangers, an incident occurred in the town, of which the following letter from my brother will give the best account, showing upon what a volcano one may walk unknowingly :—

"Dear * * *,—We got into Celaya last night, to find the whole town topsy-turvy at the rescue of Señor S. from the "*plagiarios.*" You may remember that in my letter three weeks ago from here, I told you he had been plagiared (kidnapped for ransom): but as the story is a good one, I will give you the whole of it. S. is a relative of a rich Spanish haciendado, of whom the *plagiarios*, I believe, have been trying to get hold for some time. Finally, one evening they saw S., and thinking that half a loaf was better than no bread, they decided to take him.

"As he was riding in through the outskirts of the town just after dark, a man rode up and asked him for a light for his cigarette. As he gave it, he saw that the man was exchanging courtesies with him by handing him the muzzle of a revolver, and, glancing round, he found he was surrounded. Seeing that he had no chance, he surrendered, and was tied on the back of a horse, and carried off into the mountains of Culiacan.

"Next morning his friends, fearing that he was plagiared, began inquiries after him, and traced him from the hacienda whither it was certain he had gone, to the outskirts of the town, where they lost all traces of him. Hearing further that a body of mounted and armed men had gone out of town at about eight o'clock in the evening, in the direction of Culiacan, they felt certain that he was victim to that most unpleasant fate—a 'plagio.'

"A general call to arms of the Spaniards of the district was made; and my old friend H. was among the first to arm his mozos, and scour Culiacan. After three or four days' fruitless search, a messenger came out from town to say that $5000 had been asked for his ransom, which his relative had refused to pay; and that a message had been sent with the demand, saying that if the search was not stopped immediately he would be killed in twelve hours.

"Fearing that the plagiarios might put their threat into execution, they returned to town in the hopes of persuading poor S.'s relative to raise the money. The days passed, however, and nothing was done, till at last a friend of his determined to risk everything again, and arming his mozos, started to Culiacan to search.

"After wandering for a couple of days on the mountain, they came across a little track made by men and horses, and following it up for about two miles, they got among some large broken boulders, with bushes growing in between them, at the foot of a sandstone bluff. Pressing on, they saw a man spring from behind a boulder, and run in through a little trap-door in the face of the cliff. They charged after him, and, tearing open the door, found two men preparing their arms inside. In three seconds it was all over; and they then proceeded to search the cave, which was about 30 feet by 20, with a freshly-moulded floor. After searching round for some time, somebody's foot struck a hollow place in the floor; and tearing up the loose soil, and three or four planks that sustained it, they found in a grave, 7 feet by 3, poor S.: but in a most piteous plight: half-starved, tightly bound with raw hide, gagged and blinded, and even his ears stopped up with wax.

"As they were untying him, an alarm was given outside that the plagiarios were coming back in force. Evidently they must have been on the other side of the mountain, and underrated the numbers of S.'s rescuers, for, without parley or warning of any sort, they charged right upon the party in the cave, which far outnumbered them, and which besides was, as it were, in a strongly fortified position. After a few minutes' hard fighting, in which three of the plagiarios were killed, the rest ran. Two more were picked up in the pursuit by the lassos of the mozos; and only two, I believe, escaped to tell the tale.

"Poor S., as soon as he was sufficiently recovered to do or say anything, which was not for two or three days, told a strange tale of how he had been kidnapped by one party, and after he had been ill-treated and starved by them for a week, during which time there were some hopes of his ransom being paid, they sold him to another band for 200 dollars. He was then carried off to his new quarters, his buyers taking the chance of getting the ransom: but they, finding there was little hope of making a profitable job out of it, sold him to a third party for 300 dollars, in whose cave he was when he was rescued."

April 19.—Celaya, 5690 feet, to Queretaro, 6050.

We left at 9.45 A.M., with a capital Government escort of thirty cavalry, all splendidly mounted, and armed with carbines and spears. Outside the town we crossed the Celaya river—which was 150 feet wide, with three inches of water—by a fine cantera bridge of four arches. The road ran along a paved causeway over a grassy plain: but as a good deal of the paving was up, we were alternately shaken to a jelly or plunged into a muddy hole, so at last the cochero was persuaded to take us along the "dirt road" beside the paved one. At a bridge over some ditch we were stopped by meeting four waggons, with ten mules to each, on their way to Guanajuato, laden with iron machinery from the iron-works of the Trinidad at Pachuca. One heavy waggon had chosen to stick half-way up the bridge, and the mules from one of the other waggons had to be put on to the sticking team to help them over before we could pass.

As we drew near Apasco, the road was shaded with fine quaking aspens, and hedged with roses. The land is irrigated from a strong spring, and looks green and fertile, and the town, through which we passed at twelve, is surrounded with *huertas* full of flowers and fruit-trees.

At 12.30 we made a long halt at the Molino de Apaseo, 5840 feet, to get a relay. It is a little corn and wheat mill, and grinds $1\frac{1}{4}$ tons in twenty-four hours. It was a stupid place to stop at, so I diverted myself by making pencil-studies of nopal, cacti, and the Peru pepper (*Schinus molle*), which here becomes one of the common trees. It is an extremely pretty tree, with its long delicate leaves and branches of coral berries, and in some places grows to a very large size. The berries taste like pepper: but I cannot find that they are made much use of in Mexico, except for feeding song-birds, as they are said to improve their voices. In Peru, its native country, the Peruvians make a vinous drink by boiling them.

Our escort, all but a sergeant and four men, left us at Guachipi, where we stopped at 1.45. After Guachipi we had to pass a spur of bad land, covered with Cactus. A new species appeared here, the "*Cholla*," which, in Arizona, where it grows only too plentifully, is called "jumping cactus." Each joint is a ball of horrible spines; and they are supposed to jump off the plant as you come near it, and stick to you and your horse. As to its jumping power, I cannot give an opinion: but I know, by painful experience, that if you once get a cholla-ball on your clothes, you will have considerable difficulty in getting it off again, and may think yourself lucky if some of the spines do not penetrate to the skin. General P. told me the horses and mules on the Transcontinental survey of 1867 went nearly mad with this cactus in Arizona, the balls sticking to their fetlocks; and the more they tried to kick them off, the faster they stuck.

At La Calera, a robber-village, we passed a quantity of limekilns, from which the place is named.

The roads, after leaving the cactus-land, were deep in mud, and we got along but slowly. We were now on the great high road to Mexico, and passed quantities of waggons and mules going west and north. Eighteen mules were laden with Orizaba tobacco for La Barca; and then came twenty-six waggons, with five mules each, taking "dry goods" to Leon. These waggons carry in wet weather 1½ tons, and in dry 2½ tons.

About six miles from Queretaro we had to climb up and cross a bad bit of pedregal, with high stone walls on either side of the road, or rather lava pile, called a road. As we neared the top of the rise, I was looking out of window, for we were rather on the *qui vive* for robbers, and saw our sergeant, followed by two men gallop forward as hard as he could go, and, suddenly turning, put his beautiful little black horse right at the tremendous stone wall. It was one of the prettiest leaps I ever saw. The little horse alighted half-way up the wall, scrambled to the top and over, landing safe and sound on the other side in a cactus patch, though how he did it is a mystery to me. There was great excitement for a minute: but the sergeant, coming back again over a gap, reported that he had seen a man in a bush, who, however, proved to be harmless.

At the top of the hill we found four of the escort sent out from Queretaro to meet us, and for a few seconds were in some uncertainty as to their calling, for their attire was a curious mixture of civil and military, and they were fully armed. The officer in command, however, soon reassured us by presenting his credentials from the Governor of the city; so that, when we found a second batch of them drawn up at the bottom of the hill on each side of the road, we were not tempted to prepare for action, as the engineer party were next day in the same place. A little further on we met another detachment, making thirty in all; so we were well protected, though the only good they did us was in helping to drag the coach over a stump, into which we were driven, and where we stuck fast for ten minutes.

The approach to Queretaro is very beautiful. It stands in the midst of corn-fields, with a semicircle of hills behind. The road to it runs partly on and partly beside a causeway, through an avenue of magnificent old Peru pepper-trees. Another causeway, running parallel with the road, is the embankment for a railway, begun under Maximilian's directions during the Empire.

Our minds were full of the poor Emperor as we neared the scene of his tragic end; and, about a mile from the town, a voice called from the outside of the coach, as we passed an adobe ruin, "That's where they shot Maximilian." Of course we were greatly excited, and just as General R. was giving us some fine moral reflections on the vanity of human greatness, and my sympathies were all aroused, the voice called down a second time, "That's the wrong place." How foolish we all looked!

At the Hotel Diligencia, where we arrived at 5.30, the rooms were clean and comfortable, and there was very fair food; so we settled to stay three or four days, to get a little rest, and also to wait for the engineer party, who were now following us.

CHAPTER XVIII.

QUERETARO TO MEXICO.

A bet—The Hercules Factory—Cheap labour—Arrival of the engineers from Colorado—Las Campanas—Leave Queretaro—Spearing a dog—The Divide—San Juan del Rio—Thunderstorm—An unlucky choice of routes—Ill-requited kindness—Barred out—An Indian school—The valley of the Tula—The broken break—Gathering nopal leaves—The capital of the Toltecs—An early start—On Cortez's track—The valley of Mexico—The railroad track—Arrival in the city.

Sat., April 20.—We drove out in the morning to the Hercules Cotton Factory, which belongs to Señor R., the most enterprising man in Mexico. The way thither was down a steep hill outside the city walls, and at the bottom we got on a splendid road built by Señor R. A stream, shaded by pepper trees, ran along the side of the road, where Indian women were washing clothes, and their children were washing themselves. To the right, stretching across the valley from the town to the hills, on more than sixty arches of stone and brick, was the great aqueduct, which was built under the following circumstances :—

A gentleman of the city, which at that time was badly supplied with water, made a bantering bet with a friend, that if he (the friend) would give a silver shrine, costing $1,000,000, to the Virgin, he, on his part, would build an aqueduct at a like cost. The bet was taken, and the aqueduct built; but the builder would not allow his friend to fulfil his part of the engagement, wisely considering that the money might be better employed. The water is brought from a spring 2½ leagues up the Cañada in which the Hercules Mill stands, and the same spring supplies the mill with water.

About a mile out of town we passed the Purissima, another factory belonging to the R.'s. It stands in a beautiful garden of oleanders, oranges, and shady trees, with green turf and lovely roses beneath. Between it and the Hercules is a continuous village-street of the workpeople's houses in the valley, which here suddenly narrows into a mere cleft in the hills. Nearly every house had flowers or birds in the windows, or on the roofs. On reaching the Hercules we went first into a large court full of tropical plants mixed with the finest French roses,—a fountain in the centre, and a marble statue of Hercules, with each hand on a lion, which cost $5000, and was brought from Italy by Señor R.

Don C. R. took us first to see the great water wheel, which is the best, and the second largest, overshot wheel in the Republic. It is an iron wheel forty-eight feet in diameter, made by Wren and Barrett of Manchester. We then went all over the factory, which is the very poetry of manufacturing. High airy rooms opening on courts filled with the choicest flowers. The people all look healthy and happy; and a strike has never been known. 2050 hands are employed in the two factories, besides a host of wood-carriers who do not live there. Don C. told us they keep a private army of seventy foot-soldiers and twenty cavalry, in case of any attack in troublous times. The men are dressed in a pretty white uniform, with red and yellow facings; each man gets four "bits" (about 2s.) a day, his lodging, and one uniform a year; and for the cavalry, horses are provided and maintained. On an emergency they can arm 500 of the workmen, who are all drilled and trained. In the fire-engine room we saw two light guns, and there are regular sentry-boxes along the roofs, and at all outlets. During the war of the Empire the factory was not disturbed in any way, though Liberals and Imperialists were fighting round it for months. To the credit of both sides it was respected; as indeed it should be, as a great national benefit.

On the ground floor, below the cotton mill, is a fine flour mill; which, however, is only worked on Sundays, as during the week enough water cannot be spared from the rest of the factory. Besides the water-wheel, there are two double oscillating engines; and, connected with these, a very perfect arrangement of hose, in case of fire, to every story of the buildings. The machinery is all of the very best and newest kinds, and mostly from England.

The two mills use up 1600 tons of raw cotton yearly, which is brought from Colima, Morelia, Texas, Vera Cruz, and from the valley of the Nazas in Durango and Chihuahua. Their production is 1150 tons of cotton cloth, "*manta,*" besides yarns and wick; and 2000 tons of flour. Although water constitutes the principal power, 5000 tons of wood are used annually in the mills. It is growing scarcer every year, and has to be brought long distances. General P. saw one Indian carry 225 lbs. of wood up to the top of a wood pile thirty-five feet high. He had brought this load on his back $18\frac{3}{10}$ miles; and having had to stand the cost of timber and chopping himself, was paid 45 cents, about 1s. 10d., for the whole job.

We had been calculating that the engineer party might arrive in the evening, when we got a telegram saying they had passed Salamanca; and at seven they came, such a dirty wayworn set as never were seen, after the 1600 miles they had travelled overland since we parted at Colorado Springs. How we all talked over our adventures, escapes, and experiences, can best be imagined by those who have been in like case.

Sunday, 21*st*.—All the morning was spent in talking, making up reports, and watching the usual Sunday sights from the balconies. The most exciting of these was a procession of bull-fighters through the streets, playing the famous march of the bull-ring. There was a bull-fight of course, and two of the party went to it: but came back disgusted, saying "it was miserable; no good fighting; nothing but a mere butcher's shop."

In the afternoon, we drove out to Las Campanas to see the spot where the Liberals shot Maximilian, Miramon, and Mejia, standing side by side. It is a solitary bare hill about a mile from the Garita; and half-way up the east side, a rough pile of stones about four feet high among the cactus scrub, with two very small wooden crosses on the top, and a third cut on a stone below them, marks the place of the last act of the tragedy. From this point there is a glorious view of the city, with its ring of hills across the fertile gardens and fields between Las Campanas and the city. Just inside the walls, and buried in trees, rises the dome of the old convent of Las Cruces, where the Emperor's last days were spent, and from whence he was brought to Las Campanas. From the summit, where there are remains of earthworks, the view was one of the finest I have ever seen: up the valley, the city, with its innumerable towers and domes glancing in the sun and the delicious green of the trees which surrounded it in all directions; north, the distant mountains of Guanajuato; and west, the valley of the Lerma, with one single date-palm standing up as a sentinel against the evening sky. What a spot for the poor Emperor to see as his last view of his beautiful but unhappy empire!

It is exceedingly difficult to find out the real history of those last days: but every one who has any good feeling, even though on the Liberal side, seems to give Maximilian the credit of a will to do well and right, though he was merely a tool in the hands of Bazaine and the French Emperor.

In the evening there was a sharp thunderstorm, with hailstones as big as robins' eggs.

Monday, 22d.—General R. and Mr. Y. have gone on to Mexico by the regular diligence, leaving us in Señor A.'s hands. The engineers are going on a reconnaissance up the Lerma Valley to Toluca, which will take them about three weeks. Governor H. joins us; and we leave for the capital to-morrow. Travelling almost day and night, Mexico may be reached in two days: but we are going to take it more easily by stopping the first night at San Juan del Rio.

April 23.—Queretaro to San Juan del Rio.

We left Queretaro at 12.15 in a small private stage, by the road past the Hercules Factory. Beyond the mill we drove up the narrow Cañada filled with luxuriant orchards, the aqueduct and road running parallel. We passed a ruined church, destroyed during the war of the Empire; for all this part was fought over more than once, being the position of the Liberals. Further on there were large quarries of "*loza*," a pink stone used for paving; and mules were bringing down slabs of it to the city. The road, which was well graded, took us up out of the Cañada in about an hour, and at 1.30 we reached the hacienda of Alcarriaga on cactus-covered hills. The cattle are fond of the young leaves of the nopal, and we saw them browsing freely on it. Below the cactus in the grass I saw a pretty white and pink amaryllis, which had the effect of a crocus: but I was not able to get any.

After Alcarriaga we came to a wide cultivated plain, which extends to San Juan del Rio, with a broad road between nopal hedges. This plain is one of the richest maize-growing districts in Mexico, this year's yield being 45,000,000 lbs. The only approach to excitement as we drove along was when our escort of half-a-dozen men found an unfortunate dog that they chose to consider mad, and for want of any robbers to chase, hunted the poor beast down and speared it, only laughing at our indignant protests.

At four we reached La Palma, and halted for an hour. It is a village of palm-thatched huts, each surrounded with a hedge of organo cactus, giving it the quaintest look, and a background of purple mountains, white in places with hail, rising from the rich plain. While we waited, an escort of sixteen men rode up from San Juan del Rio, and at five we set out again.

Close to this place is the Divide or watershed between the waters of the east and west, which is remarkable for being merely a rise and fall of some fifty feet in the middle of the great plain, instead of being, as in most cases, a mountain range. The river, which runs through San Juan del Rio, flows into the Panuco, and thus into the Gulf; while the Queretaro stream, which also rises here, flows into the Lerma, and thus into the Pacific.

We were caught on this very Divide in a heavy thunderstorm, which made the roads so heavy that our already tired mules completely gave out, and we crawled into San Juan del Rio at 8.30 in the dark.

April 24.—San Juan del Rio to Aroyo Zarco.

I had most comfortable quarters, being lodged, as bedrooms were scarce, in the sala of the hotel, a long room with pictures on the walls, and actually three or four books on the table,—mostly Spanish sermons, it is true, but still they were books, and, having seen none but my own note-books for so long, it gave one quite a pleasant sensation of civilisation again. The doors of my room, which evidently were very old, were of richly-carved wood, and the shutters to the deep windows which opened on a balcony were of the same. From the windows which were over the principal entrance, and shaded by a huge tree, I got glimpses of the pretty town, the tower and dome of the church rising over the trees which lined the street. In the gallery round the patio there

s

were quantities of birds in cages, with bananas and flowers growing in large pots; and we were rather sorry to change our comfortable quarters for the misery of a thirty-five miles' stage drive. The river runs past the town under a rocky cliff, very much like the Dee at Chester; and the air being alive with swallows closely resembling the European species, made the likeness still more striking.

From San Juan del Rio, which we left at twelve, the road led up a long and steep hill, which we crawled up, over an atrocious road, so slowly that we had to submit to the indignity of being passed by a herd of beef cattle, which we had passed on the 18th between Irapuato and Salamanca.

We had an escort of five men: but we were considerably more afraid of them than of the unknown dangers from which they were supposed to defend us; and so when they announced their intention of leaving us and returning to San Juan del Rio, we let them go without much regret. A furious thunderstorm came on as we reached the top of the hill, just before the escort deserted us, and their upright spears kept me in a perfect fever, as every moment I expected they or we should get struck by lightning. While the storm was at its worst we were passing through a great maguey plantation, and, though horribly frightened, I could not help laughing at the antics of a man who had been collecting the pulque in a pigskin, and now was jumping from plant to plant like some gigantic flea, with his quivering pigskin on his back, to cover over the open cavities in the pulque plants, for fear the rain or hail should get in and injure the precious juice.

At Las Palmillas the stage road branches; the usual route going straight to Tula, and the other taking a more southerly course by Aroyo Zarco to the same point. For some inscrutable reason, we were assured that this southern route would be the best to take, so we took it, and toiled along with an exhausted train of mules, over a wide open grass plain, with a road deep in mud. At 5 p.m. we came to Soledad, which must at some time have been a fine town, but now is quite ruinate; and then, and not till then, did we discover, that the stage route we had chosen had been out of use for more than a year, so of course we could expect no relays all along it. There were but two alternatives: either to go back to Las Palmillas, several miles, and so along the northern route on the chance of getting relays; or to stick to the route we had chosen, and try to get on with our luckless mules to Aroyo Zarco. The latter course was decided upon, and we began by giving the poor animals an hour and a half's rest at Soledad, getting at the same time a fair meal in a great room in what had once been a fine hotel, but where now a stray *arriero* was looked upon as a welcome guest. Our party, therefore, created no small stir, and two Mexican gentlemen who were resting their horses seemed immensely interested in all our proceedings.

It was 6.30 when we left, and we were all tolerably tired. General and Mrs. P. tried to get a little sleep on the front seat. Governor H. was on the middle seat with his rifle between his knees; Señor A. and Pablo outside; and I on the back seat, with a little heap of rifles, pistols, etc., by my side. We had been driving, or rather creeping, for the mules refused to trot, for an hour or so, when we were startled by a clatter of hoofs; voices in Spanish called out of the darkness; and as we dimly made out two mounted men close to us, the coach stopped. Quicker than I thought possible, the Governor's rifle was out of window, and he had "drawn a bead" on the nearest man.

"Where's my pistol?" called the General. I made a dive in the darkness, got it out of the holster, passed it to him, and crouched down in silence to see what would come next. It seemed hours while we heard Señor A.'s voice on the box, and those of the two unknown speaking so fast we could not make out what they were saying. In vain the

General called to Señor A. to know what it all meant; he was too intent on his conversation to answer. At last, however, he called down—

"It is two gentlemen who saw at Soledad the ladies were tired, and want you to stop at their hacienda, close here."

Poor men; they little thought how near they were being killed for their kindness. As soon as we had recovered our fright a little, we settled not to accept their kind offer, but to go on our way to Aroyo Zarco, as we could not well be more tired than we were then. So parting from the Haciendados in a much more friendly way than we had greeted them, we drove on; and after crossing five streams, arrived at last at our destination at 11 P.M. Here fresh troubles awaited us.

The Diligence Hotel was a huge house, three stories high, with a heavy barred door, at which Pablo proceeded to knock for admittance. Not a sound was to be heard in answer; gradually all the gentlemen joined him, and the mozo and cochero lent their aid. In vain they thumped, in vain they shouted. It was like a house of the dead. After an hour they resorted to threats, in a loud voice, of breaking in forcibly; for we knew there were inhabitants, as we could see a light moving about inside; and at last a man appeared at an upper window, who added insult to injury, by saying he had thought we were robbers. When reassured on this score, he proceeded to undo the gates and let us into the patio, and then took us up some stone stairs to an empty room, where we made up a resting-place for Mrs. P. with blankets, and I waited with what patience was left till rooms were prepared for us. The man at first seemed to consider beds an impossibility, as he said the *amo* had the key of the linen, and he could not wake him; however, we had no compassion on the *amo's* slumbers, and in half an hour got some fairly comfortable rooms ready. Supper there was none, and we had no food with us; so General

P. gave us each some whisky and water to prevent chills and fever after such a day's work, and by 1 A.M. I was fast asleep.

25th.—Aroyo Zarco, 8010 feet, to Tula, 6700. I was woke at early dawn by the song of birds; and so importunate were their shrill voices, that, tired as I was, I could not get to sleep again, and at last had to get up. On going out into the corridor I found whence the sounds came. All along the open passage were hung cages of clarines, sen sontiles, and half a dozen other species. One mocking-bird amused himself by cat-calling, imitating the clarines and parrots, and then bursting forth into a perfect torrent of his own song.

The house, which had once been a large hacienda, was built round three sides of a court, which on the fourth side was divided by one-storied rooms and a gateway from a second court, where the mules and horses were kept. It stood on a small river which ran down from the hills, through rolling lands covered with pulque plantations, its course marked by a rich line of trees.

Next morning Governor H. and I took a stroll to a fine pulque plantation near by. We passed on our way the present hacienda, which stood on a rise about a quarter of a mile from the Diligence House, and attached to which was a cart and carriage manufactory. The grass was jewelled with the pink and white amaryllis we had seen at Alcarriaga, and I picked a bunch of it, with long crocus-like leaves. Our progress through the pulque plantation was more exciting than pleasant, as there were scattered huts throughout it, each of which contained one or more large and fierce dogs, who rushed out to dispute our passage, and we had to arm ourselves with the largest stones we could find to keep them at bay. But the walk was well worth the accompanying annoyance, for I had never before been in a good pulque patch, and we walked along through an avenue of plants ten feet high, their huge sword-like leaves meeting overhead with the most weird effect. As we came home, we were startled by the unmistakeable jabber of a school, and following the sound, came to an open door into a tidy room, where some twenty or thirty little brown Indians were repeating their lessons after the most orthodox fashion. They were quite as much surprised at our sudden appearance as we were at finding a school in such an out-of-the-way place.

We left Arroyo Zarco at 10.15, the barometer giving 8010 feet, and drove up a steady rise up the Cierro Zarco, a fine cattle range. The soil was rich; wheat, corn, and potatoes grew freely, and the mountains to the east were timbered. Above the Cierro open rolling land took us to San Rosal, a hacienda, 8440 feet; and passing it we struck hills covered with timber, live oak, arbutus, etc. At San Antonio we reached the highest point of the pass, 8700 feet, and there a magnificent view burst upon us. We had all got out of the coach, as the road was rough, and there were rumours of robbers in the woods, and walked along in the invigorating mountain air, under the shade of fine trees, like a bit of a Devonshire park. Turning a corner with a foreground of grey rocks and red soil, under the arbutus trees with their scarlet leaves, and the live oaks with their young purple shoots, we suddenly saw below us the rich valley of the Tula, laid out like a map—fields of golden grain and green grass, white villages and haciendas, and a background of blue mountains rising up like a wall of opal between us and our goal, the Valley of Mexico. The Valley of the Tula is entirely surrounded by mountains, with single volcanos rising up out of the fertile plain, and the river winding away to the east, falls into the gulf at Tuxpan.

At San Miguelite, which we reached at 1.15, we had dropped 500 feet, and got into the coach again, or rather upon it; for tired of the jolting and heat of the inside, General and Mrs. P. and I got outside, and had a most enjoyable journey. A few miles beyond San Miguelite we were near having a disagreeable accident. We came down a long incline, to a bridge across a deep ditch full of water. This bridge was built after the fashion of this part of the country, with an abrupt rise just in the middle. Our cochero, as the mules dragged us with a mighty effort over this hogsback, put down the brake half a second too soon; snap it went close to his foot, and away went the mules, carried along by the weight of the heavy coach, straight for the ditch, which took a sudden bend back. We all thought we were in for an upset, without any doubt: but by dint of tremendous exertions on the part of the cochero and mozo, and torrents of abuse to the mules, which luckily Mrs. P. and I could not understand, the coach was stopped close to the edge of the ditch without hurt. It took some time to splice up the brake so as to make it fit for service over the bits of pedregal which crop up everywhere, thanks to the near neighbourhood of volcanos: but at last we got on, and drove across a splendid grass plain, to Agualete, 7675 feet. Here, as there was a bad bit of road, we got out, and walked down the hill to the hacienda, picking handfuls of amaryllis and wild reseda. Agualete is a large hacienda and flour-mill, supplied by water from an aqueduct along the top of a high stone wall. The fields all round are irrigated, and were yielding fine crops of wheat. Close to the aqueduct I saw a woman standing with a basket under a big nopal bush, and on going up to her found she was, by means of a long stick, with a wire hook at the end, hooking off the succulent green leaves of the cactus to cook. These leaves, if picked young enough, make a most delicious vegetable, of the consistency of stewed cucumber: at Colima we used to have them every day at dinner.

At San Antonio de Tula, 7200, which we reached at 4.30, a large hacienda, with a fine corridor of carved brown cantera stone running along the front, we joined the regular road, and our troubles, as far as relays, were over. How thankful I was to see the last of our poor mules; for I had got to know them each for some peculiar vice! Just outside the hacienda a deep cañon begins, and we kept between it and the mountain-side for several miles. Down the cañon were quantities of brilliant flowers; but they were too far off for me to make out what they were. The roads were abominable, stones and mud alternately, till we rose again into a band of mesquite country. Then, in the setting sun, we crossed a last divide, and down a steep hill swarming with workmen going home from the stone quarries, to a wooded valley; and crossing the broad shallow river under great groups of trees, we dashed round a corner into Tula, the ancient capital of the Toltecs.

26*th*.—Tula, 6610 feet, to Mexico, 7300.

Tula is in a charming situation under the hills, surrounded by trees, and boasts one of the finest churches I have yet seen in Mexico. The rest of the town is poor, excepting the hotel, which, being on the "*camino real*" (high road) between Mexico, the West, and the North—for here the road from San Luis Potosi joins in—is a very good one. My room was over the front of the house, and when Pablo knocked at my door, calling "*las quatro*"—4 o'clock A.M., I was repaid for the exertion of getting up at that unearthly hour by the view I got of the church, with its exquisitely proportioned dome and high-walled garden rising like a great ghost in front of my window in the grey dawn. After a hurried *desayuno* of chocolate and *biscoches*, about 5.15, we at last were all prepared. The coach, with its eight horses—two wheelers, four in the swing, and two leaders—was at the door, and, just before sunrise, away we went full gallop. We had given up our private coach, and taken places in the regular stage, so that we went a good seven miles an hour the whole day, changing horses or mules, as the case might be, every dozen miles. As the coach was crowded, I and two others of our party preferred a little extra dust and shaking to the heat inside, and travelled outside all day, thereby getting an excellent idea of the country, which grew more interesting every mile as we drew nearer to the capital.

Outside Tula we passed a church where evidently some great *fiesta* was going on; for even at that early hour, the churchyard was crowded with holiday folks dressed in their best, strolling about over the grass, or amusing themselves with swings and games under the trees. The road led up a long hill from the town through fields of barley, wheat, oats, and broad leaves, with Spanish broom and erythrina growing in the hedges: but at the top of the Divide, close to Venta la Bata, we had risen nearly 700 feet, and got into a totally different vegetation, with a dwarf fan palm growing among the rocks, and stunted maguey seemingly run wild from the plantations which covered the lower slopes.

At Venta la Bata we changed our horses at 7.30 for a splendid team of grey mules; and crossing a farther divide, 7490 feet, we reached the outer valley of Mexico, and stopped at Huehuetoca, 7275, for breakfast. A poor old beggar came creeping in during breakfast with quaint little cases made of plaited palm leaf; and Mrs. P. and I, unable to resist our mania for collecting curiosities, each got one; though, small as they were, it was rather difficult to know where to stow them, so crowded were we for room. The beggars are a most unpleasant feature in Mexican travelling. The moment the coach stops, a swarm of cripples, blind, and maimed, crowd to the door, and before one has time to alight, are displaying their various disgusting wounds, and clamouring for alms, sometimes actually catching hold of one in their eagerness.

Huehuetoca is close to the Laguna de Zumpango, round which Cortez retreated on his way to the friendly Tlascala after the misfortunes of the *Noche Triste*, from los Remedios, where he took refuge the night after his escape. " He took," says Mr. Prescott, " under the conduct of his Tlascalan guides, a circuitous route to the north, passing through Quauhititlan, and round lake Tzompanga (Zumpango), thus lengthening their march, but keeping at a distance from the capital. From the eminences as they passed along, the Indians rolled down heavy stones, mingled with volleys of darts and arrows on the heads of the soldiers. Some were even bold enough to descend into the plain, and assault the extremities of the column. But they were soon beaten off by the horse, and compelled to take refuge among the hills, where the ground was too rough for the rider to follow. Indeed, the Spaniards did not care to do so, their object being rather to fly than to fight."

Our road kept to Cortez's actual route for some leagues, and we saw in fancy, as we drove on, the worn-out Spaniards struggling along the plain, living on wild cherries, a few ears of corn, or a dead horse, while their enemies, to quote Mr. Prescott again, "followed in the track of the army like a flock of famished vultures, eager to pounce on the dying and the dead."

Leaving Huehuetoca about eleven we soon passed Coyotepec, a large hacienda standing on a ridge to the right, whose name (the Hill of the Coyote) denoted that we were within the old Aztec boundaries. "Tepec" in their language means a hill, as in the case of Chapul Tepec, the Hill of the Grasshopper, at which in the old picture-maps the wanderings of the Aztec nation always end, and which is there represented as a small hill with a huge grasshopper on the top.

A good road between wheat-fields, ditches filled with familiar-looking water-plants, and shaded with straight lines of upright Humboldt willows and aspens, led us to Cuantitlan, 7360 feet, a pretty town surrounded with rose-hedges, and apparently making its living by a manufacture of black shiny pottery. And a mile or so beyond we stopped at the foot of a long rise for our last *remuda* into Mexico. Eight white horses were harnessed in a moment, and away we flew at break-neck speed, only slackening about half way up the hill, as one of the middle horses got his head down and pulled so frantically against the collar as nearly to choke himself. The road down from the *Questa* was steep as a house-roof, and we swung from side to side so that every moment I expected to be shot off into a cactus-bush: but down we came in safety into a narrow valley with a stream and rows of Peru peppers and aspens; and emerging from the hills found ourselves at Tlalnepantla, in the actual valley of Mexico. But our impatience to see the famed valley was doomed to the most aggravating delay; for the streets of Tlalnepantla had, I should imagine, never been repaired since the days of Cortez, and were in such a state of mud, gulches, rocks, and holes that it took us more than half an hour to struggle through the wretched little town. Some market or feast was going on, as the Plaza was swarming with people, who had ample time during our slow progress to satisfy their curiosity by staring at me, and making audible remarks on my hat, my dress, and my extraordinary behaviour in going outside the coach.

At last we got free of the horrid streets and their scarcely less unpleasing inhabitants, and trotted away across the beautiful valley, along straight roads through green meadows, planted with upright Humboldt willows and Lombardy poplars, with dikes on either side; and past ruined Aztec villages and flourishing haciendas towards the famed city. The air was fragrant, like England in June, from damp grass, and the roses which lined the ditches everywhere. Popocatapetl was in an ill-humour, and hid his head in clouds, so that we only saw the grand slope up towards the snow-peak: but even that was enough to give one an awful feeling of unknown size and height; for the great blue ghost carried one's eye up and up till it seemed to mingle with the very clouds themselves. The roads were crowded with pack-mules, waggons, carts, horsemen, and coaches, and here and there a small body of troops. My task had been to count the mules and waggons, to get some idea of the traffic for a railroad; and in the journey since Tula we had passed or met 350 mules and 127 waggons, all carrying full loads, besides innumerable ones returning unpacked from various points, and Indios who were carrying half a mule's load packed on their shoulders.

It was three o'clock before we neared the city, which lay in the midst of the vast plain, its glittering towers and domes rising above the flat buildings; and the dark rock of Chapultepec, crowned with its white palace, away to the right, under the Ajusco mountain, which stands up strikingly out of the line which encircles the valley. At 3.30 we passed the Garita, and made our way through ruined suburbs, past dismantled convents, now turned into barracks, and waste open spaces half covered with sheets of water from the overflow of open sewers, which would breed a pestilence in any other climate, till we heard—oh wonder and delight!—the shriek of a locomotive, and coming to an open railway-crossing, jolted once more over real iron rails. I never thought I should have rejoiced so to see a railroad: but the ugly American engine, with its wide smoke-stack, seemed to us, after two months of bad roads and stage-coaches, like a harbinger of law, order, and civilisation; and we all indulged in frantic congratulations to each other on the joyful sight.

A quarter of an hour more and we raced down one of the principal streets, turned short in under a doorway, Señor A. crying to us to duck our heads or we should be killed; and pulled up in the patio of the Hôtel Iturbide.

CHAPTER XIX.

LIFE IN MEXICO.

The Hôtel Iturbide—Flowers—Tacubaya—The Paseo—Aztec calendar stone—The Inquisition—Cathedral of Mexico—A ride round the city—*Cinco de Mayo*—Chapultepec—The *Pronunciamiento* of October 1871—El Peñon del Agua Caliente—Executions by the Liberals—Breakfast at the San Cosme—Speeches—The Habanera—Mexican salutations.

Hôtel Iturbide, May 1, 1872.—Another chapter of my little history begun, amid flowers and birds, and comforts of all kinds. What a contrast to the records of the last two months! I have been too busy writing for two English and American mails to be able to take up my journal before; and also we have been resting a good deal, so a brief sketch of the last six days must suffice.

We arrived on Friday the 26th at about 4 P.M., and found that General R. and Mr. Y. had engaged most delightful rooms for us, opposite their own, in the old palace of the Iturbides; ours overlooking the Calle San Francisco, while theirs look into the patio or inner court. My room is about 30 feet by 25, and 18 feet high, with an iron balcony of its own, a prettily painted ceiling, large mirrors, and comfortably furnished; and now, with a hanging basket of flowers swinging in the window, round which an emerald humming-bird flutters, and bouquets on the table, it looks charming.

Saturday.—After a cup of delicious coffee and bread with

fresh butter, a luxury unseen since California, General P. and I took a stroll about 7.30 A.M. up the Calle San Francisco. At one of the cross-streets we came upon a crowd of flower-sellers, men and women, and in a moment were surrounded, and had the most exquisite bouquets thrust into our faces. One was offered for a *real* (6d.), which in London would have cost a guinea. Certainly anything more lovely or in more perfect taste I never saw. It reminded one of Prescott's account of the flowers of the plateau in Cortez's time.

A capital French restaurant is attached to the hotel, to which we go down for breakfast and dinner, beginning the morning with *desayuno* in our own rooms. The dining-rooms open on a small garden enclosed by walls thirty feet high, planted with eucalyptus trees, which grow ten and fifteen feet a year, and flowering trees and shrubs among which the humming-birds flash in the sunlight. A little stream two or three feet wide runs through the lawn in the middle, crowded with ducks, water-fowl, and *chichiquilotes* (the fly-catching snipe from Lake Tezcoco); in the trees cages of singing birds are hung. There are little kiosks all round, in which if one does not mind the chance of spiders, one can have one's meals. But it is a pretty and pleasant place, and, what is perhaps more to the point, the food is excellent.

At breakfast Mr. M. came in, and Major C., editor of the *Two Republics*, who kindly sent in later in the day a heap of New York papers, which were a perfect feast to us, as we have heard nothing from Europe or the East since leaving San Francisco. I got an English letter at breakfast, of the 11th of March, and spent part of the day in answering it, and the rest in reading Prescott, which is intensely interesting now one is on the actual spot. In the evening we got a telegram from M., asking for an escort from the Governor of Michoacan.

28th.—The day began delightfully by Pablo arriving at

the door with his arms literally full of flowers from Mr. Y.; sweet-peas, double seringa as large as a rose, and bunches of "Flor de San Juan" (*Bovardia*), far fuller and more fragrant than the meagre specimens we have in English hot-houses. It grows on the mountains, and the Indios bring it down packed in "*huacals*" on their backs. My room has been like a greenhouse ever since.

After breakfast, Mrs. P. and I, the General, Governor H. and Mr. Y. drove out to Tacubaya, westward from the city, the favourite suburb of Mexico, where all the rich residents have their country houses. A more charming spot can hardly be imagined; the cool airy houses are buried in trees, and surrounded with beautiful gardens in which flowers from every climate grow side by side luxuriantly. The Tlalpam Railroad, a local line of sixteen miles, running to Mixcoac, San Angel, Coyoacan and Tlalpam, has its first station at Tacubaya; and, with a line of horse-cars, puts it within easy reach of the city.

Coming home we turned down past the handsome depot of the Tlalpam Railroad, and drove to the Garita Porfirrio Diaz, by the side of the old aqueduct of the Agua Gordo, and then along the Paseo. We stopped at the Tivoli des Fleurs, a pretty cottage with a ditch round it filled with white arums, to get some ice-cream, and then went on the San Cosme, close to the old bull-ring, now quite falling to decay, as bull-fights are prohibited, though I believe they are sometimes winked at still. We drove home through the Alameda, which is on the Calle San Francisco. It is very pretty, with twelve different fountains under fine trees, native and foreign, and beds of flowers; a carriage drive all round the outside, and broad walks, some of them paved, run in all directions across it.

The streets of the city are straight, and cut each other at right angles, with here and there a Plaza planted with trees and flowers. The houses are all flat-roofed, and are built round a patio, which is reached from the street by a *porte cochère*. In the patio the carriage is kept; the stables also being often on the ground floor. The living-rooms are on the first floor; and outside them round the patio runs a balcony filled with flowers and bird-cages. At one end of the principal street, called in one part the Calle Plateros, and in another the Calle San Francisco, is the great Plaza, turned by the Empress Carlotta from a heap of rubbish into a beautiful labyrinth of trees, flowers, and fountains. On the north side stands the Cathedral, a noble building, with its two great towers and exquisitely proportioned dome, which rise above everything else in the city. The whole east side is occupied by the Palacio, containing within its walls all the Government buildings, the Congress Hall, and the President's house. The south and west sides are surrounded by shops shaded with deep *Portales*, under which a constant clatter of buying and selling goes on.

29*th*.—Wrote all day, and in the afternoon drove on the Paseo, and watched all the pretty Señoritas driving, and the *Pollos* (dandies), on their fine horses with silver-mounted trappings, and silver-embroidered hats and pantaloons, making their graceful bows, and then just tickling their fiery steeds with their ponderous spurs to make them caper and curvet before the Señoritas.

One could almost fancy one's-self in Hyde Park, from the crowds of carriages standing round the great fountain of Liberty at the end of the Paseo. The idea of danger did not enter one's wildest fancy: but since then we have heard this disagreeable fact :—

Not three months ago three young ladies of one of the very highest Mexican families here were driving on the Paseo. Their carriage happened to be the last of all coming home. They were suddenly stopped by several armed men on horseback, who asked the coachman whom he was driving. He, being a shrewd man, gave a false name, as, had their real name been known, they would have been *plagiared* (carried off for ransom). As it was, the robbers took all their jewels, and after debating whether they should kidnap them, at last decided, as the leader of the band did not come, to let them go home. In gratitude for this one of the girls kissed the chief's hand; and so the adventure ended.

We are told that it is quite unsafe to drive to Chapultepec (not three miles) unarmed.

April 30.—Before breakfast Mrs. P. and I went out for a walk along to the Plaza to look at the birds the Indios bring in for sale, and to poke about for curiosities. At the stands under the Portales all sorts of toys, silver filigree work, baskets, bowls of calabash prettily painted, pottery, and glass, are sold; and we are getting quite a large collection of all sorts of odds and ends, which though common enough here will be valuable at home. Coming back, we got some flowers and strawberries.

In the evening Governor H. and I took a walk all round the Plaza and behind the Cathedral, and examined the great Aztec Calendar Stone, which was disinterred in 1790 in the Plaza, and is now let into the north wall of the Cathedral. It is a huge circular block of black porphyry, about eight feet in diameter, weighing originally nearly fifty tons. On this the Calendar is engraved, "and," says Prescott, "shows that the Aztecs had the means of settling the hours of the day with precision, the periods of the solstices and of the equinoxes, and that of the transit of the sun across the zenith of Mexico. . . . It was transported from the mountains beyond Lake Chalco, a distance of many leagues, over a broken country intersected by water-courses and canals. In crossing a bridge which traversed one of these latter in the capital, the supports gave way, and the huge mass was precipitated into the water, whence it was with difficulty recovered. The fact that so enormous a fragment of porphyry could be thus safely

T

carried for leagues in the face of such obstacles and without the aid of cattle—for the Aztecs had no animals of draught—suggests to us no mean idea of their mechanical skill and of their machinery; and implies a degree of cultivation little inferior to that demanded for the geometrical and astronomical science displayed in the inscriptions on this very stone."

May 2.—Yesterday morning we drove at nine with Mrs. Y. to the Plaza San Domingo. It and all the buildings round it used to belong to the Inquisition, which was in existence till ten years ago. At the west side now is the Custom-house; on the east some conventual buildings, dismantled by the Liberals, and a chapel full of the most revolting figures. Outside the chapel is a long wall, against which political prisoners condemned to death are shot. The wall was full of bullet-holes, with a little cross scratched wherever any one had fallen. It seems horrible to shoot them there in the open Plaza.

On the north side is the Church of San Domingo. It must have been gorgeous in old days: but the Liberals have taken away all the jewels. The altar is carved up to the very ceiling, and decorated with figures and Venetian glass. Right and left are altars carved and gilded, with pictures let into the panels. Some of these pictures are very good. Service was going on when we went in, and the church was crowded. A priest was preaching in Spanish. We were not sorry to get out into the open air away from the scowling priest, who saw we were foreigners and "*hereticos,*" and the mass of listeners, who knelt and sat all over the floor; especially as we were told that the chances were rather serious in favour of the whole building falling down some day, as it was so shaken by earthquakes as to be quite out of the "plumb."

From thence we went to some charming public baths belonging to the Y.'s, in one of the old Inquisition buildings, and I shuddered as I thought what those thick walls must have seen. About two years ago, somewhere between the baths and the Plaza, a chamber in the wall was discovered which had no entrance except by a hole at the top, and in it were five dead bodies half mummied, evidently of some victims of that horrible institution, who had just been dropped in from above and nothing more heard of them. I saw a photograph of the group when it was discovered, rivalling Doré's Inferno in horror.

Down the same street was the Palace of Justice, originally a convent. There are two double courts, three stories high. A chapel between them is all that now remains of the convent, with so many carved and gilded shrines all round that it had the appearance of golden walls.

Thence we went to the Cathedral, which stands on the north side of the Plaza Mayor, as some say, on the site of the great teocalli of the Temple of Montezuma. The Cathedral consists of the main church, a triple nave, supported on very high pillars and rounded arches; and a large side chapel, seemingly of older date than the main building, as it is covered outside with elaborate stone carving, evidently by Aztec workmen. We went into it, but it was so crowded with a mob of the "great unwashed" that we soon came out and went round to the main entrance. The *coup d'œil* is very much spoilt by the choir, which fills up the centre of the nave, and leads to the high altar, by a pathway with a massive brass railing on either side, decorated by brass figures two to three feet high, at regular intervals.

The high altar is very gorgeous. It is supported on twelve green marble pillars, with a second row of smaller ones above. On each side of the steps are two magnificent pulpits, entirely made, stairs and all, of a kind of greenish alabaster, very clear and beautiful, and strangely carved with figures of angels, etc. They must be very old. The basins for holy water are of the same material. A great "Fonction" was going on, as it was the 1st of May, the month dedicated to the Virgin, and all her shrines were covered with flowers, and crowded with worshippers. The organ played lively tunes, which sounded more suitable to an opera-house than a church, the choir sang by snatches, and a wheel of bells on the screen was spun round and round, jingling as the Archbishop elevated the Host.

The Cathedral, Mexico.

At the back of the high altar is an apse of exquisite carving—all gilded, of course. The Liberals stripped the cathedral of all its jewels, and the silver chandeliers by which it was lighted have been replaced by commoner ones.

Outside, all along the wall of the raised ground on which the Cathedral stands, are groups of Indios selling birds under the trees, and women with picturesque stands of cakes and sweet drinks, draped in flowers and reeds. They have a pretty fashion here of hanging a kind of shade of fresh green reeds along the tops of the shop doorways, dotted with flowers. Flowers everywhere!

May 3.—We were up by eight, and took a walk in the Alameda, and then up to the flower-sellers. It is so disagreeable having to bargain: but as foreigners we are generally asked double if not treble what the people will take. The most flagrant instance of this I have met with was yesterday on the Plaza. A man had a cage of "Canarien de Siete Colores," nonpareil birds, four hens and three cocks. He asked six dollars a pair, and we said "No." He came down and down in his price, and at last, as we walked away, sent a little boy to offer us the cageful for six dollars.

In the same way the flower-sellers offer one a bunch for a *real*.

"*Es demasiado*" (It is too much).

"*Entonces Señorita, que daré usted?*" (Then what will you give?), and you get the whole for a *medio*, threepence.

May 4.—As usual, we took an early stroll along the streets; there is always something new and strange to be seen. The "*Aguadors*" or water-carriers are strange objects. A broad leather strap passes round their foreheads, supporting an immense water jar on their backs, while a second strap round the back of the neck supports a smaller one hanging in front of them. They wear a leather cap and leather apron, over white shirt and trousers.

After breakfast Governor H. and I went up on the *azotea*, the flat roof of the hotel, and got a fine view of everything except the top of Popocatapetl. Not once have we seen the great volcano entirely since we came; his head has been hidden in clouds in the most provoking way. I counted over thirty domes about the city, and the towers must have been double as many.

It was the fête of the Santa Cruz, and all the workmen of Señor ——'s new house, half a block up the street, were assembled on the roof, where an immense cross covered with flowers was erected, round which they were firing innumerable rockets and fire crackers. A more silly proceeding I never saw.

For the last two days it has been quite chilly, and several of our party have got colds on the chest. It is intensely hot on the sunny side of the street, but crossing to the shady side one is quite cold, so that chills are very common. This however is the hottest time of year, and the climate is most charming, as one is never too hot; and a shawl over one's shoulders, with a summer gown, is all one needs in the evening out walking. The Mexican ladies all wear a lace shawl or mantilla when walking in the morning, but a few are taking to hats. Foreigners dress usually after their own fashion; but Mrs. P. and I have discarded hats, as it is much pleasanter to wear a mantilla.

This afternoon, General P. being quite unwell with chills and fever, Governor H. and I took the horses, and, escorted by Pablo, started for a ride. We went through the Plaza, past the market, down the most filthy streets, each with an open black ditch of horror stagnating down the centre ; over the canal; and at last out on an open causeway running round the city. The great plain, once covered by the waters of Lake Tezcoco, which have now retreated three miles from the Garita of San Lazaro, lay beyond us covered with cattle, separated from us by a deep unfinished canal with running water in it. And towering up opposite to us, rose the beautiful Istaccihuatl (the White Woman), with a single pink cloud behind the peak, which brought out its snowy covering in strong relief. We turned to the right and rode along the causeway through gardens and orchards, with here and there a ruined church or a strong earthwork, reminding one unpleasantly of the possibilities of war and revolution in this troubled country. Pablo was armed; and in a state of such overflowing importance at the possession of a revolver, that we felt tolerably secure for ourselves as to robbers.

Alas for one's dreams of the floating gardens! One object of our ride was to try and find some trace of them. In vain had we asked all our friends: no one could tell us where they were, and all we could discover were oblong patches of garden, with a slimy ditch between each, which shake, it is said, if you jump on them, and—worst of all, they are covered with onions.

We came round to the canal again, higher up, and crossed by the Garita, where the port-dues are taken from the barges. The traffic by this canal from the south and southwest is enormous.

In twelve months, from 1st July 1865 to 30th June 1866, 102,541 tons of goods, paying duty, entered the city by this canal, besides 29,231 head of cattle:—

	Total weight in lbs.
Goods of the 1st class,	37,979,600
,, 2d class,	81,453,100
,, 3d class,	6,691,325
Timber and the finer woods,	10,876,275
Building-stone, etc.,	32,195,375
Goods in transit to the interior,	9,887,050
Total,	179,082,725
Which quantity, reduced to tons, equals .	89,541 tons.
Of eggs, sand, and other articles on the free list, are brought in at least	3,000 ,,
Articles coming in without the knowledge of the respective offices (contraband) amount at least to	10,000 ,,
Total,	102,541 tons.
Cattle entering the city by the canal during the same period,	29,000 head.

In the 1st class are included, among other articles, sugar, coffee, brandy, cocoa, hides, dry goods, flour, tobacco, furniture, glass, etc.

In the 2d class—beans, cotton, charcoal, wheat, pepper, fruits, pulque, soda, fish, etc.

In the 3d class—carts, straw bags, matting, ropes, straw, hats, etc.

We rode from the Garita up the great causeway, by which, I believe, Cortez entered the city of Mexico, along the side of the canal. Half-way up, towards the city, stands, on a pedestal, a fine bust of Guatemozin, the last of the Aztec kings. It was erected by President Juarez in 1869, with an inscription, on one side, in Aztec; on the other, in Spanish. Close by is one of the many fountains of water one finds all over the town. An old soldier was filling a little *jarita*, and I asked him for a drink, which of course he gave me, with the usual courtesy of the lower orders here. I really believe it is a pleasure to them to be asked to do one any little favour.

All the streets were full of preparations for the 5th of May; and little boys, with green, white, and red calico flags, were getting up processions of their own, and terrified our horses with cries of "*Abajo los Franceses*"—Down with the French!

May 5.—I was awoke before dawn by men singing, or rather yelling, patriotic songs in the streets. At sunrise a salute of twenty-one guns was fired, with an accompaniment of fire-crackers, and then the noise was incessant till ten at night.

And all this patriotism, display, excitement, and boasting, what does it commemorate?

"It is because 3000 sick Frenchmen could not take a very strong position, defended by 15,000 Mexicans."

Such was the explanation of the great and glorious Cinco de Mayo, which Mr. —— gave me.

The event was in reality the battle of Puebla, when the French, in 1862, advanced from the coast, and tried to take that city. And ever since, the 5th of May has been to the Mexicans what the 4th of July is to Americans.

After breakfast, about 10.30, we all adjourned to the balcony of my room to see the great procession through the Calle San Francisco.

First came the public schools, all the boys in new clothes, with a small advanced guard of cavalry; three bands; then the members of Congress, two and two, looking, in their black trousers, tail coats, and tall hats, as if they were going to a funeral; then, strongly guarded by a large body of police, came the Cabinet; and last, between the minister of war, and some other distinguished member of the Government, walked a short thickset ugly man, with a smooth face, who I knew in a moment to be Juarez, as thorough an Indio as any who sells birds on the Plaza. The police kept closely round him, so fearful are they of assassination; then followed more bands playing; and, lastly, the troops, a much more soldierlike and well-dressed body than we have seen heretofore.

After the whole Government had gone on to the Teatro Nacional to make speeches and orations, Mrs. P. and I went to see the S.'s, who asked us to go with them out to Chapultepec. I drove with Mr. S. and Father ———, a German, who was the Emperor Maximilian's confessor and private secretary, a most charming old gentleman, courteous and simple, with that *savoir faire* which a thorough knowledge of the world gives.

He talked to me a great deal about the sad state of this country, in which he has lived for more than twenty years, and told me that when he was in prison four years ago, he and some of his friends met together one night, and said to each other, " Well, what next?" Then he told them the story of the Indian who was caught in the rapids above

Niagara, and how, when he found that all efforts to save himself were useless, he wrapped himself in his blanket, and, standing up, went over the Falls without another movement. "Now," said he, "we are in the state of that Indian; and every man in Mexico must wrap himself in his blanket, and allow himself to be swept down with the stream."

I did not like to ask him much about the Emperor and Empress. It was the first time he had ever been to the Castle since the fall of the Empire, and he evidently felt it very much.

But I am forgetting, in the Father's conversation, the road by which we drove out. The Paseo del Imperador, a fine macadamized road, made by Maximilian, and planted with rows of poplar, cotton-woods, and willow trees, leads over flat green meadows which used, in Montezuma's time, to be covered with water, to the Royal Hill of Chapultepec, which the successive rulers of Mexico have kept as their country palace.

The rock of porphyry on which the castle is built rises abruptly out of the dead flat, and around its foot are the groves of "Ahuahuetes," the famous cypresses under which the Aztec kings held their court. Their boughs are covered with masses of the grey "Spanish moss" (*Tillandsia usneoides*), hanging down in streamers and festoons yards long from every twig, and giving the trees a weird look which is quite indescribable.

Driving round to the western face of the rock, up which the Americans stormed in 1847, a new road, built by Maximilian, winds up to the summit. On it stands the castle, built at the end of the last century by the Viceroy Galvez, thereby arousing the jealousy of the Government, and hastening the end of the Spanish rule.

We first came to a mass of buildings, once the military academy, but now unused, with beds of flowers in front, round which the carriage-drive runs. Getting out, we walked through a gateway and along a flagged open passage, passing the Emperor's private entrance through a low

The Palace of Chapultepec.

postern to our left, over which grew a passion-flower in full bloom—strangely appropriate, I thought, to those who so often passed in and out of that doorway.

From the eastern side a winding stair led us up to the

beautiful garden, round which are the rooms of the house on the side facing the city, and a broad portico open to the west and north. At one end is the Empress Carlotta's bedroom, opening into a small sitting-room, and looking over the plain away to the volcanos, then a *salon*, a library, and, opening into the latter, Maximilian's bedroom and study. None of these rooms are large; and their decorations, though in perfect taste, are simplicity itself. In the garden, nearly all the trees were planted by the Emperor and Empress's own hands—Australian Eucalypti, oranges, and the finer kinds of pines. Round the portico, and scattered about the ground, are exquisite bronzes from the antique; and it did my heart good to find the Venus of Milo and the Apollo Belvedere underneath that tropic sun; and the walls of the portico decorated with Pompeian frescos. The present occupants have had them all draped, considering them too little clothed to be fit for Mexican eyes. The effect may be imagined better than described!

We climbed up to the Observatory, which stands in the garden, and there a view burst upon us which made us at last realize the beauty of the far-famed valley. To the east, up the green-fringed Paseo del Imperador, lies the city, with its countless domes and towers glistening white in a rich setting of green trees. Beyond it lies the hill of Guadalupe, and the sacred place of Mexico, where the Virgin first appeared on the Western continent. To the right of it again is the Lake of Tezcoco, with the town of Tezcoco just visible below the mountains on its farther side. Following the lake round, a purple volcanic hill, rising abruptly from the plain, cuts it off, and hides Lake Chalco, forming a low foreground to the two giant volcanos, Istaccihuatl and Popocatapetl, who rear their heads, covered with eternal snow, 17,712 feet into the blue tropic sky. From the slopes of Popocatapetl a range of mountains extends right round the valley, with the Ajusco, the highest of them, directly west of the city, till the circle is completed at Guadalupe again. Lines of upright Humboldt willows and Lombardy poplars, marking some road, run in all directions over the green and golden plain; and from masses of trees rise, even on the lower slopes of the mountains, the white towers of scores of churches or haciendas. Below us feathered the weird "Ahuahuetes," with their grey garlands of moss, and Maximilian's unfinished lake sparkled in the setting sun.

We drove down and round the rock once more, stopping to measure "Montezuma's tree," the king of the grove. It is said to be forty-five feet in girth; but we all agreed that measurement to be under the mark. It is a triple tree, without a sign of decay. A group of three or four more close by are almost as large, and to the west of the rock are four avenues of them converging from a common centre. Under these trees Montezuma held his court, sipping his "*chocolatl*" in golden goblets, or smoking "*tobacco*" mingled with Liquidambar; while the rock above was used as a watch-tower and place of sacrifice. What strange and sad thoughts filled one's mind as we turned away to the Royal Hill! First the favourite home of the proudest of Indian monarchs; then in the hands of the Spaniards for nearly three centuries, who, in their zeal to obliterate all memory of the past, actually destroyed the statues of Montezuma and his father cut in bas-relief in the porphyritic rock; assaulted and taken by the Americans in 1847; then the scene of Maximilian's brief reign; and now once more, strangest of all changes, the home of a pure Indian,—for there lives Don Benito Juarez, President of this great and unhappy Republic; using the rooms, and eating off the porcelain plates of a Prince of Austria. Truly truth is stranger than fiction!

6th.—This afternoon I called on Mrs. ———, and she gave me a curious account of the Pronunciamiento last October.

I could hardly realize that only six months ago the guns had been pointed up and down the street we were in; and that the bullets were flying over the *azotea* so fast that her husband, who had gone up there to see the state of affairs, had to beat a hasty retreat.

In May 1871, the temporary peace of Mexico, which had lasted since the Emperor Maximilian's death, was once more disturbed by a presidential election. The candidates were Don Benito Juarez, Señor Lerdo de Tejada, and Don Porfirio Diaz. Juarez was elected (for the fourth time). Señor Lerdo (the present President of Mexico) retired quietly from the contest, and lived in the city of Mexico. But Diaz, persuaded against his will by over-zealous friends, most unfortunately for himself and Mexico, consented to put himself at the head of a revolutionary movement, and, as they say here, "pronounced" against the Government in October 1871.

It was on a Sunday morning. The President was at Chapultepec. The Ministers all out of town. A regiment in the barracks close to the Alameda were the first to "pronounce." Their colonel was at church. When he came back he found the whole barracks in an uproar. He mounted the stairs, and tried to bring his men to reason—they shot him dead.

Before the President heard of the *pronunciamiento* the rebels had possession of the citadel. He behaved with the greatest firmness, sending at once for General ——, at that time in the city; who vowed that he would "retake the citadel before midnight, or die in the attempt." Accordingly, as soon as it was dark, he commenced an advance over the *azoteas* of the houses, and by 12.30 had kept his word, for the citadel was once more in possession of the Government troops.

The contest has proved more serious than was at first anticipated; and for between eight and nine months the whole country has been overrun with guerilla bands, who make the revolution an excuse for wholesale highway robbery and murder, besides requisitions on every estate for food, forage, arms, and money.

A letter to-night from the engineers from Morelia, and a telegram from Acambaro; so we may soon expect to see them.

7th.—This morning we rode out to the Peñon del Agua Caliente, on the shores of the Laguna de Tezcoco. We left the city by the Garita de San Lazaro, and turning from the Vera Cruz high road, rode across a flat, in some places covered with turf, in others incrusted with salt, soda, and potass, reaching, in about three miles, a solitary cone of volcanic rock. It is an old volcano: but some convulsion seems to have tipped it over, so that the crater is now low down on the south-west side, forming a cave.

Round the foot of the Peñon are salt-works, of a most primitive kind. They are on this fashion :—A quantity of the earth is placed in a round hole at the top of a raised heap. Upon this water is poured, which, escaping by means of a small pipe through the side of the heap into an earthen pot, crystallizes into salt or soda as the case may be.

There is a hot spring here, as the name of the place denotes. It is inside a square of buildings, in the centre of which stands a fine and very old church. Invalids come hither and stay for the sake of the baths. We got off our horses and went into the bath-house, a low dark building, with baths of different degrees of heat; the bubbling water in the last being so hot I could only just bear my fingers in it.

Mounting again and riding round the foot of the hill, we tried to get down to the lake: but its shores were too marshy to bear our horses' weight. So we rode up to the old crater. In the mouth of it, which forms a large cave, live a quantity of most hideous Indians, who talk little or nothing but Aztec. They crowded round us for quartillas, driving away their innumerable dogs, who rushed out barking and bristling. These people live by catching tiny fish, about an inch long, that abound in the lake; and these they cook over a fire of dried manure, and sell to their fellow Indians farther inland, who live chiefly upon it. The ground all round sounds unpleasantly hollow to the horses' tread, and great alarm has been felt several times at strange noises heard in the Peñon, as people in the city fear it may take it into its head to explode again some day. Riding home across the flats, which in the rainy season are covered with water, the sun was intensely hot, for it was past 10 A.M., and my little horse fretted me, as he would not do the regular pacing gait like the others, but either walked like a snail or jogged. Coming through the city we passed the gas-works, where gas is made from resin.

We passed also a splendid old church, which, with a large piece of ground round it, has just been sold by the Government for $5000. It is now used as a factory of some kind. Smoke was coming out of the little windows at the top of the beautiful dome, a great proof that the Church-party is not in the ascendant just now.

Since the Liberals came into power by the death of the Emperor Maximilian, the power of the clergy has been entirely taken from them. The churches are despoiled; the convents dismantled; poor old nuns of eighty are turned adrift homeless and penniless in the streets; and the clergy, who now are not allowed to appear outside the church-walls in their robes, are paying back four-fold the debt they have been laying up ever since the conquest. Their punishment is heavy; but their crimes have been heavy also. During the last century two-thirds of the real estate of the country was in their hands; and the vast quantities of silver and gold produced annually used by them for "church purposes," instead of the further development of the land.

In one Plazuela, against a blank wall, are some hundreds of bullet-holes and crosses rudely scratched in the plaster. At every cross a man has been shot—among others, General Doran, one of the Imperialist generals. Mr. ——, as we rode by, pointed out the spot where he had seen him fall. In the Plaza San Domingo, General ——, an old man of seventy, was shot about five years ago. The wretches tied his elbows together, and put him up against the wall on a heap of dirt, and shot him in the open square.

Three of the churches we passed were quite out of the perpendicular from earthquakes, and also, I believe, from the shifting soil on which the city stands, owing to the gradual drying up of the lake. Two on the opposite sides of one street looked most absurd, leaning towards each other as if making a bow.

In the evening we went to a party given by the American Minister. Most of those present were American or English: but there were several French, a few Mexicans, and we had some charming music.

May 8.—After receiving several very pleasant visitors we drove out to the American Cemetery. It is just beyond the English Cemetery, in the outskirts of the city. Mr. S., the U. S. Consul, found it in shocking repair, overflowed constantly by the water from the ditches. So he has put up a wall all round, and keeps it in the most perfect order. The first part is a garden with a pretty cottage where the man in charge lives, and farther on are the graves, planted with flowers; the monument to the American soldiers who fell during the Mexican war, a plain and rather ugly erection, stands at the end under the tall trees, which shade the whole cemetery. We came away loaded with flowers which the gardener gave us.

Fresh facts about this curious country come under one's

notice every day. To-day I was told that till quite lately a favourite method of making money among some members of the community, has been stealing the gravestones from the different cemeteries and selling them. We drove down to Chapultepec by a fine Calzada, alongside the aqueduct of the Agua Delgado. At every leak in the masonry grow masses of maidenhair fern, and pretty little flowers. A little while ago this Calzada was thought unsafe, and no one would drive on it; which was a pity, for it is the best-made road I have seen in Mexico : but now there is no danger, and as the coachman had a revolver in his belt, we had a safe and pleasant drive out, and home by the Paseo, which was crowded.

9th.—We went to a breakfast at the Tivoli de San Cosme, given by Mr. ——, an American. The G.'s, Madame R., and her mother, Señora ——, a daughter of the President, who was extremely pleasant, her husband and several others, about thirty in all, were there. We began by a game of bowls in the Tenpin Alley, and at one o'clock went to breakfast in the open gallery of the main building. On one side we looked down into the wood of beautiful trees which shade most of the garden, with a great tame monkey swinging about the branches; and on the other over a pretty flower garden, with a stream running through it, to the blue mountains. An excellent military band played all breakfast-time, and drove the dancers of the party nearly crazy by playing valses and habaneras. I sat between Madame R. and Señor C., with the Minister of War and the President's daughter opposite. Señor C. could not speak a word of French or English; so I had no alternative between taking a fearful plunge into the quagmire of my bad Spanish, or silence. I chose the quagmire : and to my utter surprise and delight, found I could actually make myself intelligible to the Señor, and that I could also understand him. It was very encouraging, and I find the Mexicans so merciful and patient with one's blunders, that I mean to work hard at my Spanish, about which I have been quite in despair lately.

After fourteen courses of meat, with hardly any vegetables, had gone round, in true Mexican fashion, the toasts began while *dulces* were served. Some of the speeches were admirable. An old gentleman of eighty, who forty years ago was United States Consul here, made the prettiest speech in Spanish in proposing "the Ladies:"—"To the only aristocracy we tolerate, who rule us without laws, and from whose judgment there is no appeal." "Leaving us with only a *suplica*," added the Minister of War, which means the prayer for mercy of a condemned criminal.

The Governor of Mexico made a capital speech also. Speech-making, so tedious usually, seems a natural gift to Mexicans; and is as pleasant to the listeners as it is easy to the speech-makers.

After breakfast, that is to say about 3.30 P.M., we all went into the garden. Then the large dancing hall was opened, next to the gallery where we had breakfasted, and adjourning there, we danced till half-past five, and I at last learned the "Habanera."

Of all dreamy easy dances it is the most charming, with the strangest changes of time, and the strangest time for dancing all through. I found when I had once gone through the figure that I knew it. It opens by two couples doing a very slow *chaine des dames* without turning; then your partner takes you round the waist, giving his left hand to the other lady, and you giving your right to the other gentleman, and thus you *balancez* three or four times forward and back; and then comes the delicious half valse, half polka, half walk,—I do not know how to describe it. Then you begin with another couple, and so on all round the room. One custom they have is that during the crossing in the first figure, a gentleman, if he has no partner, may slip in and take a *paloma* (dove), that is, steal a lady from her first partner: but everything is done so quietly, lazily, and gracefully that you hardly seem to move.

After the dancing was over we parted from all the ladies with the regular Mexican salutation,—a stage embrace, one hand on the shoulder, the other round the waist; and a kiss on both cheeks. It took me completely by surprise with strangers, Señora ———, the President's daughter, for instance: but it is the correct thing; and must be gone through as a matter of course.

CHAPTER XX.

LIFE IN MEXICO—*continued.*

Indios and their costumes—Street cries—Guadalupe—Arrival of the engineers—Trying a gun—An *agua cerro*—Drainage—The Academia—Aztec arts—The Palacio—A Mexican debate—Chills and fever—Gizzard tea—The Monte Pio—The tree of the *Noche Triste*—A narrow bridge—Departure of the engineering party—Feast of Corpus Christi—Tacubaya—The Museum—A "useful man"—The considerate *compadre*.

ONE can never be dull in Mexico if one's window looks on any thoroughfare. The passers-by are a continual amusement, and remind one of the changing patterns in a kaleidoscope. The gaily dressed and well-mounted Caballeros riding out to the Paseo, or starting for some journey to the country, with a well-armed troop of servants behind them; the rumbling diligencias, with their eight horses, tearing over the ill-paved streets at full gallop, and turning corners in safety where you expect to see them overturn bodily; the mule-waggons coming in laden with bales of cotton from the north; long trains of pack-mules, with quaintly dressed "*arieros*" in leathern apron and drawers, coloured shirt, and broad sombrero, starting with loads of goods for the interior; and the little burros trotting into market, entirely buried, save their heads and tails, in a load of alfalfa grass, vegetables, or chickens from the country round.

Then there are the Indios, who ply their various trades

in the streets. Each class has its distinguishing dress, often very picturesque.

The *carboneros* jog along in ugly dark-blue cotton clothes, with narrow white stripes, a grey serape over their shoulders; the women with a bit of coarse cloth on their heads, put on like a Roman peasant's head-dress, their long braids of hair bound with red, twisted round it, and their heavy packs of charcoal, covered in coarse grass, supported by a leather strap across the shoulders.

The fruit-seller, in a blue striped petticoat and man's straw sombrero, carries a tray of tempting fruits—bananas, water-melons, oranges, limes, mangos, zapotes, chirimoyas, avocates, from the Tierra Caliente, and strawberries, figs, pears, apples, and all the temperate fruits from the plateau.

The "*aguador*," water-carrier, has a leather yoke and apron over his white shirt and blue trousers, carries a huge red earthen jar on his back, and a smaller one hanging down between his hands, each hung by leather straps on his head, which is covered in a close-fitting peaked leather cap.

Sombre—almost grotesque—as his dress appears, the pulque carrier exceeds him in quaintness. He too has the leather apron, but his shirt is often a dark blue, with red or white stripes; he wears leather drawers coming just below his knees, and over a bit of cloth on his head, which once was white, a leather strap supports the quivering pig-skin full of pulque on his back, while under his arm he carries the "*acojote*," or long gourd, used as a siphon to suck the juice from the maguey plant. Anything more unpleasant than the appearance of a cart full of pulque skins shaking over the rough roads, like pigs made of light brown jelly, cannot well be pictured. The popular account of the way the skins are obtained is so entirely novel I may as well recount it.

A pig is selected, shut up by himself, and starved for several days. He is then taken out, tied by one hind leg to a tree, and in front of him at some distance an ear of maize is laid. The ravenous pig espies the tempting food, and struggles to get free: but his hind leg is much too firmly secured. At last—so says the historian—his frantic efforts succeed, but how? He pulls himself out of his own skin!

The "*Mantequero*," lard merchant, is an important person, for in Mexico lard is used instead of butter in all kitchens. He stalks along all in grey, grey shirt, short drawers, and strip of grey cloth round his waist like a short petticoat, carrying the tub of lard piled up in a white pyramid on his head.

The "*Galopinas*," kitchen-maids, go out to market each morning to get the provisions for the day's consumption—nothing is bought in large quantities. Their plain dark brown or blue stuff gowns and blue rebozos look dingy, though respectable: and one is glad of a bit of bright colour in the dress of some of the other women of the city, who wear the universal white shift, embroidered round the neck, and a full petticoat which is of some bright red stuff three quarters of its length, while the upper part is brilliant yellow.

But after all, the most interesting of all the Indios are the bird-sellers, who bring their "*huacals*," or packs of birds, up from the Tierra Caliente, and sit in crowds in the Plaza outside the cathedral. They bring "*Sen sontiles*" or mocking-birds; *clarines* with their quiet grey plumage and ringing metallic voices; *pito real*, or royal whistler, a green and blue bird the size of a thrush, dirty and greedy when kept in confinement, devouring an unbelievable amount of "*moscas*," small black flies, which are found, I believe, near the Lake of Tezcoco, and sold by the pint measure; "*cardinals*," with brilliant red plumage; and the lovely "*canario de siete colores*," or nonpareil as it is called in the southern States, a canary with seven different colours on its tiny body; parrots and paroquets from Vera Cruz and Oaxaca; and sometimes, I grieve to say, a cage of little humming-birds, lovely as the flowers put at the bottom of their cage, who generally beat themselves to death in a few hours.

In the evening, the streets, though deserted by these traders, are anything but quiet. Their place is taken by more noisy vendors, who rend the air with cries of "*Tamales con puerco,*" a very uninviting hot and greasy kind of sausage-roll. And one woman about 9 P.M. every night chanted in piercing tones a long recitation, of which I could only distinguish the words—"Hot ducks, O my soul! O hot ducks!" Later, when all these sounds are stilled, and the streets are deserted, as the clock strikes 10 P.M. one is startled by a hideous din, which continues the whole night through. At every street corner a "*sereno,*" watchman, with a lantern is stationed. At each quarter of the hour he blows a whistle, shriller than words can describe, which is answered by all the other watchmen on his beat, and each hour he sings to a sort of Gregorian tone the time and state of the weather, "*Las doce, y sere-e-no.*"

At first I found sleep impossible, as a *sereno* unfortunately was stationed close to the hotel; and also I was continually roused in the middle of the night by what I took to be a boy of wakeful habits whistling the Mexican "*retraite,*" that most unmelodious of all bugle-calls. Time, however, accustomed me to the watchman's shouts and whistles, and I discovered that the little boy was a mocking-bird belonging to Señor Lerdo de Tejada, the present President of Mexico, whose house was opposite, that woke up at intervals during the night to pour forth this call in the darkness.

Monday, May 13.—General P. and I rode in the afternoon out to Guadalupe, famous for two circumstances: firstly, as being the first and only spot, till a year or two ago, where the Virgin is supposed to have appeared on the western continent; secondly, as being the scene, on the 2d February 1848, of the signing of the Treaty of Guadalupe

Hidalgo, by which New Mexico and Upper California were ceded to the United States.

Guadalupe lies about four miles from the city, up a long straight road, with trees on either side, through green meadows covered with white herons. To the left of the road runs the old causeway, up which the pilgrims used to crawl to the shrine on their knees, with twelve "stations" of carved stone and images on it, where they stopped to rest and pray. This causeway has now been sold to the Mexico and Vera Cruz Railroad Company, and trains run along it in place of the pious pilgrims, who must now make use of the train, or go up the muddy road—another proof of the decadence of priestly power in the country.

Guadalupe is built round the foot of a projecting spur from the mountain range on the northern side of the Mexican basin, which ends abruptly within half a mile of the Lake of Tezcoco.

The place consists of three churches;—a little sky-blue one on the top of the hill, over the spot on which the Virgin appeared; two in the town below, decorated with quantities of delicate stone carving and coloured tiles; about sixty houses; and, as far as we could see, about the same number of inhabitants.

How such a miserable little hole can warrant trains almost every hour in the day is a miracle indeed; yet the Indios troop there in such numbers that ten special trains run every day between Mexico and Guadalupe, taking first class passengers the single journey for a "*real*," 6d., and second class for a "*medio*," 3d.

Coming home it was quite dark, and we came at a sharp hand-gallop all the way. A thunder-storm was raging in the western mountains, and the bright flashes lit up the whole country in pink and blue light every moment. A little way out of Guadalupe the General pulled up:—

"Have you a pocket in your habit?"

"Yes."

"Then you had better take this," pulling a Derringer from his coat; "when you fire it, full cock it and pull the trigger."

It struck us as so absurd to have to take these precautions in a quiet afternoon ride three miles from a great city, that we both burst out laughing. But nevertheless I buttoned my little protector inside my jacket, putting an extra cartridge in my pocket, and rode on at a good pace with my hand on the hilt. The General had his trusty six-shooter in readiness, and we both kept a sharp look-out behind the trees and in the ditches, full of green bushes. A mounted patrol of two men and a sergeant were keeping guard; but notwithstanding this protection there have been a good many robberies along this bit of road in the last few months; while a mile beyond Guadalupe, where the route runs along the Lake shore, there is a point where the chances are so heavy in favour of your being robbed, that for some time it has been almost deserted by travellers, unless they are strongly escorted.

Going straight in to dinner in my habit when we got home, I pulled the little pistol out and laid it beside me on the table; and was greeted with a shout of laughter from all our party.

What would people in England think of a young lady producing one of these deadly weapons after a quiet ride down to Richmond on a summer afternoon! I was very glad to restore the Derringer to its owner; for the saying is, that if you carry one you are sure to shoot yourself or your best friend before six months are out, as they require such careful handling.

14*th.*—I had a most pleasant surprise to-day. We were going out in the afternoon for another ride—this time on a safer road—when, as I was sitting waiting, Señor A. looked in and said some one wanted me. I, thinking it was a visitor, who might keep me from my ride, said in Spanish, with I fear no very amiable tone of voice, that the "some one" was to come in. However, as he or she did not obey, I went out: and there in the passage, more burnt and dusty than can be described, stood my brother. He had just arrived with the engineering party from Toluca, having made another most satisfactory reconnaissance, up the valley of the Lerma from Salamanca to its source in the Lago de Lerma, near Toluca. They had seen robbers, but had not been robbed; and found timber and riches of every kind in the country,—the only misfortune being that one of the party sickened with fever on the trip, and by the time he arrived at the city was seriously ill.

General P. and I rode out by the Garita of San Lazaro and down the Vera Cruz stage road for about three miles. Just outside the Garita, in some adobe fortifications, were a company of soldiers, a waggon, and a quantity of lookers-on, a class very common in Mexico, where people always seem to have time, whatever the occupation they are engaged in, for a lounge, a gossip, and a "*cigarro*," whether the object of interest be an execution or a tumble-down mule.

"There is a row there," said my companion; and I galloped past, looking the other way, with a horrible fear lest some one was being shot.

Coming back, as the crowd was still there, I suggested that this might be the case, and General P. said the same idea had struck him. It was too horrid to be in uncertainty any longer; so with my best bow and in my best Spanish I asked a man in the road, "*Que succede?*"

"*No mas que provar una Canonazo*,"—only trying a gun, was the answer. How relieved I was! But we found afterwards, on inquiry, that my fears had been quite needless, as the authorities have still a little respect for the feelings of the civilized inhabitants, and have all executions at half-past four or five A.M.

The P.'s and I dined out in the evening, and on the dinner-table were a collection of the most splendid carnations I have ever seen. In one bouquet there were sixteen varieties, of every shade, from palest yellow to one which was almost black. The country seems to suit them specially, and it would be well worth while for English gardeners to get seed from here. During dinner we had what is here called an "*agua cerro,*" which, in plain English, means a regular deluge; and such it was—the rain coming down in sheets, reminding one of Schnorr's picture of the Flood, where the angels are represented pouring water out of buckets on the world below. These *agua cerros* are the forerunners of the rainy season, which is beginning this year unusually early. The Feast of St. John is generally the time it commences, and this year it is nearly six weeks before its time. As we drove home, the streets were in many places a foot deep in water; and with the queer foreign houses and churches, narrow streets, and the lights reflected in the water, of whose depth one could not judge, one might have imagined one's-self in Venice, except that the "*coche*" was hardly as smooth and easy a conveyance as a gondola.

Next morning the effects of the storm were much less poetic. When M. and I went out for an early walk the water had subsided, and the streets were covered with a slippery, slimy mud, most disgusting to touch and smell. Indeed, instead of mending matters by washing the town clean, the rain seems to have made things even worse than before.

The system of drainage here is primitive. Each house, as I have said before, is built round a *patio,* a square paved court, six inches to one and a half feet below the street level. Across the centre of this court to the main drain in the street runs the principal sewer of the house, covered, it is true, with flat paving-stones: but these are generally merely laid side by side across it without cement or mortar, so that a poisonous gas rises from innumerable cracks between the badly-fitting stones. When a rain-storm comes the *patios* are flooded, these drains are all flushed, and the consequences may be imagined.

One of the engineers, as I said, came in yesterday with a bad attack of fever beginning, and this atmosphere is not likely to improve it.

On Wednesday afternoon we went with a large party of friends to the Academia—a very good art-school, with a picture-gallery attached. Señor Obregon, a young Mexican artist, who was educated in the Academia, met us there and took us all over it. The pictures of the old Mexican school, which filled several rooms, were simply atrocious, mere replicas of the very lowest Spanish art; and in the two rooms of European pictures, I only found three productions worth looking at, though we were shown (*not* by Señor Obregon) endless "real Murillos." I am sorry for poor Murillo's reputation if he ever touched them.

But the really interesting room was that of the modern Mexican school. It is a fine room, well proportioned, and decorated with fresco medallions of all the old masters round the roof, and some of the pictures are really beautiful. Señor Obregon holds a deservedly high place among Mexican artists, and he had several of his pictures there. One of Columbus as a youth was fine enough to establish any artist's reputation; and I was delighted to find from him that he intends ere long to come to Europe, where I hope he may make himself a name.

The Mexicans seem to have a natural talent for art. Even the poor Indios show extraordinary aptitude in doing anything which needs taste in arrangement of colour. The painted gourds and calabashes in which the "*chia*" and other sweet drinks at the street-corners are sold are often extremely pretty, painted in bands of black and colour, with patterns in gold and silver, brilliant but not gaudy.

The pottery I have already mentioned: but lately I have been getting, thanks to Mrs. Y., a collection of "*Typos del País,*" little pottery figures four inches high, of all the different costumes of the country; for here each occupation has its distinguishing dress. They are exquisitely made, in the most perfect proportion, all coloured exactly according to life; and so delicate is the workmanship, that in the features of two tortilla makers, one from the city of Mexico, the other from Puebla, you can at a glance distinguish the two distinct races of the Aztec and Tlascalan; and these figures, worthy of coming from the hand of a first-rate artist, are made for two *reales* (1s.) each, by a poor old Indio, crippled, ill, and half-starved, who has no tools to work them with, save his nails and little bits of stick! Poor old Manuel; if he lived in Europe or the States, his fortune would soon be made; and now his old wife, Manuela, tells me that, as he is very ill and can only do a very few of these little statuettes in the week, they often do not know how to get their next meal.

These are far superior to the wax and rag figures, which are also made in the city. The latter are larger and more effective, but they look unnatural, and are so easily broken, or melted, in the trajet through the Tierra Caliente and Cuba, that very few arrive safely at the end of their journey.

Another art here is that of silver and gold filigree work, some of which is most beautiful and delicate. I have constant invasions of silver workers to my room, bringing napkin-rings—which, if a little larger, would make beautiful bracelets,—ear-rings, butterflies for the hair, necklaces, and crosses, for which they ask an exorbitant price at first, and end by coming down to an absurdly small sum for such delicate workmanship.

The most characteristic art, however, which remains in

Mexico, is that of making feather-pictures. Prescott says, "The art in which they (the Aztecs) most delighted was their *plumaje* or feather-work. With this they could produce all the effect of a beautiful mosaic. The gorgeous plumage of the tropical birds, especially of the parrot tribe, afforded every variety of colour: and the fine down of the humming-bird, which revelled in swarms among the honeysuckle bowers of Mexico, supplied them with soft aërial tints that gave an exquisite finish to the picture. The feathers, pasted on a fine cotton web, were wrought into dresses for the wealthy, hangings for apartments, and ornaments for the temples. No one of the American fabrics excited such admiration in Europe, whither numerous specimens were sent by the conquerors. It is to be regretted that so graceful an art should have been suffered to fall into decay.

"This art held an honourable place among the trades of the Aztecs. 'Apply thyself, my son,' was the advice of an aged chief, "to agriculture, or to feather-work, or some other honourable calling. Thus did your ancestors before you. Else how would they have provided for themselves and their families? Never was it heard that nobility alone was able to maintain its possessor."

But though feather-work, like its Aztec inventors, has lost its high place in the land, yet it is still carried on in a small degree; and from the humbler productions of the present day one may imagine the gorgeous robes of the Aztecs, which dazzled the eyes of the rough Spanish conquerors as they entered Mexico on the 8th of November 1519. In these degenerate days, the feather-pictures are chiefly prints or photographs of the costumes of the country, which are entirely covered with feathers, looking in the distance like brilliant paintings. I gave one of the feather-workers a photograph of M——, in a South American gaucho dress, telling him the colours of the clothes. In a week he brought it back to me, entirely covered in feathers, except the face and hands. The handkerchief on the head is done in the tiny plumes from the "ruby-topaz" humming-bird's throat; the *ponchilla* in scarlet cardinal's feathers, with stripes of other colours running across it; the *chiripa* and white trousers in black and white; and the curtain which hangs behind the figure is a green glory, from the emerald humming-bird's breast. It is quite a gem, yet the man apologized very much for asking a dollar for it, as he said there were so many *plumajes de colibris* (humming-bird's feathers) used in it.

I have seen one or two *rebozos* from 200 to 300 years old, woven of cotton and gold or silver threads, as fine and soft as silk, exquisitely coloured, and, as their present state proves, almost indestructible. The *rebozos* of the present day are all alike, dull brown or blue, without any beauty of design or colour. The *serapes* are very picturesque, woven of wool and cotton, in well-chosen colours, the prettiest having white or black grounds, with coloured borders and centres. Some of the finer ones, which are made in wool and silk, with gold and silver threads, are most beautiful; and a young dandy will often give $500 (£100) for a serape of this kind, to strap behind his saddle.

But to return to our sight-seeing. On leaving the Academia we went to the Palace, which occupies the whole of the southern side of the Plaza Major. We went first up a long flight of stone stairs—most wearying work in this air —to the Sala of the ambassadors, where the receptions used to be held at the time of the Empire. On the dais at the end are the same chairs under the red and gold canopy which Maximilian and Carlotta used. The room is very long, with a polished floor that made us long for a dance; and is beautifully fitted with evidences of the poor Emperor's taste. On the walls are full-length portraits of all the leaders of Mexico since it shook off the Spanish yoke—the Padre Hidalgo in a dress half warlike half ecclesiastical, Iturbide, Bustamente, etc. Out of them all only one had died a natural death; and he had fled the country. The others were all shot!

We penetrated to the President's rooms, in which are beautiful vases and statues from Italy, brought by the Emperor. Whatever may be the "indignant feelings of the Mexican nation at the extravagant outlay on works of art," which is one of the commonest complaints against the unhappy Maximilian, the present possessors of the said works of art do not seem to object in the least to benefit by them as they are here.

Señor C., a most charming "*diputado*," who was educated in Europe, then took us into Congress, which is within the palace precincts. We were taken to the diplomatic box, and listened to a very good and animated speech on some Church-matter for quarter of an hour. The Congress Hall is in a semicircle. In the centre of the flat side, on a little dais, sit the Speaker and four others. Señor C., the Governor of Mexico, was one of these, on the Speaker's right. On the floor of the house are tables, and two rostrums, from which most of the speeches are made. The present speaker, however, was in his own seat in the double tier of members round the semicircle. The upper galleries and boxes were crowded with listeners. Everything was extremely quiet and dignified.

After we had listened to the debate, we went down into the patio and saw the magnificent state-coach, costing 40,000 dollars, which the workmen of Milan gave the Emperor. He and the Empress never once drove in it, and Juarez is the only person who has ever used it, driving in it from the Oraciones on the 5th of May. A very vehement republican who was present remarked, for the benefit of the party, "Well, a man who has a carriage like that in this country *deserves* to be shot!" The logic of the remark I failed to see, and Don Benito Juarez seems to have appropriated the Milanese workmen's gift with much complacency.

18*th*.—The P.'s, General R., and I, went to-day to make our formal calls on the wives of two of the Ministers, and on the President's daughters, as it is etiquette that strangers should make the first visit. The latter we found at home, and were very much charmed with them. Their mother was an Italian; and having lived some four years in the States, they speak English very fairly, so that we got on, with the help of a little Spanish, without any difficulty.

May 21.—We are in a sea of troubles. Mr. V. M. came in off the Lerma reconnaissance with fever, which has since turned typhoid in almost its worst form. Three days ago Mr. H. also sickened, and we have been in great alarm about him. To-day, however, he is better.

Governor H. now is in bed; and I too have had the enjoyment of a touch of intermittent chills and fever.

What a horrid sensation it is! I could not imagine at first what had happened to me. There is a prince in one of Grimm's fairy tales who is always saying, "Oh, if I could but shiver!" and at last his wish is gratified by his wife, who pours a dish full of little fishes down his back, which produces the desired effect. I felt just as if the little fish were slipping and wriggling all over me; my teeth chattered and my hands shook. Then in a little while came a hot rush of blood, up went my pulse, jumping and then dying away, my head ached like a furnace, and then again came the chill. It has skipped the alternate days with me, which makes me all the more uncomfortable, as intermittent fever, if it once gets hold, is so apt to return for years. But I have taken such quantities of quinine that I hope it is almost baffled.

22*d*.—Our hospital is improving. To begin with myself: I am quite well again; Mr. H. up; and the Governor mending. Mr. V. M. also is a shade better, thanks to an extraordinary remedy which our good friend Dr. S. ordered as a last resource—tea made from the peelings of chickens' gizzards. It is an intense astringent, and more unpalatable than words can describe. I went down to the kitchen of the restaurant to order it myself to prevent mistakes; at the same time desiring one of the waiters to take the Governor a cup of real tea, which we had procured from a chemist's with the greatest difficulty, as tea is not usually to be had here. Now, if a Mexican waiter can make a mistake, he will; and after waiting an interminable time for the arrival of the real tea, I went to see if it had reached the Governor. I found him, poor man, perfectly raging, declaring that he was poisoned, and demanding in no measured terms what these Mexicans had given him that they called tea. My dismay was great when I found that the gizzard-tea had been brought to him instead of Mr. V. M., and that he had taken a good draught of it, being parched with thirst. I could not help laughing in spite of his misery, and as no real harm was done, soon set matters right by despatching poor old Trinidad, the author of all the mischief, for a fresh brew; and the gizzard-tea has acted like magic on the patient for whom it was destined.

May 23.—Some American friends called for us at 1 P.M., and we went with them to the *Monte de Piedad*, the national pawnshop of Mexico. It is in Cortez's palace, facing the north side of the Cathedral, at the top of the Plaza. The ground of what is now the Palacio was originally granted to Cortez: but was ceded by his descendants to the Government. In exchange they were given the ground formerly occupied by the palace of the Aztec Kings, and built upon it the present edifice.

We went into a long narrow room, with a table down the centre. The walls were lined with cupboards with wire grating, in which the valuables in pawn are kept. Señor ——, the head of the Monte Pio, was with us, with five assistants, who unlocked the most magnificent sets of diamonds and pearls, some of immense value, and handed them to us as we sat round the table. Some were quite new, others equally old. These jewels are put in "*en deposito*" at half their value, and if not redeemed at the end of six months, are put up to auction at their full value. If they do not realize this, they are put up again after a certain time at reduced value, and so on till they are sold. It is entirely under the Government, and is admirably managed.

Besides the jewels, plate, and valuables of all kinds, in the grated room, there were several rooms filled with furniture, and one very large one full of pianos and sewing-machines of every possible make. Altogether, however, the place, except for the jewels, was not so interesting as we had been led to believe.

25th.—M. and I, followed by his mozo, a smart-looking fellow, rode out to Tacuba to see the famous old tree of the Noche Triste. It was a lovely morning, after torrents of rain the night before, and the scent from the rose hedges was delicious as we rode along the shady Calzada de San Cosme, on the very track of Cortez and his soldiers, as they fought their way along this same causeway, when they were driven from the city.

As it was Saturday morning, the road was crowded with Indios trooping in to the great market,—men, women, mules and burros laden with fruit, vegetables, alfalfa grass, poultry, and charcoal, in one continuous stream. The fowls are sometimes packed in an absurd way, which at first sight seems horribly cruel, for they are sewed with string in layers with their heads out, on a flat board, which is carried on their owner's back. However, I hope they are not really as uncomfortable as they look, for the string, instead of going *through* their bodies, as it appears, is only passed under their wings, and fastened to the board underneath.

The most curious sight are the "*Carboneros*" from the mountains, who trot along—men and women—carrying a pack of charcoal some 200 lbs. weight on their backs, for a distance sometimes of as much as forty miles.

The Tree of the Noche Triste.

There is a line of street cars running out along this road all the way (three miles) to Popotla, and three cars with two mules each start from the Plaza every half-hour, going all three close together at full gallop, which has the most absurd effect. It would be much more convenient to passengers if they ran singly and at shorter intervals: but I fancy it is safer if they all run together, as there is less chance of their being stopped by "*ladrones.*" The old tree stands close to the road, in the churchyard of a small church, and till within the last month was in perfect preservation. Some little time ago, however, it was sold, so the story here goes, by the Government to a Frenchman for some small sum. He immediately sold it again for $1500: but on the authorities denying his right to do so, or, as a Westerner would say, "going back on him," he, to spite them, on the 2d of May spread petroleum over the tree and set it on fire. It is not so much injured as was feared from first accounts, some few branches being still green and unhurt: but I am afraid it will never recover such a shock. It is a huge old *Ahuahuete*, quite hollow now, and is of the same age as, or even older than, those of Chapultepec.

Turning westwards from Popotla we rode through narrow lanes between pulque plantations out into open fields covered with flowers. A low lilac verbena, French marigolds and salvias, were the only ones I knew, except of course wild roses, which flourish everywhere. We tried to cross a deep watercourse between high artificial banks, as our object was to reach Chapultepec across country: but the heavy rains of the night before had flooded every ditch, so that we had to turn back, and with some difficulty made our way to open grass pastures full of cattle and horses, between Tacuba and San Cosme; and crossing the Toluca narrow-gauge railroad, of which a few miles of track are laid, followed it up to the Calzada from San Cosme to Chapultepec.

Here we were completely stopped by a great dike which runs down the side of the road, and is about thirty feet broad, twenty feet deep, and full of water. The mozo however was determined not to turn back, and was also rather anxious, I fancy, to show off his own pluck and M.'s new horse, which he was riding, so he said if the "*niña*" could follow, he would lead the way over the railroad bridge, the only way of crossing. It was but three feet wide, and made of boards laid between the rails. M. followed on a pretty little barb pony, and I brought up the rear on a great long-legged American trotter, which was not by any means sure-footed on smooth ground. I felt considerably relieved when he bore me safely over, as a slip on the bridge would have been disastrous.

We turned up the Calzada to Chapultepec, along the side of the aqueduct of the "thin water," through whose grey stone arches, fringed with maidenhair ferns and a hundred delicate flowers, we caught glimpses of the beautiful Teja, the Empress Carlotta's hacienda. This hacienda was confiscated when the Liberals came into power again, and is now sold to the lawyer who defended the Emperor, and who bought it to prevent its going into hostile hands. It is wonderfully rich ground, and I was told three crops can be got off it in the year.

The sun was partly hidden by clouds, and the fresh pure air, laden with the scent of young leaves and roses, was quite enchanting. We caught a good view of the peaks of the two volcanos, though their slopes were hidden in white clouds; and we got home at 11 A.M. by way of the Paseo del Imperador.

26th.—Our party broke up to-day, alas! General P. and Governor H. have gone out with M. and the engineering party on a reconnaissance down the Rio Lerma to Salamanca and Guanajuato. They intend joining us again in a fortnight, just in time to sail in the French packet of the 18th of June; leaving M. and the rest to make further explorations of the country. Meanwhile Mrs. P. and I are left here under General R.'s care.

We spent the whole morning in "fixing up" in various ways, such as sewing cord on sombreros, and the hundred and one little things which are always needed at the last minute before a start. M.'s dress was perfect for the purpose; though as Mrs. Y. said, if she had met him on the road she should have prepared her purse and her prayers instantly. Dark trousers and short cloth jacket, Holland blouse over flannel shirt, fastened at the waist with a blue *faja*, over which went cartridge-belt with revolver and ivory-mounted dagger given him by a Spanish friend (of whom more anon). The whole costume was completed by a broad grey felt sombrero, with silver cord and tassels,—the "*sombrero ancho*" of the song.

His horse was a beauty, cream-coloured,—the most esteemed barb colour—and looked very handsome with his Californian saddle, a Mexican bridle of white maguey fibre and red wool, and his repeating Winchester carbine slung at the saddle-bow.

Several of our friends came to see the whole cavalcade off, and at 3.30 they started. The six gentlemen in front, followed by two mounted mozos leading the two pack-mules, — a goodly array: but

"I wish them safe at home."

29th.—We were going out driving, but an *agua cerro* came on which lasted an hour and a half. It began with thunder and heavy hail, which quite whitened the pavements, lying in heaps three inches high against the steps; and then turned into a torrent of rain. All the streets were inundated, and the S.'s coachman, who went out to get a carriage, came in with the news that the patios of the hotels were swimming in water a foot deep. So I had to wait till the water went down a little, and at seven Mr. S. walked home with me, and by means of an impromptu pathway of planks we managed to get across the patio at the Iturbide, which was still nearly covered, being a good deal lower than the street level, though the street was dry.

May 30.—The Feast of Corpus Christi—a great day among the Mexicans. All the shops were closed, and the air before dawn was full of the sound of bells. We went out early to the Plaza, and found the flower-sellers in the side streets from the Plateros sitting on the curb-stone in their usual places with hundreds of beautiful bouquets before them.

Mrs. Y. took us to inspect the various wonders of the day. On each side of the pathways up to the different doors of the cathedrals sat Indios with toys, which are only sold on this day; surrounded by swarms of children and nurses, spending their *medios, quartillas*, and *clacos*. The great favourites are "*huacalitos*," small models of the packs the Indios carry on their backs. They are made of bits of wood, filled with fruits or "*dulces*," and covered with split reed looking like sugar-cane, into which are stuck gay flowers.

The next toys in favour are the "*mulitas*," donkeys, made of corn-shuck, each carrying two *huacalitos* an inch long filled with *dulces*.

Then come innumerable coloured wooden and earthen toys, all representing a hideous dragon, who generally carries a figure of the Virgin standing on his back, or drawn by him in a rude car.

The Indios could not explain the reason or meaning of these toys—" only it was the day of Corpus Christi, and so they had them of course."

We went into the Cathedral : but the incense, the jingling bells as the host was raised, the shrill voices of the choir bursting out by fits and starts, apparently without connexion with the service the priests were conducting; the crowds of people, fine ladies and filthy *leperos* all jostling against each other and eyeing us *hereticos* with no friendly glances ; the heavy odour of the incense ; and the far less agreeable smell of humanity from the vast crowd, soon drove us out into the fresh hot air in the Plaza.

Before the priests lost their power, this Fiesta was one of

the greatest days in the year. "The host," says Madame Calderon de la Barca, "is carried through the city in great procession, at which the President, in full uniform, the archbishop and all the ministers, etc., assist," and woe to any *heretico* who did not fall on his knees as they passed. Now, however, all this is gone by, and the service in the Cathedral is all that is allowed.

In the afternoon Señora —— called on us. She is a beautiful Baltimorian; tall, with a magnificent figure, fair hair, dark eyebrows, and those wonderful violet eyes which you hardly ever see except in Baltimore.

May 31.—After *desayuno*, the S.'s and Mrs. Y. called for us, and we drove out to Tacubaya. It was a perfect morning, with changing lights, tender and pearly, and a cool wind. We drove first to Señor E.'s villa, which is very lovely, with ponds, streams, and bridges, under thick trees leading up to the house. It stands on a terrace, a perfect bower of flowering creepers, bignonias, honeysuckles, passion-flower, jessamine, and roses. The house itself is very pretty, and looks more European than any other Mexican house I have been into. But Mr. ——'s, which lies a quarter of a mile on, is the real British house. When we came to the hall-door, the first thing I saw were two old coloured engravings of the Derby and Ascot Grand Stand, hanging in the portico. Inside, the passages were all hung with dear old hunting and stage-coach coloured prints, so familiar in English houses. From a gallery up-stairs the finest view over the Valley of Mexico is to be had, with Chapultepec as a foreground.

We were in the humour for sight-seeing, so after breakfast we went off to the museum and spent a most pleasant time there. The collection of minerals is very fair; but many of the trays were empty, the contents (being very valuable) having disappeared in a mysterious manner, which some people hint that the officials in charge could account for if they liked.

The birds and beasts of the country occupy two large rooms, but are not well set up. There were several fine specimens of the "Pito-Real," or Quezal—*Trogon imperialis*, the royal bird.

But the most interesting room of all was that containing the antiquities. There we saw the original picture of Cortez, the same which is engraved in Prescott's History. It is a grand, calm face, great strength and beauty: but with a certain touch of either fanaticism or charlatanism—I cannot make out which. There were portraits of all the viceroys after him, down to the last. The early ones of the real old Spanish type had for the most part fine noble faces: but a more thorough set of ruffians than the later ones would be difficult to find. Small blame to the Mexicans for wishing to free themselves from such governors.

There were a number of the old Aztec picture maps, and Aztec remains of all sorts; among others, some good obsidian (volcanic glass) weapons and mirrors; alabaster bowls exquisitely carved in high relief, with flowers and fruits, to catch the blood of the victims of sacrifice; and the wooden instruments which the priests used to beat on the top of the Teocalli, or mound of sacrifice, to call the people to arms. There were of course innumerable idols of every degree of hideousness, which looked very Egyptian. The more one sees of Aztec remains, the more tempted one is to believe in their connexion with Egypt; and our guide the librarian, an extremely intelligent young gentleman, held this view strongly. The best European authorities, however, seem to think that there is no real connexion, but only an outward likeness between them.

Cortez's standard was there too, carefully preserved under glass, side by side with the brilliant standard decorated with the picture of the Virgin of Guadalupe, which the Emperor Maximilian brought over. And there, too, was the old flint-lock the Padre Hidalgo fired off in 1810, at the village of Dolores, near Guanajuato, when he shouted "Liberta!" at twelve o'clock at night.

It was a strange jumble altogether of old and new, Aztec, Spanish, and Austrian.

We were caught in a perfect deluge going home, and had to "walk the plank" again to get into the hotel.

Count ——, the minister, and Mademoiselle ——, dined with us. It is very pleasant finding such delightful Europeans on the further side of the Atlantic. He had just been to see Congress disperse, which it did amid firing of cannons and floating flags, and black looks from the President, who was furious at the whole session being wasted, and at last getting a refusal to his wish of sending Ministers to Austria and Spain.

Little did we dream at the time I wrote the above, that this would be Don Benito Juarez's last public appearance, and that before Congress could reassemble for its September session he should have gone to his account. He died of apoplexy in July 1872.

June 3.—Most exciting news! The revolution has been burning up again lately in the north; and to-day we heard of the defeat of Corella at Monterey, and the total rout of the Government forces. There are rumours afloat of *pronunciamientos* in the States of Vera Cruz and Puebla. I hope it is not true, as it might seriously interfere with our journey down to the coast.

4th.—As I was sitting with a friend to-day, her agent came in with a story which would be startling enough in any country but this. It was as follows:—

Last week, as an inoffensive tenant of Mrs. —— came out of his house in the Calle Perpetua—a particularly peaceable, quiet street—he was knocked down, stabbed in the arm three or four times, and robbed by a man who, it is supposed, took him for Señor N., the agent, and imagined he had been collecting rents, and was therefore worth robbing.

This, however, is hardly as bad as another story which a young Mexican, whom I shall call B., told my friend.

One day, riding on the Paseo, B. was joined by a young gentleman from Guadalajara, whom he knew slightly: but did not like, as he was a low vulgar fellow. He had a very ill-looking common sort of man riding with him, to whom, to B.'s great disgust, he introduced him, saying, "You ought to know him, for he is such a useful man. If you want to get rid of any friend you have only to send for this gentleman; and in two days your friend has disappeared, and nothing more is heard of him." B. detached himself from such delightful companions as soon as possible. Two years later the "useful man" was killed at the head of a band of robbers in the interior!

And now for one more anecdote, and we will take leave of this disagreeable subject.

Once upon a time there existed in the environs of the town of Zacatecas the most desperate robber-band that perhaps ever flourished in Mexico. No carriage, no diligencia, no hacienda, was safe from their depredations; and people going out of Zacatecas thought it as natural to be robbed in the Mesquital (acacia grove) as to put on their night-caps and go to bed.

This summer, just before M. went up there, a most complete change took place. One of the two chiefs of this robber-clan, on being given $500 by the Governor, turned what is usually called king's evidence; and instead of having, as M. expected, a most desperate fight for life on entering Zacatecas, his mind was considerably relieved by the driver of the diligence saying that no robberies had taken place during the last month,—as from the 3d to the 28th instant, 119 robbers had "died with their boots on," as a Westerner would elegantly express it.

"In one instance, however," to use M.'s words, "the better traits of the Mexican character were brought out. The informer was told by the Governor that the man of all others he wanted to get rid of was his (the informer's) old partner, co-chief, and *compadre*.

"It must be understood that the ties of one compadre to another are closer and more respected by Mexicans than that of brother, though all that the word means is fellow godfather. The informer left Zacatecas one afternoon with a couple of armed servants, and went down to see his compadre, who lived in a hamlet of Zacatecas, called Guadalupe. After chatting for half an hour in the most affable manner with his unsuspecting compadre, he said—

"'Compadre, will you accompany me up to Zacatecas?'

"'Oh, yes,' said the compadre; 'but what for, compadrito?'

"'Just to take a little Paseo.'

"'*Con mucho gusto*' (with much pleasure).

"He saddled his horse, and mounting, accompanied his compadrito up towards Zacatecas.

"About half-way they came to three cotton-wood trees; whereupon the informer stopped, and turning to his companion, said—

"'Compadre, which do you like best of those three trees?'

"'What do you ask me for, compadrito?'

"'Why,' said the other, 'haven't you any particular fancy?'

"'No,' said the compadre; 'but that one looks the prettiest.'

"'Well,' said the informer, 'you know, compadre, the fact is that I have got an unpleasant duty to perform, and so, as we are compadres, I thought I would grant any last favour you might ask, and let you choose the tree to be hung on.'

"The wretched compadre put his hand to his sword and was going to object, but he found the other in earnest: for, at a sign from the informer, the two armed servants, who were up to the game, put a brace of bullets into his back, strung him up with a lasso to the tree of his choice, and left him there as a warning to all such as might hereafter wish to follow in his footsteps; while his compadre, the informer, rode into Zacatecas quite unconcerned, as, whatever might be the sin of killing his compadre, it was fully atoned for by having carefully attended to his last will and testament."

CHAPTER XXI.

LIFE IN MEXICO—*continued.*

Visit to Guadalupe—Origin of the miraculous serape—The collegiate church—Votive offerings—Church of Tepayac—Sulphur spring—Letter from M.—Popotla and Tacuba—Molino del Rey—The battles of August and September 1847—An unfortunate haciendado—Last evening in Mexico.

June 7.—To-day we made our long-talked-of expedition to Guadalupe, as our time here is getting short. The weather looked so threatening, and the roads through the city were so deep in mud, and so full of holes, that we were strongly tempted two or three times to turn back: but we persevered and were rewarded; for, thanks to good driving, we escaped an upset; and once outside the Garita the road improved, the rain held off, and the clouds which remained shaded us pleasantly from the scorching sun.

Arrived at Guadalupe, we went first into the great Collegiate-church at the foot of the hill, built in commemoration of the miracle, and in which the wonder-working picture of the Virgin is now preserved. We entered, with an old priest, by the Sacristy, which is full of wardrobes and chests of drawers containing the priests' clothes, of which they must be very vain, judging by the number of looking-glasses on the walls, below a series of miserably painted pictures representing the life of our Lord. The church, or rather cathedral, is magnificent, with its painted and gilded roof and gorgeous high altar, in the centre of which—at a safe height to avoid detection from the eye of the unbeliever —hangs the famous serape.

The following is the story of its miraculous origin, taken partly from what was told me on the spot, and partly from the graphic account of Madame Calderon de la Barca:—Early in December, in the year 1531, ten years after the conquest of Mexico, a poor and pious Indio, named Juan Diego, a native of Cuautitlan, went to the suburb of Tlatelolco to learn the Christian doctrine, which the Franciscan monks taught there. As he was passing over the barren hill of Tepayac (now Guadalupe), the Virgin Mary appeared to him, and told him to go in her name to the Bishop, the Ilustrissimo D. Fr. Juan de Zumarraga, first Bishop of Mexico, and tell him that she had appeared in Mexico, and wished to have a place of worship erected in her honour on the spot.

He obeyed her: but could not obtain an audience of the Bishop. The next day the Virgin appeared in the same place; and on his telling her of his failure, "Return," she said, "and say that it is I, the Virgin Mary, the Mother of God, who send thee."

Juan Diego did as he was desired: but the Bishop would not believe him, merely desiring him, if it were as he said, to bring him some sign or token of the Virgin's will.

On the 12th of December he carried this message to her, and she "bade him climb to the top of the rock of Tepeyac, to gather the roses he should find there and bring them to her. He obeyed, though well knowing that on the spot were neither flowers nor any trace of vegetation. Nevertheless he found the roses, which he gathered and brought to the Virgin Mary." She threw them into his serape, and bade him return to the Bishop and show them as the token he had asked. Juan Diego set out for the Episcopal house, and when he found himself in presence of the prelate, he opened the scrape to show him the token; when, lo! instead of roses there appeared imprinted on it the miraculous picture of the Virgin!

It was conveyed by the awe-struck Bishop to his own oratory; and soon after, this splendid church was erected in honour of the patroness of Nueva Espagna, in which the scrape has hung for upwards of 300 years.

It was uncovered for our special benefit, and a row of candles were lighted in front of it. A more palpable fraud I never saw. Even at the distance we stood we could, with aid of an opera-glass, see that it was merely an oil-painting, and a poor one into the bargain; and Dr. S., who has examined it closely, assured me you can see the paint on the canvas as clearly as possible. The painting represents the Virgin in a blue cloak covered with stars, a garment of crimson and gold, her hands clasped, and her foot on a crescent supported by a cherub.

It is held in such reverence throughout the Republic that hardly any house is without some representation of it; and even in the poor Indios' dwellings, where often there is not a chair or a table, a little coloured print of "Nuestra Señora de Guadalupe" is stuck up on the wretched walls. The moment it was known in the town that the picture was uncovered for "*los Americanos*," the Indios came trooping in; and, casting themselves on their knees, said their prayers to it with the utmost devotion, thinking themselves highly favoured at having a chance of seeing the sacred relic at any but the usual times.

The high altar is surrounded with massive silver rails, which lead down to the choir. This is the only church which has not been despoiled by the Liberals: but even they did not dare lay hands on anything in a place so bound up in the hearts of the whole Mexican people. The choir is the most beautiful piece of wood carving I have seen in the country; and the screen is quite unique, of dark carved wood richly inlaid with silver work, which has a most charming effect.

In one corner of the church was an extraordinary collection of votive pictures; and, had not disgust overpowered all other feelings, it would have been hard to keep one's countenance. They are miserable daubs, in the coarsest style of art, descriptive of the dangers from which people have been delivered by the aid of "Nuestra Señora de Guadalupe de Mexico," who always, let it be remembered, appears in each in the exact form of the picture.

In one there is a street-fight; and she is seen in the clouds over the houses by the unlucky man who is getting the worst of it, and who calls upon her just in time to save himself from a stab. In another a man is being *plagiared* (carried off by robbers for ransom), sitting dolefully bound under a tree, with the robbers all round him, and the Virgin again comes to the rescue. Another man is upset in a raging torrent, with a heavy cart and the mules on the top of him. His companions of course are killed; but he looks placidly out from under a wheel, with nothing save his head above water, and calling on "Our Lady," is miraculously saved.

But perhaps the most absurd of all, was the picture of a stage-coach which has come in two; the eight white horses tearing off in the darkness over a narrow bridge with the front wheels; the cochero and muchacho thrown from the box and lying dead on the ground; while the happy and pious man, who has been miraculously preserved by the blue and golden Señora in the right-hand corner of the clouds, drags his lady-love with her mother and sister, out through the windows of the prostrate body of the coach.

Besides these pictures, so thoroughly characteristic of the dangers of Mexico, there are here, as at every wonder-working shrine, wax arms, legs, heads, and whole figures of those who have been cured of various diseases; pairs of crutches stand in the corner; and, among other votive offerings, a single head of maize, from some Indio I suppose, too poor to give more. There are altars all round the church to the principal saints. On that of St. Joseph is a grotesque representation under a glass case, in pottery figures, of the birth of our Saviour. Mary and Joseph are nearly twice the size of the surrounding shepherds and shepherdesses; and from the ceiling hang little tin candelabra, such as we put on Christmas-trees, and cherubs of the rudest kind. It was a relief to get out into the fresh air, and shake off the impressions which the sight of such superstition could not but inspire. But there was more to be seen yet.

We painfully climbed up the narrow and steep way between low walls to the little blue church, built over the actual spot on the hill of Tepayac, where the Virgin appeared. The stones that paved the path, which is zigzagged up the face of the hill, were slippery with age, and the wear of those millions of weary feet and knees which have dragged themselves up to the top of the hill. Only four years ago the Señora ———, mother of one of the members of the Cabinet, an old lady of past sixty-five, crawled on her knees the whole distance from Mexico to the church, on the 12th of December, the great fiesta in commemoration of the event.

We were amply repaid for our climb when we reached the summit, by the superb view over the great Cathedral Church to the towers and domes of beautiful Mexico, and the rim of mountains beyond, and the Lake of Tezcoco to the left, between us and the great volcanos. The church is very small, and not particularly pretty: but close to the door is a fine portrait of the blessed Juan Diego, as he walked over the mountain that December day three hundred years ago, with the birds flying around his head and settling on his shoulders. It seemed to me to be by the same hand as the portrait of Cortez in the Museum.

A miserable diseased child was selling medals and pictures and strips of holy ribbon, some of which we bought for a *real*, inscribed, " *Medida del sagrado rastro de nuestra señora de Guadalupe de Méjico*,"—measure of the sacred neck of Our Lady. The only other occupants of the little chapel were an Indian man and woman, who, lighted taper in hand, were slowly crawling on their knees up the altar-steps and back again to a side altar, kissing the hangings of the altars each time they reached them. The poor creatures seemed so completely absorbed in their performance, whatever it was, that they hardly even glanced at us; though foreigners always create a sensation among the inhabitants, even so near the city.

We descended the hill by a paved walk on the opposite side, like that we had come up by, passing a curious monument—a mast and sail of a full-rigged ship, as large as life, built of adobe, and plastered; which a wealthy inhabitant of Mexico, during a storm at sea, vowed to put up to the Virgin of Guadalupe if he were saved. He was wrecked: but his life was saved, and he kept his vow more honourably than another gentleman of whom I heard, who vowed $100,000 to Sta. Maria de Guadalupe; and when the time came for payment, repented of his bargain, and managed to pay half, and get the receipt from the priest for the whole amount! Our stony path led us down to the Holy Sulphur spring, over which an exquisite little chapel, the "Pozito de Guadalupe," is built. The dome is covered with blue and white glazed tiles, divided by yellow stripes, which run down from the top. We entered among a crowd of devotees and beggars, and drank some of the bright yellow muddy water; and, after this last very disagreeable experience, thought that we had seen all we need see of the most sacred spot of Mexico, and returned.

On reaching the hotel late in the evening, we were greeted by General R. :—

"Well, have you heard what your husband and brother have been about? They have had a fight with the robbers, and cleaned them out."

Pleasant news indeed for us! For we had received letters every day saying that they were prospering, and having an excellent journey, without a word of robbers. It appeared, however, that this afternoon's coach from Toluca had brought word from the diligencia authorities at Maravatio or Morelia, to the chief of the diligencias here, that some of *"los Señores Caballeros"* had been attacked by robbers, killed several, and driven on unhurt themselves; which last item set our minds a little at rest.

A few days later I received the following letter from my brother, which may serve to give some idea of the chances of the road in Mexico:—

"SALAMANCA, *June* 10.

"MY DEAR * * *,—... We left Maravatio in the diligence at 3.30 A.M., the Governor inside, Gen. P. and I on the box. Of course it had been raining, and was horridly dark, so we kept a good look-out. About five miles out of town, we ran down into a gully, with a stone wall on the left, and high tree cactus to the right. Suddenly from a break in the wall, and from behind a grove of cacti, out sally—without speaking, and at a walk—five men on horseback. It was the queerest sight—it seems a dream now.

"A ghostly figure walks across the horses' heads; they stop: we have a vague feeling of uncertainty what to do; when the sharp whisper of the cochero breaks the spell—'*Ahi riene! ahi riene!*' here they come!

"The next thing I remember was taking a cool shot at a man about ten yards from me, while Gen. P.'s pistol was cracking right and left, blinding me with smoke. Alas! I had forgotten to throw in a cartridge from the magazine before starting. I throw it in, and drop the man over his saddle-bow; while, at the same instant, Gen. P. and the

Governor do likewise for two others. They reel past the coach *hors de combat*, while the two remaining ones we dose with bullets as they slink away: but without apparent effect.

"Gen. P. was polite in the extreme to one of them who stopped behind a cactus for a minute. I think in thirty seconds he put half-a-dozen bullets in through that old tree in a way that made the fellow clear out as if he didn't like it. I contented myself by scaring my man once: but I don't think he'll forget it. He went back up the road, and stopped 200 yards up the hill to have a look. I let loose, and the ball hit the hard sandstone below him, and ricochetted up the road past him, making it ring every twenty yards. You should have seen him go for it. . . . Well, we jumped down, and commenced skirmishing till it was light alongside the coach. Would you believe that there were *seven* men on board besides us, and one woman; and only one of them was game to take one of our pistols and help us. The woman said to me afterwards, when I spoke to her, that 'there was no time to be afraid.' After we had skirmished about a mile, I was astonished to see the Governor creeping along under cover of a wall some 300 yards off, just as if he was 'birding.' Away I went for him, and as I got within 100 yards, he let loose over the wall. He had spotted two more reconnoitring, and if you have ever seen G. at home creeping on a blackbird, you will have an exact idea of his movements. Unfortunately he missed, and they cleared out; so we went back to the coach, and found that out of the three shots the robbers had fired, one had torn the sleeve of Gen. P.'s coat, and grazed his arm, passing over the mozo's head, and past my ear. So ended the great conflict. . . .

"From Morelia, after a very pleasant time with the Prefect, we went to ——'s hacienda. He, ——, provided us with an ex-robber, Gabriel by name,—the mildest man who ever robbed a coach or cut a throat,—to take Gen. P. and me, as the others were to follow in a body, through the worst robber country. The first ten miles were the most dangerous, and about four miles from ———'s we came to a little robber-hamlet on a hill. Directly we got in sight, we saw the look-out on the top of the hill give the alarm, and in a moment it was like a swarm of bees. Horses driven up men crowding out of a little stone *tienda* (shop), and most unusual activity shown. Gabriel said, 'It is all right, I know them, and if you like will introduce Gen. P. to the chief.' We declined with thanks; so when we got within 400 yards of the house, Gabriel galloped forward to tell them who we were. When we were 200 yards nearer, with a long stone wall dividing us from them, we stopped, and then it came out somehow that we were each of us in a horrid funk. The utter feeling of uncertainty as to whether our robber-friend was to be trusted or not made it very kittle. In a minute, however, we decided that we might go on; so in through the gate we rode, and past the house, where Gabriel was standing chatting with about forty of them. Whereon they off with their hats, and, with a mighty cheer, burst out, '*Que viva Don Porfirio Diaz.*' I took off my hat with a low bow, in some perplexity at this strange greeting, and we rode on. In fifty yards Gabriel joined, saying when he got up, they asked him if we had any money, and who we were. Yes, he answered, we had money: but that I was Porfirio Diaz's First General, and that Gen. P. was a Californian capitalist come down to see the country, with a view of negotiating bonds for Diaz. As luck would have it, I looked my assumed character fairly well, being beautifully mounted, and dark enough in complexion to satisfy the most critical.

"On Gabriel led us in pelting rain through robber-hamlets, bypaths, and woods till it got quite dark, and we halted at 10 P.M. at the house of a friend of his in a really respectable little village, on a sort of island in the flat land, strongly defended. After some food, and having a yarn about robbers, we chucked ourselves into bed, and as he said there was no danger, left our arms lying about the room. We were just dozing off when there was a violent scuffle in the tienda next door, and a woman rushed past our door to get out through the big gate, shouting, 'Gabriel! Gabriel! *ladrones.*' We all jumped up. Gabriel seized his rifle and tore open the window, while we began hunting for arms in the darkness, not knowing what was going on. In a second I heard Gabriel's rifle miss fire—and again—and again. He yelled for another rifle, and I found the General's and gave it him. Out of the window he jumped into the darkness, in his shirt. In the meantime Gen. P. found his pistol and I mine, and out we went. There was a light in the store, and suddenly we saw Gabriel fire about 100 paces away, and run on with a couple of other armed men after him.

"Just about that time we became aware that we were up to our knees in mud, in nothing but our shirts, and it was raining. On finding at the store that there were only three robbers, who had tried to rob the till, we went back and armed ourselves for further mischief,—Gen. P. in the darkness getting hold of the mozo's rifle, and filling it with Smith and Wesson pistol-bullets from my belt, and I getting by mistake into Gabriel's pants. I armed one of the mozos with my pistol, and the other, an old fellow of about eighty, with an enormous sword which I found in the corner. Meanwhile, I had got my gun. The sight of the old man, whose teeth were chattering with mingled cold and fear, in a scant shirt and drawers, poising his gigantic sword's point on the ground with palsied hand, makes me burst with laughter while I write. Out we sallied: but found Gabriel coming back, without having caught anything except a violent cold. Then we looked over our arms, laughed for about half an hour over the scare, and slept till morning. Gabriel guided us well to Salamanca, and thence we went to Guanajuato, coming back here to-day."

June 8.—At 7.30 A.M. we started for Tacuba, some of the party driving, and Mr. G. S. and I riding. I rode Mrs. S.'s beautiful cream-coloured barb "Dicky," whose paces are perfect. He does the peculiar Spanish *sobre passear* gait enchantingly, so that one has nothing to do but sit still without moving in the saddle, and be carried along quite smoothly at seven miles an hour, by a sort of half run, half canter, the horse moving both legs on the same side at once like an elephant. This is the easiest pace for man and horse alike; and a well-trained horse will keep up this gait for twelve and fourteen hours on a stretch.

It was a bright morning, and the road, as on the last time I rode along it with M., was swarming with Indios coming in to market. After taking a farewell look at the old tree at Popotla, and getting some bits of charcoal, remains of the Frenchman's fire, from below it as a *recuerdo*, we rode on to Tacuba, about a quarter of a mile.

Here stands an enormous church inside an olive yard, and beyond, on a green open space somewhat like an English village-green, is one of the *Teocallis* where Cortez and his men halted, to gain time after the Noche Triste, and re-form.

Mr. Prescott thus describes the scene:—

"Cortés and his companions now rode forward to the front, where the troops, in a loose, disorderly manner, were marching off the fatal causeway. A few only of the enemy hung on their rear, or annoyed them by flights of arrows from the lake. The attention of the Aztecs was diverted by the rich spoil which strewed the battle-ground; fortunately for the Spaniards, who, had their enemy pursued with the same ferocity with which he had fought, would in their crippled condition have been cut off probably to a man. But little molested, therefore, they were allowed to defile through the adjacent village, or suburb, it might be called, of Popotla.

"The Spanish commander there dismounted from his jaded steed, and, sitting down on the steps of an Indian temple, gazed mournfully on the broken files as they passed before him. What a spectacle did they present! The cavalry, most of them dismounted, were mingled with the infantry, who dragged their feeble limbs along with difficulty; their shattered mail and tattered garments dripping with the salt ooze, showing through their rents many a bruise and ghastly wound; their bright arms soiled, their proud crests and banners gone, the baggage, artillery—all in short that constitutes the pride and panoply of glorious war,—for ever lost. Cortés, as he looked wistfully on these thinned and disordered ranks, looked in vain for many a familiar face, and missed more than one dear companion, who had stood side by side with him through all the perils of the Conquest. Though accustomed to control his emotions, or at least to conceal them, the sight was too much for him. He covered his face with his hands, and the tears which trickled down revealed too plainly the anguish of his soul. . . .

"Meanwhile the advancing column had reached the neighbouring city of Tlacopan (Tacuba), once the capital of an independent principality. There it halted in the great street, as if bewildered and altogether uncertain what course to take; like a herd of panic-struck deer, who, flying from the hunters with the cry of hound and horn still ringing in their ears, look wildly around for some glen or copse in which to plunge for concealment. Cortés, who had hastily mounted and rode on to the front again, saw the danger of remaining in a populous place, where the inhabitants might sorely annoy the troops from the *azoteas*, with little risk to themselves. Pushing forward, therefore, he soon led them into the country. There he endeavoured to re-form his disorganized battalions, and bring them to something like order."

The *teocalli* outside Tacuba is a good deal destroyed by age: but we rode up to the top, which still is quite large enough to allow ample room for our two horses, and our three companions on foot. We found a few bits of broken pottery upon it—how old, who can say? Perhaps those scraps of red earthenware with black painted lines in barbaric patterns, may have held the blood of the victims of sacrifice, at the very time that Cortez and his men were halting in the great street outside.

The Spaniards after this halt marched out to a hill at some few miles' distance, called then the Hill of Otoncalpolco, where they took possession of a large *teocalli* with strong outworks of stone, in which they entrenched themselves for a day and night; and there, in later times, was built a church dedicated to the Virgin, under the title of "*nuestra Señora de los Remedios*," whose miraculous image was supposed to be brought over from Spain by the followers of Cortez.

"It is said that this image was brought to Mexico by a soldier of Cortez's army called Villafuerte; and that the day succeeding the terrible *Noche Triste*, it was concealed by him in the place where it was afterwards discovered. At all events, the image disappeared, and nothing further was known of it until, on the top of a barren and treeless mountain, in the heart of a large maguey, she was found by a fortunate Indian. Her restoration was joyfully hailed by the Spaniards. A church was erected on the spot. A priest was appointed to take charge of the miraculous image. Her fame spread abroad. Gifts of immense value were brought to her shrine. A treasurer was appointed to take care of her jewels, a *camarista* to superintend her rich wardrobe. No rich dowager died in peace till she had bequeathed to Our Lady of Los Remedios her largest diamond or her richest pearl. In seasons of drought she was brought in from her dwelling in the mountains, and carried in procession through the streets. The Viceroy himself on foot used to lead the holy train. One of the highest rank drove the chariot in which she was seated, ... and plentiful rains immediately followed her arrival."[1]

[1] Madame Calderon de la Barca.

We were most anxious to pay a visit to the hill of Los Remedios, and talked of extending this very expedition thither: but the road to it and its neighbourhood were reported as being so unsafe, that unless we went a large party very strongly armed, we should infallibly fall in with the *ladrones;* so our project had to be abandoned. After leaving Tacuba we rode down a bypath to a rather suspicious-looking village, where there was another large *teocalli,* one side of it now forming the wall of a house. Being very thirsty, we bought from an Indian woman in the village about 200 small apricots for a *medio* (3d.), on which we feasted ourselves and the horses; and then started home by a long muddy road leading us back into the Calzada de San Cosme.

June 9.—Paid our farewell visit to beautiful Chapultepec. It was as usual a delicious morning. Nothing can be found more delightful in the way of climate than the fresh cool air of the Mexican plateau after sunrise at this time of year—every leaf and blade of grass sparkles with rain or dewdrops of the night before; the flowers fill the air with fragrance; the birds sing; the *colibris* and gorgeous butterflies dart past one like living jewels; the glorious tropic sun pours down on the valley; while any idea of oppressive heat is dispelled by the white gleaming heads of the snow-crowned volcanos against the clear blue sky.

We wandered for the last time through the mysterious avenues of *ahuahuetes,* gathering quantities of small grey-leafed orchids with pink flowers, and masses of the streaming Spanish moss; not as a *recuerdo:* but for the much more prosaic purpose of packing our various treasures; as it is so soft and yet elastic, that it makes the best stuffing, next to horse-hair.

Then we turned westwards, and leaving the castle and its groves behind us, walked up a green road, past the Emperor Maximilian's buffalo-grove, which he destined to be the beginning of a great Zoological Garden: but which, like most of his intended improvements, is fast relapsing into its original waste. Our point was Molino del Rey, a large flour-mill a mile off, belonging to the priests of Mexico, the scene of the famous battle on the 8th of September 1847, between the Americans and Mexicans.

We drove up to the Molino; and the *Padron*, a very pleasant and gentlemanlike young Mexican, showed us all over it. From the top story—it is five stories high, and stands on a hill—we got a view it is as impossible to describe as to imagine, all over the valley, with Chapultepec and its dark groves of giant trees at our feet as a foreground. The battle-field, with its monument to the Mexican generals who fell on that day, lies outside the large enclosure of the Molino, which really is more like a village inside walls than a mill.

The Mexicans were inside the walls, and covered the flat roofs or azoteas; so that the Americans could produce no effect on them, as they were well sheltered, while the Mexicans were inflicting heavy loss on their assailants. General Scott therefore ordered his men to storm the position, which they did with magnificent gallantry, forcing their way through a low narrow doorway.

Mexican affairs in the spring of 1847 were somewhat in the following position :—

California and New Mexico were already in the hands of the Americans. Tampico was also theirs; and General Taylor, left with a comparatively small army of occupation, along the line of the Rio Grande, had pushed forward to Saltillo, and there gained the brilliant victory of Buena Vista.

General Santa Anna, who had returned from exile in the previous year, had been elected President of the Republic of Mexico, in place of General Salas. Undeterred by previous disasters, he determined to withstand the advance of the Americans to the utmost, deceiving the masses of the people by accounts which left the public mind in doubt as to whether he had not after all been victorious.

Meanwhile, on the 9th of March, General Scott landed his troops on the coast below Vera Cruz, and by the 26th, after a vigorous bombardment, General Landero, the commander, capitulated; surrendering into General Scott's hands the principal commercial port and most renowned fortress of the Republic.

Leaving this important capture in the hands of General Worth, Scott marched with 10,700 troops towards the capital. The first opposition he met with, was where the road from the coast first enters the rugged passes of the Sierra. Here he encountered the Mexican troops, who were entrenched in a strong position; and on the 18th of April gained the decisive victory of Cerro Gordo, by which he opened the way for the American forces to the upper plateau of Mexico.

Jalapa and Perote were abandoned by the Mexicans without firing a gun; and from Perote, General Worth, who had joined the army, advanced towards Puebla.

The indomitable Santa Anna, meanwhile, had not been idle. In spite of these disheartening reverses, he had gathered together nearly 3000 men from his broken armies, and with these advanced from Puebla to give battle to General Worth at Amozoc. Unable, however, to check him, he retired upon the capital. Puebla in the meantime yielded submissively to General Worth on the 22d of May; and here the American forces were assembled.

In August, General Scott being reinforced by the arrival of fresh regiments, resolved to march upon the capital, and on the 11th concentrated his forces in the valley. Of the four possible routes by which this object might be accomplished, Scott chose that which, turning south from the hacienda of Buena Vista, and passing the town of Chalco, led along the narrow strip between the shores of Lake Chalco and the foot-hills of the mountains forming the southern rim of the Mexican basin, till it fell at Tlalpam into the main road from the city of Mexico to the southern Tierra Caliente. On the 15th of August this movement was commenced; and on the 17th, Worth, after an advance harassed by the light troops of the Mexicans, reached Tlalpam.

On the 21st Valencia was defeated in the brilliant battle of Contreras; while, at the same time, the left of the American army was engaged in the equally successful attack on Churubusco. After these crushing defeats, a short armistice was proposed. To this General Scott consented. But as the conditions were not adhered to, he sent word on the 6th September to Santa Anna, calling attention to the infractions of the compact, and declaring that, unless reparation were made before noon the next day, he should consider the armistice at an end. Santa Anna replied by recriminations, and a bombastic appeal to the people; so on the 7th preparations were made for the final attack.

On the 8th General Worth advanced on a strongly fortified position behind Chapultepec—the Molino del Rey—which was now used as a cannon-foundry, and the fortified Casa Mata close by, which contained a large quantity of powder.

The Molino was assaulted with heroic courage, and defended with equal gallantry. The havoc made by the guns of the Casa Mata among the Americans was terrific: but they were undaunted; and at last, hand to hand, they forced their way into the Molino, while a heavy cannonade reduced the fatal Casa Mata, and drove its occupants for shelter under the guns of Chapultepec. A series of strategic movements were now commenced, which had the effect of completely deceiving the enemy; and meanwhile preparations had been going forward for the attack on Chapultepec. Early on the 12th the bombardment commenced, and on the 13th the position was carried by assault, after a staunch opposition under the gallant old Bravo, who, fighting to the last, was taken prisoner with 1000 combatants.

The end was near. The routed troops retreated fighting, across the meadows and along the causeways, to the capital. Worth seized the causeway and aqueduct of San Cosme, while Quitman advanced by the other from Tacubaya to the Garita of Belen; and by nightfall these gallant officers had established themselves in the suburbs of the city, and awaited the return of daylight under the walls of the unsubdued citadel. But before morning, Santa Anna—at last convinced of the impossibility of continuing the struggle—had closed the panic-stricken Council of War, by announcing that the citadel must be evacuated; soon after midnight General Scott was apprised of the fact that the Government and troops had fled from the capital; and on the morning of the 14th the American army were in possession of the city. The war was now virtually at an end, though many engagements of more or less importance ensued during the few following months.

In January the New Congress assembled. Santa Anna, deposed and defeated, fled for refuge to Oaxaca; and finally, early in April, one year and eight months after his return to Mexico, embarked for Jamaica in voluntary exile. But ere he could leave, the peace he had so determinately opposed was concluded; and on the 2d February 1848 a treaty was signed at Guadalupe Hidalgo, confirming the southern boundary of Texas, and ceding New Mexico and Upper California to the United States.

But to return to our expedition.

The fortifications round the Molino were all rebuilt during the French occupation of the country, and are in good preservation. We walked down a steep hill, as the road was so bad we thought it safest to trust to our own feet: but as the carriage arrived safely at the foot, got in again, and drove on through maguey plantations and orchards to Tacubaya. The Indios were holding a great market, and we sauntered up the street looking at their goods, which for the most part consisted of vegetables and fruits. Among the latter were quantities of pears, and some excellent green figs, of which we laid in a good supply, as they were rare luxuries, and drove on three miles through rolling pulque plantations to the hacienda of Mr. P.

The owner, though born in Chili, was an American citizen. He married a wealthy American lady, and lived on his fine estate in great prosperity. In 1847 General Pillow's brigade was quartered in his barns, which compromised him seriously with the Mexicans; and he gave further offence at the battle of Molino del Rey, when he took breakfast to the American Generals before the fight, and, after it was over, took care of the wounded.

From this time ill-luck pursued the unfortunate man. The people of Mixcoac, a village between his hacienda and the mountains, cut off his water supply in either 1858 or 1859, and thereby destroyed his whole crop for the year. He, at least, got damages from the Government for this injury. At the beginning of the Intervention, however, the chief officer of the Government repaid himself in some small degree; for, the day President Juarez's family escaped from Mexico, they caught the ladies from Mr. P.'s going to church, turned them out of the carriage, put two soldiers on the box, and drove off. The mules alone were worth $1000, and of course were never heard of again by their owner. As soon as the French left the country, the persecution began afresh; and in 1868, 1869, and 1870, the Mixcoac people cut off the water again. When Diaz's troops came in front of Mexico they quartered themselves on the hacienda. The robbers killed his administradors and robbed his house repeatedly; and at last the unfortunate gentleman had to give up the struggle and retire to safe quarters, leaving his beautiful home to its fate.

It is now completely deserted. The paper is falling off the walls of what were once splendid salas. The only living creatures in possession are swallows and doves, who build unmolested in every room. The pretty garden is a tangled wilderness. Two of the fountains in it, of Artesian water, clear and pure as crystal, are dry; and the third is almost completely covered with a mass of roses, bignonias, and a dozen other flowering creepers run to waste. The walls in front of the hacienda are broken down; and the roofs of two immense granaries have fallen in. A fine road which Mr. P. built from the house towards La Piedad he was obliged to block up, as it was only used as an entrance for the robbers.

A short distance from the hacienda we passed a smaller house, where one of his administradors (an Englishman) used to live. One day it was attacked. The ladies of the family entrenched themselves on the *azotea*, where they remained in comparative safety. The administrador defended himself bravely below: but after killing several of his enemies, at last was killed himself, and the house was rifled.

We left the hacienda with relief. Anything so utterly depressing as the whole aspect of this once beautiful estate cannot be imagined.

Thursday, 13*th*.—Once more we have struck our tents, and are prepared to march.

The last four days have been consumed in paying and receiving farewell visits, and packing up our numerous treasures—no easy work where one has to explain every want to people who generally contrive to misunderstand directions if given by one of their own countrymen in purest Castillano, and much more by foreigners in halting speech. We felt somewhat inclined to follow the example of the man who came raving one day to the alcalde of a village, talking three languages in hopes of making himself understood:—" Señor Juez and Alcalde, dispense me s'il-vous plait. Last noche three hombres, called Gringos, entrada'd me casa, rompido'd me chairs, broke me vasos, and knocked down Margarita tampoco. Hang the country and the language! I wish I'd never learnt it!"

However, all is accomplished at last. I have spent my last evening with Mrs. Y., walking home, attended by a pompous coloured servant, through the quiet streets I have learnt to know so well. No lights, save the summer lightning playing overhead, or the lamps of the sleepy *serenos*, who were waiting till 10 P.M. to begin blowing their hateful whistles. And now my trunk is packed, and all is ready for a fresh start to-morrow, with England before me in five weeks more.

CHAPTER XXII.

A RECONNAISSANCE IN THE SOUTHERN TIERRA CALIENTE.

Preparations—Breakfast at Santa Fé—The unreasonable Commandante—Over the Sierra—"*Escolta*"—*Pueblos* of the Toluca valley—Tenancingo—My new guide—The *barrancas*—A bad ford—The old pack-horse takes a swim—A curious phenomenon—The cave of Cacahuamilpa—Bananas and sugar-cane—The Mexican Sindbad—An army of bats—Stoning iguanas—Hacienda of San Gabriel—Ixtapan de la Sal—"A bad place"—The romance of the skunk—Back to Mexico.

THE shortness of our stay in Mexico, and other reasons, made it impossible for us to visit—as I longed to do—the southern "Tierra Caliente," or tropical lowland of Mexico. But M., my brother, made about this time a railway reconnaissance thither, which he has described in the following letter; and which contains, I believe, many facts new to English and American readers :—

"DEAR R.,—It must not be imagined that our preparations for a reconnaissance in Mexico are very great, as from my journal I see that I was told off for southern service at about 4 P.M. on the 1st. A few provisions in the shape of cartridges were laid in, rifles cleaned, saddles and pack-saddles looked to, and barometers compared. My servants, three in number, had ten dollars apiece given to them to leave with their families; and at ten o'clock on the morning of the 2d I took the barometer-reading and time at the door of the hotel. Of course my horse insisted upon standing first on his head, and then on his tail, much to my own discomfort and the delight of the sundry friends who were waving '*adios*' to me from the window. I flattered myself on starting that such a ruffianly-looking band had never before ridden down the Calle Plateros. My own outfit consisted of a grass '*sombrero ancho*,' the invariable Mexican short jacket, and a pair of goat-skin overalls; while the bells on my Texan spurs jingled a merry tune to the horses' quick step. A carbine, revolver, and big knife completed the picture.

"The mozos, in their yellow leather jackets and trousers, also armed with carbine, pistol, and sword, chattered gaily to their accompanying *compadres*, who were giving them the last *noredad* or robber-story from our proposed route. Even the old white pack-horse caught the infection, and backed into carriages, or spluttered the remains of last night's shower over the pavement, to the undisguised disgust of the *catrinas*, the young swells of Mexico, who were ogling certain dark eyes that peeped through the gay sunblinds on either side of the street.

"Past the barracks and into the Paseo, meeting the late risers coming in from their morning ride; through the Chapultepec Gate, and up the street of Tacubaya, where the train runs past us, to the great disgust of our horses, till we strike the first descent of the long limestone road leading from Mexico to Toluca.

"Twelve o'clock, and we stop at the little hamlet, or rather long street of Santa Fé, where we are to pick up an ex-Pronunciado, my companion and guide. He is all ready saddled: but presses me to come and breakfast, which, considering that I have had nothing except a cup of chocolate at 5 A.M., and that there will be no chance of getting anything more till 5 P.M. on the other side of the mountain, I accept most willingly, and sit down, after profuse apologies on his part for his offering such a meal to his '*querido amigo*,' to vermicelli soup, a noble piece of steak; roast chicken; '*molle*,' which is turkey parboiled and fried in a sauce of Chile hot enough to set a dry man on fire; washed down with a tumbler of very fair *vin ordinaire*, and topped up with a little cup of *café noir* and a *puis café* of '*mescal*.' It may well be imagined that, starting directly after this, one is rather given to meditation, solid, but altogether too heavy for the subject, which consists of a steadily ascending foot-hill of brownish-yellow as a foreground, going up and up till it loses itself in blue green pine woods, their heaviness relieved by patches of yellow wheat, and capped with the long broken line of the sierra. That is beautiful enough: but let us see what we are leaving. Mexico, nestling in a corner of its broad valley, half-hidden in trees and shrubberies, lies like a map 1500 feet below us. To the north we follow the valley for sixty miles, dotted with lakes and hamlets, till we lose it in the blue distance of the sierra; while east, across Tezcoco, in whose blue water they are reflected, Popocatapetl and Istaccihuatl shut out the view by 8000 feet of sombre mountain side, the varied tints of which are set off by 3000 feet more of dazzling snow, standing out sharp and clear in the blue sky.

"Up and on past El Contadero, the last outpost of the Federal district, which my revolutionary companion thinks prudent to avoid, as the Commandante is still suffering from the effects of a scrimmage three months before, in which my friend had the great misfortune to put a rifle-ball through the said Commandante's leg. The delicate way in which he told me he did not care to meet him rather amused me.

"'Don't think,' he said, 'that I have any ill-feeling towards the man : but he is so unreasonable ; I cannot understand his dislike to me after I have submitted to the amnesty.'

"I told him to meet me a mile on; thinking, as I saw the Commandante limping about giving his orders, that after all it was not so wonderful if he did harbour a little spite against my unlucky friend.

"Here my passports are carefully looked over; and, after folks have convinced themselves that I am on a pacific errand, I jog along to where C. meets me, under the first straggling pines. From here the road changes into short broken zigzags, winding through the deep gulches, trying alike to man and horse. Here we pass a train of ten mule waggons, bringing grain into Mexico. The front waggon has its front wheels mired down so deeply that the united efforts of thirty mules are unable to get it out. Just half a mile above we overtake the three diligences 'doubling up' their teams over a rough piece. The reader has no doubt a vision before him of four gallant greys racing up a long English turnpike-road, up a gradient of 1 in 100 feet; but let him imagine one coach at the bottom of the hill, whose six lead-mules have been put on to the other team, making fourteen mules in all, which are now toiling with another diligence up a gradient of 1 in 16, over rocks and stones that would not disgrace the side of Snowdon.

"Up and onward, till the barometer marks 10,400 feet above sea level; and we see, 2000 feet below us, the broad wheat lands of Toluca blushing under the setting sun. Here we breathe our horses, tighten up our girths for the descent, and ask the escort, who are waiting for the coach, the 'news.' There is none; and after telling them not to take us for robbers when they catch us up with the coach down below, we jog down the road in the last gleam of sunset, which, striking a cloud in the western horizon, is reflected on to the snow peak of the Nevado de Toluca, lighting it up with a crimson glow. Down and across an open plain, with its scattered ranches; past the monument to the famous Hidalgo, the liberator of the Mexican people, on the place where he made his first and most decisive stand against the Spaniards; down again through a vista of fine trees till twilight changes to night, and we are reminded of the diligences we left behind us by the sharp crack of a whip, the heavy lumbering of their wheels, and the clatter of the sabres of the cavalry who escort it. We turn aside, and they rattle past us, their eight mules doing their twelve miles an hour down a hill over which nobody but Mexican drivers would dare to do more than four; while we laugh at the 'insides,' who, taking us for robbers, hide their pistols in their hand-bags, and call on the escort and '*la santissima Virgen*,' to protect them,—though both would have proved useless if we had really been what they thought us. We canter along with the escort for the next mile, till we reach the top of the descent into the Toluca valley: and jog slowly down into the little town, or rather street, of Lerma, the city of the Lake.

"Here a hasty council is held as to whether it is better to push on twelve miles to Toluca, or stay where we are. Having letters of importance to deliver there, I decide to go on, being slightly biassed in my decision by the quarters, as I prefer a comfortable room in the Toluca Hotel, hardly second to the Iturbide in Mexico, to a miserable lodging in the Meson at Lerma, where a few months previous I had passed a sleepless night on account of hungry bed-fellows. So after a *petit verre* with some friends whom we met opposite the little tavern, we settle ourselves down in the saddle for a twelve-mile trot across the level plain, through the darkness. The servants, who up till now have been riding in open order, close up with us; and a general conversation ensues on the topic ever dear to Mexicans, namely, robbers; and really a fitter place than the long straight road we were now travelling, with its deep dikes on each side, and a cross road cutting in at intervals, could scarce be imagined. Suddenly C. bends low over his saddle-bow, and I see his hand busily slipping the carbine slung along his saddle, while the servants slip theirs out of their cases. I slip my pistol out of the holster, and peer through the darkness ahead, at five or six forms which appear to be horsemen coming towards us. Just then we catch the clink of a sabre, and I hear a thankful sigh behind me from one of the boys, which finds an echo in my own breast of ' *Escolta*,' the escort. It was amusing to watch their movements when they caught sight of us, which was not till they were within about twenty yards. The two leaders pulled up short, to let the rest get up. Out rattled their carbines, while the two last half-wheel their horses, in order to run in case we should prove awkward customers. ' *Quien vive?*' challenges the sergeant. ' *Méjico*,' I reply. ' *De quel regimiento?*' ' *Americano.*' ' *Passen*,' in a sort of voice that showed his uncertainty still as to who we were. The ambiguity of this challenge is patent, as any robber could call himself ' *Paisano*,' or ' *Americano*,' and the escort would pass him without further inquiry.

"This was the only excitement that beguiled our road; and about 8 P.M. we were clanking up the streets of Toluca to the hotel, where the fatigues of forty-eight miles in nine hours were soon forgotten in a warm bath, a good supper, and bed. Next morning early, I did my business with the Governor and the Gefe Politico (chief of police), who objected so strongly to my revolutionary friend, that I thought it best to send him back, and continue my route alone. That day I made a short and broken journey, to let the horses recover from their long trip of the previous day, and was very kindly entertained by the Gefe Politico of Tenango, who gave me all possible information about the country, and accompanied me next morning up to the head of the Tenango Pass, the southernmost and highest point of the Toluca Valley, and indeed of the Central Mexican plateau. It is this pass that forms the watershed of the Rio Lerma, which from here runs through a series of large valleys, divided from each other by deep and rocky cañons, to the Pacific at San Blas, opening out into the large valley called the Bajio at Salamanca. Toluca is 8600 feet; the upper portion, known as the Toluca Valley, comprising an extent of some 50 miles by 30, is all under cultivation, and is by far the most thickly populated part of Mexico. Here the land does not belong, as is generally the case, to private individuals. It is owned by Indian '*Pueblos*,' or corporations, each family having its little plot of land, and working by co-operation under the direction of the '*Juez*' or judge. A large number of these Indians do not speak Spanish; and those who do, do so very imperfectly. From what I know of them, they belong, I fancy, to one of the older Mexican races before the Toltec or Aztec came in. Socially, they are a quiet, well-conducted people, working in the summer on their farms, and in the winter at small industries, one of the principal of which, at the upper end of the valley, is the weaving of baskets and mats made from the rushes growing in the lagoon of Lerma. These mats, together with earthenware, pottery, eggs, chickens, and charcoal, they take over to Mexico for sale. The means of transportation is on their own backs; and an Indian will carry from 150 to 200 lbs. thirty miles a day for almost any distance. On this trip, two Indians with empty packs, whom I had as guides some months before, happened to leave the gate of Mexico at the same time as I did, and kept up with me to within about two miles of Toluca, where they turned off to their own little Pueblo without the slightest signs of fatigue.

" But now we are on the summit of the Divide; and before us the Tierra Caliente is losing itself in the far distance in a blue haze. Down through a deep cañon, past little Indian villages and a couple of flour-mills, and '*aguardiente*' distilleries, we fast leave behind us the cold zone, and I hail with delight the last scrub oak at about 7000 feet above sea-level, and see a thousand feet below me the luxuriant leaves of banana peeping through the dark green of the orange-trees in the Plaza of Tenancingo. After finding a lodging in a tumble-down old palace, which formerly belonged to the great folk of the place, and is now used as a sort of inn, I wander down to the river with an acquaintance. From the town it seems just across a level plain shut in by two ranges of mountains, which converge about twenty miles below; and I am congratulating myself on a good railroad line for at least that distance, when, on the outskirts of the town, I suddenly come upon a chasm 200 feet deep, into which I find the river fall, about 200 yards above the spot we stand on.

"The beauty of the scene before me is almost indescribable. Six miles up stream a thin white ribbon over a wall of grey rock marks where the river debouches on to a flat grass plain, through which it meanders sluggishly till it reaches the end of the volcanic strata, where it drops over a perpendicular black wall of trap rock into a circular basin 100 feet across, which it has eaten out of the soft sandstone that here comes to the surface; and when my companion tells me that this is only the beginning of one of the smallest of the barrancas of the plain, which stretches southward, I become aware of the fact that engineering in the Tierra Caliente is not quite so easy as it looks.

"After smoking a cigarette or two and watching the curtain of spray which hung over the fall, we wander back to the inn, where I find waiting for me a short, thickset, dark man, who places himself at my disposition, and gives me a letter from the Governor of Toluca, in which he says that 'he has much pleasure in introducing to me the bearer, Q., as a man whose thorough knowledge of the Southern country and people would make him doubtless an invaluable guide to my party.' Which surmise has been fulfilled to the very letter.

"As, however, Q. has some little business to settle, we do not start next day; and I amuse myself by prospecting for coal, which is said to exist there, but only find veins of cinnabar. The following morning (the 6th), accompanied by a goodly cavalcade of enthusiastic railroaders, we cross the bridge above the fall, and keep down the eastern bank of the stream, which seems to be considered the best. I find that my friend was not mistaken in his description of the plain. The river-channel, or, as I will call it and its like for the future, 'Barranca,' de San Geronimo, deepens 200 feet in the next three miles, and the fall of the plain itself is very considerable. Our friends proposed to accompany us to a little pueblo called Sumpahuacan, distant fifteen miles, and lying, at the extreme south-eastern edge of the plain, in a sort of cove. This we reach about mid-day, after passing one desperately deep barranca called San Pedro, which skirts the range on the eastern side of the plain. As we canter up the further slope, we see a considerable commotion astir in the pueblo; and some of our party draw back; fearing a '*Pronunciamiento*,' or a disturbance of some kind or another. I however innocently cantered on with Q. into the little Plaza, where we were suddenly confronted by about thirty well-armed Indians, who halt us sharply, and in no civil way ask what the dickens we all want. Before I have time to reply, however, they recognise Q.; and warm greetings take the place of a warmer but less pleasant welcome which might have ensued had I been accompanied by any one else. When I look back at our well-armed little troop, I can hardly blame their mistaking our errand. The Indians, too, have a hearty welcome for railroad interests, which they show by preparing a sumptuous repast under the grand old ash-tree in the Plaza; and after dinner, when our friends leave us, provide us with a good escort and sure guides for the next fifteen miles.

"With many regrets we say goodbye to the Indians, and part with our friends on the further side of the Barranca, which we have to recross; and I must say I feel rather queer as I see them canter off across the plain. My position is this: Myself and three servants, whom I feel I could depend on utterly, in a country new to all of us, inhabited by Indians who seem entirely at the beck and call of Q. Can I trust him? I was a good prize, I knew; which endangered still more my position. 'Well, I'll try him at all events!' and giving a cigarette to each of our Indian escort, I pave the way to a long conversation about the troubles of the last revolution, as we make our way towards the junction of the Barrancas de San Pedro and San Geronimo.

"About half a mile from the junction the trail we have been following strikes the edge of the San Pedro Barranca again, which has now deepened into a chasm 500 feet deep, dropping sheer down on our side, and bounded on the opposite side by the Range, which rises some 4000 feet above us. An Indian trail three feet wide, with a perpendicular wall below, and where one false step would send one 500 feet on to the jagged rocks of the stream-bed, is not an inviting field for soliloquy; but I could not help feeling awe-struck at the almost inconceivable power which had, geologically speaking in a few years, hewn this chasm out of solid sandstone rock.

"The first glance at the trail decides me that I would sooner trust my own legs than the horse's; and down I get, utterly regardless of the Indio's assurance that there was no fear yet, and relinquish my horse into the hands of one of them. My mozos do the same; but Q. says that his old grey went down it the last time at a hand-gallop, after an unpleasant encounter with the Government troops on the plain above. So giving him the rein, he lets the old horse pick his way down the zigzag path, over loose boulders, a sheet of sandstone worn smooth by the barefooted Indios, or —what is more dangerous than either—a rut worn through the sandstone a foot deep and a foot broad, through which a horse has not room to pass one foot before the other, unless he lifts them clean out of it. Down we go, through shrubs, clinging here and there to the face of the cliff, till the sound of the water below us, scarcely noticed above, deepens into a low roar, and we find ourselves at the actual junction of the two barrancas, 550 feet by my barometer below the plain. Here the trail crosses the eastern barranca, which, owing to the previous night's rain, is in flood, and up to our horses' stomachs. We pass, however, in safety, with the exception of an Indio who chooses a line for himself, and in jumping from one rock to another in mid stream, slips, and if he had not been brought up by hitting one of the mozo's horses, would most probably have had his brains dashed out in the rapids below. But he joins in a good laugh at his own expense on the further bank, when I give him two dollars to get some more powder, as his own had been thoroughly soaked.

"The trail now keeps low along the edge of the river. On our left hand the range rises in a perpendicular crag some 3000 feet high, from whose top a man might drop a stone amongst us. In all my mountaineering, which is not a little, I have never seen such a sheer wall: still less can I account for its formation. Its stratum, or rather strata, are curved, broken, and lying at every angle. The rock itself is one of those strange intercalations of sandstone, shale, and limestone that are sometimes met with, and from its position with regard to the range on the western side of the plain, it would seem to have been upheaved simultaneously with it, but cut off from it at a more recent epoch by the action of water.

"Keeping down the bank of the river, or rather a long series of rapids, we came in a couple of miles to the junction of the barranca which we had been following with another coming in from the west; and on looking at the troubled 100 yards of water between us and the further bank, I feel my heart sink when Q. tells me that this is the only ford. But in spite of his advice to go back to Sumpahuacan, and cross the range to the east, I determine to get to the plain on the further side if possible; and tell the mozos to make their preparations accordingly. They unpack the old horse, and repack very carefully. Fortunately, as will be seen hereafter, my body-servant is sharp enough to take my papers and maps out of the pack and strap them round his own shoulders, while we girth up our horses; and I put my barometer and watch into the crown of my hat for fear of casualties.

"When we are all ready, an Indio dashes in, and just manages to reach the point between the junction of the two streams. He says we can make it; and in another ten seconds Q.'s old grey is in the middle of it. Suddenly he makes a wild plunge forward, or rather under, which brings forth a gulp from his rider of mingled fear and cold water: but thank goodness, the old grey has only hit a big rock, and scrambles out on the sandy neck, dripping, but none the worse, with the exception of Q.'s rifle, which, as he had forgot to take it out of the holster, went right under water This served as a warning to me and the mozos to take ours in our hands, and I make my essay with a vengeance, as my horse, after refusing to go in for a minute or two, makes a sudden dive into the water, nearly unshipping me. By dint of administering a gentle dose of the butt of my rifle under his ear, I force him up-stream, so as to avoid Q.'s rock, and land safely on the little peninsula. The mozos pass, one of them driving the old pack-horse in front of him, in safety. Thinking it needless to make our escort wet themselves more than is necessary, I have fee'd them, and said goodbye on the bank we left, from which they have been intently watching our passage, and are now shouting advice to us as to the best mode of crossing the next stream, into which our guide rushes and comes out fifty yards downstream, after rolling over two or three times, with the pleasant news that it was half a yard deeper than the first one.

"In goes Q.: and about mid-stream the old horse is swimming: but gets out with a struggle. I follow safely, as does the first mozo: but judge of my horror on seeing the old pack-horse, who comes next in order, turn deliberately nearly in mid-stream! For a moment he keeps his feet, and then is swept down the rapid. Fortunately the stream sets on to the bank on which Q. and I stand, and about fifty yards below the gallant grey straddles a rock sideways that was sticking up. No man knows how he kept his head above water for the thirty seconds which it took the other two mozos to get across and uncoil their lassos. Entering the stream cautiously, one throws a lasso over the old horse's head, while the other makes two or three shots at one of his hind legs sticking out of the water, which he finally catches. Putting their horses up-stream they pull him from his rocky resting-place: but then, oh horror! his full weight being exposed to the force of the stream, the strain is so heavy on the lassos that the horses cannot find sufficient foothold on the rocky bottom. Down goes the outside horse: and he and his rider scramble to shore as best they can, while the other one slips his lasso, preferring to lose it than to run the chance of losing his own or his horse's life. But some horses were born to be hung, and not drowned. The old grey, after turning over three or four times, lands on a sandy promontory that juts out forty or fifty yards below; with, strange to say, both lassos on him. There he sits on his tail in the water, with his forefeet out in front of him, staring round with the most comically bewildered look that can be imagined. And it is some time before we can induce him to get up and come on to the bank. Here he is unpacked, and receives as hearty a benediction as men who find their clothes wetted, bread soaked, and whisky-bottles broken, can be expected to give. Happily, I carry a pocket-flask, which we now divide among the party; the guide and the mozo who has got ducked coming in for the lion's share.

"Here first I become aware that twilight deepens on us; and by the time we reach the top of the barranca, where my barometer registers 750 feet above the stream bed, along a twin path to the one we came down, it is almost dark.

"Ten miles to go, and a mighty poor chance of supper; which we prove thoroughly two hours afterwards, when we find at the little ranche that the owner has been taken off the previous week by the Government troops, on suspicion of having been connected with the stealing of a horse, and that his wife and family have been sorely straitened since for a means of subsistence. However, maize cakes, cheese, junket, and fresh milk are delicious when flavoured by that most excellent sauce of hunger; and after scattering some maize stalks, the only fodder we could get for the poor horses, who were thoroughly tired out by one of the longest and hardest day's work they had ever done, I roll myself in my cloak on the grass, and remember nothing till the sun wakes me next morning.

"With a true Englishman's grunt, I cast off my blankets, and find the horses are greedily despatching their morning meal of maize stalk.

"From inside the hut I hear unmistakeable sounds of breakfast.

"Q. is up already, and has been making love to our hostess for the last hour, much to the hindrance of her culinary operations. After a hearty breakfast, the counterpart of last night's supper, we start along the plain, which here is a perfectly level expanse of grass, about two miles wide, bounded on the east by the barranca we crossed last night, and on the other side by a still larger one coming in from the north-west. Beyond the latter, a long range looms up, in which is the very valuable mining region of Tasco, from which the range takes its name. We follow the plain down for the next ten miles, where it is shut in by two mountains, under which, to my intense surprise, I find the two barrancas disappear. After an examination, I find that both of these barrancas have outlets, one to the right, and the other to the left of the mountains; but of very ancient date. The left-hand barranca enters the mountain side about 1000 feet below the level of the plain, about 800 feet below its old channel, which here strikes almost due north. As far as I could judge, though I could not get to it, the entrance to the tunnel is 300 feet high by 200 broad. The western barranca, I should fancy, was 1500 feet below the level of the plain, but its own old channel is only about 200. It is not very difficult to give the reason for this curious natural phenomenon. Countless ages ago, these two rivers or barrancas ran over the bed of trap which caps the plain. In an unlucky day for engineering they wore it through, and began eating their way through the soft sandstone below it. For centuries they must have kept to their original channels, on either side of the mountain, but at last the under current of water began eating out an escape under the mountain, which escape it finally made about three miles below the entrance: with one noticeable fact, that instead of following more or less the direction of their old channels, the two streams converge under the mountain, and come out within fifty yards of each other on the further side. After explorations showed me that even the present mouth of the eastern barranca has been changed, for about 100 yards from it, to the eastward, is an enormous cavern, now known as the cave of Cacahuamilpa, which has been traced back into the mountain for some two miles or more, but never, I think, to the very end. It must evidently have been an older channel than the present one, which for some reason got blocked up, and the present channel eaten out in its stead.

"This cave has been so well described by Mr. Brantz Mayer, Secretary of the U.S. Legation to Mexico, who visited it in 1842, that I venture to make use of his words:—

"'I was one of the last to leave the entrance of the cave, which hangs in a huge arch of sixty feet span, fringed with a curtain of vines and tropical plants. Our party preceded me for some distance along the road that descends rapidly for the first hundred yards. Each one of the guides, Indians, and travellers, carried a light. . . . I lit my torch and followed.

"'The first hundred yards brings you to the bottom of the cavern; and, if not warned in time, you are likely to plunge at this season of the year (September) up to your knees in water. You cross a small lake, and immediately before you, under the vast Gothic vault of the cave, rises a lofty stalagmite pillar, with a fringe falling from the top of it, which seems formed of the brightest foam congealed in a moment. A mimic pulpit rises from the wall, covered with elaborate tracery, and hard by an altar is spread with the fairest napkins, while above it depends a crystal curtain hanging in easy folds, each one of which flashes back the light of your torch as if carved from silver.

"'We fastened the end of our twine to a pillar of the altar and struck out westwardly in the direction of the cavern. After a short distance we turned slightly to the south, and passing down a file of rocks that had fallen from the roof, entered the second chamber.

"'In the centre of this a huge stalagmite has been formed. . . . It is a lofty mass 200 feet in circumference, surrounded from top to bottom by rings of fountain basins hanging from its sides, each wider than the other, and carved by the action of water into as beautiful shapes as if cut by the hand of a sculptor. An Indian climbed to the top of it, and firing a blue light illuminated the whole cavern. By the bright unearthly blaze every nook and corner became visible, and the waters and carving of this fountain-tower stood out in wonderful relief.

'We penetrated to the third chamber. Here there was

no central column, but the effect was produced by the immensity of the vault. It appears as though you might set the whole of St. Peter's beneath it, with dome and cross. . . . An Indian fired a rocket, which exploded as it struck the top of the immense dome, the detonation reverberating from side to side of the vault with the roar of a cannonade. A sheet of stalactite was struck, and it sounded with the clearness of a bell. . . .

"'Beyond this chamber was a narrow path between the almost perpendicular rocks, and, as we passed, the guide crept through an entrance near the floor, and, holding his torch aloft, displayed a delicious little cave, arched with snowy stalactites. In the middle rose a centre table, covered with its fringed folds, and adorned with goblin nick-nacks. . . .

"'Two rocks standing beyond this retreat are the portals of another chamber, groined, like the rest, in Gothic arches, with the tracery of purest stalactites, while its floor is paved all over with beautiful little globular stalagmites. In a corner fountain we found the skeleton head of a serpent.

"'The path beyond this is nearly blocked up by immense masses that have fallen from the roof. Passing over these, you attain another vaulted cathedral, bright as the rest with flashing stalactites, while its floor is covered knee-deep with water. . . .

"'We had now penetrated nearly 5000 feet in the interior of the earth, and the guides said that the chambers were still innumerable beyond. Persons have slept here and gone on the next day, but no termination has yet been discovered. . . . From this chamber we returned to the entrance by the clue of our twine.'

* * * * * *

"On leaving the cave and gaining the plain that lies to the south of it, we, for the first time, become aware that we are in the Tierra Caliente. The sun strikes down fiercely on the lava that crops up through the soil; and a dull steamy brown grey mist rises off the plain, making a little patch of light green sugar-cane in the hacienda of San Gabriel, five miles away, look temptingly cool. But I have wandered from my railroad line in search of 'the beauties of nature;' and I have to skirt the mountain due north again to regain it, at the further end of the old northern channel of the barranca.

"After skirting the base for about five miles along the plain, I open on a sort of little oasis in the desert, formed by the river of Malinalco coming in from the north, which, just as it debouches from the mountains, opens out into an oval basin a mile and a half long, covered with sugar-cane, rice, and maize, the latter growing above the level of artificial irrigation; while the broad belt of banana that skirts the river banks, forms, with its large pendant foliage, a beautiful contrast to the delicate spikes of the cane. Here and there a ceiba or an ahuahuete rears its giant head 150 feet above the stream-bed; and beneath its shade, and half hidden in orange groves, peeps out a little low white house, with a broad verandah, and sometimes a dark spot among the bananas marks a coffee-plantation. Joyously we drop into the valley, forgetting the burning heat in the cool green foliage. Through the maize, and into the cane-brake, with its little ditches bubbling with the fresh clear water; and then we dive into the semi-darkness of the banana grove; the refreshing roar of the river deepening till we emerge into the bright sunshine on its bank.

"It seemed almost a sin to drop from the sublime to the ridiculous at such a time and such a place; but how could one help it? In mid-stream, with the water boiling and seething round their waists, was a family party,—to wit, a stalwart young man, with his aged father on his back, the two reminding me sadly of Sindbad and the Old Man of the Sea. In front of him was this young man's wife, in the treble agony of driving three donkeys, each packed down with household penates, on the top of which were perched her three round-headed boys, aged respectively five, six, and seven. An Irishman driving two pigs was nothing to it. Each donkey went separate ways; the stream, against which she could hardly struggle, threatened every moment to overwhelm one or other of them. In vain she screamed to her husband to throw off the old man, and save his own children from drowning: but the Old Man of the Sea stuck to him, and absolutely refused to be drowned. After the first burst of laughter, we saw that matters were really serious, and, charging in on horseback, got down-stream of the donkeys, and picking the children off their backs, drove them to the bank. But judgment fell upon the Old Man of the Sea, as Sindbad, tripping over a big sunken rock, dived head-foremost into the water, within ten yards of the shore. No sooner did Sindbad find himself in this plight than he cast the old man off, and '*sauve qui peut*' was the cry. Poor old Man of the Sea! We fished him out of a deep eddy, thirty yards below, half drowned, and certainly more than half full of water. It was a beautiful sight to see him sitting on the bank, and hear the flow of anathemas that bubbled out on his son's head between the gulps for breath. But his daughter-in-law was equal to the occasion; and as we crossed the stream, and plunged into the banana swamp on the further side, we could hear the old man's guttural bass and the woman's, squeaking falsetto singing a glorious duo to the rattling accompaniment that Sindbad was playing on the donkeys' backs with a thick piece of driftwood, varied every now and then by a shrill scream from one of the children, who had been nearly or perhaps quite swept off the back of one of the donkeys by one of the long hanging leaves of a banana.

"The trail we had been following soon broadened, and we

find ourselves on the remains of an old Indian *Calzada*, leading up to the little Plaza of Cuoatlan del Rio, where we decide to pass the night in the house of one of Q.'s revolutionary friends. We ride up to the door, and get a most hearty welcome from him.

"The evening passed away in eating, drinking, and chatting, and with one curious incident as we were coming up from the river at sunset, after a refreshing bathe. We saw, as we got to our host's door, an enormous cloud of what at first appeared to be black-birds, coming out of the top of the Court-house that stood opposite, a noble old pile of Spanish architecture, surrounded by a garden and some magnificent coco-nut palms. Q. immediately called my attention to them, and told me that they were an army of bats, which lived in two enormous attics on the top of the house. As far as I could form an idea, there must have been millions of them, as the next morning early, when they came in the same way, and two or three hours later in the evening, they took six minutes coming out in a continuous stream of thirty to fifty deep. Next morning we went up and inspected their domicile, or rather tried to do so, as it was utterly impossible to get near them from the dirt.

"After the bat inspection was over we followed down the river through a long chain of banana groves, which every now and then opened out into a little '*rega*,' or meadow of rice or sugar, till we came, in about six hours, to the boundary wall of the hacienda of San Gabriel, and through the scattered bushes we saw a broad low-lying flat of perhaps four miles square, the cane-lands of San Gabriel and San José. Our path here followed the outside of the wall, covered with great patches of lianas, honeysuckles, and passion-flowers. The sun was at its full height, and, to our intense delight, we found basking in the heat, on the top, numberless iguanas and teguexins (lizards). And now the fun began; by a common impulse we bent down to the ground from our saddles without getting off, and in another moment such a broadside of stones was hurled at the hapless iguanas, as perhaps never yet had surprised their weak nerves. The horses grew as excited as we did; and my old horse, who had evidently been at this work before, would point at one of them like a dog, and swing himself round of his own accord, so that I could get a fair shot with the full swing of my arm: but I am afraid there was a great deal of good shooting and very bad hitting. However, we managed to have a pretty lively time, which was increased by one of the mozos hitting the old pack-horse hard under the ear with the biggest stone he could find; and by my saddle turning round with me as I stooped to pick up a stone, dropping me on my head, having carefully chosen the hardest spot along the whole road for my exploit. I am ready to depose, on oath, that an old black and red iguana, ten yards on, was laughing at me when I caught sight of him, and, as I pulled out my pistol to have a quiet shot at him, he cocked his head on one side, as much as to say, 'The man who falls off his horse can't hit me.' Alas for his powers of divination! The ants' nest, into which he fell, told a different tale as we passed the next morning.

"As we entered the little Plaza outside the hacienda of San Gabriel, I became aware of the fact that it was Sunday, as it was thronged with Indios from the neighbouring ranches.

"The yearly yield of this hacienda is 48,000 *panes* of sugar, weighing about 25 lbs. a piece, and worth $4 each; 4000 barrels of aguardiente or rum at $18 a barrel; and about 1000 cwts. of rice, $2.50 per cwt.

"It may be curious to you to know the yield of the small State in which San Gabriel lies (Morelos):—

933,000 arobas (25 lbs.) of sugar,
68,600 barrels of rum,
37,000 cwts. of rice,
3,000,000 lbs. weight of tropical fruits,

were last year's harvest (1872), of which some two-thirds went up to the city of Mexico, at an average price of $1.50 per cwt. for freight, for an average distance of seventy miles.

"Here I was at the southernmost point of my trip, and the next day I trespassed on the well-known hospitality of the administrador of the hacienda, by resting my horses and lounging.

"On the return trip we follow back our old line for three days to Pedras Negras, where we branch off to Ixtapan de la Sal, so called from the great salt pan or lick there. On nearing a little village about two miles from it, we heard the bells ringing for mass, and Q., who had intended to go to the Padre's house in Ixtapan, said that we would wait till he had done mass here, and then ride back with him, as he is a man '*muy instruido;*' and certainly a more pleasant courteous gentleman of the world I have rarely met. It was a pretty thing to see the little children run out of the cottage doors and plump themselves down in the road on their knees to receive the old man's blessing as we trotted past with him after mass. We were soon deep in railroad politics, and a little sprinkling of natural science; and before I knew where I was, I found him bowing me into a long low nicely furnished room, which had a certain air of refinement about it that one does not often meet with in Mexican towns. As he had to perform another mass here, he persuaded me to go up to a wonderful cave about half a mile from town during his absence, adding laughingly, 'I know of old that Q. doesn't care for my blessing, and to you as " buen heretico," I would not give it if you asked me.' So off we started, past the salt licks formed by a stream which bubbles out of a crack in the lava rock, evidently being the overflow or rather escape of the pond I am about to describe.

"Leaving these, we headed for a low circular hill, say 200 feet in height, and a quarter of a mile across at the top, in which, I was told, the cave and crater lie. As we neared it the first thing that struck me about it, was the wonderful fertility of the soil. The oaks, which must have had hard work to send their roots down in the rugged lava bed, are of far larger size than any I had yet seen in Mexico, and of most brilliant foliage. The tufts of grass which find a precarious living at their feet are rank and healthy. Rising the hill by a well-beaten path through the trees, we suddenly opened on a circular glade, 300 feet in diameter, of the most gorgeous grass lawn, in the centre of which is a circular basin of 150 feet in diameter and twenty feet in depth to the surface of the water. For aught one could tell it might have been hewn by hand out of the solid lava, so straight and smooth are the sides, with the exception of one place where the bank shelves down sharply to the water's edge. At a hundred different points on the surface water heavily surcharged with gas comes bubbling up, and in one spot so strong is the jet that it makes a mound of water about a foot high by six inches through. From what I judge, the water must be very deep, and our guide told us that they had sounded it for eighteen brassadas (about 108 feet), and found no bottom, except close to the edge, about two or three yards from which there seemed to be a sudden drop off. I had nothing with me, I am sorry to say, in which to bring home any water: but the taste seemed to be almost entirely carbonate of soda, without a vestige of iron.

"'A bad place,' says Q. : 'but come on to the cave.'

"And verily, as we forced our way up through the green oak over a steep bank, and I caught sight of the blue white bubbles seething up out of the blue black water,—a fitter mouth for l'Inferno could hardly have been imagined.

"Topping the crest, we opened out on to a grass glade with a bunch of trees growing out of a sort of rockery in the middle, which was the cave.

"We were to leeward of it, and at about twenty yards'

distance I could clearly scent a smell of what seemed to me salts of ammonia.

"Tying our horses to the little rail, we jumped inside, and found a broken opening between three or four boulders that seemed to have been rent asunder by earthquakes. But I could not trace a definite line more than that the gas came from two sides of the opening, and that a straight line drawn from the southernmost one, and cutting the north one, would have, if produced, hit the pond or crater we had just left; also that the same line produced southward would have hit the salt-lick and soda-spring at the bottom of the hill.

"It seems to me that it is simply a vent of the gas, the natural channel of which carries the gas from the crater to the soda-spring, as in all three I noticed sudden strong burstings out of gas at uneven intervals.

"To show the strength of the gas, I placed a strong young game-cock in the full blast of the southmost vent, which seemed to be the strongest. In three seconds he was reeling; ten, had fallen; and in fifteen was nearly dead. After taking him out and restoring him, I tried myself, and gave myself the most exquisite bursting headache in the same time, which lasted me for the rest of the day. The smell was exactly like sal-ammoniac.

"In ten minutes I tried the game-cock again, who died in about fifteen to eighteen seconds, as I could not be quite certain as to the date of his death.

"The grass around was quite covered with bones of rats and birds; and in the opening itself was the skull and neck-vertebræ of a donkey, who, my guide informed me, had died there before the railing was put up.

"But I picked out quite a romance there. On a boulder sticking up in the opening lay a half-decomposed bird, while, with one paw on the bird, and the other clutching the rock, was a skunk at about the same stage of decomposition. Poor fellow! he paid with his own the life he would have taken.

"It was then getting late, so we cantered back to Ixtapan, and after a good breakfast (twelve o'clock), set off for Tenancingo, which we did not make till nine o'clock P.M., men and horses tired out. Here I find orders to get back to Mexico, which I do with many long farewells to the hospitable folk of the S. Tierra Caliente. . . ."

*　　*　　*　　*　　*　　*

CHAPTER XXIII.

THE CITY OF MEXICO TO VERA CRUZ.

Teocallis of the Sun and Moon—Pulque—Puebla de los Angelos—Churches and relics—Sta. Florenzia—Muddy roads—The steel-works of Amozoc—Cacti—A midnight start—The Peak of Orizaba—Down the *cumbres*—Orizaba—A wild team—The railroad again—Vera Cruz—The *Vomito* and the *Norte*—Gachupines and parrots—Farewell to Mexico.

Friday, June 14.—Our exit from the city of Mexico was at first sight much more civilized than our entrance into it; for we came in on the top of the stage-coach; and we left in a train on the Vera Cruz Railroad. But there the civilisation stops. We had come in armed with revolvers and carbines; we left protected by three car-loads of soldiers, 200 men in all. The Revolutionists six weeks previously had attacked the train at Omatusco, killing the guard who incautiously looked out to see what was the matter, and burning the station. But notwithstanding this novel experience in railroad travelling, we were all in too high spirits at being actually on our homeward road to mind any amount of possible Pronunciados.

General P. and Governor H., with Gabriel their faithful guide, arrived from the interior the night before; and at 7 A.M. we had bidden farewell to a crowd of friends on the platform, and steamed out along the old causeway to Guadalupe; the sun shining on the waters of the Lake of Tezcoco, and lighting up the dazzling snowy summits of the two great volcanos, clear cut against an azure sky.

The railroad skirts the northern side of the lake, running through green meadows and past Indian villages. At San Juan Teotihuacan, where we stopped for a minute, we got a good view of the celebrated Teocallis of the sun and moon, —the only remaining relics of the Micoatl, or Pathway of the Dead, as the plain on which they stand was called by the Aztecs. In Cortez's time, these pyramids, which stand rather less than half a mile apart, were surrounded by hundreds of smaller ones disposed symmetrically in wide streets, forming a vast burying-ground. The two great pyramids were surmounted by two stone idols covered with gold, representing the sun and moon. No trace of these remains; the gold having been appropriated by the greedy conquerors, and the vast stone images destroyed by order of Zummaraga, first Bishop of Mexico, to whose ill-directed zeal we owe the destruction of most of the relics of the Aztec civilisation. The Teocalli of the sun is 682 feet round at the base; perpendicular height 180 feet. The Teocalli of the moon is rather smaller, and 144 feet high.

I could make out faint traces of the ancient terraces round the outside of the Teocalli, though it is now overgrown with cactus and scrub, and battered out of shape with the weathering of 300 years.

The teocallis were the temples of the Aztec nation. On their summits burned the sacred fire; and there, too, those horrid rites of sacrifice were perpetrated, which made the old Spanish conquerors feel that death in any other form was preferable to the chance of falling into the hands of the Aztec priests.

From San Juan an up grade took us out of the Valley of Mexico past Otumba, historic as the scene of Cortez's great struggle with the Tlascalans; and when we had risen 1000 feet above our starting-point, we reached the Llanos or Plains of Apam. Apam, besides being the centre of one of the finest wheat districts of Mexico, is the *pulque* metropolis of the world. Here, as far as the eye can see, the country is covered with countless acres of *pulque* plantations. So vast are the quantities consumed of this very uninviting beverage, that a "*tren de pulques*" runs every day each way between Mexico and Puebla; and during the year 1871 the railroad carried 34,605 tons of it. Gabriel, who escorts us as far as Vera Cruz, brought Mrs. P. and me a large bowl of *pulque* when we stopped at Apam, of which we drank, chiefly to please him. It was neither very good nor very bad; but generally foreigners, after a short apprenticeship, get as fond of it as the natives.

Five miles from Apam we passed the hacienda where General —— was shot, whom I saw on the 5th of May walking close to the President in the procession. He was murdered by robbers on his own hacienda, a fortnight ago; and his funeral, three days before we left the city, was the most splendid spectacle I have seen in the country,—ministers and generals following the hearse, with all the troops in Mexico. The din of military bands was so deafening, that, knowing nothing of the funeral, I ran to the window as they passed to see if there was a *Pronunciamiento*. At Sultepec, a little further on, the train, last autumn, was attacked by Pronunciados, who lay flat on the roof of the little station-house, and shot at the military guard of the train.

At Apisaco, where we stopped for breakfast, the main line of the Vera Cruz railroad stopped, a branch only going to Puebla. The middle section of the road between Apisaco and Orizaba, over the edge of the plateau of Mexico, was not finished.[1] Our route to the coast took us on to Puebla by the

---

[1] This division was opened on the 29th of December 1872, and presents to the eye of the engineer the most remarkable triumph of railroad engineering in the world. "After the first four miles beyond Orizaba we get on what they call 'the grade,' which is an almost uniform one for the next twenty-five miles of 4 per cent., or 210 feet in the mile. In the last seventeen miles, from Maltrata to Boca del Monte, we ascend 3500 feet along the face of a broken hill-side, which has an average side slope of

branch line, down a rather steep grade, at twenty-five miles an hour. Tlascala, that once flourishing city which stretched along the summits and sides of the hill, the capital of "*the land of bread*," lay on the right of the track as we wound round the sharp curves of the Sierra, and across the Zahuatl by a fine iron bridge, in place of the ancient stone one, by which Cortez and his men approached on the 25th of September 1519. All that one sees of the city from the railroad is a church on the hillside.

We arrived at Puebla at 1.30, and were at once struck by its cleanly appearance. The streets are well-drained and paved. The position of the city is magnificent, lying, as it does, at the foot of the eastern slopes of Popocatapetl, so that at the end of most of the narrow streets the vista is filled by blue mountain-side. As we were in plenty of time to catch the French steamer at Vera Cruz, we decided to stay one night at Puebla, in order to see some of its beauties.

We wished to have visited Cholula, the "holy city" of the ancient Mexicans, from whose ruined Teocallis innumerable Aztec remains are still dug: but it is some miles off, so we had to content ourselves with an exploration, as thorough as might be, of its Spanish successor, "la Puebla de los Angelos."

Mr. B., the consul, kindly acted as our cicerone, and took us first to his own house, which is in a part of the convent of San Domingo, the patron saint of the Inquisition. In what

about 1 to 1. A number of rocky points, separated by deep ravines, form a continuous succession of tunnels and bridges. It seems almost incredible that the longest piece of tangent in seventeen miles is 100 feet, yet it is a fact; in many places we find curves of 350 feet radius; while in two places we find 250 feet; and when the track was opened, owing to the caving in of a tunnel, a temporary track was built round the point through which the tunnel runs, with a curve and reverse curve of 150 feet radius. Over the whole of this division the speed is limited to eight miles per hour, which is found to be the maximum speed that can be run with perfect safety."—From *Ocean Highways*, May 1873.

are now Mr. B.'s stables are cells in the thick wall, where the victims were incarcerated. During the siege in 1862 he tried to open a way through to the church of San Domingo, which adjoins, and came upon a small square chamber, which we were shown, in the massive wall, which was full of human bones. These unfortunate creatures had, as in the city of Mexico, been dropped in from a hole in the top and there left. Truly, " murder will out !"

The Church of San Domingo is very large. A side chapel, devoted to some special Madonna, has a dome of carved and gilded wood so fine and delicate it looks like golden cobwebs. This Madonna was one of the richest in all Mexico; her jewels were magnificent; and she had one string of large pearls which used to appear on *fiesta* days fifteen *raras* (yards) long. These jewels, if they still exist, are said to be in the custody of the bishop, who keeps them buried for fear of a revolution. During the siege by the French, Mr. B. and his family took refuge in this chapel, as being more out of the way of shells than his own house. What strange surroundings !—the ghosts of all those victims of the Inquisition—the superstition of the country, which could expend thousands on this tawdry image—and outside, the shot and shell of the European invaders !

Thence we made our way to the Cathedral, which stands on the pleasant Plaza. It is outside almost a facsimile of the Cathedral of Mexico. The columns inside, were covered up to the capitals in crimson velvet in honour of some feast, and had a most striking effect. The high altar is supported by sixteen columns of marble of the country, and richly adorned with silver and gilding. Under the canopy —*el Ciprés* I believe it is called in Mexico,—stands a Madonna made in some metal, and weighing, we were told, 9000 lbs. Beneath the altar some steps lead down into a circular room lined throughout, walls, roof, and floor, with black and white marble. In this room the bishops are buried, their coffins being placed in niches in the wall, which are covered with the marble lining.

The choir is lined with stalls, the backs of which are inlaid with wood, no two of the same pattern. Over the bishop's chair at the end is a picture of St. Peter, also in inlaid wood: but so exquisitely is it executed, that not till I had actually mounted the bishop's throne and felt it over with my fingers could I believe it was not a highly-finished oil-painting.

One chapel was full of horrid relics—a bone from this saint's leg, or that saint's arm—a skull of one, and a tooth of another. Gabriel, who is a thorough *Liberale* in his dislike of the clergy, said to me, talking of relics, " If all the teeth of Sta. Apolonia were collected which are scattered over Mexico, they would fill eight railway cars !"

Hard by, another chapel was opened by the sacristan, and we were taken within the iron gates, which were carefully locked after us to keep out the *leperos*, who swarmed after us. A false back to the super-altar was unfastened by a secret spring and taken down, and before us lay enclosed in a glass case the figure of Sta. Florenzia. She was a martyr, and reposed transfixed by an arrow, in clothes which savoured strongly of a Fairy Queen in a pantomime: but they were literally incrusted with jewels. The silver and gold tissue was embroidered with seed pearls and tiny diamonds, emeralds, rubies, and turquoise. Round her neck hung magnificent pearls; and her right wrist was adorned with a bracelet of single emeralds, flat and hardly cut, each nearly an inch long. If the jewels were *bonâ fide*—and we were assured that they were so—the pretty, childish-looking little saint, who lay there so innocently unconscious of all her grandeur, must have been worth a king's ransom. We were most fortunate in getting a glimpse of her; as, owing to the value of the jewels, she is only uncovered once a year; and hardly any foreigners have been allowed to see her.

Leaving the Cathedral, a violent rainstorm put an end to our sight-seeing; and we had to run back under shelter of the Portales to the Casa de Diligencias, which was a pleasant resting-place enough, the upper gallery round the patio being full of birds and flowers, with bananas and orange-trees growing in tubs, and plenty of benches outside our rooms to lounge on, enjoying the freshened air.

Puebla being the terminus of the railroad, we had to betake ourselves once more to our old enemy, a diligence. So accordingly, on the 15th, we whirled out of the "City of Angels," with eight wild ponies, making up our minds to two days more of misery before again reaching civilisation in the shape of railway carriages.

The view from the first rise out of Puebla was superb; and as we stuck fast in a deep mud-hole at that point for some ten minutes, we had plenty of time to admire the beauties of nature. Behind us lay the white city, at the foot of Popocatapetl and Istaccihuatl, whose snowy heads, pink in the rising sun, looked so near, one almost imagined one could touch them. To our left rose the massive Malinche and the Cofre de Perote, and far away, right before us, gleamed the white needle-like Pico de Orizaba. The roads were naturally bad, and owing to the unusually early setting in of the rainy season, were rendered worse by mud. In the actual rainy season, coach-traffic is sometimes stopped for a time owing to the mud. As an instance, when President Juarez's family returned to Mexico after the fall of the Empire, the carriage in which Madame Juarez was travelling stuck fast in the streets of Cordova; and in spite of the efforts of twenty-four mules harnessed together, it was several hours before it could be extricated. Luckily, however, no such misfortune befell us; and, sitting outside the coach, the journey was pleasant enough, as there was no dust, and the scenery was splendid.

At Amozoc, the first town we reached, while we changed

horses, the coach was surrounded by a jabbering crowd of men and women, who offered for sale spurs and bits of a peculiar manufacture—steel inlaid with silver. This is, I believe, the only place in Mexico where steel is worked; and they have carried the art to great perfection. The spurs —some of them immensely heavy—were beautifully chased with elaborate patterns in silver on the steel. They and the bits were no use to me, as Mexican bits are far too severe to put into any English horse's mouth. I found, however, that among other things, the people were selling the most exquisite little flat irons of the same work, and got two or three pair, less than an inch in length; and a pair of sleeve buttons, with a silver flower inlaid in the blue steel.

Our next halt was at Tepeaca, where we hoped to get some breakfast. The people of the town, however, seemed to pay as little attention to the welfare of travellers as to the walls of their houses, which were all falling down from neglect: for we could not get a relay of mules, or anything to eat save a little sour bread; and so we had to push on hungry, and with a tired team. The road led us through a series of flat valleys, ten miles or more broad, covered with corn-fields and pulque plantations; and about 2 P.M. we reached Tecamachalco, a pretty town on the mountain-side, at the entrance of a cañon through which the road leads. Orchards and gardens full of fruit-trees, with hedges of maguey and sweet peas, surround the town, watered by streams of water which run down off the mountains.

Through the cañon, we plunged into a luxurious cactus and aloe vegetation for some miles. The Yucca of the north, or some closely allied species, grew in strange uncouth trees, with thick brown stems, surmounted by the head of narrow green leaves. Opuntias and Dasyliriums of endless varieties, mingled with the glaucous green sword-blades of the maguey, whose yellow and scarlet flower-spikes, fifteen and even twenty feet high, rose stiffly erect, like flaming candelabra, above the surrounding scrub.

After the cactus-land came a long stretch of cultivated land in a broad valley, till at 6.30 P.M. we reached San Augustin Palmar. After a tolerable supper we retired to our rooms to sleep, or try to sleep, for three hours, as the diligence was to start at 1 A.M. precisely. My room was too full of "*chinches*" to encourage much sleep; and it was rather a relief than otherwise, when the sleepy servant thumped at my door and cried twelve o'clock, to get up and plunge my head into cold water—the only equivalent for sleep in such a case.

At 1 A.M. we started; two passengers besides our own party making the coach uncomfortably full. Till daybreak we were lighted by flaming torches carried by the muchacho on the box. They shed a stream of sparks behind us, and showed us here and there the weird hedges of cactus and aloe which lined the road, and in the uncertain light took every imaginable shape, giving us not a few alarms by their unpleasant resemblance sometimes to a group of men on the watch for the coach. However, we passed in safety the "*jornadas*"—places where the road runs in a deep gulch barely wide enough for the coach to get along, while those on the box are just on a level with the surrounding ground. They are uncanny spots, and much infested by robbers; so all the gentlemen got out and walked on each side of the deep roadway.

About 4 A.M., just as the dawn was beginning to take the place of our torch-light, a view broke upon us that I have seldom seen equalled. We were winding down the face of a steep hill. Below us lay a gorge of infinite depth filled with seething blue mist, stretching away with endless windings between rocky cliffs, whose upper parts were clear cut in hard blue shadow, while their base was lost in the blue cloud below; and beyond, against the blue-grey sky, rose the peak of Orizaba, its everlasting snow faintly pink with the first rays of day, while we were still shivering in the shadows of night; and close to us, on the edge of the cliff, throwing the whole picture into shape, by force of contrast, stood a single *maguey*, its tall flower-spike rising hard and scarlet against the pale snow.

At dawn we reached La Cañada, a town at the bottom of the valley we had looked into, and found it crowded with waggons and hundreds of mules transporting a Government " *Conducta* " of $4,000,000 from the mines down to the coast. Then, rising 500 feet up a long hill, with superb views of the Peak on our left, we found ourselves on the very edge of the great Mexican plateau.

Below us was one of the *cumbres* or steps, by which in a few miles the stage-road descends nearly 4000 feet. This first *cumbre* was about 800 feet, down which the road was zigzagged; and when we reached a few huts at Vallé below, and stopped to change mules and get some excellent chocolate, looking back one hardly knew how we had come down, so sheer was the cliff and so steep the turns: but that was nothing to what was to follow. On starting again I got outside to see better; and because I thought that the very small chance of being pitched off the coach was preferable to being quite flattened between a very fat Mexican and a very sleepy Spaniard inside. From Vallé, a pretty sharp rise leads to the top of the great Cumbre de Aculcingo; and here, in four miles, you drop suddenly 1900 feet, and change from the cactus-vegetation of the plateau at the top, to the tropical of the Tierra Caliente below.

At the summit of the Cumbre, the two leading mules were taken off, and trotted down loose in front of us; the cochero managed the four mules in the "swing," and the break, which is worked by his right foot; and the muchacho held the two wheelers, on whom, poor beasts, came all the weight of the coach.

'*Vamonos!*" Down goes the break! Gabriel, who is beside me, seizes my arm with one hand, and holds me in my place by main force. We squeeze ourselves into the smallest compass possible, to give the cochero and muchacho room for the free play of their elbows; and down we plunge. The cliff is almost perpendicular; the road takes twenty-two sharp turns down it; and being utterly unprotected by any kind of railing, and swarming with pack-mules, and long waggon-trains from the country below, the descent is neither safe nor easy. Once or twice, at a particularly sharp corner, I thought we should not be able to turn, and must go clean over, as the coach was very heavily laden: but, thanks to the magnificent driving of our cochero, we reached the foot in safety, and breathed again.

At the village of Aculzingo, where we saw our two leaders quietly trotting into their stable, we changed mules in a moment, and then went off full gallop with our new team along a splendid road. It was the strangest change from the barren cactus-land above the Cumbres. The cañada or valley, down which our road lay, is twenty miles long, and one to one and a half broad, between wooded mountains from 1000 to 3000 feet high. A little river, shaded by cypress and sub-tropical trees, ran through rich fields of maize and sugar-cane, with hedges of huge aloes in full flower, and past palm-thatched huts, with green parrots crawling about the door-ways, surrounded by neat gardens full of bananas and pine-apples. Then the valley narrowed into a pass. We crossed the line of the Vera Cruz Railroad, saw it winding up the mountain-side to Maltrata, and met a group of English engineers riding out to inspect their track, their unmistakeable British attire contrasting queerly with their Mexican saddles and little Spanish horses. We whirled round the corner of a hill; and there was the pretty town of Orizaba right in front of us.

We pulled up at the door of the Diligence Hotel—a great

improvement on our previous resting-places,—and sending on our baggage under Señor A.'s care to await us, decided to stay twenty-four hours in the attractive little town, as we were all tired with our rough stage journey, and glad to spend as short a time as possible in the ill-omened Vera Cruz.

The well-dressed Mexican visitors at the hotel must have wondered at my appearance as I walked in to inspect our rooms. Every one was in a great hurry and confusion, as the coach only waited to put us down, and then went on to join the railroad at Fortin, seven miles on; so in order to make myself useful, I caught up the first of our possessions I could lay hands on, and carried them off to my room. As luck would have it, they happened to be a couple of rifles, and never shall I forget the horror and amazement with which the good people sitting at *almuerzo* in the dining-room regarded me. I can excuse them; for I must have been a strange figure, with a crimson and purple bandana handkerchief, which Gabriel had given me, knotted, robber-fashion, over my cotton Garibaldi, to keep off the dust, a short woollen gown—a deadly offence to Mexican feelings,—sunburnt and dusty, and laden with the two heavy carbines!

The town of Orizaba nestles at the foot of the great snow-capped Pico, fairly buried in lime and orange groves. One cannot tell where the streets end, and the orchards begin, so mixed together are they. Little streams of water dash across the roads, and the old stone walls are alive with ferns of endless variety. After a siesta in the middle of the day, we walked up to the market, and bought pine-apples for a *real* apiece, which I have never seen equalled for size and flavour; and in the evening we wandered out of the town through cool shady groves, where oranges, mangos, and bananas, mingled with scarlet erythrinas, and huge aloes, and a hundred other beautiful plants and flowers, growing with that prodigal luxuriance one sees only in the tropics, had the delicious fragrance of our hothouses. The night at Orizaba, however, did not pass quite as pleasantly as the day. The mosquitos, delighted to find a new-comer, swarmed into my room through the iron-barred window, which was, like almost every other in the town, quite guiltless of glass; and having no mosquito-net, I was so devoured as to be almost unrecognisable when I appeared at breakfast next morning.

At 10 A.M. on the 17th we left in the diligencia for Fortin, seven miles off, and our last experience of "staging" was certainly an exciting one. The mules, when once harnessed, are always impatient to be off; so two men turn the two leaders at right angles to the other six, with their heads against the wall, and a bit of rope, eight or nine feet long, passed through their bridles. When all is ready, they turn them out into the road, run beside them till their heads are quite straight, then let slip the ropes, and away the whole eight go, heads down and crouching low, as hard as they can fly for a quarter of a mile. On this occasion the mules—a magnificent greyish roan team—were very fresh; and being kept waiting for a few minutes, the wheelers began to amuse themselves by a kicking match, which ended in their kicking over the traces, throwing themselves and the middle mules down, and breaking the harness. When fresh harness was brought, and all the passengers were ready, they were once more put in, and starting with two or three good kicks, we went down the narrow paved streets of Orizaba like Lützow's wild hunt, the heavy coach whisking round corners and flying over ditches in a way that took one's breath away.

One glimpse more we caught of the Pico de Orizaba, which will never be effaced from my mind. It had been hidden in clouds all the morning, but as we flew along the excellent road, through sugar and coffee fields, we happened to look up, and far overhead towered the snowy peak like a great white ghost looking out on us from the clouds which rolled round its base above the blue foot-hills; while we below looked up to its calm coldness through a frame of bananas, aloes, and palms, in blazing steaming heat.

At Fortin we reached the temporary terminus of the railroad, and were soon comfortably established in English carriages for the run of seventy miles into Vera Cruz. The first part of the road lay through banana, coffee, and tobacco fields, at Cordova plunging into tropic forest, with the trees covered with lianas, and clouds of yellow butterflies dancing in the sun. Just beyond Atoyac, a little station above a beautiful rocky river, we came to the Chicahuiti Pass, where river and railroad make their way through a narrow gap out of the mountains. The road is blasted along the cliff, some 200 feet above the river, which falls in a cascade fifty feet high, through a narrow cleft of rock completely overarched by fine trees, wooded hills rising on either side a thousand feet from the stream. Once out of the pass you are clear of the mountains; and as you cross a wide open plain to Paso de Macho they stretch away south as far as eye can see, an almost impassable wall, till lost in the misty Atlantic atmosphere.

The journey thence became tame and tiresome, over wide plains covered with volcanic boulders, with here and there a tree-bordered gully, through blinding dust and broiling sun, till at Soledad we struck the belt of wooded swampy land which runs along the coast. So dense is the forest through which the road has been cut, that a calf which got upon the track galloped down in front of the train for more than a mile, before it could find a place to turn off. The swamps were full of two kinds of white cranes, and as we neared the coast low palms grew among the underwood. About 4.30 P.M. lines of coco-nut palms appeared; then white buildings; and plunging through an opening in the old battered walls, which, by the way, for want of stone, are built entirely of white coral and madrepore, we steamed along inside the ramparts of Vera Cruz.

The very name of this ill-omened city brings unpleasant associations with it. Besieged and bombarded countless times, it appears as if fate had tried to sweep from the face of the earth the headquarters of that most horrible disease, the "*Vomito*," which rages in the city for several months of the year. It only disappears at the approach of a second plague, the "*Norte*," a furious wind which, though driving away "Yellow Jack," often prevents vessels approaching the coast for days, if they escape being driven ashore when caught in it suddenly: a severe remedy.

It was therefore with no small feeling of relief, as we had to sleep there for one night, that we heard Dr. S.'s greeting when he met us on the platform at Vera Cruz:—

"City quite healthy; not a single case of fever."

Hot and tired as we were after our journey, we were thankful for a few hours' respite before a sea-voyage; and were soon comfortably established at the hotel, looking on the pretty Plaza with its group of tossing coco-nut palms and hedges of scarlet hibiscus. But though the hotel was excellent, and we got an unlimited amount of ice which of course comes straight down from the States, yet the remembrance of the heat of that night haunts me. In vain I tried to sleep. I pulled my bed into the middle of three or four thorough draughts, with a breeze rushing in through the high open windows. But the breeze was a sirocco, pouring hot air upon one, and by its very violence heating instead of cooling one's skin. I tried fanning myself: but that made matters much worse. At last, towards morning, in despair I got up, and sitting at the window, passed what remained of the night in watching the wakening life of the city, and especially the antics of the ugly *Zopilotes*, the black Turkey buzzards, who swarm about the streets, acting as aide-de-camps to the *norte*, in keeping the streets clean.

Soon after sunrise I sallied forth with Dr. S. to see the town. It is very small, being about five blocks long by three blocks deep, and entirely surrounded with the coral walls. We went outside the walls to the north of the town, near the great sand-hills which extend for miles along the coast: but the heat was so fierce, we soon had to beat a retreat. The only attractions in the city itself were the market and some charming baths. These baths were built round a patio, full of tropic flowers of every hue, and great banana plants, and fitted in the most luxurious way possible: and Mrs. P. and I came away not only refreshed by our bath, but laden with bouquets which the courteous proprietor picked for us on seeing our delight with his garden.

The market, just off the Plaza, is well worth a visit; for there, besides the fruit and vegetables, which are always of interest in a tropical country, the Indios bring in quantities of birds, especially parrots, from the neighbouring forests.

Apropos of these parrots, I heard an absurd story, which, of course, turns against the "*Gachupins,*" as the Mexicans call the Spaniards from old Spain. These Gachupins are supposed to be exceedingly "green" when they first arrive, and to do all sorts of foolish things. One Gachupin, so the story goes, had heard much of the parrots of Nueva Espagna, and on landing at Vera Cruz made straight for the forest to try and catch some. He soon reached a wood full of them, and seeing one sitting quite quiet in a tree by himself, began to climb the tree to secure him.

The parrot, as it happened, was a tame one, which had escaped to the forest again: but had not lost the power of speech. As our Gachupin put out his hand to seize him, he cocked his head on one side, and exclaimed—

"*Que . . . quieres?*"—which, being interpreted, means, "What do you want?"—with a very strong Spanish expletive.

The Gachupin took off his hat, and, with a low bow, replied—

"*Dispense-me, V. Senor:*" "Excuse me, Sir, I thought you were a parrot."

Not being a Gachupin, I went no further than the market in quest of parrots, and soon found an irresistible "Lorito," a little red-headed fellow, who, far from insulting me, was crying helplessly in a palm-leaf bag, with three small brothers and sisters out of the same nest. He proved an excellent traveller, and reached England in safety. At 4 P.M. we embarked on board the 'Nouveau Monde,' which was lying on the glassy waters of the gulf beneath the guns of San Juan de Uloa. Señor A., and one of the engineer's party, who had come with us as far as the coast, with our faithful friend Gabriel, came on board, and only left us when the pilot's boat returned to shore, some few miles out at sea,— Gabriel taking leave of us in true Mexican fashion, kissing General P. on both cheeks, and giving Mrs. P. and me a stage embrace, as he patted us on the back. True-hearted friend! Were there more like him in the country, beautiful unhappy Mexico might take the place she ought among the nations of the world.

Three days of indescribable heat and misery brought us across the gulf to Havannah, where we spent nearly a week; thence in a small steamer we crossed to Key West, and up the coast of Florida to Cedar Keys, where we took the cars, running through the palmetto groves and cedar swamps of Florida and South Carolina to Savannah, Charleston, Richmond, and New York, heartily glad to be once more safe on American soil.

CHAPTER XXIV.

MEXICO AND ITS RESOURCES.

BY those who know it best, Mexico is always spoken of as a country richer in natural products than any other in the world.

This is a broad statement: but it has more truth in it than such sweeping assertions usually possess.

Lying between 21° and 14° north latitude, it would seem at first sight to be an almost exclusively tropical, or semi-tropical, country. But from its northern boundary there runs down a central plateau, gradually rising from an altitude of 3000 feet above sea-level at El Paso, till, fifty miles south of the city of Mexico, or 18° north latitude, it has attained an elevation of 8000 to 9000 feet. Thus the difference of latitude is entirely counteracted by the altitude, and the southern portion of the plateau is in reality colder than the northern.[1]

This plateau forms a connecting link between the Rocky Mountains of North America and the Cordilleras of South America, with a noticeable point of difference from these northern and southern ranges. In both of them the Atlantic slope is the most gradual, the Pacific slope being precipitous, and the mountains approaching comparatively near to the

---

[1] City of Mexico, elevation 7400 feet, mean temperature 17° 5 Centigrade, or 63° Fahrenheit.

El Paso del Norte, elevation 3900 feet, mean temperature 21° Centigrade, or 70° Fahrenheit.

coast. In Mexico this is reversed, the Pacific slope being much the longest: but still not sufficiently gradual to allow of any river-communication between the interior and the coast, as in North and South America.

This plateau is not by any means smooth, being formed of a series of basins, landlocked in every case on three sides, and very commonly on all sides by mountain ranges rising from 500 to 3000 feet, while round its southern extremity extends a volcanic rampart, south of which the landlocked basins disappear entirely, and the main watershed, which north is extremely complicated, becomes more clearly defined.

The volcanos of Orizaba, Popocatapetl, Istaccihuatl, Malinche, the Nevada de Toluca, and Jorulla, form a connecting chain, which present a remarkable exception to the ordinary mountain-chains.

"The cones of eruption," says Humboldt, " usually follow the direction of the axis of the chain; but in the Mexican table-land the active volcanos are situated on a transverse fissure running from sea to sea in a direction from east to west."[1]

Round this plateau, which will average roughly 400 miles across, lies a belt of true tropical country, varying from 50 to 200 miles in breadth. The Mexicans have divided their country into three zones:—

The *Tierra Caliente*, or Torrid Zone, from sea-level to an altitude of 5000 feet, or, in other words, the limit of sugar.

The *Tierra Templada*, or Temperate Zone, from 5000 to 7000 feet.

The *Tierra Fria*, or Cold Zone, from 7000 feet and upwards.

Taking these three zones and examining their products, we may arrive at a tolerably correct knowledge of their natural riches.

[1] Humboldt, *Essai politique*.

In the Tierra Caliente we find sugar, rice, cotton, coffee, tobacco, cocoa, indigo, vanilla, drugs, vegetable poisons, herbs of all kinds, cochineal, yarns, coquito nuts for oil, gum-arabic, gutta-percha, and all the tropical fruits, *i.e.* banana, orange, lemon, lime, pine-apples, figs, cocoa-nuts, guayava, chirimoya, zapote, chico-zapote, granaditas, mangos, etc.

In woods there are mahogany, Brazil wood, ebony, prim-avera, rosewood, zapote, orange, chijol, alzaprima, and an endless variety of hard-woods and dye-woods.

Sugar.—Throughout the Tierra Caliente sugar is largely raised, and the refined white sugar which in the city of Mexico now fetches from 4d. to 6d. per lb., is considered to be of a superior quality to Havannah sugar. The State of Morelos, for instance, which contains 3500 square miles, last year (1872) raised 233,250 cwts. of sugar, with only about 1-20th of its sugar-land under cultivation, besides 15,425 tons of molasses, which are mostly converted into rum and aguardiente.

Coffee.—The coffee supply of Mexico is at present scarcely equal to the demand for home-consumption, and this for a very simple reason—that the people are too lazy to grow it. The south-west, especially the States of Colima and Micho-acan, have, up to the present time, proved themselves the best coffee-producing districts. But through all the south there is so much land possessing just the same natural advantages that there can be no doubt that if the same care were taken there as in the two former States, just the same quality of coffee could be raised. The coffee-bean of Colima and Uruapan closely resembles that of Mocha, and quite equals it in flavour.

Cotton.—The south of Mexico cannot be said to be thoroughly satisfactory as a cotton-raising district, with the exception of the State of Guerrero, as the crops are from time to time entirely destroyed by an insect which attacks the pod just as it has bolled, and in a night will destroy a whole crop. This, however, has not occurred in the northern portion of the country, where there are large cotton districts in Southern Chihuahua, Western Durango, and Coahuila. In the city of Mexico this cotton fetches one cent per lb. less than the Texas cotton, because the latter is more thoroughly cleaned. But English and American millowners in Mexico state that the Mexican cotton is stronger and of quite as fine a fibre as the Texan; and that when properly cleaned it ought to command a market value of one to two cents per lb. more than the Texan. Sea Island cotton is universally grown throughout the north.

Tobacco.—An enormous quantity of tobacco is grown in Mexico, especially in Orizava and Tepic. But, owing to the carelessness of the Mexicans in curing it, its quality is far inferior to the Havannah, though it is naturally good. And should the Havannah crop diminish in consequence of the abolition of slavery in Cuba, some Cuban tobacco-firm might with advantage migrate to Mexico. Land is cheap, labour is cheap, and with the varied soil and climate a "vuelta abajo"[1] may be found, which will in a few years rival or surpass Cuba itself.

The products of the Tierra Templada and Tierra Fria—excepting woods—are so intermixed, that they may be taken under the same head. In these two zones are found maize, wheat, barley, maguey, grapes, all kinds of temperate fruits, such as apples, peaches, strawberries, etc.; beans, peas, Chili or peppers, alfalfa or lucern, and all kinds of vegetables. Potatoes grow above the 7000 feet level.

The Tierra Templada, lying above the tropic woods, and below the oak and pine of the Tierra Fria, is almost entirely bereft of timber, with the exception of willow and ahuahuete along the streams, and a sparse growth of poplar, ash, and sycamore.

[1] The western coast of Cuba, the best tobacco-producing district in the island.

"[1] The largest bodies of timber I have seen are those on and around the slopes of the mountain of Toluca, and those stretching south from Maravatio down into the Tierra Caliente." Following the western side of the Mexico basin, there are pine forests, from the crossing of the Mexico and Toluca stage-road, for about thirty miles north.

"On the south-west side of the valley from the Toluca mountain there is not much timber, except far back, say thirty to forty miles in the range; so that the first fine body of timber we come to is that of the Jordana, on the west side, about forty miles down. This runs down within six miles of the river; and opposite, about twenty miles distant to the east, are the forests of Xocotitlan and Trochi. From here there is no good timber for twenty-five or thirty miles, when we strike the western edge of the forest of Tlapujagua, coming in from the south. From this to within four miles of Maravatio, there is fair timber on both sides of the river. That on the south-west side runs down to the forests of Troxes and Angangeo, which are fine pineries. The northern forests follow the mountain which leaves the river; and the last point where we have good timber is on the Sierra Augustin, about twenty miles north of Acambaro, and twenty-five east of Salvatierra.

"On the south side, however, twelve miles south of Maravatio, is the Sierra Andres, which is the N.E. boundary of the range that runs down to the east of Morelia, and into the Tierra Caliente. This is the largest body of timber, and the finest that we have along the route. It stretches west down to Acambaro and Zinapecuaro, and south for thirty leagues, broken here and there. This is the furthest point west that pine grows.

"It will be seen, then, that from Toluca for 100 miles down the Rio Lerma, and distant three to six leagues from

[1] Report on Timber Resources of the Lerma Valley, City of Mexico, May 1872.

it, we have a succession of pineries varying in size and worth.

"The principal woods are two sorts of pine,—cedar, which grows something like the Washingtonia gigantea; spruce, white and red oak. The red oak grows to a large size, and is used principally for waggon work. The white oak is smaller, and in many places grows in such a way as to produce the best of ties. I have seen in one acre of ground fifty sticks twelve inches thick at the base, and not less than ten inches at fifty feet from the ground."

Of all the products of the Tierra Templada and Tierra Fria, we will examine only two—wheat, and the maguey plant.

At present only enough wheat is raised in Mexico for home-consumption: but this might be developed to a point of which perhaps neither foreigner nor Mexican has any idea. That Mexico would be a good point for production there can be no doubt, and a ready market for the surplus produce, over and above that consumed in the Tierra Caliente, where wheat will not grow, would be found at Havannah and the West Indian Islands, whose supply at present comes from far up the Missouri river. The barley, oats, and maize would also be in demand. And if California and Chili can ship round the Horn to England, Mexico could do the same much more easily from her Gulf ports. The quality of wheat grown at present is somewhat inferior, being the old Andalusian seed brought in by the Spaniards 250 to 300 years ago, which has never been renewed. Its yield, however, is very large. Humboldt states that the Mexican wheat gives seventeen to twenty-four grains for one. That of France give five to six for one, and Hungary eight to ten for one.

The principal wheat-producing districts of the north are at present the districts of Urès and Hermosilla, in the State of Sonora, which harvested 150,000 tercios of 300 lbs. each last year (1872): but were this tract thoroughly developed, it ought to yield at least half a million.

The valleys of the Carmen and Encinillas in Chihuahua, which cover an area of some 2500 square miles, ought all to be under wheat.

Further south we find great plains in the State of San Luis Potosi, which would also raise good wheat.

From Zacatecas, down past Aguas Calientes, Lagos, Leon, and Guanajuato, a series of valleys form the wheat region which supplies the mines of Guanajuato, Zacatecas, Fresnillo, and Durango.

South of this we reach the principal wheat-raising district, known as the Bajio. These wheat-lands of the Bajio lie along and adjacent to the Rio Lerma and its tributaries for a distance of 200 miles. At present not one-tenth of them are utilized. But were this district put under proper cultivation, it is almost impossible to calculate what it might produce. Its possible yield has been estimated at 500,000 to 1,000,000 tons;[1] and those whose judgment may be safely taken, say that there is no reason why it should not reach the latter figures.

To the east of the Bajio and the Rio Lerma we find another enormous wheat-raising district, that round Queretaro, San Juan del Rio, and Tula. It is now either almost uncultivated, or else devoted to maize-growing. In the Valley of San Juan del Rio, in 1872, 45,000,000 lbs. of maize were harvested.

South of this again, and due east of Mexico, lie the plains of Apam, the wheat-growing region which supplies the city of Mexico, Puebla, the mines of Pachuca, and the whole south-eastern Tierra Caliente. Here also an immense quantity of barley is produced.

Another product of the Templadas worth notice is the maguey plant, *Agave Americana*, which may fairly be

[1] California's yield for 1872 was between 500,000 and 900,000 tons.

considered as one of the most remarkable plants in the world.

At the age of from four to eight years, according to its class, before the flower-spike has grown large, the flower-stalk and the adjacent leaves are cut out, forming a hollow from one to two feet in diameter. Into this hollow, for six to ten months, a thick, sweet juice exudes from the base of the leaves, which is gathered morning and evening after scraping the sides of the cavity. This is put into vats, to ferment for eight or nine days, diluted slightly with water; and when a heavy film settles at the bottom, the liquid, which is skimmed off, is ready for drinking. This liquor, called *pulque*, forms the universal drink of the Mexicans. To give some idea of the amount of pulque used in the city of Mexico, the Mexico and Vera Cruz Railroad, over a distance of sixty miles, derive the sum of $600 daily from the transportation of pulque; which, at ten cents a ton per mile, would be 100 tons of pulque daily, and this from only one side of the city of Mexico.

But this is not the only use of the maguey plant: from its butt a sort of whisky called Mescal is distilled.

The fibre, moreover, of the leaves, after they have been dried and combed out, makes the finest hemp; and in Mexico nothing else is used for ropes, lassos, string, etc. The French navy made experiments with this fibre, and found that a one-inch rope of maguey fibre sustained the same strain as a $1\frac{1}{2}$-inch Manilla rope. This should be brought into more general use. At present Yucatan exports in a small way; about 2000 bales of 400 lbs. each, leaving the port of Progresso every month for Havannah and New York. But as the supply is unlimited, it is to be hoped that this in the future will take a large place among the exports of Mexico.

Another use of this fibre in Mexico is for mats of all sorts, especially for putting under the saddles or pack-saddles. From its power of rapidly absorbing heat and moisture, it proves the most perfect saddle-cloth, as it keeps the animal's back cool, and at the same time prevents the saddle from galling.

Having obtained a slight idea of the wealth above ground of Mexico, we must now delve deeper; and this brings us to the most important of her natural products—her mines of precious metals. The principal deposits of gold and silver lie along the whole range of the Sierra Madre as far as 21° north latitude. South of this the line of deposits divides, one head following the eastern, the other the western edge of the central plateau, until it dips into the Tierra Caliente of the south. Here, throughout the whole breadth of the country, as far south as Chiapas, the land is so dotted over with mines, that it may be described as one vast mining region second to none in the world.

Besides this central chain of mines there is a large district in the States of Coahuila, Nueva Leon, and San Luis Potosi. This has been hitherto but little explored, with the exception of the mining region of Catorce in the northern part of San Luis Potosi.

The following is an approximate estimate of the present production of silver:—

Amount coined annually at	
Guanajuato Mint,	$4,500,000
Zacatecas,	4,500,000
San Luis,	3,000,000
Guadalajara,	3,000,000
City of Mexico,	5,000,000
All the other less important mints,	8,000,000
	$28,000,000
Amount sent out of the country in bars and otherwise uncoined, including a large amount smuggled,	12,000,000
Total,	$40,000,000

The average yield of ore throughout Mexico is about

$40 per ton. But of course much richer ores are to be found. The mine of Sombrerete, north of Zacatecas, ten years ago reduced $14,000,000 of ore in eleven months. And Humboldt estimated that in 1803 Mexico was producing "two-thirds of what was annually extracted from the whole globe."

The reduction of ores is carried on in the most primitive way; and in some places old furnaces are at work, reducing by fire, which have been going ever since the Spaniards first landed.

The usual method of extracting the ore is by means of old-fashioned stamps worked by mules. The following account of the reduction-works at Parral, by one of the engineering party in 1872, will give an idea of the present state of things:—"After the ore is worked out of the vein, men break it by hand to prepare it for the stamps in the smelting works,—a *carga* (350 lbs.) is broken for three reals (1s. 6d.). The stamps are four in number, worked by mule-power. Thence the ore goes into the *arrastras*, which is worked by a little ten-horse-power engine. After it has been thoroughly worked in the *arrastras* it is allowed to run out into the patio, a paved yard. Here salt, quicksilver, and sulphur are thrown in, and it is trampled by mules till it is supposed to be ready. It is then washed, and the amalgam squeezed in a bag to get out all the possible quicksilver. An immense quantity of quicksilver is lost by this process, as only one-sixth of what goes into the retort is pure silver."

In Guanajuato fifty-two mines are actually worked at present, though the number of veins is not and cannot be known. 996 stamps with four mules each are worked there, and sixty mills with sixteen mules each. These, with a reserve of 256 mules for stamps, mills, and patios, gives 5200 mules in the city of Guanajuato alone.

Iron, lead, tin, copper, antimony, alum, saltpetre, etc., are found in Mexico in large quantities. And in a few years she may rank with California or Spain for her cinnabar (quicksilver in its natural state). Of this there are large deposits in many places only waiting development, and of late years the supply has been decreasing while the demand has increased.

A jar of quicksilver (75 lbs.), worth in Mexico five years ago $75, is now worth from $110 to $140.

Coal, too, is reported from various points in the country: south east of Zapotlan, in Jalisco; south of Morelia, in Michoacan; between Puebla and Matamoras Azucar; and in the State of Vera Cruz between Tuxpan and Tampico. It has, however, never been actually worked: but each year it becomes more important to the welfare of the country that coal-mines should be opened, as charcoal, the only fuel, is becoming more difficult to obtain. And were coal procurable, it would be used for the reduction of silver by a less wasteful process than the "arrastras," and for the working and pumping of the mines by steam instead of mule or man-power.

Here then we find a country possessing enormous natural wealth, a variety of climates, and consequently of products, unsurpassed by any other in the world,—every advantage in fact which nature can bestow on one tract of land. But it is undeveloped. To what is this owing?

The simple answer to this is of course from the inertia of the people, and from the constant political disturbances.

This is partly true. But is it even now too late to rouse the people from their inertia; to suppress the facility for revolutions?

To this there seems but one answer, given alike by Mexicans and foreigners:—

These evils may yet be overcome by rapid means of transportation—in other words, by railroads.

With a system of railroads the force of contact with other nationalities would stimulate the Mexican to action.

The very products of the country would be doubled in value by quick railroad transportation. The surplus of the home consumption could be exported; and to starving thousands would be given a living by the further development of their own country.

A pailful of water, moreover, at the right moment, might have stopped the great fire of Chicago; and in the same way fifty men might crush out a revolution, if they could be moved in a few hours to the spot where the first spark ignited.

Then again the interchange of products between the temperate and tropical zones of Mexico, now carried on with immense disadvantages, owing to the topographical difficulties of the country, would be promoted to an extent undreamed of hitherto; while all the improvements in machinery for mines, agriculture, etc., would be brought within reach of the most remote hacienda, the owner of which cannot now afford to send his crops to market, owing to the cost of transportation being as great as the return he would get for his produce.

Mexico at present only possesses one railroad of any importance—the Mexico and Vera Cruz railway, which was completed from the Atlantic to the city of Mexico on the 1st of January 1873, after (owing to causes too numerous to mention here) twenty-one years of construction.

But though this is the only railroad, it must not be imagined that the Mexicans have been behind-hand in trying to get other people to build railroads for them; they are fully alive to the fact that they cannot build them for themselves; and numbers of concessions have been granted by the Mexican Congress. But hitherto, for one reason or other, these have all fallen through.

During the last two years, however, the railroad question in Mexico has revived with more than its old vigour; and it seems probable that ere long one of the many projected companies may take solid shape, and give the country a chance of regeneration in a thorough system of railroads.

The Mexican people are now wearied out by sixty years of political intrigue and strife, in which the mass of the people—say eight millions out of nine, have neither borne nor wished to bear an active part, knowing that they are only tools in the hands of better educated and more scheming men. The cry which is now heard throughout the length and breadth of the country is, " Give us peace and railroads. By the first, we gain security for the development of our noble country. By the latter we render that peace more secure, by the increase of power which would be given to the existing government; and further, they would give us a ready market for the increased production of our land."

There may be yet a bright future for Mexico, if her rulers will but give her the chance to let her take once more the place she has lost; and make her motto like that of her neighbour the United States, " Development of the earth's riches."